# Living Language

## 3rd Edition

Series editors
**Jane Bluett** and
**John Shuttleworth**

Although every effort has been made to ensure that website addresses are correct at time of going to press, Hodder Education cannot be held responsible for the content of any website mentioned in this book. It is sometimes possible to find a relocated web page by typing in the address of the home page for a website in the URL window of your browser.

Hachette Livre UK's policy is to use papers that are natural, renewable and recyclable products and made from wood grown in sustainable forests. The logging and manufacturing processes are expected to conform to the environmental regulations of the country of origin.

Orders: please contact Bookpoint Ltd, 130 Milton Park, Abingdon, Oxon OX14 4SB. Telephone: (44) 01235 827720. Fax: (44) 01235 400454. Lines are open from 9.00am to 5.00pm, Monday to Saturday, with a 24-hour message answering service. Visit our website at **www.hoddereducation.co.uk**

**Series editors: Jane Bluett and John Shuttleworth**
**Author team: Jane Bluett, Susan Cockcroft, Grainne Costello, Mike Devitt, Keith Sanger**

© Jane Bluett, Susan Cockcroft, Grainne Costello, Mike Devitt, Keith Sanger 2008

First published in 1997 by
Hodder Education,
part of Hachette Livre UK,
338 Euston Road
London NW1 3BH

Second edition published 2000
This third edition first published 2008

| Impression number | 5 | 4 | 3 | 2 | 1 |
|---|---|---|---|---|---|
| Year | 2012 | 2011 | 2010 | 2009 | 2008 |

2006001096

Cover photo © Hal Roach/MGM/ The Kobal Collection

Typeset in Palatino and Helvetica Neue.
Editorial and production by Topics – The Creative Partnership, Exeter
Printed in Italy

A catalogue record for this title is available from the British Library
ISBN: 978 0 340 93955 0

# Contents

# Introduction

## Who are you?

If you are reading this book, then you probably

- already have some experience in studying and enjoying English Language at GCSE
- are studying English Language at either AS or A2 level
- are aware of some of the relevant ideas behind the subject and are familiar with ways of writing about it.

Obviously *Living Language* is primarily intended as an introduction to AS- and A-level English Language. However, it will also be useful if you are studying English Language & Literature.

In this introduction we explain

- the differences between GCSE and A level
- how this book relates to the Assessment Objectives for the English Language specifications.

## Bridging the gap: from GCSE to A level

You will find that moving from GCSE to A level is a big step, but not a step that you are unprepared for, nor one that will be too great. This is because there is an intermediate stage in A-level study which means that everyone has to sit an Advanced Subsidiary (AS) examination before proceeding to A level. Many people will take this examination at the end of the first year of their course, but it can be taken at other times, depending on how your course is organised. The AS exam is pitched at a standard in between A level and GCSE, so that, at the beginning of your A-level course, you are faced with less of a mountain to climb. You do not have to move on from AS to A level unless you wish to do so.

Your exams are now connected like this:

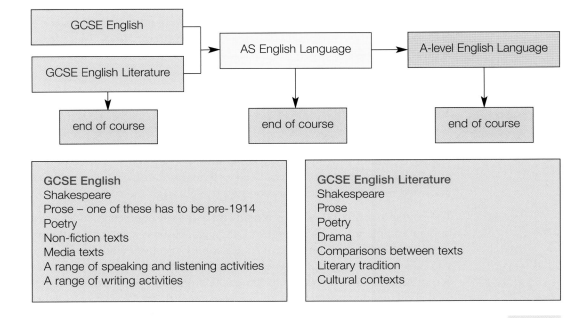

| GCSE English | GCSE English Literature |
|---|---|
| Shakespeare | Shakespeare |
| Prose – one of these has to be pre-1914 | Prose |
| Poetry | Poetry |
| Non-fiction texts | Drama |
| Media texts | Comparisons between texts |
| A range of speaking and listening activities | Literary tradition |
| A range of writing activities | Cultural contexts |

**AS English Language**
This requires you to show knowledge and understanding of

- the key features of the following areas of language study:
  - ◆ phonology (sound and intonation patterns of speech)
  - ◆ lexis (vocabulary)
  - ◆ grammar (of both spoken and written texts)
  - ◆ semantics and pragmatics (the ways meanings are constructed and interpreted in both speech and writing)
- the ways language varies according to whether it is written or spoken and according to the context in which it is produced
- the ways language varies according to personal and social factors
- the ways that variations in language can shape and change meanings and forms.

In addition you need to be able to

- write appropriately and accurately for a variety of audiences and purposes and comment on what you have produced.

**A-level English Language (in addition to AS requirements)**
This requires you to show deeper knowledge and understanding of

- areas of language study
- the ways in which historical and geographical variation shape and change meanings and forms in language
- the ways in which human language develops. (This may be a requirement of AS study depending on the specification you are following.)

You need also to be able to

- comment on and evaluate the usefulness of your application and exploration of these systematic approaches to the study of spoken and written texts, including texts from the past.

So how is GCSE different from AS and A level? Naturally, there is continuity with English Language GCSE, as you would expect. There you had to write pieces for different purposes and had to study a range of non-fiction and non-literary texts. These feature again at AS and A level, but in addition you will be studying some spoken texts. You will also be studying how spoken and written language is structured and organised.

In general terms, to succeed beyond GCSE you obviously need to enjoy studying language. You will also need to be prepared to study texts from outside your own time and culture, thus expanding your horizons. As you continue your studies, the methods you use will become as important as the content of the course. This is why how you approach a text is just as important as what you say about it. Above all, you will need to be able to make your own judgements about what you read and hear, coming closer to being an independent informed reader and listener as you progress through the course.

The course you are following is already an excellent one designed to test your knowledge, understanding and skills in English Language. However, the government has stipulated that there should also be a number of Assessment Objectives whose purpose is to assess whether you have achieved AS- or A-level standard and therefore whether you deserve an award in the subject. The mark you achieve in each component of the course depends entirely on how well you have demonstrated your ability to meet these Assessment Objectives, whether in coursework or in an end-of-module examination. It's as well, therefore, to know what these Assessment Objectives are.

Here they are in full for AS and A level. Below each objective is a user-friendly explanation of what exactly the objective requires.

## Assessment Objectives

**AO1** – Select and apply a range of linguistic methods, to communicate relevant knowledge using appropriate terminology and coherent, accurate written expression.

Here you are being asked to show that you can write about language in a way that shows you have studied it at an advanced level. You must be able to use technical terms effectively and precisely and show your understanding of the areas of language study to which you have been introduced. Your own written language must also be effective. You should learn to apply your knowledge of language to your own writing. As a student of A-level English Language you need to show that you can use accurate and well-constructed sentences.

**AO2** – Demonstrate critical understanding of a range of concepts and issues relating to the construction and analysis of meanings in spoken and written language, using knowledge of linguistic approaches.

Language concepts and issues are the ideas and opinions that surround the use of language in all its forms. You need to understand a range of theories about language use as well as the attitudes and values language expresses or provokes. You must show that you have engaged with these ideas in a critical way and are able to challenge them – for example, political correctness, how we acquire language, attitudes to accents.

**AO3** – Analyse and evaluate the influence of contextual factors on the production and reception of spoken and written language, showing knowledge of the key constituents of language.

All language use, written or spoken, is dependent upon the context in which it occurs. Here you must show that you are aware of the contextual factors at work. These will always include audience and purpose as well as more specific contexts you may be asked to consider, such as gender, power, occupation.

**AO4** – Demonstrate expertise and creativity in the use of English in a range of different contexts informed by linguistic study.

You will be expected to write effectively for a range of audiences and purposes. You need to explore the writing process and develop your own skills as a writer. You need to show that what you have studied in the course informs the writing you produce. Your creativity should be shown in the way that you can manipulate language in a variety of ways. For example, how would you present a complex idea to a non-specialist audience?

## Addressing the new specifications

Whichever English Language specification you are studying, you will be required to produce coursework and complete examination tasks that allow you to demonstrate the skills and understanding outlined in the Assessment Objectives. Each specification will ask you to do this in different ways. However, every A-level English Language student will be involved in the following activities:

- writing for different audiences and purposes
- analysing a wide range of written and spoken texts and data
- applying systematic approaches to the study of language
- exploring how language is used in a wide variety of social contexts
- evaluating theories and concepts to do with language use
- learning about the way language develops.

*Living Language* addresses each of these modes of study, providing you with a range of resources and activities designed to support you in your A-level course. As well as guiding you towards exam success, *Living Language* will help you develop your own ideas about language use and improve your skills as a language practitioner. We hope that you will find this book a practical and informative guide to your journey through the English language.

## Technical terms

Key technical terms are highlighted in blue the first time they occur in each chapter; these terms are defined in the Glossary at the end of the book.

# Key Concepts for Studying English

> ## At the end of this chapter you should be able to
>
> - select and apply a range of linguistic methods, to communicate relevant knowledge using appropriate terminology and coherent, accurate written expression (AO1)
>
> - demonstrate critical understanding of a range of concepts and issues relating to the construction and analysis of meanings in spoken and written language, using knowledge of linguistic approaches (AO2)
>
> - analyse and evaluate the influence of contextual factors on the production and reception of spoken and written language, showing knowledge of the key constituents of language (AO3)
>
> - demonstrate expertise and creativity in the use of English in a range of different contexts informed by linguistic study (AO4).
>
> For a more student-friendly version of these Assessment Objectives, turn to page vii in the Introduction.

## Introduction

One of the most irritating things when you start a new academic subject is that you don't know the words, you can't 'talk the talk', and you feel tongue-tied at best and totally mystified at worst. This can happen all too easily when you are introduced to the study of A-level English Language. Not only are you expected to know what people are talking about when they refer lightly to grammar, lexis and syntax, but alarming phrases like language concepts, diachronic change and phonological features may trip off the tongue of your teachers. How will you ever manage, you wonder? Maybe you should have taken AS Philosophy, Physics or PE instead?

The aim of this chapter is to create a sense of calm confidence in the face of any relevant concept, term or theoretical position associated with the study of English Language so that by the end of the chapter you can not only 'talk the talk' but understand and – when required – apply these concepts to real texts in English, whether they're literary or non-literary, spoken or written.

We start with the basic premise that language is either expressive (creative, conveying feeling and mood, literary) or functional (pragmatic, getting things done, non-literary) communication. (We shall be considering spoken and written English in this chapter, but most of the ideas, concepts and terminology can be recognised in all human languages.) Every language is structured in predictable patterns so that other speakers and writers recognise those patterns and can start to make sense of what is being spoken or written. (Babies learn from very early on to recognise the predictable patterns in the speech of their carers, initially of sounds, but soon of grammatical patterns as well as individual words. For more on child language acquisition, see page 232.) These structured patterns or systems can be categorised as grammar, syntax, phonology and lexis. In order not to start off by creating the confusion we're anxious to avoid, here are some working definitions.

- Grammar and syntax are broadly interchangeable terms which describe the ways in which the sentence (written) or utterance (spoken) is organised into structures like words, phrases and clauses.
- Phonology means the individual sounds or phonemes which make up a particular language.
- Lexis is the vocabulary or word-stock of any given language

But patterns of words and predictable word order don't really convey meaning in themselves. A classic example of this is the following sentence cited by the American linguist Noam Chomsky:

'Curious green ideas sleep furiously.'

Can we make sense of this? The language is English, the patterning of words and the word order are recognisably English, the words are all part of our normal vocabulary – and yet the sentence doesn't mean anything! The simple explanation is that the words have meaning individually, but not when placed together in this particular sentence. Below we have taken each word from the Chomsky sentence and written a new sentence of similar length in which this word now makes sense.

**Curious** French children stare unblinkingly <u>at the visitors.</u>
Beautiful **green** trees sway rhythmically <u>in the wind.</u>
Exciting new **ideas** spread rapidly <u>through the company.</u>
Exhausted airline passengers **sleep** restlessly <u>on the benches.</u>
Busy financial traders chatter **furiously** <u>on their mobiles.</u>

In each new sentence the 'Chomsky word' is placed into a context where its meaning is relevant. The underlined phrase added to each sentence clarifies the specific context and elucidates the meaning further.

We can conclude that meaning does lie in the individual word (lexical item). But meaning is also determined by the word order (or patterned arrangement). Look what happens if we muddle up the order of the Chomsky sentence.

Furiously curious green sleep ideas.
Ideas green furiously curious sleep.
Sleep curious ideas green furiously.

Are you beginning to feel slightly disoriented? It's disconcerting to say the least to lose any ability to make sense of your own language because the word order is wrong and the grammar/syntax unguessable!

So where does meaning lie? Is it in the way language is visually represented on the page (graphemes)? Is it in the way in which the graphemes themselves represent the sounds of words (phonemes)? Is it linked with context, audience and purpose? These are urgent questions which will have to be addressed in this chapter. But before we bite the bullet and wade into the ocean of concept and theory (and we'll be talking about mixed metaphor a little later), let's look for a life-raft if not a life-boat.

The diagram on the facing page models the way we use language to communicate, whether in spoken or written modes. Two axes intersect: the horizontal or syntagmatic axis (representing the structure of language); and the vertical or paradigmatic axis or axes (representing language choices/variants available). The diagram uses the Chomsky sentence as a starting-point. Which of the sentences work in English?

|  | | | | | | | | | |
|---|---|---|---|---|---|---|---|---|---|
| 1 | | Curious green | ideas | sleep | furiously | | | | |
| 2 | | Bizarre red | thoughts | snooze | crossly | | | | |
| 3 | | Strange purple | theories | snore | angrily | | | | |
| 4 | The | | cat | sat | | on | the | | rug |
| 5 | The | | tiger | prowled | | through | the | | jungle |
| 6 | The | | seal | swam | | under | the | | ice |
| 7 | The | deliciously soft and furry ginger | cat | sat | serenely | on | the | Persian | rug |
| 8 | The | sleekly striped and spotted | tiger | prowled | restlessly | through | the | silent | jungle |
| 9 | The | silver coated, brown mottled | seal | swam | swiftly | under | the | clear blue green | ice |

*paradigmatic axis* (vertical) — *syntagmatic axis* (horizontal)

The Chomsky sentence (1) on the syntagmatic axis fails to convey meaning, despite its grammatical correctness, because it lacks context and relevance. Similarly, sentences 2 and 3 on the paradigmatic axis fail to work, because the alternative words also lack context and relevance. To create recognisable meaning, the paradigmatic choices have to be relevant and appropriate to context.

The next three sentences (4–6) demonstrate that the relationship between the syntagmatic and the paradigmatic axes can represent the communication of meaning in a sentence if the factors of context and relevance are in place. In sentence 4 the cat, a domestic animal, is sitting on the mat, a domestic item, hence the context is domestic. In sentence 5 the tiger, a predatory animal, is slinking through tropical terrain, hence the context is exotic. In sentence 6 the seal is exhibiting normal behaviour in a polar context. In other words, although sentences 4, 5 and 6 are as identical in form and structure as were sentences 1, 2 and 3, the former do communicate recognisable meaning whereas the latter don't. The reason is that the lexical choice on the paradigmatic axes for sentences 4, 5 and 6 is relevant to context.

What this model represents is the instantaneous nature of meaningful communication, whether spoken or written. All the time we are talking, we are making meaningful lexical choices according to context (and if people don't understand us, we have to choose again). What else it shows is that, however clear the structure of sentence/utterance, without communicating relevant meaning, nothing happens.

The last three sentences (7–9) show how meaning can be enriched by adding new descriptive and sound elements to the basic sentence structures in sentences 4–6. As you can see, the picture created in sentences 7–9 is becoming richer in detail and more powerfully imagined. What has happened is that words communicating sensuous detail (visual, tactile and aural) have been added, and the overall meaning enriched.

## Exploring the structure of written language as it relates to meaning

Working in pairs, make up a short sentence on the Chomsky model that is grammatically correct but doesn't mean anything.

Rewrite your sentence until you have turned it into a sentence of similar length and structure which does make sense.

What is the context of your new sentence? What kind of changes (paradigmatic choices) did you have to make before it had recognisable meaning?

# Semantics

The first key concept we shall examine is semantics (the study of meaning) conveyed via lexis rather than grammar, syntax or phonology.

The term 'semantics' derives from the Greek word '*seme*' meaning 'sign'. Meaning is communicated via verbal and non-verbal sign systems, and the study of meaning is called semiotics. Thus, whatever you chose today to wear (your favourite jeans, a T-shirt with a particular message, chunky jewellery, a woolly cap) all signalled to your friends, and to anyone else looking, something particular about you. Most of us, whatever age, try to communicate in our dress the person we want to be (professional lady, yummy mummy, absent-minded professor, cool media personality). These non-verbal sign-systems, such as codes of dress, convey meaning in exactly the same way that the Highway Code conveys meaning about our roads and motorways via another kind of semiotic system. The semiotics of verbal language utilise the sign-systems of speech and writing (phonemes in spoken language and graphemes in written texts) to convey meaning. In this section we shall only be looking at lexical semantics – the meanings of words – and leave the other systems till later.

There are two kinds of linguistic meaning conveyed in semantics – denoted meaning and connoted meaning. Denoted meaning is roughly equivalent to a dictionary definition of a word, but connoted meaning involves associated meaning, meanings based on points of similarity including metaphor. In the following edited examples from the *Chambers Dictionary*, the first part is the denoted meaning of each word (marked DM) and the second half is the connoted meaning (marked CM).

- **crocodile** noun. (DM) a large long-tailed tropical reptile … with powerful tapering jaws and a thick skin covered with bony plates; (CM) a double file of school pupils taking a walk; *crocodile clip* a clip for making electrical connections with serrated jaws that inter-lock; *crocodile tears* hypocritical grief, from the old story that crocodiles … shed tears over the hard necessity of killing animals for food …

- **crook** noun. (DM) a bend, or something bent; a staff bent at the end as in a shepherd's or a bishop's; (CM) a professional swindler, thief or criminal in general; a curved tube used to lower the pitch of a wind instrument: adj. (Austr. and NZ colloq.) ill; unfair; wrong, dubious; inferior, nasty, unpleasant …

Charles Dickens makes a famously grim joke about denoted (or literal) meaning in *Hard Times* (1854), a novel criticising the negative effects of the philosophy of utilitarianism and mechanical industrialism on society. The schoolmaster, Mr Thomas Gradgrind, asks a question:

'Bitzer,' said Thomas Gradgrind. 'Your definition of a horse.'

'Quadruped. Graminivorous. Forty teeth, namely twenty-four grinders, four eye teeth and twelve incisive. Sheds coat in the spring; in marshy countries sheds hoofs, too. Hoofs hard, but requiring to be shod with iron. Age known by marks in the mouth.'

Dickens is well aware that Bitzer's is an accurate definition for his day: however, he is making a point of contrast with Bitzer's inarticulate school fellow, Sissy Jupe, whose father is a circus equestrian and who actually knows about horses, their reality and their beauty, not just their teeth. The passage is a lesson in semantics!

## Activity 2

**Pair work**

## Investigating denoted and connoted meanings

Choose a good dictionary which includes a range of meanings and provides an etymology or word history, such as the *OED online* or the *Shorter Oxford Dictionary*, *Chambers Dictionary*, or *Collins Cobuild Dictionary*. (Avoid student dictionaries which may provide only basic definitions.)

Look up three words from the list below (or as many as you can) and in pairs discuss the differences between denoted and connoted meaning in each definition. You may also notice that your word has changed its meaning over time. (For more on how words change over time, see page 281.)

- apron
- barm
- tart
- wicked
- villain
- hilt
- fox
- doldrums
- silly
- sinister
- career
- wardrobe

## Semantics and society

Although it's interesting and useful to know that meanings of words change over time, what is really important is the reason why such changes happen. The explanation is that language reflects society. Communication between human beings, whether spoken or written, does not take place in a vacuum. Whatever we talk about today (the World Cup, the obesity crisis, politics, global warming, new clothes, iPods, flat-screen televisions, drugs, green issues, the post-code lottery, space travel, the war in Afghanistan, …) our lexis is up to it, and we have words available to construct and convey meaning. In the Middle Ages, when society was very different and no-one in Europe ate tomatoes or potatoes or drank tea and coffee or knew about DNA and the deep holes in outer space, the lexis was also different.

Social attitudes were different too, especially in relation to sex and gender, with significant effects on language, as we shall see. Overall, however, the point to remember here is that meaning in language is individually, socially and environmentally determined. A classic example is the fact noted by American linguist Benjamin Whorf that Eskimos have many different words for snow (they live in polar regions). Similarly in British English we have more words linked with rain and bad weather than with sunshine and clear skies, reflecting our different weather expectations. In other words, language reflects society, including the environment. (For more on how social context affects language, see Chapter 2.)

If the vocabulary of any language reflects the social practices and environment of that society, it follows that the vocabulary of individual speakers will reflect their personal circumstances (family, friends, education, occupation, region, etc.). Sociolinguists have come up with some useful terms to describe the ways people talk.

- Idiolect is an individual's unique way of speaking (comparable to style in written language).
- Sociolect describes the variety used by a speaker in his or her speech communities and social networks (friendship group, age group, occupation, social class, etc.).
- Genderlect has been coined to describe the lexical choices made by women or men.

Of course, spoken language is more than just vocabulary – grammatical choices also have to be made. In this section, however, the focus is on semantics and the way meaning is communicated via lexis. Indeed, whoever we're talking to, whether it's family or friends, people at work, people in shops, the bank, the supermarket, the surgery, the careers office or the travel agency, and wherever we go to seek information, exchange goods and services or just chat with friends, we must choose the right vocabulary to guarantee a successful interaction. Similarly when we are writing, whether it's a holiday postcard or a letter of application or an essay, the lexis we use will reflect our own lexical preferences or style, but also our sensitivity to context, audience and purpose. For example, a letter of condolence which uses trite clichés of 'sympathy' will mean less to the recipient than a few words reflecting genuine understanding of the person who has died, and empathy with how the recipient might feel.

| Activity 3 | Investigating lexical choice in spoken and written language |
| --- | --- |
| **Pair work** | Working with a partner, imagine you have both been on holiday to the same destination at different times. One of you has had a good experience, the other less good. |
| | Each describe your experience as if you were talking to a close friend at home. |
| | Each write a postcard to a family friend who has paid your airfare describing your experience. |
| | Discuss the different spoken and written lexical choices you used in relation to audience/purpose. |

## Semantic field

An important aspect of semantics is the concept of semantic field. Semantic field means the range of vocabulary/lexis associated with a particular subject, topic, situation, profession, etc. For example, the semantic fields of education might include institutions (nursery, primary and secondary schools, college and university), the curriculum, the exam system, the inspection organisation (including Ofsted), teachers, pupils and teaching assistants, and physical equipment ranging from whiteboards to goal-posts. The list of possible areas within this enormous semantic field is mind-boggling.

| Activity 4 | Exploring the concept of semantic field |
| --- | --- |
| | Choose five areas of education from the list above. Write down ten words from each semantic field. Are these semantic fields very different from each other or does each list 'run into' another? |

Within a semantic field as broad as education, there are many separate discourses. The term 'discourse' has a range of meanings, but in relation to semantics, it is associated with more specialised lexis. So, for example, we might refer to the discourse of educational theory, the discourse of citizenship or pastoral care, as well as the discourses of history, physics or English studies. In the semantic field of medicine, examples of particular discourses might include the discourse of paediatrics, cardiology, geriatrics or sports medicine. In the semantic field of music, the discourse of reggae is very different from the discourses of world music, classical music, heavy metal and country and western. The discourse of journalism might include the subdiscourses of different ideological groups (right- and left-wing press), as well as the discourses of broadsheet and tabloid newspapers – all within the semantic field of publishing.

A final point. The examples given here of semantic fields are very broad: the term can also be applied to much smaller areas of specialisation, from skateboarding to surfing. So when can a semantic field be described as a discourse (and vice versa)? Katie Wales (in *A Dictionary of Stylistics*) suggests that this may happen when people are not only using similar lexis, but are also members of the same discourse community and 'engaged in the same communicative pursuit, united by common public goals'. There are real discourse communities like the world of advertising or the world of horseracing, where everyone involved is a confident user of the lexis. Ultimately applying the term 'discourse' to vast areas like education or medicine seems like putting a quart into a pint pot.

## Activity 5
**Pair work**

### Identifying a range of semantic fields and discourses

Working in pairs, choose three or four topics from the list below and write down as many lexical items as possible associated with each one.

- sailing
- football
- fashion (clothing)
- tabloid journalism
- parliament

- cakes
- climate change
- cars
- percussion
- ICT

- rail travel
- fly-fishing
- weddings

As co-authors, write 150–200 words on one of the topics above to be published in a specialist journal. Compare your texts with those of others in the group, and decide which texts address specific discourse communities.

## Semantic change

Semantic change is the final aspect of semantics we need to address. We noted earlier that language reflects society, and that, as society changes, the lexis mirroring the physical, social, intellectual and cultural experience of its speakers will also change. A key factor here is the way social attitudes affect how people talk about basic human life experiences associated with gender, age and social hierarchy. For example, in country A, words like 'milk', 'bread', 'water', 'rock' may remain unchanged over centuries. But if country A is invaded by country B, and forced to use language B, a different lexis will be introduced which over time may lead to language A being lost.

Social attitudes within a country can lead to lexical change. Words in English whose meaning has changed in a negative way (pejorative change) tend be associated with women, age, folly and criminality, suggesting changing social attitudes over time. For example,

- 'hussy', derived from 'housewife', a former indicator of status, now means 'promiscuous woman'
- 'biddy', formerly a word for a hen or chicken, now means 'old woman'
- 'silly', originally 'sely', meaning 'happy', 'blessed' or 'innocent', now means 'foolish'.

Less frequently, change is ameliorative, meaning 'for the better'. Examples include

- 'mischief' – former meaning 'serious harm', current meaning 'playful misbehaviour'
- 'praise' – former meaning to 'judge, appraise', current meaning to 'express approval'.

---

| **Activity 6** | **Investigating some examples of semantic change** |
| --- | --- |

Look up the following words in a good dictionary (one providing an etymology or word history), and note, first, whether the changes are positive or negative, and, secondly, whether any words have either broadened or narrowed their meaning.

- harlot
- notorious
- fair
- girl
- spinster
- sinister
- enthusiasm
- boor
- egregious
- tart
- politician
- sophisticated
- lewd
- knight
- starve
- crafty
- annoy
- churl
- villain
- awful

For more on broadening and narrowing see pages 281–282.

---

## Synonyms, antonyms and hyponyms

Here are three more useful terms associated with meaning.

Synonyms are words with the same or similar meaning (buyer/punter/customer; beautiful/lovely/glamorous; sad/miserable/fed up). We used synonyms earlier in this chapter when discussing the syntagmatic/paradigmatic axes (page 3). Which word we choose often depends on context and levels of formality (register). Thus 'punter' is informal, whereas 'beautiful' or 'miserable' are more formal choices.

Antonyms are sets of words with opposite meanings, either of degree (narrow/wide, strong/weak), of absolute contrast (alive/dead, true/false) or word pairs or converses representing two sides of a common semantic pairing or process (give/receive, husband/wife, borrow/lend).

Hyponyms are associated with the way we categorise meaning. The general or superordinate category 'animal' has subordinate categories such as 'cat' or 'bear'. These in turn have further subordinate categories like 'Siamese', 'Russian Blue', 'tabby', or 'grizzly bear', 'polar bear', 'brown bear'. Thus 'animal' is the superordinate hyponym of 'bear' and 'tabby' is the subordinate hyponym of 'cat'.

You may wonder whether it's remotely useful to know these terms – the answer is yes, absolutely. First, if you are a creative writer, the more you know about subtle variations of meaning the better; and secondly, any writer or speaker benefits from access to a wide range of lexical options, as well as being able to create better coherence and cohesion when they speak or write. (For more on this subject see pages 40–41.)

# Lexis or vocabulary

It's not a big jump to move from the meanings of words to the words themselves, whether we refer to them individually as lexical items, or to the lexis, the lexicon, vocabulary or word-stock of a language. English has an extraordinarily rich and ever-expanding vocabulary, recorded in dictionaries both online and on paper, enriched by borrowings from other languages, or loan words (pizza), and enlarged by neologisms (i-Pod), blendings (smog), clippings (fax), acronyms (NATO), compoundings (skinhead), affixations (healthwise) and back formations (burgle/burglar) – among other methods. (For more on how new words are formed in English, see page 279.)

This huge lexicon provides a remarkable resource for people in all walks of life, whether they're novelists or nuclear scientists, cooks or CEOs, engineers or athletes, journalists or geologists, retailers or rose-growers. This vocabulary includes recently established colloquialisms as well as new scientific, technological and economic lexis. Usage is the criterion that determines entry into 'the dictionary' and lexicographers (dictionary writers) have access to corpora (computer 'banks' of recorded speech) as well as all published texts, as they observe the changes and developments in this amazing living entity, the English language.

## Content and function words

In English, by far the highest proportion of words in our vocabulary are content words (that is, nouns, adjectives, verbs and adverbs) which convey meaning. Function words on the other hand provide connections and maintain coherence and cohesion between content words. They are pronouns, prepositions, determiners (including definite and indefinite articles) and conjunctions, and they will be discussed in more detail in the section on grammar.

Now read Lewis Carroll's nonsense poem 'Jabberwocky' from *Through the Looking-Glass* (1871).

'Twas brillig, and the slithy toves
    Did gyre and gimble in the wabe:
All mimsy were the borogroves,
    And the mome raths outgrabe.

'Beware the Jabberwock, my son!
    The jaws that bite, the claws that catch!
Beware the Jubjub bird, and shun
    The frumious Bandersnatch!'

He took his vorpal sword in hand:
    Long time the manxome foe he sought –
So rested he by the Tumtum tree,
    And stood a while in thought.

And, as in uffish thought he stood,
    The Jabberwock, with eyes of flame,
Came whiffling through the tulgey wood,
    And burbled as it came!

One, two! One, two! And through and through
    The vorpal blade went snicker-snack!
He left it dead, and with its head
    He went galumphing back.

'And has thou slain the Jabberwock?
    Come to my arms, my beamish boy!
O frabjous day! Callooh! Callay!'
    He chortled in his joy.

'Twas brillig, and the slithy toves
    Did gyre and gimble in the wabe:
All mimsy were the borogroves,
    And the mome raths outgrabe.

9

This poem offers opportunities for many interesting activities, ranging from semantic investigation of Carroll's made-up or 'portmanteau' words like 'slithy' (slimy/writhing) to neologisms that have become part of our lexicon (burbled, galumphed, chortled). It also demonstrates very clearly that even if the lexis is unfamiliar, we can work out which are the content words and which the function words – in other words, the grammatical relationships.

## Activity 7
### Pair work

## Identifying the content words and function words in 'Jabberwocky'

Working in pairs, make two lists, one of content words, the other of function words in the poem. (Identify, if you wish, the individual parts of speech.)

Rewrite the poem as a short prose narrative, keeping to the story but replacing any content words you wish to.

How many conjunctions have you used to make your prose narrative flow smoothly (cohesion)? Another useful word to describe these words is discourse markers.

So far in this section we have looked at the richness and flexibility of English, touched on some of the ways in which its vocabulary is increased, and presented the lexical relationship between content and function words. To go further down that road at present would take us into grammar and syntax in more detail. Before we go there, here are a few useful terms you will encounter throughout your A-level course relating to lexis.

- Lexeme – this means a word or lexical item. A lexeme can have many different variants (dance/danced/dancing).
- Morphology – this means the structure or form of a word.
- Morpheme – this is the smallest viable grammatical unit. Morphemes that make independent sense (dog, car) are called free morphemes. Morphemes that don't make sense on their own are called bound morphemes (for example, prefixes like 'in-', 'un-', 'dis-', plural markers like 's').

## Activity 8
### Pair work

## Investigating the morphology of words

Look at the words below and list the morphemes in each word. Decide which are free and which are bound morphemes. You may find it helpful to look up the words in a good dictionary.

- conscience
- incomprehensible
- remarkable
- jejune
- frozen
- fight
- borrow
- seizure
- cart

Collocation is another word which needs explanation. A collocation is a group of words (phrase) which is readily recognised by most speakers of that language. It's not the same as a cliché (a worn-out expression like 'sick as a parrot', 'over the moon', 'at the end of the day', 'at this moment in time'). Collocations like 'cold front', 'soaring house prices', 'fish and chips', 'get the message', 'the mind boggles', though familiar, remain useful. Indeed, collocations are often used creatively by writers, poets, and comics to surprise the audience with unexpected insights. The Monty Python 'Pet Shop' television sketch reverses audience expectations using normal collocations and subverting them for comic effect. In this extract, collocations are underlined.

| Praline (John Cleese) | Hello, <u>I wish to register a complaint</u> … Hello? Miss? |
| Shopkeeper (Michael Palin) | What do you mean, <u>miss</u>? |
| Praline | Oh, I'm sorry, I have a cold. I wish to <u>make a complaint.</u> |
| Shopkeeper | Sorry, <u>we're closing for lunch</u>. |
| Praline | <u>Never mind that, my lad</u>. I wish to complain about this parrot what I purchased not half an hour ago from <u>this very</u> boutique. |

The audience laughs at the absurdity of this complaint (the parrot is 'stone dead', not 'resting', as the shopkeeper tries to assert) made more amusing by the comic seriousness of the opening conversation.

# Grammar and syntax

In this section we shall be looking at grammar and syntax from a rather different angle. Instead of investigating the detail of English grammar and syntax, we shall focus on broader principles, showing how understanding grammatical relationships helps us to make better sense of spoken and written texts. We hope this will transform the process of textual analysis into a creative exploration of language and literature, rather than a mechanical procedure in which you simply tick features from a checklist.

On pages 2–3 of the introductory section, grammar is linked with the concept of structure in language. Experience of learning a new language confirms to most people that different languages have very different grammatical structures and rules (never mind differences in vocabulary!). Although languages that belong to the same 'language families' may have some grammatical elements in common, each language has its unique grammatical system and structures. If you think about the Romance language family, which includes French, Italian, Spanish and Portuguese, there are numerous differences between these languages and not just

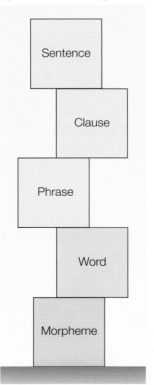

in the lexis. Similarly, English, part of the Germanic language family, is significantly different from its 'relatives' Dutch, German, Swedish, Danish and Norwegian. Languages evolve according to what happens to their speakers socially, politically, economically and geographically. The grammar of a language spoken by a small number of speakers in a mountainous and inaccessible area will not change much over generations; indeed, grammar is always the slowest element in a language to be affected by change. Because English is so widely used by millions of first- and second-language speakers and has many different versions (Indian English, American English, West Indian English as well as Australian, Scottish, Irish and Welsh English!) its grammar *is* susceptible to some degree of change. Nevertheless, the basic grammar of English remains the same, and we shall be focusing on this.

**Rank order** or hierarchy may seem a strange concept to apply to grammar, but if you think in terms of a tower of children's bricks, it should make more sense.

In the diagram, at the top we have the sentence, next down is the clause, next the phrase, then the word, and finally the morpheme. Obviously the sentence is the largest unit and the morpheme the smallest. The rank order is just the same in spoken language, except that utterance replaces sentence. Why is it relevant to talk about rank order at all? Our purpose here is to

**11**

demonstrate that the term 'grammar' is a way of describing relationships between words, while 'syntax' is a way of describing relationships between different structures within the sentence/utterance. If you can remember the overall relationship between words and structures, it will help you to speak, write and analyse more effectively.

We have now established that for any writer/speaker, choices are not only lexical and content based (paradigmatic axis) but also order and structure based (syntagmatic axis). We'll look now at some aspects of grammar and syntax that students of language need to know about.

# Syntax

Under this heading we include structural features such as word order, phrase and clause patterning, right- and left-hand branching sentences, and the role of pronouns – all used by writers and speakers alike, according to context and circumstance.

### Word order
The normal word order in English, whether spoken or written, is SVO (subject–verb–object):

> Mary (S) teased (V) the tiger (O).

However, for particular purposes, such as focus or emphasis, we sometimes invert subject and object:

> That band (O) I (S) really hate (V).

This is called fronting. Samuel Pepys does something similar in his diary entry of 9 March 1666:

> Music and women I cannot but give way to (OSV), whatever my business is.

So does Wordsworth in one of the mysterious 'Lucy' poems:

> No motion has she now, or force (OVS, O)
> She neither hears nor sees (SVV)
> Rolled round in earth's diurnal course
> With rocks and stones and trees.

### Sentence patterning
Sentences which pile up phrase and clause together until the final point is made are called left branching: the reader waits with increasing interest as more information is given. E.g.

> Although we had watched the lightning playing over the horizon and seen the palm tree branches swooping violently in the gale, we were not prepared for that icy, solid curtain of rain.

Right-branching sentences, on the other hand, give you the key information quickly and then elaborate on it.

> The car was packed, after we spent hours carefully positioning my pot plants and pictures so nothing would break, and squeezing the duvet and pillows round the boxes of books (not all read as thoroughly as they might have been) together with the carton of kitchen junk I hadn't managed to sort out in time.

Writers have the time to experiment with word order, but it's surprising how much variety there is in spoken language – worth listening for when people are chatting around you. Watch out for syntactic parallelism in speech or writing, from the simple 'Out of sight, out of mind' to the more complex

> I could not love thee, Dear, so much
> Loved I not honour more

> (Richard Lovelace, 'To Lucasta, Going to the Wars')

## Activity 9

**Pair work**

## Creating different effects through word order and sentence structure

Working in pairs, choose one or two of the following options and write the opening paragraph, using a range of word-order variations/syntactic structures to create the appropriate effects for each genre:

- murder mystery
- tabloid news report
- children's story (age 7–11)
- space fiction
- broadsheet editorial or feature article

This example of a children's story is an extract from Roald Dahl's *The BFG* (1982).

> Sophie couldn't sleep.
>
> A brilliant moonbeam was slanting through a gap in the curtains. It was shining right on her pillow.
>
> The other children in the dormitory had been asleep for hours.
>
> Sophie closed her eyes and tried to doze off.
>
> It was no good. The moonbeam was like a silver blade slicing through the room on to her face.
>
> The house was absolutely silent. No voices came up from downstairs. There were no footsteps on the floor above either.
>
> The window behind the curtain was wide open, but nobody was walking on the pavement outside. No cars went by on the street. Not the tiniest sound could be heard anywhere. Sophie had never known such a silence.

Turn to page 48 for a commentary on this example.

# Grammar

Here (as an exemplar) we shall focus on a range of different grammatical verb forms including modality, tense and aspect, transitivity, mood and voice. But why choose verbs? Verbs constitute one of the most remarkable elements in English grammar because they can tell us so much, whether we are reading or listening.

At this stage you need to know only a few basic facts about verbs. They can tell us about what is happening to the 'subject' in a given situation, at a given time, who is taking action or receiving it, and how long that action lasted. Dynamic verbs describe action (running, walking, singing), whereas stative verbs describe states of existence (being, seeming, becoming).

### Tense and aspect

Tense and aspect tell us when something happened (past, present, future), and whether the action was completed (perfect aspect) or ongoing (continuous aspect). These two examples show the difference between tense and aspect.

- He <u>was</u> hungry, so he <u>turned</u> the left-overs into a giant Spanish omelette and <u>ate</u> it all himself.

Past tense – 'was', 'turned', 'ate'; third person singular – 'he'; perfect aspect – 'turned' and 'ate' are completed actions.

- She <u>was</u> <u>grilling</u> the steak when the smoke alarm <u>went</u> <u>off</u>.
  Continuous aspect – 'was grilling' is action continuing; perfect aspect – 'went off' is action completed.

Aspect is useful for the writer because it conveys further information about time to the audience without need for a more wordy explanation.

---

## Activity 10 — Practising the use of tense and aspect in creative writing

Choose two of these situations:

- a wedding
- climbing a mountain
- going out with friends
- an English lesson
- walking in the country

Describe one situation using the past tense and either perfect or continuous aspect. Describe the other situation using the present tense and either present or continuous aspect. What different effects are achieved by varying the use of aspect?

---

### Mood and modality

Mood and modality are not too hard to understand, because they relate to what verbs are doing: making statements (indicative mood); asking questions (interrogative mood); issuing commands (imperative mood). It's more difficult to understand the relationship between the grammatical subject and modality. Modal verbs themselves convey attitudes and express possibilities rather than certainties. For example:

- You <u>ought</u> to catch the train if you run.          (Obligation/expectation)
- You <u>should</u> get a high grade if you work hard.       (Obligation/logical necessity)
- You <u>might</u> pass if you put in some revision time.     (Possibility)
- You <u>would</u> enjoy that film.                          (Prediction/likelihood)
- You <u>must</u> go now or you'll get drenched.             (Obligation/compulsion)
- You <u>may</u> leave early for that dental appointment.     (Permission)
- You <u>will</u> be our first choice if Mary/Daniel resigns.  (Prediction/insistence)
- You <u>can</u> be confident that we will support you.       (Are allowed to)

In literature, modal verbs are often used to reveal character, or provide more subtle description of a scene. In conversation, modal verbs tend to soften or mitigate comments, conveying politeness and protecting face ('Should you really be going out tonight when you've got such a terrible cold?'). There is an important relationship between the modal verb and the grammatical subject, whose subjectivity is thereby emphasised.

---

## Activity 11 — Investigating the literary use of modal verbs

**Pair work**

Read the following passage from *Macbeth* in which the murderous king sees that all is nearly lost. Identify the modal verbs and, with a partner, decide what effect Shakespeare might be seeking by using them.

> I have lived long enough: my way of life
> Is fall'n into the sear, the yellow leaf;
> And that which should accompany old age,
> As honour, love, obedience, troops of friends
> I must not look to have; but, in their stead,
> Curses, not loud but deep, mouth-honour, breath
> Which the poor heart would fain deny and dare not.

## Transitivity and voice

Verbs can tell us who did what to whom (SVO). If the grammatical subject (S) in a sentence is taking the action we call this a transitive verb. For example,

- The bird (S) ate (V) the worm (O).
- John (S) enjoyed (V) the walk (O) in North Yorkshire.
- The learner driver (S) narrowly missed (V) the low wall (O).

If the action of the verb is received by the grammatical subject (who is acted upon, not acting) we call this an intransitive verb. The verb has no object. For example,

- The worm (S) was eaten (V) by the bird.
- The sneezing child (S) was sent (V) home by the teacher.
- The weather forecast (S) was read (V) by a new presenter.

Voice is another important grammatical concept associated with transitivity. If the verb is in the active voice this means that the grammatical subject/real subject is taking the action. In literature (as well as in spoken interaction) sentences which convey information tend to use the active voice and have an object. The passive voice is when the action happens to the grammatical subject, who is acted upon. In literature, sentences which convey emotion or create mood tend to use the passive voice and have no object. The following sentence shows the use of transitive and intransitive verbs and therefore of active and passive voice.

The exhausted detective trailed [transitive verb, active voice] the alleged suspect [object] for hours: then suddenly the man was surrounded [intransitive verb, passive voice] by a crowd of protesters and disappeared [transitive verb, active voice] from sight.

## Activity 12 — Practising the use of transitivity

**Pair work**

Working in pairs, take turns to tell each other the story of your day so far, using transitive verbs only. Then each write a shortened version of the other person's story, using intransitive verbs only. What kind of differences in effect did you observe?

## Activity 13 — Investigating ways in which grammar conveys meaning in a poem

**Pair work**

Read the following poem by W.H. Auden. He wrote it at the beginning of the Second World War, having seen Pieter Breughel's painting of the fall of Icarus at the Musées

Royaux des Beaux-Arts in Brussels. According to Greek legend, Icarus was the young son of the master craftsman Daedalus. His father crafted wings for them both, secured by wax, but Icarus flew too near to the sun, the wax melted and he fell to his death. The story has been used to symbolise the dangers of over-ambition, but Auden also points at human indifference to others' suffering.

Working in pairs, underline all the verb forms you can find in the poem. Look for one example of each of the following:

- past tense
- present tense
- perfect aspect
- modal verbs
- transitive verb
- intransitive verb

Try to work out together how his grammatical choices strengthen Auden's meaning.

Turn to page 48 for a commentary on this activity.

### Musée des Beaux Arts

About suffering they were never wrong,
The Old Masters: how well they understood
Its human position: how it takes place
While someone else is eating or opening a window or
Just walking dully along:

How, when the aged are reverently, passionately waiting
For the miraculous birth, there always must be
Children who did not specially want it to happen, skating
On a pond at the edge of the wood.
They never forgot
That even the dreadful martyrdom must run its course
Anyhow in a corner, some untidy spot
Where the dogs go on with their doggy
Life and the torturer's horse
Scratches its innocent behind on a tree.

In Brueghel's *Icarus*, for example: how everything turns away
Quite leisurely from the disaster; the ploughman may
Have heard the splash, the forsaken cry,
But for him it was not an important failure; the sun shone
As it had to on the white legs disappearing into the green
Water; and the expensive delicate ship that must have seen
Something amazing, a boy falling out of the sky,
Had somewhere to get to and sailed calmly on.

# Sound patterning and phonology

Every language has its own system of sounds represented by phonemes in speech and by graphemes in writing. This is what is meant when we talk about the phonology of a language. Every language has a unique set of phonemes, but each phoneme can be subtly varied according to where a speaker lives (**accent** and **dialect**). These slight variants are called **allophones**. For example, if you live in North Yorkshire some of your phonemes may be different depending on whether you live in the west of the county or the east. These allophones can be recognised and differentiated both by local residents and by linguists.

The technical study of speech sounds and how they are produced is called phonetics. The human articulatory structure (mouth, teeth, tongue, etc.) is the same worldwide, so the International Phonetic Alphabet (IPA) represents in graphic symbols the actual sounds made in whatever language is being spoken or studied. The phonemes of English include 24 consonants, 12 vowels and 8 dipthongs (double vowel sounds), as follows:

| Consonant sounds | | | | | | | | | |
| --- | --- | --- | --- | --- | --- | --- | --- | --- | --- |
| /p/ | as in *part* | /g/ | as in *get* | /θ/ | as in *thing* | /ʒ/ | as in *measure* | /l/ | as in *let* |
| /b/ | as in *but* | /tʃ/ | as in *chin* | /ð/ | as in *this* | /h/ | as in *has* | /r/ | as in *red* |
| /t/ | as in *too* | /dʒ/ | as in *joke* | /s/ | as in *see* | /m/ | as in *mat* | /j/ | as in *yes* |
| /d/ | as in *did* | /f/ | as in *food* | /z/ | as in *zoo* | /n/ | as in *not* | /w/ | as in *will* |
| /k/ | as in *kiss* | /v/ | as in *voice* | /ʃ/ | as in *she* | /ŋ/ | as in *long* | | |

| Vowel sounds | | | | | | | |
| --- | --- | --- | --- | --- | --- | --- | --- |
| **Long vowels** | | **Short vowels** | | | | **Diphthongs** | |
| /iː/ as in *each* | | /ɪ/ as in *it* | /ʊ/ as in *put* | | | /eɪ/ as in *day* | /ɪə/ as in *near* |
| /ɑː/ as in *car* | | /e/ as in *then* | /ə/ as in *again* | | | /aɪ/ as in *by* | /eə/ as in *there* |
| /ɔː/ as in *more* | | /æ/ as in *back* | | | | /ɔɪ/ as in *boy* | /ʊə/ as in *truer* |
| /uː/ as in *too* | | /ʌ/ as in *not* | | | | /əʊ/ as in *no* | |
| /uː/ as in *word* | | /ɒ/ as in *much* | | | | /aʊ/ as in *now* | |

Because sound is the first thing a baby responds to, it's no surprise that we all delight in patterned sound, from nursery rhymes to rap, rhythm and blues to Rachmaninov. Indeed, our everyday conversation is sound patterned much more than we realise ('I'm a poet and I didn't know it!'). Sound patterning is central to all literary genres, from lyric and epic poetry to fiction and drama, and in many non-literary genres too, like advertising and political speech-making. Indeed, as we shall see in the section on rhetoric later in this chapter (page 42), sound patterning lies at the heart of all persuasion.

## Some sound-patterning devices

One of the most accessible devices is onomatopoeia, when the sound of a word directly expresses its meaning (sizzle, bang, splash). A more general term for this is 'sound symbolism' or phonaesthesia. The poet Tennyson was particularly skilful with this kind of sound patterning, as you can see from the following texts. The first is an extract from 'Mariana', a poem imagining the situation of the deserted lover of Count Angelo in Shakespeare's play *Measure for Measure*. The second is from *Morte d'Arthur*, Tennyson's version of the death of King Arthur, whose loyal knight Sir Bedivere is seeking the death barge which will take the dying king to 'the island valley of Avilion'.

**Text A**

About a stone-cast from the wall
   A sluice with blackened water slept,
And o'er it many, round and small,
   The clustered marish-mosses crept.
Hard by a poplar shook always,
   All silver-green with gnarled bark:
For leagues no other tree did mark
The level waste, the rounding gray.
   She only said, 'My life is dreary,
     He cometh not,' she said;
   She said, 'I am aweary, aweary,
     I would that I were dead!'

**Text B**

He heard the deep behind him, and a cry
Before. His own thought drove him, like a goad.
Dry clashed his harness in the icy caves
And barren chasms, and all to left and right
The bare black cliff clanged all around him, as he based
His feet on juts of slippery crag that rang
Sharp-smitten with the dint of armed heels —
And on a sudden, lo! the level lake,
And the long glories of the winter moon.

## Activity 14 · Investigating some poetic uses of sound patterning

In both extracts, look for examples of the following types of sound patterning:

- onomatopoeia, including phonaesthesia
- alliteration
- assonance
- consonance
- dissonance

**Reminder**

- Alliteration refers to repetition of the initial consonant (red rag).
- Assonance refers to repetition of a vowel sound with different consonants (fat cat).
- Consonance means repetition of a consonant group with different vowels (whistle/rustle/hassle/wrestle).
- Dissonance means use of clashing consonant sounds for dramatic effect.

What emotional and descriptive effects is Tennyson attempting to create in each extract? How successful is he?

## Rhyme and rhythm

The other major areas of sound patterning which must be considered are rhyme and rhythm. Rhyme refers to the repetition of a group of sounds or phonemes, while rhythm refers to the regular patterning of light and heavy beats (stressed and unstressed syllables). These repeated patterns usually are found in poetry, but can appear in prose, as well as in spoken language (formal or informal).

Initially lots of people find rhyme and rhythm confusing simply because of their awkward spelling (both words begin with the admittedly bizarre consonant cluster 'rhy-') and then lose heart. However, if you can master the spelling and remember the meaning, you will understand the powerful effects achievable by these types of sound patterning. Types of rhyme include end rhyme, internal rhyme, half-rhyme and eye rhyme; under the heading of rhythm we can include metre and metrical patterns.

### Rhyme

End rhyme is easily recognisable in this nursery rhyme, with an interesting non-rhymed variation in lines 4 and 5.

> Hey diddle <u>diddle</u>
> The cat and the <u>fiddle</u>
> The cow jumped over the <u>moon</u>
> The little dog laughed
> To see such fun
> And the dish ran away with the <u>spoon</u>.

Internal rhyme refers to 'phonetic echoes' within the poetic line itself (or the prose fiction sentence or even in conversation):

> The curfew <u>tolls</u> the <u>knell</u> of passing day,
> The <u>lowing</u> herd winds <u>slowly</u> o'er the lea.

Half-rhyme conveys a sense of rhyme and rhythmic patterning to the audience by using the same final consonant with different vowels and initial consonants (band/bind/found/wind).

Eye rhyme is visual rather than aural, in that the pattern is realised via graphemes, not phonemes. Examples include cough/bough/rough/slough.

You may also encounter the terms masculine rhyme and feminine rhyme, referring to end rhymes. This will make more sense when you've read the next section, but in brief, a poetic line ending with a strong stressed syllable is called masculine rhyme (Humpty Dumpty sat on a <u>wall</u>/Humpty Dumpty had a great <u>fall</u>), and an end rhyme which is weak or unstressed is called a feminine rhyme (Little Jack Horn<u>er</u>/Sat in a corn<u>er</u>). These terms are plainly sexist and reflect past attitudes. We use them simply for descriptive convenience.

### Rhythm

The word itself comes from the Greek *rhuthmos*, meaning flow, and refers to the patterning of sound not only in language but also in music. However, in terms of language, whether spoken or written, rhythm refers to the regular patterning of sound. We talk about certain languages being 'musical' and these tend to be languages from the Romance family like French, Italian and Spanish. Closer to home, people view certain regional varieties of English as being 'musical' or not (Newcastle/Liverpool, Welsh/Birmingham). People's individual idiolects also vary in their musicality. Nevertheless, poetry is the most obviously 'musical' or rhythmic literary genre, and metre is the name given to the regular patterning in verse of stressed and unstressed syllables.

Poets have a range of choices: they can choose to write in a regular metre, or an irregular metre (free verse). The choice seems to be partly a matter of individual preference, and partly poetic fashion. The most popular metre for English poets from Chaucer until the twenty-first century has been iambic pentameter or blank verse. This metre consists of 10 syllables, 5 of which are stressed and 5 unstressed. The reason for its popularity seems to be that it fits the ebb and flow of English speech. If you read aloud the lines on page 20 from Shakespeare's Sonnet 18, you can hear the way the voice (underlined) modulates the stressed/unstressed patterning. Stressed syllables are numbered in bold.

1 **2** 3 **4**    5 **6** 7 **8**    9  **10**
<u>Shall</u> I com<u>pare</u> thee to a <u>summer's</u> <u>day</u>?
  1   **2**   3   **4** 5 **6**   7   **8** 9 **10**
<u>Thou</u> art more <u>lovely</u> and more <u>temperate</u>.
Rough <u>winds</u> do <u>shake</u> the <u>darling</u> <u>buds</u> of <u>May</u>
And <u>summer's</u> <u>lease</u> hath <u>all</u> too <u>short</u> a <u>date</u> …

Tetrameter (8 syllables, 4 stressed, 4 unstressed) is a metre which was popular with eighteenth-century poets. Here Dorothy Wordsworth writes about the cottage she and her brother shared at Grasmere in the Lake District.

  1   **2**   3   **4** 5   **6**   7     **8**
Peaceful our valley, fair and green,
And beautiful its cottages,
Each in its nook, its sheltered hold,
Or underneath its tuft of trees

An example of trimeter (6 syllables, 3 stressed, 3 unstressed) is

  **1**   2   **3**   4   **5** 6
Land of hope and glory
Mother of the free … .

Much less frequently encountered is dimeter (4 syllables, 2 stressed, 2 unstressed), the unwieldy hexameter (12 syllables, 6 stressed, 6 unstressed) and the even heavier fourteener (14 syllables, 7 stressed, 7 unstressed). Byron was a wonderfully inventive user of metrics, and this extract from 'The Destruction of Sennacherib' is hexameter at its most exciting.

  1   **2** 3 **4**    5    **6**   7 **8** 9   **10** 11 **12**
The Assyrian came down like a wolf on the fold,
And his cohorts were gleaming in purple and gold;
And the sheen of their spears was like stars on the sea,
When the blue wave rolls nightly on deep Galilee.

The best way to be confident about metre is to try it out on poems you know, from nursery rhymes to Sylvia Plath. You may find that modern poets don't use as much regular metre as poets in the past, but there usually are patterns to be discovered. Watch out too for syllabic verse where the number of syllables in a line counts, rather than the number of stresses.

## Activity 15 — Looking for sound patterns created by rhyme and rhythm

Group work

Go back to the W.H. Auden poem on page 16. Half your group should focus on the broad area of rhyme and the other half on rhythm. Look for sound patterns and explore how effectively sound patterning enhances meaning. Share your findings.

# Language functions

What are the functions of human language? Many theorists, in fields ranging from linguistics and philosophy to anthropology and sociology, have attempted to address this key question. For early humans the function of language was probably to exchange information and perhaps express feeling. The linguist Michael Halliday suggested that language has three overarching metafunctions:

- the ideational metafunction, by which information about the world is communicated
- the interpersonal metafunction, which concerns the personal relationships between speakers/writers in an exchange
- the textual function, which refers to the actual language mode used (spoken or written) and the genre chosen.

Looked at in more detail, these broad metafunctions can be linked with language functions identified by other theorists.

- The ideational metafunction includes the referential or descriptive function.
- The interpersonal metafunction includes conative, expressive and phatic functions.
- The metalingual or poetic function is part of the textual metafunction.

Halliday noted that when children talk, these metafunctions disappear. Instead we have separated functions:

- instrumental function – 'I want' ('Me want apple.')
- informative function – 'I've got something to tell you' ('Daddy home now.')
- imaginative function – 'Let's pretend' ('You be the engine driver.')
- regulative function – 'Do as I tell you' ('Granny fetch my book.')
- interactional function – 'Me and you' ('You and Henry my friends.')
- personal function – 'Here I come' ('I'm swinging higher.')
- heuristic function – 'Tell me why' ('What's that?').

As children's language develops, all these individual functions meld back together, and they ultimately acquire the metafunctions of adult language. (For more on child language acquisition, see page 232.)

Having outlined the theoretical background of language function, we can turn to those aspects of language function particularly relevant to your A-level English course. We shall be looking at the pragmatic and expressive functions of spoken and written language, and in particular how they relate to the creative function in literary and non-literary language.

The pragmatic function of language is covered by the ideational metafunction, in that it is related to the world and its affairs, from shopping to cooking to climate change, school dinners, iPods, taxi-drivers, football and sausages. In other words, talking and writing about any aspect of the world is part of the pragmatic function of language, by which things get done, meals are prepared, conversations are concluded, doctor's appointments are made and kept, and service encounters of all sorts happen. Pragmatic language functions include

- to inform
- to advise
- to persuade
- to get something done (transactional)

- to argue (expository)
- to collaborate
- to socialise
- to evaluate

These purposes or functions tend to be associated with non-literary spoken and written language.

## Activity 16
**Individual**

## Exploring a range of texts with pragmatic language function

List each spoken exchange you took part in during the course of one day (for example, talked to sister at breakfast, said hello to neighbour, bought bus ticket). Then identify each exchange in terms of its function from the list above.

The expressive function of language, included within the interpersonal metafunction, reflects the individual act of communication between speaker and audience or addressee, and writer and audience or reader. Its subfunctions are interactional, social and evaluative and convey feelings and emotions, express relationships and reveal attitudes and opinions. There is also the associated phatic function, which at the most basic level communicates human recognition of other humans as part of the same social world, thus creating a kind of social lubrication ('Hi, how are you?' 'I'm fine thanks. You OK?'). The expressive function appears in casual conversation as well as in more complex interactions, and it is a key aspect of literature. In literature the writer is

- expressing his or her emotions
- creating emotional response in the audience
- crafting and communicating emotion via a character, situation or description to affect the reader or audience
- exploring subjective and emotional experience via a particular literary genre, such as poetry.

## Activity 17 — Investigating a range of language functions

**Pair work**

In this activity we shall look at some examples of pragmatic and expressive language function in action across a range of text types. Text A is a transcript of a conversation in a shop. Text B comes from the *Times Educational Supplement* (October 2007). Text C is from Shakespeare's *Twelfth Night*. Text D is from 'At the Bay', by Katherine Mansfield (1932).

Working in pairs, look at each of the four texts in turn and decide

- how the ideational, interpersonal and textual metafunctions are realised in each
- which texts seem predominantly pragmatic and which expressive
- what other functions you can identify in each text (there will be several in each)
- how the creative function is demonstrated

### Text A

(.) indicates a short pause – a number in the brackets gives the length of a pause in seconds.

| | |
|---|---|
| Customer | er love (1.0) how come these in here are so cheap are they seconds or something |
| Salesperson | oh (2.0) it's just because they're white |
| Customer | what do you mean |
| Salesperson | well erm last year's stock summer (.) you know |
| Customer | oh I see so there's nowt wrong with them then |
| Salesperson | oh no |
| Customer | OK then I'll have this one please |
| Salesperson | thank you (.) there you go two ninety nine please thanks there's your receipt and your penny |
| Customer | thanks love |
| Salesperson | bye |

### Text B

**Conduct 'state of the nation research'**

We invite experienced researchers, either individuals or consortia, to tender for a 'state of the nation' research project about teachers' continuing professional development (CPD). This project is intended to inform our strategy in this area.

The successful bidder will report on recent research that influences current CPD strategy. Using focus groups and surveys you will also gather and analyse teachers' experiences of CPD.

The contract will start on 7 January 2008 and will last 4–6 months.

### Text C

**Orsino**  If music be the food of love, play on,
Give me excess of it, that, surfeiting,
The appetite may sicken and so die.
That strain again! It had a dying fall.
O, it came o'er my ear like the sweet sound
That breathes upon a bank of violets,
Stealing and giving odour.

### Text D

A few moments later the back door of one of the bungalows opened, and a figure in a broad-striped bathing-suit flung down the paddock, cleared the stile, rushed through the tussock grass into the hollow, staggered up the sandy hillock, and raced for dear life over the big porous stones, over the cold, wet pebbles, on to the hard sand that gleamed like oil. Splish-Splosh! Splish-Splosh! The water bubbled round his legs as Stanley Burnell waded out exulting. First man in as usual! He'd beaten them all again. And he swooped down to souse his head and neck.

'Hail, brother! All hail, Thou Mighty One!' A velvety bass voice came booming over the water.

Great Scott! Damnation take it! Stanley lifted up to see a dark head bobbing far out and an arm lifted. It was Jonathan Trout – there before him! 'Glorious morning!' sang the voice.

'Yes, very fine!' said Stanley briefly. Why the dickens didn't the fellow stick to his part of the sea?

# Pragmatics

Pragmatics is an area of linguistics which is closely connected with language function or purpose, and with language in use. (This will lead us in the next section to consider another key concept, context.) Pragmatics is primarily associated with spoken language, and focuses on the ways in which people use language to 'get things done'. David Crystal (1987) puts it well: 'pragmatics studies the factors that govern our choice of language in social interaction and the effects of our choice on others'. Pragmatics theorists are therefore interested in how successful conversation works (for example, H.P. Grice's conversational maxims), and how direct and implied meanings are conveyed (for example, conversational implicatures). A further aspect of pragmatics is the way expectations work in the structuring of pragmatic interactions.

Erving Goffman (1974) was an early exponent of frame theory applied to interaction. J.J. Gumperz (1982) argued that whilst we are talking, we pick up contextualisation cues (or frames) enabling us to recognise the situation and structure our responses appropriately. These mental frameworks help us to interpret the current situation and anticipate what is going to happen. Thus going to see the doctor or attending a job interview have particular frames leading to particular discourse structures. If these frames of expectation are disrupted (for example, the doctor insists on giving us an account of her symptoms, or the interviewer confides that the job isn't worth applying for) we are completely wrong-footed and don't know how to respond.

Schema theory develops the idea of the effect of expectations further. 'Schema' means a mental model or knowledge structure in the memory, with its own patterning of expectations, frames and assumptions. Deborah Tannen (1993) links frame theory with schema theory, and in the following extract from a fascinating case study demonstrates how conflicting frames can produce miscommunication between a paediatrician, a child patient who has cerebral palsy, her mother, and an unseen video audience of fellow doctors. Here each speaker uses different frames of communication. These range from a medical register (examination frame), a friendly register (paediatric consultation frame), and a register appropriate for addressing the mother (consultation frame). Each frame creates and fulfils its own discourse expectations – unless someone slips up and uses the wrong register (which is what happens). To make matters worse, in the same consultation, mother and doctor have totally mismatched schema. For the mother (mental schema: wheezing means illness) the child's noisy breathing at night is worrying; for the doctor (mental schema: wheezing signifies a specific medical problem, which is not present) noisy breathing at night is nothing to worry about. Result – mismatched schema and a significant problem of communication!

**Pediatric consultation frame**
Doctor    Let me look in your ear. Do you have a monkey in your ear?
Child    [laughing] No
Doctor    No? let's see … I … see …a birdie!
Child    [laughing] No …

**Consultation frame**
Doctor    Her canals are fine, they're open, um her tympanic membrane was thin, and light … As you know, she does have difficulty with the use of her muscles.

**Paediatric consultation frame plus examination frame**
Doctor    [examining child's stomach] Okay? Okay. Any peanut butter and jelly in here?
Child    No
Doctor    No? Is your spleen palpable over there?
Child    No

**Examination frame plus consultation frame**
Doctor    Once more. Okay. That's good. She has very coarse breath sounds um … and you can hear a lot of the noises you hear when she breathes you can hear when you listen. But there's nothing that
Mother    That's the kind of noise I hear when she's sleeping at night.
Doctor    Yes. Yes. There's nothing really as far as pneumonia is concerned or as far as any um anything here. There's no wheezing um which would suggest a tightness or a constriction of the thing. There's no wheezing at all.

| Activity 18 | Investigating the registers associated with different frames |
|---|---|
| **Individual** | How many registers are employed in these doctor-patient exchanges? Match the lexis with each register. |

In most examples of pragmatics or language in use, the interaction works reasonably well, and if it doesn't there are obvious reasons why not, as in the Tannen case study described above. 'Language in use' encompasses many interactions of everyday life, often called service encounters (going to the supermarket, the bank, the hairdresser, student services or even the examinations office), where we tend to know what to expect. In Activity 17 we looked at an example of a service encounter in a shop. In the next activity there are two examples of pragmatic exchanges. One is entirely practical with only minimal phatic function, the other is more purpose driven and persuasive in function.

| Activity 19 | Comparing different kinds of pragmatic exchanges |
|---|---|

Read both texts carefully. Identify the purpose(s) of each interaction, the participants and the situation. How did you reach your conclusions?

Compare the lexical choice in each text, including use of specialised jargon, evaluative lexis and any interpersonal language.

Assess the success/failure of each interaction, giving reasons for your decision.

**Text A**

| A2 | London afternoon MIDLAND 58 heading 335 |
|---|---|
| ATC | MIDLAND 58 good afternoon climb flight level 180 |
| A2 | flight level 180 MIDLAND 58 |
| ATC | SPEEDBIRD 32 GOLF contact London on 131.05 routing direct to Pole Hill |
| A3 | 131.05 direct Pole Hill SPEEDBIRD 32 GOLF |
| ATC | SHUTTLE 75 heading 340 |
| A4 | 340 for SHUTTLE 75 |
| A5 | SHUTTLE 340 approaching flight level 200 |
| ATC | SHUTTLE 40 thank you climb now flight level 280 |
| A5 | climb flight level 280 SHUTTLE 40 |
| A1 | AIRFRANCE 046 maintaining level 290 |
| ATC | AIRFRANCE 046 roger |
| ATC | UK 618 continue present heading until advised |
| A6 | continue present heading until advised UK 618 and heading 325 |
| ATC | MIDLAND 58 climb flight level 280 |
| A2 | climb level 280 MIDLAND 58 |

[passage omitted]

| ATC | AIRFRANCE 046 contact London 131.05 goodbye |
|---|---|

[passage omitted]

| A7 | London good afternoon BRITANNIA 444B passing 260 descending flight level 200 |
| ATC | BRITANNIA 44B thank you |
| | |
| ATC | UK 618 contact Manchester 124.2 goodbye |
| A6 | 124.2 goodbye |
| ATC | SHUTTLE 40 direct to Trent call London 128.05 goodbye |
| A5 | 128.05 direct to Trent SHUTTLE 40 bye |
| ATC | MIDLAND 58 contact London 131.05 goodbye |
| A2 | 131.05 MIDLAND 58 goodbye |

**Text B**

| Sarah | Mr A let me introduce you to Michael Smith (.) he's our customer adviser (.) he'll be looking after you this morning [pause] what would you like to drink (.) tea or coffee |
| Michael Smith | good morning Mr A (.) come through to my office (.) have a seat (.) I understand from Sarah that you've got some credit cards that you haven't managed to pay off in full (.) and I've noticed that you've got a small personal loan and you make a lot of use of your current account (.) is that correct |
| Mr A | yes it is (.) but I also owe some money to um Suite Ideas (.) who I got a three piece suite off recently |
| Michael Smith | how much are we talking about |
| Mr A | oh about two thousand two hundred pounds |
| Michael Smith | so apart from the things we've talked about already (.) and the money to Suite Ideas (.) what other outstanding debts have you got |
| Mr A | that's it (.) apart from my mortgage really |
| Michael Smith | so what we're going to do this morning (.) is to spend twenty minutes doing what we call a customer service review (.) and find out a bit of background information about you (.) and see if we can save you any money on a monthly basis (.) organise your overdraft (.) and make sure that if anything were to happen to you (.) all those debts were protected with insurance (.) how would that make you feel |
| Mr A | oh well that would be great (.) a big relief (.) I didn't think you'd be able to do that and save me money (.) |

# Context

The importance of context in any written or spoken exchange should now be crystal clear. Without an understanding of the situation, events, participants and purpose of any spoken exchange we are lost. Without an understanding of the audience and purpose (and possibly genre) of any written text, whether literary or non-literary, it will be hard to make sense of it. Context is clearly of the utmost importance, as indicated earlier on pages 2–3.

## Context in spoken language

Whether we're talking with friends or strangers, almost the first thing to be established is the context of the discussion. Without contextual clues, we can feel excluded from the interaction, until someone helps out ('We're talking about the film that was released last week.'). Frame and schema theory can help, if we recognise a familiar situation ('Can I help you?' or 'I'm not trying to sell you anything but ...'). Once we've recognised the context, we can usually work out the audience and purpose.

In other situations, there are similar patterns of expectation, sometimes linked to the actual physical environment in which an interaction takes place (a bus stop, a train station, a supermarket, a classroom, the Strangers' Gallery in the Houses of Parliament, a public meeting, a travel agency or a bank). What can derail us in exchanges is if we have one set of expectations from an encounter and the reverse happens. Every situation has its own generic expectations, and if these are flouted or subverted, the end result is disturbing at best and disruptive at worst.

## Context in written language

Context is important to all written language, as many theorists have demonstrated over the last two decades. We also need to understand some different approaches to author, text and context which theorists have teased out. For example, there are clear differences between readerly and writerly texts and between reading and writing positions in relation to context.

- A readerly text is one where the reader and author share expectations, recognise the genre expectations and rely on them being present (for example, any detective story or romantic Mills and Boon novel).
- A writerly text is one where literary and generic conventions are violated, expectations are flouted and the reader has to work hard to understand the text (for example, James Joyce's *Ulysses*).
- Reading position refers to the fact that we all read from our own personal experience (including gender) as well as from our experience of society.
- Writing position refers to the individual author's desire to be creative, within the context of their personal life and their experience of society.

The concept of interrogating a text has also emerged. Although the word 'interrogation' has some negative overtones, the idea of vigorously asking questions of a text, rather than simply looking at it, gives the reader an active rather than passive role. Likely questions are predictable enough, however (Who wrote the text? For whom? When was it written? What was going on in the world at the time?).

The following constructed model is a useful and more developed way of approaching context. This breakdown of different contexts can be applied to any text, literary or non-literary, spoken/heard or written. Where appropriate, the term 'listener/speaker' can be substituted for 'reader'.

- Context of immediate situation: Who is reading the text and from what position? Is it a text suited to objective reading or empathetic, creative reading? What other readings might be possible?
- Context of reception: Who were the first readers of the text and how would they have read it?
- Context of production: Who is/was the author/ producer of the text? How and why was it written? What is/was the author's own attitude?
- Context/larger cultural frame of reference: The social, historical, political and cultural environment in which the author wrote the text and readers read it.
- Context of text: What is the genre? What is the text about? Does it reflect the writer's individual and social experience? Does it appeal to the reader's individual and social experience? What literary influences or models are reflected in the text?

We shall now explore four texts, two literary and two non-literary, and apply the context model on page 27. Text A is a soliloquy by Hamlet. In Text B, from 'Mrs Midas' by Carol Ann Duffy, Midas's wife discovers that her husband's touch turns everything to gold. Text C is part of a speech by Martin Luther King (1963). Texts D, E and F are short extracts from Christmas circular letters from Simon Hoggart's collection *The Cat That Could Open the Fridge* (2004).

**Text A**

**Hamlet**  To be, or not to be – that is the question;
Whether 'tis nobler in the mind to suffer
The slings and arrows of outrageous fortune
Or to take arms against a sea of troubles
And by opposing end them. To die, to sleep –
No more – and by a sleep to say we end
The heartache and the thousand natural shocks
That flesh is heir to. 'Tis a consummation
Devoutly to be wished ....

**Text B**

He came into the house. The doorknobs gleamed.
He drew the blinds. You know the mind; I thought of
the Field of the Cloth of Gold and Miss Macready.
He sat in that chair like a king on a burnished throne.
The look on his face was strange, wild, vain. I said,
What in the name of God is going on? He started to laugh.
…
It was then I started to scream. He sank to his knees.
After we'd both calmed down, I finished the wine
on my own, hearing him out. I made him sit
on the other side of the room and keep his hands to himself.
I locked the cat in the cellar. I moved the phone.
The toilet I didn't mind. I couldn't believe my ears:

how he'd had a wish. Look, we all have wishes; granted.
But who has wishes granted? Him. Do you know about gold?
It feeds no one; aurum, soft, untarnishable; slakes
no thirst.

Note: Miss Macready was the narrator's history teacher. Henry VIII of England and Francis I of France had a magnificent but unproductive meeting in 1520. 'Burnished throne' is an intertextual and ironic reference to Cleopatra in Shakespeare's *Antony and Cleopatra*.

**Text C**

I have a dream that one day this nation will rise up and live out the true meaning of this creed: 'We hold these truths to be self-evident; that all men are created equal.'

I have a dream that one day on the red hills of Georgia the sons of former slaves and the sons of former slaveowners will be able to sit down together at the table of brotherhood.

I have a dream that one day even the state of Mississippi, a desert state sweltering with the heat of injustice and oppression, will be transformed into an oasis of peace and justice.

I have a dream that my four little children will one day live in a nation where they will not be judged by the color of their skin but by the content of their character.

I have a dream. ...

### Text D

This year's stress has been my neighbour's wind chimes. I can hear them clearly in my bedroom, even with the window closed. It drives me mad. My neighbours do not respond to polite requests, they will not take part in mediation and they are merely indignant at letters from the Council. I am a Quaker and a pacifist, I have training in conflict resolution – well now I have first-hand knowledge too. I have discovered what hate is, and that I was blessed in not hating anyone for the first 33 years of my life.

### Text E

July and August were incredibly hot, and on the 21st, right on cue, the potato crisp hullabaloo broke out, since when the village has been at various times in an uproar, pitting brother against brother, and we still await a decision from the planning authority.

### Text F

This year Snugs (Mr Snugglekins, our cat) has kept us on our toes. He has learned to open the door of our new large fridge.

### Commentary on Text A

The extract comes from Hamlet's soliloquy after he has learnt that his father was murdered by his usurping uncle, Claudius. The text is currently read, studied and performed by actors and students worldwide; the tragedy of the protagonist, the Prince of Denmark, draws audiences into empathising with the witty but damaged hero (*immediate situation*).

The play was first published in the Quarto in 1603 and presumably performed at about the same time. Although we are short of contemporary evidence about its reception, there was a second Quarto edition 1604–1605, another in 1623, and many others since, so we can assume that the play's popularity has lasted (*reception*).

Our information about Shakespeare's life is limited, except that we know he had a grammar-school education, was an actor as well as a writer, and often wrote parts for fellow actors (*production*).

The play would have appealed to an audience keen on ghosts and familiar with Senecan tragedy, and to a society where the royal succession had only just ceased to be a burning issue, but where the murder of a king was truly shocking (*historical/cultural background*).

Contemporary audiences would have been aware of its sources in Jacobean revenge tragedy, as well as earlier historical texts which Shakespeare may have used, such as Saxo Grammaticus's twelfth-century *Historiae Danicae*, and Francois de Belleforest's sixteenth-century *Histoires Tragiques* (*text/genre*). Shakespeare's skilful reworking of his many sources has created a play where audiences, producers and readers can still find new ways of interpreting the character of Hamlet (see Tom Stoppard (1966) *Rosencrantz and Guildenstern are Dead*). The way Shakespeare uses powerful images of warfare, the sea and sleep to represent life and death, as well as the magnificent handling of iambic pentameter, and particularly the caesura and enjambement to convey Hamlet's mental struggle, are fruitful areas for further discussion.

### Commentary on Text B

'Mrs Midas' comes from *The World's Wife* (1999) by Carol Ann Duffy, in which the poet uses the voices of famous 'other halves' (Mrs Darwin, Mrs Aesop and Anne Hathaway) to provide a new perspective. The readership is contemporary, with perhaps particular interest from women. The construction of the poem makes it difficult, however, to read from any perspective other than that of the female narrative voice (*immediate situation/reception*).

In terms of the *production* of the text, Duffy has a strong interest in interpreting the world through a feminist perspective and exploring the breadth of women's experience. The collection, *The World's Wife*, and this particular poem represent a development in her work in that there is a common theme uniting the poems, namely women's relationship with men. Duffy is avowedly feminist; born in 1955, she grew up as feminism became politicised in the 1970s and 1980s (*larger social/cultural frame of reference*). The poem itself (*text*) is in relatively regular six-line stanzas, with variable line length. Duffy has a powerful ear for the rhythms of natural speech, so that the ironic voice of Mrs Midas conveys to the reader a kind of confessional, confidential quality, with allusions ranging from the mundane ('I moved the phone') to historic and literary allusions.

### Commentary on Text C

People who read or hear recordings of this speech today will respond differently depending on their national, political and personal attitudes both to the speaker and to his message. Most people who abhor slavery and its consequences will empathise completely with Martin Luther King's speech (*immediate situation*).

When the speech was given in August 1963 to celebrate the centenary of President Abraham Lincoln's emancipation proclamation, the supporters and members of the NAACP would have wholeheartedly supported King, as would other Americans who rejected segregation. Elsewhere in America, particularly in the South, very different views might have been held (*reception*).

The Reverend Martin Luther King (later a winner of the Nobel Peace Prize) was a well-known Civil Rights activist in the early 1960s, leading various demonstrations and marches in the Southern United States. In August 1963 he led a Freedom March from the Washington Monument to the Lincoln Memorial, and made this speech to an audience of over 200,000 marchers (*production, social/political/cultural frame of reference*). It is a masterpiece of rhetoric, and thought by many to be the greatest speech of the twentieth century (*text*).

### Commentary on Texts D–F

Hoggart selected these extracts as amusing examples of self-revelation (D), inadvertent mystification (E) and the climactic end to a narrative of family medical disaster (F). He seems fascinated by the combination of smugness, 'showing off', lack of self-awareness, and obsessive detail characterising this genre. The contexts of *immediate situation/reception* are complicated, in that the 'reader' is not the intended recipient (who disloyally sent the letter to Hoggart!). We can assume that by the time Hoggart's book was published many more people would have read the letters. We can only speculate about whether there might have been more sympathetic readings by other recipients.

The context of *production* is interesting here – why would the family/family representative write in such detail? The explanation seems to differ with each text. Text D is absurd and yet one sympathises with the writer, equally tortured by wind chimes and his conscience! Text E is funny because the imagination runs riot as to what the 'potato crisp hullabaloo' could possibly be about (the writer quite oblivious to a reader's mystification). Text F is comic within the context of the previous narrative of medical disaster. The bathetic image of the dextrous cat is unintentionally comic. The writing position in each text is entirely author focused, with zero awareness of audience. Egocentricity and one-upmanship prevail.

The *social/cultural frame of reference* is the social networking middle class. The genre of the round-robin letter (*text*) has become increasingly popular as a lazy way of telling people family news at Christmas. Hoggart tells of travelogues and medical histories 9000 words in length, as well as catalogues of spectacular achievement by the writer's children/grandchildren. Readers find this genre appealing, appalling or a combination of guilty enjoyment, fascinated horror and straight embarrassment.

## Activity 20 · Investigating context further

Use the model on page 27 to write a contextual commentary.

Choose the first page of a short story or a 'coffee break' magazine story, and analyse the ways in which context is used to make the story appeal to the reader.

Select a one-page advertisement, with more text than image, and analyse how the use of context supports its persuasive purpose.

# Text and discourse

There is some discussion among linguists as to which is the superordinate category, text or discourse. The term 'discourse' can be applied to the specialised 'discourse of advertising' as well as to a passage of continuous written text beyond the sentence. The term also is used with general reference to spoken language, and the practice of discourse analysis explores stretches of spoken interchange, focusing in particular on the structures and patterns of interaction.

Text is a term also associated with the concept of structure. The word derives from the Latin noun *textum* meaning 'structure', which in turn derives from the Latin verb *texere*. This verb had four meanings:

- literal meaning 'to weave'
- transferred meaning 'to twine together, intertwine'
- 'to put together or construct'
- 'to compose speech or writing'.

It's not at all difficult to see how readily the word 'weave', associated with cloth, transferred its meaning to constructing spoken and written language into a web of words. Even today we use similar words to describe language, such as the 'fabric' of an argument or the 'texture' of the poem. So perhaps text is a superordinate category above discourse, both historically and philosophically?

Today the term 'text' is applied by linguists and post-modern theorists not only to written and spoken language, but also to graphic and multi-modal forms, such as film or installation art. In this section, however, we shall use 'text' to refer to any genre or form of spoken and written language. The transferred image of text as a woven structure remains useful, because all communication in language is in effect a woven structure of words, sound patterns, grammar, syntax and imagery. You may also have noticed that 'context' is related etymologically to 'text'. Both share the same root form, with the prefix 'con-' (together with) representing the extra information that context gives to a text.

## Activity 21 — Identifying audience, purpose and context

**Pair work**

Read the following texts carefully. Text A is a telephone conversation between friends. Text B is an extract from a twentieth-century American short story, 'New York to Detroit' by Dorothy Parker. Text C is a nursery rhyme. Text D is from the *Observer* newspaper (2007). Text E is a computer desktop message. Text F is an extract from a letter dated 1859 from a young woman (Sarah Ellen Gaukroger) to a young man who, she suspects, is trifling with her affections.

Working in pairs, identify audience and context for each text then consider how the language choices (including lexis, grammar, syntax and discourse features) match the purpose of the speaker or writer.

### Text A

| | |
|---|---|
| Stephen | Ian |
| Ian | Yes |
| Stephen | Hello |
| Ian | What did you do in English? |
| Stephen | We didn't do anything really. |
| Ian | Did you do your projects? |
| Stephen | No, because he was away. |
| Ian | Was he? |
| Stephen | Yes. |
| Ian | That was fortunate. |
| Stephen | Well I walked into the classroom and … |
| Ian | He's never away. |
| Stephen | No, but he's supposed to have a really bad cold or something |
| Ian | Oh that's a shame will he be there tomorrow? |
| Stephen | Er, well if he wasn't there today and he's got a really bad cold, I doubt it. But you've still got to go to the lesson though. |

### Text B

'All ready with Detroit,' said the telephone operator.

'Hello,' said the girl in New York.

'Hello?' said the young man in Detroit.

'Oh, Jack!' she said. 'Oh, darling, it's so wonderful to hear you. You don't know how much I –'

'Hello?' he said.

'Ah, can't you hear me?' she said. 'Why, I can hear you just as if you were right beside me. Is this any better, dear? Can you hear me now?'

'Who did you want to speak to?' he said.

'You, Jack!' she said. 'You, you. This is Jean, darling. Oh, please try to hear me. This is Jean.'

'Who?' he said.

'Jean', she said. 'Ah, don't you know my voice? It's Jean, dear. Jean.'

'Oh, hello there,' he said. 'Well. Well, for heaven's sake. How are you?'

'I'm all right,' she said. 'Oh, I'm not either, darling. I – oh, it's just terrible. I can't stand it any more. Aren't you coming back? Please, when are you coming back? You don't know how awful it is, without you. It's been such a long time, dear – you said it would just be four or five days, and it's nearly three weeks. It's like years and years. Oh, it's been so awful, sweetheart – it's just –'

'Hey, I'm terribly sorry,' he said, 'but I can't hear one damn thing you're saying. Can't you talk louder, or something?'

## Text C
Hickory dickory dock
The mouse ran up the clock.
The clock struck one,
The mouse ran down,
Hickory dickory dock.

## Text D
The BBC is being urged to appoint a language chief by critics who claim that its reputation as a bastion of the Queen's English is fading fast.

They claim that presenters and correspondents on both television and radio routinely misuse words, make grammatical mistakes and use colloquialisms instead of standard English.

Sir Michael Lyons, chair of the BBC Trust, will receive an open letter tomorrow calling for a 'democratic airing' of the proposals, which advocate the creation of a new post to scrutinise 'the syntax, vocabulary and style' of thousands of staff heard on air.

## Text E
Unable to connect you to preferred wireless network
Windows could not connect you to any of your preferred
wireless networks. Windows will keep trying to connect.
To see a list of all networks, including others you can
connect to, click this message

## Text F
I have heard (and from good authority) of your making an offer of your honoured self (not a month since yet) to a lady that I know would not deign to speak to you but no matter she has as you no doubt suppose plenty of the shining metal, and that leads me to think you are determined to have money, it is of more consequence to you by far than love affection and domestic happiness. And if you take a wife without money it will be the last recourse, I pitty [sic] the woman you get on that score, for you will ever repine at her want of <u>gold,</u> pardon me if I have said more than I ought but when we feel we have been slighted if we have any spirit we shew it, and I hope I am not without nor without common sense either. I think it a very serious matter talking of love and marring [sic] to much so to be trifled about; you need not think because you have got a <u>cage</u> you can have any woman for the asking for I would have you remember they don't all want you that looks at you ...

# Intertextuality

The concept of intertextuality emerged in the 1960s, reflecting the interest of French critics in the theories of the Russian linguist and philosopher Mikhail Bakhtin. He regarded all language, spoken or written, as dialogic. He not only believed that spoken language reflected conversations between individuals but he saw our relationship with our society as dialogic. Bakhtin famously used the term heteroglossia (meaning 'multiple voices') to describe the rich texture of social and personal interaction.

Use of the term 'intertextuality' recognises the fact that all texts have links with each other over time, in subject-matter and in the lexis available. One American critic, Harold Bloom, coined the phrase 'the anxiety of influence' to describe this state of mutual indebtedness. He was trying to convey the burden of the past felt by many creative artists.

Since the 1960s, the idea of influence, of textual echoes, allusions and references in literature has broadened considerably. As recording technology has advanced, and corpora of spoken language become established, it has become clear that people use intertextual reference freely in their everyday conversations, and not just in literary high culture. We all see patterns of analogy and make connections as ways of understanding the world. Furthermore, as the concept of 'text' widens to include multi-modal and visual genres, we recognise other sorts of visual patterns and analogies, and intertextual links can be made between visual images in film and other art forms. One kind of powerful intertextual reference is the terrifying shower scene in Hitchcock's film *Psycho* – a visual echo which many subsequent directors have exploited to chilling effect.

Here are three examples of intertextual references in literature.

- In Shakespeare's sonnet the line 'My mistress' eyes are nothing like the sun' deliberately subverts the courtly love tradition of rosy lips and sparkling eyes.
- Aldous Huxley borrowed a phrase from the lines 'How beauteous mankind is! O brave new world/ That has such people in't', from Miranda's speech in *The Tempest*, as the title for his novel *Brave New World* (1932).
- T.S. Eliot made an intertextual reference to Enobarbus's magnificent description of Cleopatra in his portrait of a modern woman in 'A Game of Chess' in *The Waste Land* (1925).

| Activity 22 | Exploring how intertextuality enriches a text |
| --- | --- |

**Pair work**

Text A is from Shakespeare's *Antony and Cleopatra*. Text B is from 'A Game of Chess', from T.S. Eliot's poem *The Waste Land*.

Working in pairs, read both texts carefully. Your task is to look for connections between them, to see what points Eliot might be making about twentieth-century society in his use of intertextual references. Here are some suggestions about aspects/features to consider.

- Compare the setting, situation and action in each text
- Lexis – try listing equivalent or semantically related words and phrases. For example, why does Eliot change 'burn'd' to 'glowed'?
- Syntax – look at comparable phrase and sentence structure, and word order
- Sound patterning – compare the metre and any other sound patterns.

**Text A**
The barge she sat in, like a burnish'd throne
Burn'd on the water: the poop was beaten gold;
Purple the sails, and so perfumed that
The winds were lovesick with them; the oars were silver,
Which to the tune of flutes kept stroke and made
The water which they beat to follow faster,
As amorous of their strokes …

**Text B**
The Chair she sat in, like a burnished throne,
Glowed on the marble, where the glass
Held up by standards wrought with fruited vines
From which a golden Cupidon peeped out
(Another hid his eyes behind his wing) …
In vials of ivory and coloured glass
Unstoppered, lurked her strange synthetic perfumes,
Unguent, powdered, or liquid – troubled, confused
And drowned the sense in odours …

(**Note:** 'Cupidon' is a variant name of Cupid, son of Venus and god of sexual love.)

# Narrative

Everyone can tell a story: narrative is part of everyday existence, whether it's an account of what happened at work, or a visit to yet one more university, or whether it's a funny story about friends or about a perfect stranger on the bus. We even narrate our symptoms to the doctor, and expect the diagnosis to provide a further explanatory narrative. Stories are told in travel journals or historical documents. Long-established genres like history, biography and autobiography are also narratives. As we tell our story, we are critically reassessing our social and physical environment and making new interpretations of the world. In other words, narrative combines both the ideational and the interpersonal metafunctions of language (see page 21). In the public context, news bulletins, journalism and advertising are all different kinds of storytelling. Some of these narratives are relatively impersonal and objective (national news broadcasting), others are full of 'human interest' and melodrama (tabloid press).

Storytelling or narrative in everyday life is universally recognised, but storytelling about imaginary or imagined characters and situations has an equally long tradition, going back to purely oral cultures when human beings made up stories to explain the mysteries of their terrifying world to each other, or told the adventures of tribal heroes. Many ancient cultures maintained written as well as oral versions of their history, stories and myths on vellum, papyrus, stone and even wood. We call this literature.

# Narrative voice

The narrative impulse is integral to human communication, but how does narrative actually work? We must start with the 'voice' of the storyteller. The concept of narrative voice is familiar to most people, and it is the voice that determines point of view or narrative perspective. In non-literary contexts like casual conversation, the narrative voice is first person, simply because the narrator is telling the story. However, the moment the narrator begins to tell someone else's story, the narrative voice becomes third person. In non-literary genres like advertising, second-person voice can be used as part of a strategy of synthetic personalisation (pretending friendliness to sell something – 'It's winter and you're fed up? Imagine yourself on a tropical beach …').

In literary genres like prose fiction and poetry, first- and third-person narrative voices are the norm. In drama, the situation is different, because dialogue between characters and the plot creates the overall narrative. Sometimes a character may step out of role to tell the audience more about the action. In *Henry V* and *Murder in the Cathedral*, Shakespeare and Eliot revive the Greek tradition of the chorus for their own purposes. In *Henry V* the audience is to imagine itself transported with the young king to France; in *Murder in the Cathedral* the women of Canterbury comment on events leading to Thomas Becket's martyrdom.

What are the advantages of first-person narrative voice? The reader benefits from insight into the character of the central narrator, as we can see in novels such as *Jane Eyre, Wuthering Heights, Huckleberry Finn* and *The Catcher in the Rye*. The reader also experiences events from the point of view of the narrator, the only disadvantage being that the narrator may not see the full picture or be reliable. Indeed, an author may exploit an unreliable narrator who holds back information, as Nellie Dean does in *Wuthering Heights,* to create suspense.

The third person or omniscient narrator is probably the most frequently used narrative voice because there is no intrusion of opinion or evaluation of events and character. The disadvantage is that the narrator is totally detached from the events and characters involved. A strategy counteracting this is the introduction of an authorial voice commenting on event, character or situation, and thereby drawing the reader into a more interactive relationship. Novels using third-person narrative voice include *Bleak House, Tom Jones, A Farewell to Arms, The Great Gatsby* and *Atonement*. Novels including an active authorial voice include *Middlemarch, Pride and Prejudice, Jane Eyre* and *North and South.*

# Point of view

It's also important to define 'point of view', which differs from narrative voice because it describes the 'angle of vision' through which plot and character are perceived and presented to the reader. It is not the voice speaking the narrative. A useful term which describes how point of view works is focalisation; the focalising eye of the narrator provides a crucial perspective for the reader. It is, of course, possible for an author to use a whole range of different points of view. If, alternatively, one point of view and one narrative voice are used throughout, this is called interior monologue or stream of consciousness. Every action, event and character is mediated through the direct words and thought of the focalised and subjective first-person narrator.

We can see how speech and thought are expressed in first-person narrative voice, but how are they represented in third-person narrative voice? These sentences illustrate the difference between how direct speech/thought and how indirect speech/thought are represented.

- The waiter said, 'Would you like to see the menu?' (Free direct speech – FDS)
- The waiter thought, 'I must remember that special order.' (Free direct thought – FDT)
- The customer said that she would prefer mineral water. (Free indirect speech – FIS)
- The customer thought that the service was excellent. (Free indirect thought FIT)

We have considered narrative voice, point of view and the representation of speech and thought mainly in relation to fiction. You should be aware that poetry can also use a range of narrative voices and different points of view.

## Narrative structure

The final aspect of narrative we need to explore is narrative structure. Although there have been other theorists, such as Vladimir Propp (1928) writing about structure in Russian fairy tales, we shall investigate William Labov's (1972) theory of narrative structure. Having undertaken studies of oral narratives of Black New York teenagers, Labov defined narrative as a unit of discourse with clear boundaries, linear structure, and recognisable stages in its development.

| Labov's narrative stages | Key Stages 3 & 4 |
| --- | --- |
| abstract – summary | introduction |
| orientation – context | development |
| evaluation – point of interest in the story | complication |
| narrative – storytelling, involving a series of complicating events | complication |
| result – what finally happened | climax |
| coda – signals the end | resolution |

You can compare this model with the one you may be familiar with from Key Stage 3 and Key Stage 4, shown in the right-hand column. Another interesting similarity can be seen between Labov's stages and the ordering of arguments by Roman rhetoricians (see page 43 for comparison of models). Even more interesting is the fact that the narrative stages in Labov's model are not all obligatory – some features can be optional. This allows for the narrative flexibility needed by storytellers of all kinds and in all contexts. Here is an example of how the narrative structure model can be applied to a nursery rhyme.

| | |
| --- | --- |
| Jack and Jill went up the hill | abstract + orientation |
| To fetch a pail of water | evaluation |
| Jack fell down | narrative |
| And broke his crown | result |
| And Jill came tumbling after. | coda |

The relationship between reader and narrator/author is an interesting one, ranging from Jane Eyre's triumphant 'Reader, I married him' to Tristram Shandy's collusive invitation to the reader to 'Shut the door' whilst he tells the delicate story of his conception. Much thought has been expended by theorists on reader-response theory. Here are some of its basic principles in simplified form:

- There is more than one reader of a text.
- The implied reader means the reading audience the author expected; it can also mean the audience the text 'created' itself (because readers responded to it).
- The inscribed reader means the reader who 'fits' the text and who is comfortably at home with it.
- The intended reader is whoever the author says s/he wrote for.
- The ideal reader means the reader who will extract maximum value from a particular text.
- The informed reader is every writer's dream – s/he knows the language of the created text, understands its range of meanings as well as the relevant literary conventions.
- The empirical reader means someone capable of reading texts in a variety of ways.

## Activity 23
**Pair work**

# Investigating theories of narrative and narrative structure

Here is a range of texts to investigate. Text A is from *Jane Eyre* (1848). Text B is a transcript of a conversation between a mother and her six-year-old child. Text C is an extract from Lawrence Sterne's *Tristram Shandy* (1760). Text D is an early version of a poem by Emily Dickinson. Text E is from Zadie Smith's novel *White Teeth* (2000). Text F is an extract from George Eliot's novel *Middlemarch* (1872).

Read these texts carefully, paying attention to the different kinds of narrative demonstrated.

Working with a partner, explore the ways in which the narrative functions in each text, using this list to help you:

- narrative voice
- point of view
- narrative structure
- authorial voice

What is the relationship between the reader and the narrator/author in each text?

---

**Text A**

The next thing I remember is waking up with a feeling as if I had had a frightful nightmare, and seeing before me a terrible red glare, crossed with thick black bars. I heard voices, too, speaking with a hollow sound, and as if muffled by a rush of wind or water: agitation, uncertainty, and an all-predominating sense of terror confused my faculties.

---

**Text B**

| Child | do you know what |
|---|---|
| Mother | (1.0) what |
| C | (3.0) I found (.) a fossil today |
| M | really |
| C | I mean a tooth |
| M | a tooth |
| C | yeah |
| M | wasn't one of yours was it |
| C | no (2.0) no it was off a dinosaur |
| M | a dinosaur where in school |
| C | no not inside |
| M | outside |
| C | erm |
| M | in the play area |
| C | yeah I saw a hole and then I looked in it and then I saw a (.) saw one |
| M | a tooth |
| C | yeah (.) and then I digged in with my finger (1.0) and then I saw one |
| M | are you sure it just wasn't a piece of stone |
| C | (.) no |
| M | why did you think it was a tooth |
| C | (3.0) because it was |
| M | (2.0) well sounds interesting enough to me |

## Text C

I wish either my father or my mother, or indeed both of them, as they were in duty both equally bound to it, had minded what they were about when they begot me; had they duly considered how much depended upon what they were then doing; – that not only the production of a rational Being was concerned in it, but that possibly the happy formation and temperature of his body, perhaps his genius and the very cast of his mind; – and, for aught they knew to the contrary, even the fortunes of his whole house might take their turn from the humours and dispositions which were then uppermost: –

## Text D

**The Chariot**
Because I could not stop for Death,
He kindly stopped for me;
The carriage held but just ourselves
And Immortality.

We slowly drove, he knew no haste,
And I had put away
My labor, and my leisure too,
For his civility.

We passed the school where children played,
Their lessons scarcely done;
We passed the fields of gazing grain,
We passed the setting sun.

We paused before a house that seemed
A swelling of the ground;
The roof was scarcely visible,
The cornice but a mound.

Since then 'tis centuries; but each
Feels shorter than the day
I first surmised the horses' heads
Were toward eternity.

(1891 version)

## Text E

For his second marriage [Archie] had chosen a mohair suit with a white polo-neck and both were proving problematic. The heat prompted rivulets of sweat to spring out all over his body, seeping through the polo-neck to the mohair and giving off an unmistakeable odour of damp dog. Clara, of course, was all cat. She wore a long brown woollen Jeff Banks dress and a perfect set of false teeth; the dress was backless, the teeth were white, and the overall effect was feline; a panther in evening dress; where the wool stopped and Clara's skin started was not clear to the naked eye. And like a cat she responded to the dusty sunbeam that was coursing through a high window on to the waiting couples. She warmed her bare back in it, she almost seemed to *unfurl*. Even the registrar, who had seen it all – horsy women marrying weaselly men, elephantine men marrying owlish women – raised an eyebrow at this most unnatural of unions as they approached his desk. Cat and dog.

**Text F**
Nor can I suppose that when Mrs Casaubon is discovered in a fit of weeping six weeks after her wedding, the situation will be regarded as tragic. Some discouragement, some faintness of heart at the new real future which replaces the imaginary, is not unusual … That element of tragedy which lies in the very fact of frequency, has not yet wrought itself into the coarse emotion of mankind; and perhaps our frames could hardly bear much of it. If we had a keen vision and feeling of all ordinary human life, it would be like hearing the grass grow and the squirrel's heart beat, and we should die of that roar which lies on the other side of silence. As it is, the quickest of us walk about well wadded with stupidity. However, Dorothea was crying …

# Cohesion and coherence

These closely linked terms follow on well from the previous section on narrative structure. Labov's narrative-structure theory is plot based and sequenced. Texts which are less strongly narrative based are structured by other means. The question 'How?' is answered by the terms 'cohesion' and 'coherence'. Cohesion describes the specific means by which sentences and larger units of text 'stick together' and communicate meaning. Coherence looks beyond the sentence/utterance and describes the way in which a whole passage of speech or writing makes sense. We shall now look at the following range of cohesive devices:

- plot (in narrative genres)
- semantic and grammatical relationships in a sentence/utterance
- substitution
- anaphoric and cataphoric reference
- ellipsis
- repetition of lexis, syntax and sounds
- use of conjunctives and discourse markers.

**Plot:** Obviously events and action create the overall structuring of narrative, as we have already discussed.

**Semantic and grammatical relationships:** We have already looked in some detail (page 9) at the distinction between content and function words. The link between content words is semantic, creating basic cohesion, even if the function words are absent:

hungry child eagerly ate red apple picnic asked.

We need the function words to create complete cohesion (and thus coherence):

<u>The</u> hungry child eagerly ate <u>my</u> red apple <u>at</u> <u>the</u> picnic <u>and</u> asked <u>for another</u>.

So the content words provide coherent meaning and the function words explain the relationships.

**Substitution** is another cohesive device used in this example, where the pronoun 'another' substitutes for 'red apple'. Substitution occurs frequently in both speech and writing, without people being conscious of it. It's invaluable because it avoids unnecessary repetition and makes a sentence/utterance more fluent.

Anaphoric reference is a related cohesive device that 'looks back' to a previous noun. For example,

'Did you enjoy the <u>film</u>?' 'Yes, <u>it</u> was great, especially the car chase.'

'It' refers back to 'film', avoids repetition and provides cohesion and coherence.

Cataphoric reference is a cohesive device which 'points forward'. For example,

She just couldn't take <u>it</u> in. Her <u>dream</u> of being elected to Parliament had come true!

**Ellipsis** is another useful cohesive device also avoiding unnecessary repetition. For example,

James missed the bus, [he] arrived late and [he] spilt his coffee – but [he] got the job.

**Repetition** of lexical (L), grammatical (G), syntactic (S) and phonological (P) features is a frequently used cohesive device, both in spoken and in written language. Dickens is a particular master of this kind of cohesion, as we can see in the following extract from *Great Expectations* (1861). A commentary is provided on page 48.

> My first most vivid and broad impression of the identity of things, seems to me to have been gained on <u>a memorable raw afternoon</u> [S] towards evening. At such a time I found out for certain, that <u>this bleak place overgrown with nettles</u> [S] was <u>the churchyard</u> [S]; and that <u>Philip Pirrip</u>, late of this parish, and also <u>Georgiana</u> wife of the above, were <u>dead and buried</u> [L]; and that <u>Alexander, Bartholomew, Abraham, Tobias,</u> and <u>Roger</u> [L], infant children of the aforesaid, were also <u>dead and buried</u> [L]; and that <u>the dark flat wilderness</u> [S] beyond the churchyard, intersected with <u>dykes</u> and <u>mounds</u> and <u>gates</u> [L], with scattered cattle <u>feeding</u> [G] on it, was <u>the marshes</u> [S]; and that <u>the low leaden line</u> [S,P] beyond, was <u>the river</u> [S]; and that <u>the distant savage lair</u> [S] from which the wind was <u>rushing</u> [G], was <u>the sea</u> [S]; and that <u>the small bundle of shivers</u> [S] <u>growing</u> [G] afraid of it all and <u>beginning</u> [G] to cry, <u>was Pip</u> [S].

| Activity 24 | Explaining how repetition creates cohesion |

Reread the passage from *Great Expectations* and look at the suggested examples of lexical, grammatical, syntactic and phonological repetition. What effects does Dickens achieve by using these cohesive devices?

**Conjunctives and discourse markers:** These sound complicated but are easy to recognise and understand. They act as linking or listing devices (because, although, however, therefore, moreover, furthermore, firstly, secondly, next, finally, etc.). They clarify meaning, structure argument and create cohesion and coherence.

| Activity 25 | Investigating conjunctives and discourse markers |
| Pair work | |

Find two editorials (opinion columns), one in a tabloid and one in a broadsheet newspaper. Underline the conjunctives and discourse markers.

Try reading the passages aloud to a partner, omitting the cohesive devices. Discuss what effect this has on the overall coherence of the text.

# Rhetoric

Rhetoric is the final section in this chapter and in many ways sums it all up. Until recently rhetoric was assigned to the dusty cupboard of out-of-date ideas and practices; it's only recently become better known and better understood as a vital tool in the study of spoken and written language.

The general public, if asked what they understood by the term rhetoric, would connect it with the discourse of politics, all flashy language or 'spin' and no real substance. This perception goes back to the times of Socrates, when rhetoric was condemned by some as the mother of lies. However, since people can lie in simple as well as sophisticated language, it seems rather unfair to condemn rhetoric out of hand as automatically dishonest. Indeed, the long fight back against this labelling began then, and continues today.

The etymology of 'rhetoric' is Greek (*techne rhetorike*) and it simply means 'the art of speech'. Developed in the fifth century BC by law-court orators, it was associated with public speaking as a means of persuasion. This association with the law was, in many ways, the undoing of rhetoric's reputation: because it is the duty of lawyers to defend the guilty as well as the innocent, they were obliged to use rhetoric (manipulation of language to persuade the jury) and were damned for it! Eventually, attitudes to rhetoric partially softened, and in medieval and renaissance times it became a major component of the classical curriculum, in which the art of speaking well (*bene dicendi*) was deemed essential.

Today, two perceptions of rhetoric co-exist: the traditional view (2500 years old) that rhetoric is (at best) suspect and (at worst) dishonest, and the current view held by linguists that rhetoric is simply the art of speaking and writing effectively. Unsurprisingly, this section adopts the second view!

A key word associated with rhetoric is 'persuasion'. It's not difficult to identify spoken and written genres with a strongly persuasive purpose (advertising, political speeches, even family arguments). However, persuasion is a powerful component in less overtly persuasive contexts. If you persuade a friend to come for coffee, go out clubbing with you or lend you a book, you have had an effect on them which should lead to your desired outcome. How did you persuade them? By rational argument? ('I really need that book for my essay – you could borrow my lecture notes tonight, and we could swap back tomorrow.') Or by affective arguments based on emotion? ('I'm really lonely since I broke up with … . Do come and keep me company!') Although your friend will use his or her own judgement in making their decision, they will have been affected by your persuasion.

The importance of what modern linguists call **affect** in language immediately broadens our understanding of the nature of rhetoric. It is no longer simply associated with politics, the law, or with that supreme world of artifice, advertising; it is a central aspect of every kind of text, spoken or written, which aims to affect or influence its audience. Even reference and information/fact-based texts, like scientific articles or instruction booklets, aim to have some kind of effect on their readership. We may conclude that persuasion (and hence rhetoric) is central to all human communication, with the persuasive element stronger or weaker, depending on the audience, genre and context. Hence the claim in the opening sentence of this section that rhetoric 'sums up' this chapter.

## But how does rhetoric work?

Some rhetorical strategies and techniques can be deployed across the whole spectrum of spoken and written texts. Our aim is to show you how to recognise these strategies when you are reading/listening and how to use them yourself when speaking/writing. These strategies include

- the marshalling and application of argument
- the ordering and structure of persuasive texts
- the application of a range of techniques from the persuasive repertoire (for example, lexical choice, sound patterning), from figurative language or trope, and from schematic devices (including syntactic effects).

## Marshalling and application of argument

This can only be mentioned briefly, because this chapter's overall focus is on method, not content. We therefore refer you to the Aristotelian concepts of rhetoric (*ethos* – personality and stance; *pathos* – emotional engagement; *logos* – the resources of reason), and suggest that you read these up for yourself if you are particularly interested in philosophy or critical thinking. The models of argument covered by the term *logos* are not difficult to understand, and are well used today. Here are some examples:

- definition model of argument – 'What it boils down to is …' or ' She's the kind of teacher who … .'
- oppositional model of argument – 'Don't blame the children, blame the parents.'
- place/function association model of argument – 'You don't come to school to stare out of the window! You come here to get on with your work.'

## Persuasive ordering

The way any text is structured and organised determines its effectiveness. When you add the element of persuasion (however strong or weak this might be), structure is even more important. In the table below, Labov's theory of narrative structure, with its obligatory and optional elements, is set beside the Roman rhetoricians' model of persuasive ordering.

| Roman rhetoricians | Labov |
| --- | --- |
| Introduction | Abstract |
| Narrative | Orientation |
| Determination of the point at issue | Orientation |
| Enumeration and summary of points | Complicating action |
| Proof or refutation of case | Complicating action |
| Conclusion (case proven) | Evaluation |
| Conclusion (response to points proved) | Result or resolution |
| Conclusion (call to action) | Coda |

Look at the optional and obligatory elements within the table. The function of evaluation or judgement must be an obligatory element in persuasion. For example, whether we are being persuaded to buy some magnificent car, or we are trying to write a convincing A-level essay, or telling our friends about a brilliant/appalling concert we went to, an expression of subjective opinion is inevitable. Other obligatory elements may include an opening statement of some sort ('The assertion that monetarism is an outmoded policy needs to be examined closely' or 'I thought … would be rubbish last night but actually she was fantastic!') or a closing statement ('I would argue that there is still room for monetarism in our economic policies' or 'and I was really glad that I wasn't put off by that terrible review in NME').

**Activity 26**

## Investigating persuasive ordering in a range of texts

You can return to any of the passages already quoted in this chapter to investigate persuasive ordering. However, you will find it particularly interesting to look at the extracts from Martin Luther King's speech (page 29) and Sarah Gaukroger's letter (page 33).

## Persuasive repertoire

By now you should be well aware of the potential of lexical choice and sound patterning to create particular effects in a variety of texts. In the next activity you will see how two eighteenth-century writers, the playwright Richard Sheridan (Text A) and the poet Alexander Pope (Text B), harness these features to increase the persuasive effect they intend.

**Activity 27**

## Exploring the persuasive effects of lexical choice and sound patterning

Read both passages carefully. Identify the lexical features selected to reveal the character of Sheridan's Mrs Sneerwell in Text A. Identify the phonological features selected to convey Pope's opinion of the named writers in Text B.

How persuasive are the authors?

Turn to page 48 for a commentary on this activity.

**Text A**
Mrs Sneerwell

I confess, Mr Surface, I cannot bear to hear people attacked behind their backs; and when ugly circumstances come out against our acquaintance I own I always love to think the best. By-the-by, I hope it is not true that your brother is absolutely ruined?

**Text B**

'Twas chatt'ring, grinning, mouthing, jabb'ring all,
And Noise, and Norton, Brangling, and Breval,
Dennis and Dissonance; and captious Art,
And Snip-snap short, and Interruption smart.

## Figurative language or trope

Although figurative language may be a familiar term, trope is unlikely to be. The latter is a rhetorical umbrella term that includes not only metaphor but also metonymy, synecdoche and irony.

### Metaphor

Metaphor is used when we want to explain something we see or imagine by comparing it with something different. Metaphor is an implicit comparison, unlike simile, which is an explicit comparison. To say 'She is a rose' is an implicit comparison; to say 'She is like a rose' spells out (makes explicit) that comparison. The attributes the woman shares with the rose, however, are the same in both metaphor and simile (beauty, softness, scent). Even so, the poetic power of Burns' use of simile in the following verse is as effective as the starker, more dramatic statement 'She is a rose'.

> O my Luve's like a red red rose
> That's newly sprung in June:
> O my Luve's like the melodie
> That's sweetly play'd in tune.

Modern theorists have shown that everyone uses metaphor in everyday conversation, without being aware of it. Cognitive linguists propose that there are certain basic metaphors (conceptual metaphors) that are rooted in our imagination. Some examples are

- Life is a journey – 'She'll go far!'
- Love is war – 'the battle of the sexes'
- Death is sleep – 'Night, night, grandma'
- Good is up – 'up-beat' or 'I'm really on top of the world'
- Bad is down – 'He's quite down in the dumps' or 'It's the pits'
- Anger is heat – 'It made my blood boil' or 'She blew her top'.

### Metonymy

Metonymy is based, not on semantic association as in metaphor, but on structural association. So we have 'The White House issued a denial' – the President's official residence stands for everyone who works there.

### Synecdoche

Synecdoche involves a relationship between an expressed idea, and an unexpressed one – so the part represents the whole. An example is 'I see a sail!' – the captain knows that it will be attached to a ship!

### Irony

Irony is one of the most frequently used tropes, not just in texts like fiction or journalism, but in everyday conversation – for example, saying 'You look as though you've had a miserable summer!' to a friend sporting a glorious rich tan.

## Schematic devices

Scheme is a classical rhetorical term, not to be confused with schema (discussed earlier in this chapter, page 24). Its meaning is more closely related to structure than to semantics. Use the table to explore a range of structural devices, including antithesis, listing, amplification, diminution and some other tricks and ploys. You already know more about schematic devices than you may think, since we all recognise the effectiveness of puns and wordplay (Beanz means Heinz) and earlier in this chapter (page 12) we examined the effects of syntactic parallelism and right- and left-branching sentences.

| Device | Explanation | Example |
|---|---|---|
| **Antithesis** | Contrasting directly opposed ideas and/or emotions | It was the best of times, it was the worst of times, it was the age of wisdom, it was the age of foolishness … (*A Tale of Two Cities* by Charles Dickens) |
| **Listing** | 'Heaping up' of detail which creates a powerful tension in an audience | All whom the flood did, and<br>   fire shall o'erthrow,<br>All whom war, dearth, age,<br>   agues, tyrannies,<br>Despaire, law, chance, hath<br>   Slaine …<br>(*Holy Sonnets 4* by John Donne) |
| **Hyperbole** (amplification) | Exaggeration or overstatement; in drama, expresses strong emotion. Here Macbeth's emotion is pretended. | Here lay Duncan,<br>His silver skin lac'd with his golden blood.<br>(*Macbeth* by Shakespeare) |
| **Litotes** (diminution) | Understatement or playing down a situation for different reasons (politeness, modesty, not being unkind). Here down-playing is for ironic effect. | She was <u>not uninterested</u> in the prospect of a free trip to Australia accompanying his Stradivarius cello in economy class. |
| **Incrementum** (amplification) | Building up increment by increment | On his last skiing holiday not only did he miss the flight and arrive a day late, which was bad enough, but he also broke a ski, lost his expensive sunglasses and then, to cap it all, he slipped and fractured his leg near the ski-lift. |
| **Paradiastole** (whitewash) | Flattering vice and error by the use of neutral or positive terms | Using 'severe' instead of 'cruel', 'tired and emotional' for 'drunk and incapable', 'free spirit' for 'irresponsible person' |
| **Occultation** (passing over) | Saying you won't mention something, so actually drawing attention to it, often with comic effect | Don't mention the war!<br>(*Fawlty Towers* by John Cleese and Connie Booth) |
| **Interrogatio** (rhetorical question) | Asking a question that does not require an answer from the reader/listener | If Winter comes, can Spring be far behind? (from Shelley's 'Ode to the West Wind')<br><br>Isn't this a case in point? |
| **Pysma** | Asking a barrage of multiple rhetorical questions | Hath not a Jew eyes? Hath not a Jew hands, organs, dimensions, senses, affections, passions? … If you tickle us, do we not laugh? … and if you wrong us, shall we not revenge?<br>(Shylock speaking in *The Merchant of Venice* by Shakespeare) |
| **Subjectio** | Asking a series of rhetorical questions and then answering them yourself | Do we know the solution to our problems? Yes, we know what to do, but will it be done? Yes, if we have the courage! |

## Activity 28

**Pair work**

# Investigating a range of texts from a rhetorical perspective

Working in pairs, select one or two literary and one or two non-literary texts or short extracts. Identify the genre, audience and purpose of each text. Identify the degree of persuasion in each (strongly persuasive to mildly persuasive). Assess how effectively the text structure, lexical choice and use of tropes/schematic devices work to support the persuasive purpose of each text.

## Activity 29

**Pair work**

**Group work**

# Persuading, using a range of rhetorical devices

Work in pairs or small groups. Select a genre, audience and topic from these lists.

| Genre | Topic | Audience |
|---|---|---|
| speech | gangs | general public |
| newspaper editorial | socialising | teenagers |
| magazine article | political satire | left/right-wing supporters |
| facebook entry | being green | friends |
| blog | travel | parents/family |
| text message | old age | the Prime Minister |
| sketch | religion | Richard Branson |
| monologue | celebrity | outsiders/droppers out |

Write at least the opening section of your chosen genre (approximately 200–250 words). Your purpose is to persuade the audience, using whatever persuasive techniques and strategies seem appropriate.

Present your text to the group, asking them to assess its effectiveness on a scale of 1–5.

## Review

In this chapter you have been given the opportunity to

- discover how language is structured
- investigate how meanings are commmunicated via word choice, grammatical strategies and sound patterning
- explore the functions of language and some definitions of discourse
- discover the differences between text, context and intertextuality
- learn how to analyse stories and their structure
- investigate the story of rhetoric, past and present
- explore the role of persuasion in texts
- learn a range of persuasive techniques
- test out your own rhetorical skills.

**Commentary**

**Activity 9**

The focus of the passage keeps shifting from Sophie's voice, to her perspective on the scene, to the narrator's account. All the sentences are simple (one finite verb) or compound (two finite verbs linked with a conjunction, reflecting the child's view). The word order is SV, SVA or SVO throughout – again, reflecting the child as central consciousness. The repeated phrases 'No voices … no footsteps …No cars …Not the tiniest sound' all contribute to the extraordinary silence being conveyed before the initiating event – the arrival of the BFG!

**Commentary**

**Activity 13**

There are many examples of continuous-aspect verb forms – 'is eating … opening … walking … waiting … skating …disappearing … falling'. Auden uses continuous aspect to create a sense of suspended action for the reader, as the moment of tragic fall is caught by the artist (and no-one else, seemingly). The poignant contrast of continuous life with imminent death is suggested here by grammar.

**Commentary**

**Page 41**

This is the opening passage of the novel and the first cohesive feature is Dickens' introduction of the first-person narrative voice ('*My* first … impression … seems to *me* …', 'At such a time I found out …'). Immediately we recognise an adult perspective on the child's increasingly frightening experience in the graveyard. The lengthy compound sentence reaches a climax as the reader focuses on 'the small bundle of shivers …' and learns his name – 'Pip'. Dickens also creates a sense of threatening gloom by lexical and phonological repetition of noun phrases ('raw afternoon', 'bleak place overgrown with nettles', 'churchyard', 'dark flat wilderness', 'dykes … mounds … gates … marshes', 'low leaden line … the river', 'distant savage lair … the sea'). There is also the grammatical cohesion of features like past and present participles, differentiating between the grim past ('dead and buried') and the mournful present ('cattle feeding', 'wind rushing' and the child 'growing afraid …' and 'beginning to cry'). Overall the passage is skilfully constructed to create a sense of the central consciousness, adult or child, refracting the gloomy and frightening landscape of the churchyard in the marshes, and preparing the reader for worse.

**Commentary**

**Activity 27**

Richard Sheridan's comedy *The School for Scandal* (1777) shows the self-revealing hypocrisy of the outrageous gossip Mrs Sneerwell through her own word choice.

Similarly, Alexander Pope in his ferocious attack on foolish writers uses dissonance and a range of harsh consonants to persuade his readers of their individual folly.

# Language and Social Contexts

2

## At the end of this chapter you should be able to

- select and apply a range of linguistic methods, to communicate relevant knowledge using appropriate terminology and coherent, accurate written expression (AO1)

- demonstrate critical understanding of a range of concepts and issues relating to the construction and analysis of meanings in spoken and written language, using knowledge of linguistic approaches (AO2)

- analyse and evaluate the influence of contextual factors on the production and reception of spoken and written language, showing knowledge of the key constituents of language (AO3)

For a more student-friendly version of these Assessment Objectives, turn to page vii in the Introduction.

In this chapter you will

- be introduced to the main concepts in language and social contexts
- investigate your own language use
- consider how language influences thought
- examine how language varies with gender, region and occupation
- examine how language is influenced by technology
- examine how language is influenced by power relationships.

Language is a social tool. It exists for communication between individuals and social groups. The study of language variation as a result of social context is called sociolinguistics and has a range of technical terms and concepts related to it.

There are two main aspects to language and social contexts:

- the variation that exists in language use between different social groups
- the attitudes and values that are conveyed through language choices, both attitudes towards different social groups and attitudes to different language use.

# Exploring language variation

Let's start by defining a variety of English. All texts, whether spoken or written, arise from particular situations and all texts have distinctive linguistic features. If these distinctive features appear in a number of texts because a similar situation gives rise to them, then we can say that this set of features is a variety of English. So, for example, if the situation is that all speakers of English who were born within the sound of Bow Bells in London use a distinctive set of linguistic features, such as their pronunciation and their use of rhyming slang, then it is permissible to say that this is a variety of English, known as Cockney. Or, to give another illustration, if all TV weather forecasters use a distinct set of features (a very restricted lexis being, perhaps, the main one), then we can speak of this as a variety. So you can see that there is an 'infinite variety' of Englishes and why it is not possible to examine them all in this chapter.

In general, there are two types of feature that identify a variety: the sociolinguistic and the stylistic. David Crystal, in his invaluable *Cambridge Encyclopedia of the English Language*, defines them thus:

- **Sociolinguistic features** relate to very broad situational constraints on language use and chiefly identify the regional and social varieties of the language (for example, Canadian, Cockney, upper-class, educated). They are relatively permanent, background features of the spoken or written language, over which we have relatively little conscious control. We tend not to change our regional or class way of speaking as we go about our daily business, and usually do not even realise that it is there.

- Stylistic features refer to constraints on language that are much more narrowly delineated, and identify personal preferences in usage (poetry, humour) or the varieties associated with occupational groups (lecturers, lawyers, journalists). They are relatively temporary features of our spoken or written language over which we do have some conscious degree of control. We often adopt different group uses of language as we go through our day (for example, family, job, religion, sports) and frequently change our speaking or writing style to make a particular effect.

| **Activity 1** | # Varieties of discourse |
| --- | --- |

**Pair work**

People are remarkably good at identifying a particular variety of discourse. Often it takes only a very few words for us to realise that we are encountering legal or religious discourse, for example. We are very sensitive to the codes and conventions that writers (and speakers) use in particular discourse.

Here are fragments from fifteen different discourses. For each one, list as many clues as you can that enable you confidently to identify the variety the fragment comes from.

1 Babies in Drug Test Overdose
2 Dear Sir or Madam
3 Sirloin steak pan-fried in a classic sauce flamed with brandy presented on a bed of crushed herb potatoes
4 Non-payment will result in prosecution
5 Almighty God, our heavenly Father, who of thy great mercy hast promised forgiveness of sins to all them that with hearty repentance and true faith turn unto thee
6 There was an Englishman, an Irishman
7 Does the Right Honourable gentleman agree that the report of the Select Committee
8 These varicosities, whilst containing synaptic vesicles and granules
9 The responsibility for the initial communication of the company's corporate culture lies with the local company training centre
10 When did anyone ever tell you you had beautiful specs?
11 Weather lovely. Wish you were here.
12 2 hours allowed
13 'Big, hilarious, intricate, furious, moving' – *Guardian*
14 During the day our light comes from the sun. The sun is brightest in the middle of the day.
15 And they're off

Now imagine that you are responsible for writing entries in a language encyclopedia on 'Types of Discourse' in which you briefly have to describe and illustrate three or four different types. Base your entries on the work you have just been doing, though you will need to find more extended examples than those given above.

Here, for example, is the beginning of an entry on religious discourse, based on fragment 5 above:

> Religious discourse is marked by relatively archaic language. This can be seen in its pronoun (thee and thou) and possessive adjective (thy, thine) systems and in its retention of archaic tenses (hast, hath). Much religious language begins with a direct invocation (Almighty God) …

Complete this entry and then write some entries of your own.

Our choice of language features will always be influenced by the social context in which we find ourselves. All aspects of our lives and experience influence the ways in which we use language: factors such as age, gender, occupation, region, time and ethnicity. The modes we choose to use, such as speech, writing, telephone, TV, computer or radio, will all influence the way that the message is conveyed and the way that language is used. The relationship we have with other people will also influence the language choices we make.

In this section you will examine some of the ways in which language use varies according to social factors, with specific focus on gender, region, occupation and technology.

## Key terms of language variation

- Sociolinguistics: the study of language variation according to social context
- Sociolect: the language features belonging to particular social groups
- Idiolect: the language choices of a particular individual
- Dialect: how lexis, grammar and accent vary from Standard English in particular regions.

These terms are also sometimes used:

- Prolect: the language of a particular profession
- Genderlect: the study of language related to gender, usually women's choices in language use.

## How to examine and comment on your own language use

Before examining a range of social contexts, you are going to take a close look at your own language use. In the next activity you will learn how transcripts work, how to analyse speech discourse and how your language use demonstrates idiolect, dialect or sociolect.

Analysing speech texts is different from analysing written texts because different speakers construct a conversation but you will study it as a whole text.

In your analysis your aim is to explain how these different speakers construct a whole text and the specific features of each speaker's style and contribution. Transcripts can be difficult to follow as it isn't always clear who is being addressed or how the contributions follow each other. It may be difficult to make sense of them out of context.

This is an example of a spontaneous conversation between a group of girls, aged seventeen to eighteen, having a chat about an evening out. The whole transcript represents less than 30 seconds of conversation.

| | |
|---|---|
| Girl 1 | No! They went off! \| Where did you go? |
| Girl 2 | \| Who did? |
| Girl 3 | I went Walkabout |
| Girl X | She went \| Walkabout |
| Girl 2 | \| What time did you go there? Laura … |
| Girl 5 | Err, Emily came with me |
| Girl X | An then I went home 'coz they wouldn't let me in |
| Girl 2 | Why? Have you got an ID? |
| Girl X | [laugh] Yeah! |
| Girl 6 | Why'd everyone split up then? |
| Girl 1 | Don't know. Where did you go? \| |
| Girl 5 | I pulled this guy as well \| |
| Girl X | \| Walkabout |
| Girl 2 | \| Did ya? |
| Girl 5 | Yeah |
| Girl X | Did ya? |
| Girl 1 | Did you stay with Beth? |
| Girl X | Who? Where? |
| Girl 5 | I told ya |
| Girl X | Ooh! |
| All | [laugh] |
| Girl 1 | Did ya? |
| Girl 2 | who? |
| Girl 5 | [contented sigh] Ahh, it was good wasn't it [laugh] |
| Girl 2 | What did you do? |
| Girl 5 | [laughing] I'on't know! |
| Girls 2+X | Yeah ya do! [Both laugh] |

These are the features you are looking for.

| Features | Example from transcript | How to comment on the features |
|---|---|---|
| Context | The whole conversation, the place and circumstances in which it takes place | This transcript takes place in a social situation, amongst people who know each other well. (You should expand this as you look at specific features and show both what you can work out from the language choices and how the circumstances have influenced the language choices.) |
| Topic setting: Who sets the topic and how? How are new topics introduced? How are others included? | **Girl 1** No! They went off! Where did you go? | Girl 1 sets the topic by asking questions and encourages others to contribute. |

| Features | Example from transcript | How to comment on the features |
|---|---|---|
| Turn taking: How are turns organised? Who takes the most turns? Are there adjacency pairs (turns that clearly follow because they are question/answer or set phrases)? Are there interruptions? Who interrupts/why? | **Girl 2** Who did? | Turns are short, indicating a fast-paced conversation. Turn taking is not easy to follow, Girl 2 speaks over Girl 1's question, in response to her first statement (They went off). Girl 3 follows with an adjacency pair to answer Girl 1's question, creating two simultaneous conversations. |
| Are there non-standard features? Ellipsis is where words are missed creating non-standard grammar. Elision is where sounds/letters are missed. These terms are sometimes used interchangeably. | **Girl 3** I went Walkabout (Walkabout is a bar.) | This seems to continue throughout. She misses out the preposition 'to' (I went [to] Walkabout), showing the casual nature of the conversation. |
| Are there non-fluency features like repetition, repairs (where speakers correct themselves), or interruptions? | **Girl X** She went Walkabout | Girl X answers Girl 1's question for Girl 3, creating repetition of the same point, indicating that they are all talking at once rather than using organised turn taking. |
| How are sentence types used: interrogatives (questions), declaratives (statements), imperatives (commands) or exclamatives (exclamations)? | **Girl 2** What time did you go there? Laura … | Girl 2 contributes to the conversation by asking questions, which encourages other participants. This conversation is interpersonal and phatic, that is, although they are exchanging information, the purpose is primarily to reinforce their social ties, their shared experiences and knowledge about each other. In places the conversation is constructed through short statements. |
| Include non-fluency features like fillers. Comment on the discourse structure – how the speakers use their turns to follow each other. Comment if there are problems following it. | **Girl 5** Err, Emily came with me | Girl 5 starts with a filler 'Err' to give herself time to think. The structure of this conversation is such that it is difficult to follow in parts. This could be part of a response to Girl 1. |
| Include non-standard pronunciation/elision. | **Girl X** An then I went home 'coz they wouldn't let me in | The casual, interpersonal and social aspects of the conversation are shown by the use of elision: an/coz/wouldn't. |
| Features showing back-channel or feedback – this is where the listener shows they are listening and encouraging more speech. It might be verbal (yeah) or just noise (mmm) or repeating points or asking questions. | **Girl 2** Did ya?<br>**Girl 5** Yeah<br>**Girl X** Did ya? | The interpersonal aspect is shown through the back-channel where Girl 2 asks rhetorical questions to show that she is listening and interested in getting more information. |

| **Activity 2** | Investigate your language use |

1   Collect your own data. In groups of four or five, record 5–10 minutes of spontaneous conversation. You might find it easier to decide on some topics in advance.

2   Listen to your tape and write down everything that is said, exactly as it is on the tape.

- Write the speakers' names in the left margin, like a play script.
- Mark simultaneous speech with a line and set directly underneath.
- Mark pauses with (.) and show the lengths of pauses by numbers. For example, (2) is a pause of 2 seconds.
- Write down everything, including fillers like 'err' or 'emm', often used to give the speaker time to think.
- You could represent some of the non-standard pronunciation through the spelling: 'coz', 'an', etc,
- If you cannot hear what is said mark it as '(inaudible)'.
- You can represent your speakers anonymously or by name.

3   Make notes on the following points to organise your ideas. For an examination question you should show that you

- understand how the context influences the language choices and the meanings created
- understand linguistic concepts and can explain them using technical terms.

### Key points for analysing transcripts

- Explain fully the circumstances surrounding the conversation. This means looking carefully at the context and showing how this might influence the way language is used. For example, what is the relationship between the participants, what are the circumstances of the conversation, what is the conversation for?

- Look at the dialogue as a whole (the discourse). What is it about, how does the topic progress? Is the conversation interpersonal or transactional?

- Look at each person's contribution separately. Look at the participants who present arguments or ideas, those who encourage others to speak, those who show active listening through feedback. Who dominates the conversation? How does it create the discourse?

- How is turn taking organised? Comment on interruptions, overlaps, simultaneous speech, turn taking.

- Which non-fluency features are present? How do the non-fluency features affect the progress of the conversation? Non-fluency features include pauses, false starts, repairs.

- Is there anything significant or interesting in the grammar choices – for example, non-standard grammar such as ellipsis, particular sentence types such as interrogatives, imperatives, exclamatives or declaratives?

- Is there anything interesting or unusual about the lexical choices – idiolect, sociolect or dialect features? Is there any interesting use of colloquial or technical lexis?

- Are there noticeable differences in the way males or females participate in the conversation (if it is a mixed conversation)?

4 Evaluate this activity. You will probably find that it was difficult and time consuming to transcribe speech and you may have had difficulties following either the tape or the written account despite the fact that you had no difficulty following the conversation in context. You might have found that speaking 'spontaneously' into a tape recorder is quite difficult in itself. Was the transcript a limited representation of the original speech activity? Was there anything that surprised you in your speech or the speech of other people in your group?

**Group work**

5 As a group present your findings to the rest of the class. When you have heard the presentations from the other groups write a summary of the common features within your class. Is your speech fairly similar or is there wide variation?

## How is language linked to the way people perceive the world?

Many commentators are concerned with the interrelationship between thoughts and words. George Orwell, in both his journalism and his fiction, examined the way language is corrupted. Here he is discussing political writing.

*Politics and the English Language*, 1946
The writer either has a meaning and cannot express it, or he inadvertently says something else, or he is almost indifferent as to whether his words mean anything or not. This mixture of vagueness and sheer incompetence is the most marked characteristic of modern English prose, and especially of any kind of political writing.

He presents the argument, which is quite often shared by others, that if language becomes imprecise, then this indicates a lack of precision and rigour in the thoughts behind it. Does this seem familiar to you? If you examined modern political discourse do you think you would find the same features?

An alternative viewpoint on language and thought is that presented in the Sapir Whorf hypothesis. These two researchers examined differences between languages and what this suggests about the way the world is perceived. Their hypothesis, called linguistic determinism, states that our thinking is determined by language: the thoughts we have are restricted by the language at our disposal

Political correctness has aspects of this point of view. It is primarily a means of challenging racist and sexist language that is intended to give offence or to exclude some groups of people. It also attempts to challenge attitudes. It is very much centred on how attitudes are embedded in the language we use.

Consider these issues.

- Do you think it is possible to have an idea, a belief or concept that couldn't be expressed in words?
- Do you think the way you perceive the world is influenced by the way your language chops it up and represents it?
- Do politically correct terms make sexist or racist attitudes disappear?

- Do politically correct terms make people more aware of the effect of their choice of words and therefore avoid 'casual' racism or sexism?
- Does changing the language change people's attitudes, or are changes in attitudes reflected in the language people use?
- What evidence could you use to support your views?

Euphemisms are an important aspect of social attitudes and language. A euphemism is a polite term substituted for a more blunt word, which might be offensive. The words that are deemed taboo and the euphemisms a society uses will show the values of that group of language users. Terms that are considered offensive or things you are not allowed to discuss in polite society reveal the sensitivities of that particular society. For example, euphemisms in English relate to concepts such as death. For example, 'kicked the bucket', 'passed away', 'lost' (as in 'I lost my husband'), 'gone to meet his maker' all avoid using the blunt word 'died'. Euphemisms are also common for topics such as sexual activity, parts of the body or bodily functions.

Euphemisms can also be used to manipulate attitudes to certain topics. Here's Orwell again.

*Politics and the English Language*, 1946
Thus political language has to consist largely of euphemism, question-begging and sheer cloudy vagueness. Defenceless villages are bombarded from the air, the inhabitants driven out into the countryside, the cattle machine-gunned, the huts set on fire with incendiary bullets: this is called *pacification*. Millions of peasants are robbed of their farms and sent trudging along the roads with no more than they can carry: this is called *transfer of population* or *rectification of frontiers*. People are imprisoned for years without trial, or shot in the back of the neck or sent to die of scurvy in Arctic lumber camps: this is called *elimination of unreliable elements*. Such phraseology is needed if one wants to name things without calling up mental pictures of them.

Does this use of language seem familiar to you?

Explore this issue:
- collect euphemisms that are familiar to you
- examine the concepts and words that are being avoided through the use of euphemism.

This way of looking at language use moves beyond knowing the names of people, places and things to being able to think and talk about things virtually created by language. This is what is meant by the idea that language does not just name reality; it actively constructs it. For example, the compound noun 'Greenpeace' hardly existed 20 years ago, yet in constructing that word, one section of society has constructed an idea of caring for both the natural environment and the human race which has entered everybody's mind/vocabulary whether they believe in it or not.

Binary opposition is the tendency to divide people and things into two contrasted or opposing groups. You will have noticed already some binary oppositions that are very common in the English language: us and them; right and wrong; mine and yours. Many English idioms (everyday sayings) consist of similarly paired words: black and white; ins and outs; the long and the short of it; give and take; more or less; on and off; his and hers; haves and have-nots. There are hundreds in everyday use.

A term given to these paired words is binomials. There are also many trinomial constructions in idiomatic English, such as the popular expression 'left, right and centre'. Notice the customary word order; it would cause a slight surprise if anyone said 'left, centre and right', yet there is a certain logic to it.

## Activity 3 — What are idioms?

Collect as many binomial and trinomial expressions in idiomatic English as you can.

- How helpful are binomial and trinomial constructions to the way you look at life?
- Is there any significance in the fact that they sound very odd when reversed (for example, 'forget and forgive' or 'the ugly, the bad and the good')?
- Why do you think trinomial phrases and slogans are so popular with advertisers and politicians? Why are these expressions satisfying and powerful, even when, in the back of your mind, you don't believe a word of them?

A society at any time will have dominant discourses or lexical terms or semantic fields (words that are linked by meaning) that reflect the concerns of the time, and that will change. For example there is much talk at the moment related to the environment: carbon footprint, carbon offsetting, climate change, global warming, emissions, recycling, environmentally friendly products or practices. These terms all belong to the semantic field of 'the environment'.

# How does language vary?

In this section you will look at the ways in which language use varies from the Standard English form. The main areas of language varieties examined here are:

- gender
- regional variation
- social variation
- technology
- occupation.

But before you look at the concepts and theories related to language variation, you should investigate the language varieties of a language group or speech community with which you are already familiar.

## Key terms of language variation

Speech community means a group of people who share a similar social experience, and hence share similar vocabulary and grammar. They could be

- people who live in the North of Scotland in an isolated fishing village
- fans of heavy metal or jazz living at opposite ends of the country
- local football supporters
- supporters of Manchester City from around the world
- friendship groups
- neighbourhood groups
- work-based associations.

All could be described as speech communities. Most of us are part of more than one speech community – probably several.

Social contexts: When people meet, talk, consult, ask advice, argue, discuss problems or make plans, their exchanges will take place within a social situation (for example, a family meal, doctor's consulting room, classroom, supermarket, job interview, restaurant). Linguists describe these situations as social contexts, and they make an enormous difference to the way we actually use language. For example, we avoid taboo language at home; we give the doctor clear information about a health problem in the consulting room; we are polite at the job interview for the position we want!

Communicative competence is the term for someone's ability to use appropriate language within a particular speech community. To do this we must recognise the community's linguistic 'rules' (norms), and how far changes (variations) can be made to fit any new situations. Note that competence has a particular meaning here, which is different from its usual one (that someone does a job well). It means here that someone knows and can use the language of a particular community.

To sociolinguists the term code has a specific meaning: a variety or style of spoken or written language used in a particular social context. We all use a variety of linguistic codes in everyday conversation, and code switch almost without thinking as we adjust to new social situations (for example, chatting casually to a friend in class, then responding to a complicated question from the teacher or lecturer). If you are bilingual, you probably code switch from one language to another in casual conversation, without even being aware you're doing it.

Social networks are the connections one individual has with other individuals or groups. Social networks frequently cut across class boundaries, and measuring the relative strengths of the networks can tell us a lot about individual members of speech communities. For example, one person's social networks may include family, friendship group(s), fellow class members, sports club, drama group, church or similar religious group, internet chat-room.

There are different ways of describing social networks, depending on the differences in people's informal social relationships. For example, if your best friends are also members of your extended family and you all work together and socialise together, you are part of a dense social network. If the members of your network interact with each other in more than one context (at work, playing badminton, at church), it is called a multiplex network. If you meet a wide variety of people who don't know each other, yours is a loose social network.

Linguistic variables are features of spoken language that vary from individual to individual, depending on factors like age, gender, status and social context. An example of a linguistic variable is the 'ng' consonant form used at the end of words like running. In Norwich this is pronounced in two ways: running or runnin'. In 1974 a linguistics researcher, Peter Trudgill, studied Norwich residents' differing pronunciations of '-ing' (running/runnin'). He tabulated his findings, taking into account the social class and gender of his subjects, and found that women and men in the higher social classes preferred '-ing' to '-in'. He deduced that the regional pronunciation (runnin') had less prestige than the Received Pronunciation form (running). So Trudgill's study is an example of a linguistic variable forming the basis of a research project.

Accommodation theory: Howard Giles (1975, 1991) developed this theory to explain the way people converge towards or diverge from the speech and accent of the person they are talking with. He suggested that convergence expresses social solidarity with the other speaker; divergence expresses a wish to increase social distance from the other speaker.

Most of us are aware of this unconscious tendency to 'fit in' accent-wise when we visit another part of the country. Giles suggests that power is also involved. In an interaction the person with less power is more likely to converge with the more powerful person's speech. This is also seen as significant when considering politeness strategies – accommodating your language to reduce the linguistic distance between yourself and the other person. Social context seems to provide the clearest explanation for either convergence or divergence.

## Activity 4

Individual

# Investigating a speech community

Your task is to investigate a speech community – less daunting than it sounds! Choose one speech community that you're part of yourself (for example, one of your A-level classes, a friendship group, a sports club or band). Listen to the normal conversation within this particular community over a period of approximately a week, but try not to be too obvious about it. (William Labov realised that people did not speak naturally if they were aware of people recording them and called this the observer's paradox.)

Note down, under the following headings, any characteristic language features you can remember (preferably, do this at the end of each day).

- **Vocabulary:** Was it specific to your chosen group (for example, subject specific, use of slang, taboo language or dialect)?
- **Non-standard grammar** or **syntax:** How frequent was it (for example, 'We was late for the match' [plural subject, singular verb]; 'I never did nothing' [double negative])?
- **Code switching:** Were there any examples of this (vocabulary or grammar) taking place in your chosen group?

Write a brief report of your findings using the headings above.

**Note:** If you have the chance to tape-record some of the conversations within your speech community, the spoken data would form an excellent basis for an investigation.

## Review

This section has introduced you to the ideas and concepts connected with language and social contexts. You should now know

- how language varies
- how discourse choices demonstrate social context
- the technical terms that describe aspects of social context
- how to analyse spoken texts.

Explain in detail what these terms mean:

Revision

- speech community
- social contexts
- communicative competence, codes, code switching
- social network, linguistic variables, loose, dense and multiplex networks
- accommodation.

If you have completed the activities in this section, you should now have a good grounding in the technical terms that describe aspects of social context and language and have examined aspects of your own language experience. You also need to be able to analyse texts produced in a range of social contexts from business web pages to a transcript of a local dialect.

Depending on the situations in which we find ourselves, our language use can be determined by cultural factors such as

- our gender role (whether we are male or female)
- our role as an adult or as a child (whether we are young or old)
- our role as a member of a majority or a minority group
- our ethnicity or culture.

You are now going to look at some of the diversity of language that is involved when people are forced to adopt these culturally defined roles. In some cases, you will also consider the attitudes that are associated with such culturally defined uses of language.

# Language and gender

In this section you will be learning to

- understand and apply a range of terms and theoretical ideas about gender and how it influences language use
- analyse texts that show gendered language use
- analyse texts that represent men and women.

## What does language and gender mean?

Here are two entries in the *OED online* for 'gender'.

1 Kind, sort, class; also, genus as opposed to species.
2 In modern (esp. feminist) use, a euphemism for the sex of a human being, often intended to emphasize the social and cultural, as opposed to the biological, distinctions between the sexes.

It is the second entry that is relevant to the study of language and gender: social or cultural ideas about men and women. Much of the study of language and gender looks at how men's and women's language use varies and how attitudes are encoded in texts. This is important as social and cultural differences between men and women change over time and this may be reflected in the theoretical position of any commentators.

Before looking at texts, you are going to examine a range of theoretical views from different times, as they show changing attitudes to gender. The focus, methods and findings of different theorists may be influenced by their culture and social attitudes. You need to be aware of the influence of cultural attitudes when studying theoretical views and when you are analysing texts – because you have culturally defined attitudes too. You also need to consider how being male or female influences your ideas.

## Do men and women use language differently?

**It has been suggested that women**

- talk more than men
- talk too much
- are more polite
- are indecisive
- complain and nag
- are hesitant
- ask more questions
- support each other
- are more co-operative

**Whereas men**

- swear more
- don't talk about emotions
- talk about sport more
- talk about women and machines in the same way
- insult each other more frequently

- are very competitive and try to outdo each other in conversation
- dominate conversations
- speak with more authority
- give more commands
- interrupt more

In a much challenged American study, Robin Lakoff identified these ten features of women's language:

1 hedges – sort of, kind of, I guess
2 super polite forms – would you please, I'd really appreciate it if
3 tag questions – don't you, isn't it, shouldn't we?
4 emphatic intonation – on words such as 'so' and 'very'
5 empty adjectives
6 hypercorrect grammar and pronunciation
7 lack of a sense of humour – poor at telling jokes
8 direct quotations
9 specialised vocabulary – for colours, for example
10 question intonation on statements – the voice rises at the end.

## Activity 5
**Pair work**

## Investigating the claims about male and female language use

In pairs, classify these sets of claims into two groups:

- **Group 1:** statements that seem subjective, such as 'women talk too much'
- **Group 2:** statements that are objective and can by verified by evidence, such as 'men insult each other more frequently'.

Conduct an investigation to verify some of these claims. This is important, as you need to be clear about how reliable claims about language use are.

## What the researchers say about language use...

The following texts are excerpts from writings about gender and language.

### A  Otto Jespersen
*Language: its Nature, Development and Origin*, 1922

The same paragraph was presented to various well-educated persons, who were asked to read it as rapidly as they could, ten seconds being allowed for twenty lines. As soon as the time was up the paragraph was removed, and the reader immediately wrote down all that he or she could remember of it. It was found that women were usually more successful than men in this test. Not only were they able to read more quickly than the men, but they were able give a better account of the paragraph as a whole ... But it was found that this rapidity was no proof of intellectual power, and some of the slowest readers were highly distinguished men. Ellis (*Man and W.* 195) explains this in this way: with the quick reader it is as though every statement were admitted immediately and without inspection to fill the vacant chambers of the mind, while with the slow reader every statement undergoes an instinctive process of cross-examination; every new fact seems to stir up the accumulated stores of facts among which it intrudes, and so impedes rapidity of mental action.

## B  Peter Trudgill
*Sociolinguistics and Introduction to Language and Society*, 1974

Most of the evidence we have for gender differences in English has come from some of the urban dialect surveys carried out in Britain and America that we have already mentioned. The sets of data these surveys have provided have one striking feature in common. In all the cases so far examined, it has been shown that, allowing for other factors such as social class, ethnic group and age, women on average use forms which more closely approach those of the standard variety or the prestige accent than those used by men, although we cannot predict which form a given man or woman is going to use on a given occasion. In other words, female speakers of English ... tend to use linguistic forms which are considered to be 'better' than male forms.

## C  Dale Spender
*Man Made Language*, 1980

Framing questions in terms of the silence of women leads to an examination of the language which excludes and denigrates them, and it also leads to an examination of their access to discourse. When the only language women have debases us and when we are also required to support male talk, it is not unlikely that we shall be relatively silent. When the only language men have affords them the opportunity to encode meanings and to control discourse, when they have made the language and decreed many of the conditions for its use, it is not unlikely that they will use it more and that they will use it more in their own interest; thus they assist in the maintenance of women's silence.

## D  Jennifer Coates and Deborah Cameron
*Women in Their Speech Communities*, 1989

The fact that women and men differ in terms of their communicative behaviour is now established sociolinguistic fact. The problem remains of *explaining* such difference. How and why do women and men come to be in possession of different communicative norms? There are two conflicting views of women's status in society: one sees women as a minority group which is oppressed and marginalised; the other sees women as simply different from men. The two main approaches to sex differences in communicative competence reflect these two views. The first – the dominance approach – interprets linguistic differences in women's and men's communicative competence as a reflection of men's dominance and women's subordination. The second – the difference approach – emphasises the idea that women and men belong to different subcultures; the differences in women's and men's communicative competence are interpreted as reflecting these different subcultures.

## E  Deborah Tannen
*You Just Don't Understand*, 1990

Many experts tell us we are doing things wrong and should change our behavior – which usually sounds easier that it turns out to be. Sensitivity training judges men by women's standards, trying to get them to talk more like women. Assertiveness training judges women by men's standards and tries to get them to talk more like men. No doubt, many people can be helped by learning to be more sensitive and more assertive. But few people are helped by being told they are doing everything all wrong. And there may be little wrong with what people are doing, even if they are winding up in arguments. The problem may be that each partner is operating within a different system, speaking a different genderlect. ...

Understanding genderlects makes it possible to change – to try speaking differently – when you want to. But even if no one changes, understanding genderlect improves relationships. Once people realize that their partners have different conversational styles, they are inclined to accept differences without blaming themselves, their partners, or their relationships. The biggest mistake is believing there is one right way to listen, to talk, to have a conversation – or a relationship. Nothing hurts more than being told your intentions are bad when you know they are good, or being told you are doing something wrong when you know you're just doing it your way.

## Activity 6

Pair work

### Examining the sources

Read the five texts and make a list of the main findings of each theorist.

Make a judgement on how subjective or objective their findings are.

Examine in detail the language each theorist uses – their use of pronouns to show partisan views; their use of emotive or objective language; use of technical terms.

Comment on what they are telling us about gender differences. Are they attempting to

- quantify observations
- identify causes
- examine consequences of differences in male/female language?

Evaluate each proposition based on how it is presented here and on your own experience of men's and women's use of language. In other words, do you agree with the findings?

Gender theories tend to separate themselves into

- the deficit model – women's language is inferior to men's
- the difference model – men and women are socialised differently
- the dominance model – men and women have different status

Which of these theorists fit these descriptions?

Turn to page 108 for a commentary.

## Activity 7

Individual
Homework

### Researching this topic further

**Either:** Find more information about the theorists who wrote Texts A–E.

**Or:** Investigate others who have researched this topic, such as O'Barr and Atkins, Pamela Fishman, Geoffrey Beattie, Deborah Jones, Susan Githens, David Graddol.

## Summary of ideas on how gender influences conversational styles

Research on conversational style has focused on the areas of grammar, lexical choice and politeness markers. But you need to listen to people and check these out for yourself!

- **Grammar – intensifiers and boosters:** Women are thought to use more extreme intensifiers and boosters in conversation (terribly, awfully, disgustingly, amazingly, etc.).
- **Grammar – use of modals:** Modals are should, could, would, might, may, can, must, will, ought. Women apparently use different sorts of modal auxiliaries in directives (*'Would* you answer the door?'), in declaratives (*'I'd* just like to say …'){ } and in compound requests ('When you've finished those case-notes, *would* you like to look at this, and then *could* I possibly ask you to contact his GP?'). These uses might be interpreted as 'female tentativeness' (deficit model and dominance model), context bound or as politeness strategies. For more on modals see page 14.

- **Lexical choice – evaluative lexis:** Evaluative words are ones that in one way or another express an opinion. Women are thought to use more strongly positive and negative evaluative lexis ('That's a really great outfit – you look fantastic!' 'It's such a bad idea to go for that option.'). This usage may, however, be dependent on social context, as well as class and age.

- **Lexical choice – taboo language, euphemism and expletives:** There are stereotypical assumptions about male and female use of this kind of lexis (men swear more than women and use more taboo language, women prefer euphemisms, etc.). Both Jesperson (1922) and Lakoff (1975) agree about this. Coates (1993), however, notes that their opinions were based not on evidence but on what they thought ought to be true! She also observes that swearing – using expletives – is class linked and that both sexes swear more in same-sex situations.

## A closer look at gender conversational styles

A key researcher in the area of conversational style is Jennifer Coates. She described the difference between competition and co-operation in male and female conversational styles. This model claims that men's conversational style tends to revolve around each person holding the floor, telling anecdotes or jokes or giving opinions. Men tended to interrupt each other until other speakers backed down and 'conceded the floor'.

In contrast she found that women spoke co-operatively, their interruptions were supportive rather than to stop the previous speaker from talking. She described the discourse as co-constructed so that several speakers combined to make a point, rather than what might usually be expected – that each person would take a distinct turn.

## Theories on gender and politeness: facework

Using politeness strategies is called facework. Brown and Levinson called their theory of politeness 'positive and negative face'.

- Positive face is the desire to be valued. To ensure people's face needs are met, we employ positive strategies ('Hi! Great to see you looking so good.').

- Negative face is the desire not to be imposed upon and uses negative strategies ('Excuse me, would you mind checking your ticket – I think you may be in the wrong seat.').

Are women better at facework than men? Holmes (1995, p.7) argues that women use more positive politeness strategies. She lists the explanations offered by linguists:

- Women are concerned to involve others and make connections.
- Men are more detached and autonomous.
- Girls and boys are differently socialised (difference model).
- Men and women are differently empowered (dominance model).

Politeness strategies include such features as compliments and apologies, back-channel behaviour and hedges.

Holmes (ed. Coates, 1997) examined male and female compliments in her New Zealand study (confirmed by other research evidence). Her findings were that

- women tend to perceive and use compliments 'to establish, maintain and strengthen relationships'
- men are less comfortable about them, particularly if complimented by women of lower status.

Compliments like these face-threaten men, in just the same way that 'stranger compliments' (such as remarks and wolf-whistles from building-site workers) face-threaten women.

Research has shown that in mixed-talk situations, women use more back-channel behaviour or minimal responses (mmm, yeah) than men. The function of minimal responses is to encourage a speaker to continue by indicating interest and attention (thus fulfilling face needs). Delayed minimal response shows that the listener's attention is receding and that s/he wants to speak!

## Activity 8

**Individual**
**Homework**

## Writing an analysis

This text is one of Jennifer Coates' examples of women talking together. C is discussing her decision to go to Australia for a family funeral.

Examine the text with reference to the features of women's use of language explained in this chapter. Use the prompt questions in Activity 2 to gather your ideas about this text then write up an analysis.

Make sure you cover the following key features:

- the pragmatics of the text (what it tells you about the context of the conversation, the relationship of the participants, their knowledge of the situation/topic, their attitudes)
- the discourse (how the speech is structured and particular features of speech)
- the grammar (sentence types, use of modals, use of pronouns, any non-standard grammar)
- the lexis/semantic fields (words linked by meaning, technical or colloquial lexis).

Because there is a lot of overlapping, simultaneous speech is shown in square brackets within the dominant speakers' turn.

Turn to page 109 for a commentary.

### Notation
(.) brief pause
[A: mmm]  simultaneous speech by another speaker
/  turn follows immediately from previous speaker

C  I probably I mean it would have also would have been if (.) I'd go now Daniel was sort of (.) 18 months old and [A: mm] it would have been rather difficult [A: yes] and this [A: yes] kind of thing /

D  that's right I suppose there's two [C: um] things there's /

C  I think I would go now because probably because I would want to go [E: mm] cos it would be be very easy to go/

D  yeah

C  [A: yeah] it would have been I don't know /

D  there's two things aren't there there's [C: anyway] the the other people like [C: right] your mother or father who's left and or or siblings and there's also how how about the easiness of going

E  mm

C  mm

A  mm

B  yeah

D  I mean I would I

A  well to go to Australia seems a bit over the top

# How gender is represented in texts

Here are some ideas.

### Lexis
There is often a difference in the words chosen to refer to men and women, for example in

- terms of endearment (to show affection)
- terms to describe an attractive person
- pejorative or derogatory terms.

Do the terms 'man' and the pronoun 'he' refer to males or all humans?

### Connotations
- Adjectives that are used for men and women and what they suggest
- Different connotations of 'mismatched pairs' or 'asymmetry' in terms that apply to men and women, such as master/mistress, governor/governess, lord/lady
- How terms used to refer to women gain negative connotations, or undergo semantic derogation over time

### Grammar
- Do writers choose significant nouns, verbs, adjectives to apply to men or women?
- Are they presented differently in terms of the subject or object of a sentence?

### Discourse
- Are men and women represented in stereotypical roles?
- Women are often referred to in terms of their appearance, their clothes, their age, their relationship to others, as daughters, wives, mothers. Whereas men are often referred to in terms of status, jobs, actions.

### Attitudes and values
- Does the writer have a bias represented in the text?
- Does the writer assume attitudes in the reader?

## Activity 9    How words reveal attitudes

Explain the issues demonstrated by the following examples of language use.

- These paired terms: wizard/witch, chef/cook, landlord/landlady, baronet/dame, governor/governess, sir/madam
- These terms used to refer to both men and women: slut, slattern, harlot, wench.
- The order of these pairings: male and female, husband and wife, brother and sister, son and daughter, Mr and Mrs.
- The word 'tart' was originally used as a term of endearment to women in the way 'sugar' or 'sweetie' might be used now.
- These terms: girl talk, talking man to man, locker-room talk, lady-like language, gossip.

In an examination you may be given texts that show examples of language use or you might be given data like that above, or research opinions or general opinions about language and language use. You should tackle them the same way, showing that you understand linguistic methods and knowledge; that you can use terminology (AO1) and have a critical understanding of the concepts and issues (AO2); that you understand how context – in this case the broader social attitudes – influence the meanings and attitudes behind language use (AO3).

You need to bring your awareness of language techniques to your reading of any text, to evaluate critically how the writer is conveying his or her opinions and how they are 'positioning the reader' to accept certain ideas.

The attitudes and values in some texts are not very difficult to discern – for example in certain types of fiction.

## Activity 10 — Analysing the representation of gender

**Individual**
**Exam preparation**

How is gender represented in the text on the book cover below? You should include how males are represented as well as females.

Make your notes under these headings.

- Nouns
- Verbs
- Adjectives
- Adverbs
- Graphology
- Discourse
- Lexical Choice
- Pragmatics

Compare it to Text B, Beth Ditto's column from the *Guardian* (June 2007) on page 68. Comment on the target audience and the attitudes and values presented in both of these texts. (Turn to page 109 for a commentary.)

*Breathtaking romance & adventure*

**A royal request…**

Aid worker Katy McMann was tending to the wounded in a war-torn country when she stumbled upon the cause of the conflict – the king of Baraq. The enigmatic Nikolas Ramsey was hiding among prisoners until he could find a way to rescue his kingdom. In the confines of the prison the chemistry between them sizzled, and Katy wished circumstances were different.

She kept his dangerous secret, but then he asked her to make a sacrifice for the Baraqi people – have his child for the future of his kingdom. Fulfilling his request might save the country and Nick, but would it cost Katy her heart?

UK £3.10    Rs. 99
ISBN 978-0-263-85767-2

*Season's Greetings from*
**MILLS & BOON**
*Pure reading pleasure*

The Lost Prince
Cindy Dees

MILLS & BOON
INTRIGUE

**Text B**

# What would Beth Ditto do?

**Today's dilemma for Beth How should I respond to catcalls in the street?**

I have been 130lb as well as 215lb. I have had blond, strawberry blond, green, pink and purple hair, and none of that has ever exempted me from having lewd comments flung at me in the street. This happens to all women, and it can be really upsetting, but we shouldn't feel hopeless about it — I really believe that if men and women start communicating about this, it's something that we can tackle together.

First things first . . . we have to stop referring to this as a "catcall". Women aren't cats, we aren't pets, we are just people trying to cross the freaking street to get an ice-cream cone. (Well, in my case, anyway.)

I struggled with this question, asking, "Beth, what *would* you do?", and then I remembered all the times I've shouted back: "Show us your cock! That's right — let everyone here see how huge it is! Oh wait! What's that? I didn't hear you! You're walking away?!" Using my voice is always my first instinct. In good conscience, though, I know that this kind of harassment happens in varying degrees and that shouting back isn't always appropriate. Harassment can also stir up strong feelings, which can ruin your day. So, taking all that into consideration, I've written a handy list of scenarios and sketched out exactly how to respond!

*No 1:* If you find yourself on the receiving end of some crude dude's remarks, it is up to you to decide how much energy to give the jerk. It's understandable to feel too tired, or afraid, or even embarrassed to confront a stranger who hasn't the sense to respect you as a human being. If you feel up to it, though, go right ahead! Just be careful and know how to protect yourself.

*No 2:* If you find yourself feeling powerless after someone has shouted at you, you need to remember that this is the masterplan of sexism. The guys in question may not know it, but every time they "catcall" a girl they are reminding her of her vulnerability in a system designed to do just that. As women, we need to remember the power that lies within.

*No 3:* If a friend or partner tells you that catcalls are a fact of life and to "just get used to it", it's worth recognising that they are fuelling the harasser's fire and extinguishing yours. It can be particularly annoying when a boyfriend does this — it's not fair for someone who has the privilege of taking a risk-free stroll in the park, day or night, to dismiss your reaction. The next time he says something like that then you should arrange to get some of the most annoying, frightening women, young and old, ugly and beautiful, thin and fat, to stare at him for a week, pointing and remarking on his body. He'll just have to get used to it! Seriously, though, I suggest that you nip any comments like that in the bud. You can't be yourself with a partner who writes off your feelings.

*No 4:* This advice is for the boys . . . If you want to give a woman a compliment, there is nothing wrong with just saying, "You look beautiful." The over-the-top stallion attitude is intimidating, though, and, let's face it, doesn't really work for anyone. I mean, seriously? When was the last time it actually got you a date?!

Beth would love to answer your one-line questions or dilemmas in her fortnightly column. Please email them to **beth.ditto@guardian.co.uk**

The Guardian 08.06.07 **17**

# Key features in written text

To analyse a written text ensure that you

- show you understand how the context of the text – the situation of the writer and the situation of the reader – influences the language choices.
- use the following language-based concepts and terms to describe, analyse and explain the text.

### Pragmatics and discourse

- What is the most interesting feature of the text? How is this achieved in terms of language features?
- How does the text work as a whole? Who is it communicating between? What is it for? Is it successful? What attitudes and values does the writer have? What assumptions does the writer make about the reader? How does the writer try to influence the reader?
- How is the text structured? Comment on the cohesion of the text (how the ideas link together). Does it present an argument? How has the writer organised the ideas in the text? How does the writer address the reader? Does the text conform to specific conventions? Does the text use features from a range of genres? Or use an unexpected genre form?

### Grammar

Look carefully at features such as sentence choices.

- Are they simple/complex or compound and is it important? Does the writer use interrogative, imperative, exclamative or declarative sentences and how does this influence the way the text is read? Is the use of modals interesting? Does the writer use passive or active sentences? Are there interesting choices of word classes – nouns, verbs, adjectives, adverbs?

### Lexis/semantics

- Semantic choices will be dictated by the topic. Has the writer chosen interesting semantic fields in any description? Does the writer use words with specific connotations to create effects? Are there interesting choices in the lexis, for example technical or colloquial vocabulary?
- Is there anything interesting in the choices of graphology – font, layout, colours, images, use of white space?
- Does the writer use phonological features such as alliteration, rhyme, and onomatopoeia? What is the effect of these choices?

There are further ideas related to analysing texts and social contexts at the end of the chapter on page 106. For more on these areas of language study see pages 4–16 and 23–26.

# Attitudes to gender representation

The use of language to represent gender is considered important enough by many workplaces or official documents for them to have developed policies to advise on or regulate language use.

## Activity 11

# Investigating gender-neutral language

The following text is a policy for New South Wales relating to gender-neutral expression. New South Wales was the first Australian jurisdiction to adopt gender-neutral language in legislation. In 1983 the Attorney General approved a proposal from the Parliamentary Counsel's Office that in the preparation of future legislation preference would be given to the use of gender-neutral language.

Make a list of features considered in the text to show gender bias. Explain why.

Examine a range of examples of policy documents on gender language. The school or college you belong to may have such a policy, or you can find them quite easily by searching on the internet.

### Applying the Policy
In applying the Policy, the following gender-neutral terms are preferred if a general reference inclusive of both sexes is required:

- person (rather than man, woman)
- the person (rather than him, her)
- the person's (rather than his, her)
- spouse (rather than husband, wife)
- child, person under the age of... (rather than boy, girl)

No assumption is made in legislation that particular occupations or activities are exclusively carried on by men or women. Gender-neutral terms for occupations, activities and other things are preferred where these are readily available and sensible, for example:

- worker (rather than workman)
- administrator (rather than administrix)
- staffed, crewed (rather than manned)
- chairperson, presiding member, president, convener, moderator (rather than chairman)

Sex-based pronouns are to be avoided when the referent may not be of that sex.

## Review

This section has introduced you to the main ideas and approaches to studying language and gender. You should have no difficulty in

- identifying features that are supposed to be typical of male or female language
- commenting on whether a text conforms to the theoretical ideas about gender and language
- writing about the way texts represent males and females
- explaining how language reflects views about gender differences
- describing the issues connected with language and gender.

### Revision

1  Explain the deficit model, the dominance model, and the communicative competence model for examining language use. Include the names of theorists if you can.

2  What are the main features of women's language use according to researchers?

3  How have theories of language use changed over time?

4  What are politeness strategies? How are they relevant to gender?

5  What features would you look for in a text showing gendered language use?

6  What issues are there concerning how gender is represented in writing?

# Language variation across Britain

In this section you will learn to

- understand what a dialect is
- employ terms and concepts to describe how dialects vary from Standard English
- analyse how and why dialect is represented in written texts
- examine attitudes towards different dialects and accents of the British Isles
- analyse and investigate urban dialects and influences from other languages.

## What do we mean by 'dialect'?

Dialect means the specific lexis, syntax (or sentence structure) and grammar of one particular variety of English, including the way its speakers pronounce it. There are regional (including rural and urban) dialects, as well as social dialects. This can be confusing, because people think that the terms accent and dialect are interchangeable. They're not! Accent means pronunciation only. Dialect is a much broader term; it includes all the aspects of language.

- Regional dialect describes the variety of English spoken in a particular region of the UK.
- Urban dialects may derive from earlier regional and rural dialects or from other languages such as Jamaican.
- Social dialects in English today include Standard English, Scottish Standard English and Northern Irish English. Originally regional varieties, they are now the prestige standard forms in England, Scotland and Northern Ireland: the variety used in education, the government, the media, and the public domain in general.
- Dialect levelling is when dialects disappear and Standard English forms spread to all social and regional groups.

## What do we mean by accent?

Quite simply, accent means the way we pronounce the language we speak every day. Accents can also be regional or social.

- Regional accents can be described in generalised terms: 'He's got a Northern accent', or as a specifically local accent: 'You can tell she was born in Belper, not Derby!'
- Urban accents are used in areas such as London, Birmingham, Manchester, Liverpool, Newcastle, Glasgow.
- Social accents are the accents adopted by social groups which have no regional base. Received Pronunciation (RP) remains the principal social accent today although historically it actually originated in the South East of England.

Remember

- Received pronunciation refers to the accent
- Standard English refers to the dialect.

Have you travelled much within Britain? Even if you don't consider yourself an expert in regional variation, you could probably tell the difference between people who come from

Liverpool, Birmingham or Dorset. On the other hand you may think that you don't have an accent. Most people consider the way they speak is without an accent, until they come across someone from another part of the country!

**Activity 12**

Individual
Exam preparation

## How do dialects differ from Standard English?

Examine these two extracts, which both represent the Nottingham dialect. The first is from *Lady Chatterley's Lover*, written in 1928 by D.H. Lawrence, and the second is from *The Killing Jar*, written in 2006 by Nicola Monaghan.

Complete a table like this so that you can compare and contrast them.

| Text | Accent features (representation of sound) | Lexical items (regional words) | Grammar forms (non-standard grammar) |
|------|------|------|------|
| *Lady Chatterley's Lover* | | | |
| *The Killing Jar* | | | |

Why do these writers choose to represent the regional speech of these characters?

Turn to page 111 for a commentary.

### Text A

The conversation is between Lady Chatterley and Mellors, a local man who works on the Chatterleys' estate.

'It is so nice here, so restful,' she said. 'I have never been here before.'

'No?'

'I think I shall come and sit here sometimes.'

'Yes?'

'Do you lock the hut when you're not here?'

'Yes, your Ladyship.'

'Do you think I could have a key too, so that I could sit here sometimes? Are there two keys?'

'Not as Ah know on, ther' isna.'

He had lapsed into the vernacular. Connie hesitated; he was putting up an opposition. Was it his hut, after all?

'Couldn't we get another key?' she asked in her soft voice, that underneath had the ring of a woman determined to get her way.

'Another!' he said, glancing at her with a flash of anger, touched with derision.

'Yes, a duplicate,' she said, flushing.

''Appen Sir Clifford 'ud know,' he said, putting her off.

'Yes!' she said, 'he might have another. Otherwise we could have one made from the one you have. It would only take a day or so, I suppose. You could spare your key for so long.'

'Ah canna tell yer, m'Lady! Ah know nob'dy as ma'es keys round 'ere.'

Connie suddenly flushed with anger.

'Very well!' she said. 'I'll see to it.'

'All right, your Ladyship.'

Their eyes met. His had a cold, ugly look of dislike and contempt, and indifference to what would happen. Hers were hot with rebuff.

But her heart sank, she saw how utterly he disliked her, when she went against him. And she saw him in a sort of desperation.

'Good afternoon!'

Notice where D.H. Lawrence includes this comment: 'He had lapsed into the vernacular. Connie hesitated; he was putting up an opposition.' He is explicitly showing Mellors is using divergence to create distance between them and thereby to create tension in the plot. The representation of dialect here is for the purposes of characterisation, to show the social distance between Mellors and Lady Chatterley

### Text B

It were that year I started school. I should of started a year before, but my mam hadn't got round to organising it. My mommar wasn't having none of that, though and got me enrolled at the Catholic school down the road. She was Catholic, see, and said St Teresa's was a better place to go than anywhere else. All's I really knew about it were when she dressed me up in this brown pinafore and made me eat cereal one morning. I didn't want to get up cause Mam was still in bed, and I pulled a right mardy when she tried to get me out the door. But, like I said, my mommar wasn't one to be messed with. She gave me a right clout and dragged me off through the estate and onto Aspley Lane.

It were autumn and there was brown leaves all round where they'd fell off the big trees. I wouldn't look at my mommar cause she'd took me away from my mam so I crunched my way through looking at my feet. I noticed my shoes and tights were the same colour as the leaves and soon that had me so interested I stopped being in a mardy and was talking to my mommar about what'd happen when I got to school.

I got there to find this place where the chairs and tables, even the toilets, were all built at just the right height for me. I walked round fascinated. There was water and sand and a Wendy House to play in, with a toy iron and cooker and all that kind of thing. I was well impressed. There was this woman there, tall as a witch and with this silver hair in a mist round her head. She spoke to my mommar and I heard her going on about how much time I'd missed and the catching up I'd have to do.

Then Mommar left me there. I wasn't impressed about that, not one bit. I curled up in a ball on the carpet and wouldn't move nowhere. The teacher kept trying to come near me and I just screamed my head off. When she tried grabbing me I bit her on the hand. They couldn't ring my mam or my mommar ner nowt cause we didn't have a phone in them days, so they just put me in this room on my own till I calmed down.

## Why and how do accent and dialect vary?

Variation may be due to influence from a different language in a particular region. The general trend however is for dialect levelling to occur. So even if you could hear different accents, people in different regional areas will generally use the same lexis and grammar as Standard English.

Whether regional variations will be maintained or disappear over time often depends on the nature of social networks. A more closed community will have more variant features, whereas a more open community will mix with others whose language use is different and therefore language use will become more homogenous owing to convergence. Factors such as the broadcast media or newspapers will also tend to establish the standard forms. This is why you will often find that older generations have stronger accents and use more dialect forms than younger people. You may find that younger people use slang in common across regions of the country. Geographical and social mobility also have an influence on dialect levelling.

Lesley and James Milroy investigated the role of casual speech within three Belfast communities:

- Ballymacarrett (Protestant, low male unemployment)
- the Hammer (Protestant, substantial male unemployment)
- the Clonard (Catholic, substantial male unemployment).

They found that

- the stronger the social network, the greater the use of vernacular (everyday, informal, non-standard, spoken language) or non-standard linguistic features
- in Protestant Ballymacarrett and the Hammer, women used fewer vernacular features than men and preferred prestige forms
- in Catholic Clonard, younger women preferred non-prestige forms, contrary to the conventional practice of Ballymacarrett and the Hammer, as a way of showing social solidarity with their unemployed men.

These findings demonstrate the importance of social networks within a social class and their influence on the way people use language in their speech communities. They also show that apparent norms, like women's well-documented preference for prestige forms (hypercorrection), can be reversed (consciously or otherwise) by the need to express something more important (here, social solidarity).

## Activity 13 — Investigating the speech of your region

**Individual**

*Either:* Find examples of representation of your local accent in written texts.

*Or:* Write a list of regional terms and find their origins.

*Or:* Use the BBC voices website www.bbc.co.uk/voices/recordings/ or the British Library 'sounds familiar' website www.bl.uk/learning/langlit/sounds/

## Why is regional speech represented in writing?

Generally, authors do not represent the way people speak in an exact way, otherwise speech in literature or in media texts would look like a transcript. There is a range of reasons why an author might choose to include regional markers in dialogue:

- for characterisation – to indicate class, regional origin of the characters and create contrasts between them
- to create prestige for non-standard speech forms – generally written texts use Standard English, but some writers may wish to give their regional speech value and attention
- to create atmosphere or link to the topic of the text – for example, local tales, anecdotes, selling regional specialities
- to convey or create in the reader a positive or a negative attitude to the dialect.

# What attitudes exist towards British dialects and accents?

When accents are represented in writing, this is usually because the author has some attitude towards the dialect, either a positive or negative attitude. If there is no intention to show attitude, the accent is unlikely to be represented. There is a wide variation in speech patterns across England. You are going to examine your own and other people's attitudes to them.

| Activity 14 | Attitudes to language variation |
| --- | --- |

**Pair work**

### Stage 1
Read the following statements carefully. (Some are made up, some are actual quotations.)

Decide what you think the speakers were trying to say about language in each statement: the attitudes and values behind each statement.

Write down your individual or joint responses to each statement. Do you share these opinions?

*Example:* Statement A seems to show that the speaker thinks a Birmingham accent is inferior, and it made her feel inferior. When she lost her job, she assumed this was the reason. Your response might be: 'My parents come from Birmingham so I really like the accent – I don't care what people think about it.'

A  'I lost my job because of my Birmingham accent.'

B  'Why can't the BBC use Queen's English speakers like they used to?'

C  'He's only got to open his mouth and he lets himself down.'

D  'I can't stand being called visually impaired – I just can't see as well as I used to …'

E  'I wish I didn't have a local accent.' 'Oh, I really like yours – can't stand mine though!'

F  'It is impossible for an Englishman to open his mouth, without making some other Englishman despise him.' (George Bernard Shaw, 1912)

G  'You should hear his language – you can tell what sort of person he is!'

H  'When I mark essays I insist on *different from* not *different to*!'

I  'I can't stand all these Americanisms you hear on the box all the time.'

J  'I really love a Scottish accent!' 'Yes, but I hate Glaswegian – you can't understand a word they say!'

K  'He told me to make sure that the motherboard was securely attached to all the ports, but I hadn't a clue what he meant.'

L  'Linguistic prescriptivism, established in the eighteenth century, was consolidated in the nineteenth century by scholars' obsessive interest in diachronic phonological variation within the Indo-European group of languages. Today we prefer descriptive linguistics, though there remain profound differences of approach between the systemic functional methodology and the transformational generative grammar tradition.'

### Stage 2
Below is a list suggested by one linguist (D. McKinnon) of the kinds of favourable and unfavourable judgements people make about other people's English.

Match the statements in Stage 1 with this list.

I think the way s/he uses English is
1 correct/incorrect
2 beautiful/ugly
3 socially acceptable/socially unacceptable
4 morally acceptable/morally unacceptable
5 useful (for a particular purpose)/not useful
6 appropriate/inappropriate (for the context)
7 not controversial/potentially controversial (could offend)

## Activity 15 — Studying the use of accent stereotyping on TV

**Individual**

1 Select any commercial TV channel and choose either a weekday (Monday to Thursday) or a weekend day (Friday to Sunday). Look at a range of 'commercial breaks' and

- identify the expected audience (this will depend on the programmes on either side of the commercial break as well as the channel and time of day)
- list the products
- identify the accents used for each product
- suggest reasons for the choice of accent
- look for connections between accent, product and audience – for example, is RP used for financial services but Yorkshire accents for bread?

2 Do newsreaders have regional accents? If so, which ones?

3 Make notes on the way soap operas use regional accents.

4 Can you find any news articles about attitudes to accents?

5 Do you think the media reflects or perpetuates attitudes to regional speech?

Compare your findings with others in your group and create a display of your findings.

## Summary of features to look for in variation from Standard English

Phonology
- **Accent:** How is this represented in a written text – by non-standard orthography (spelling) or IPA?
- **Typical accent variation:** The glottal stop features in words like bottle/letter where the t sound is formed at the back of the mouth. Vowel sounds vary from North to South. Prevocalic r occurs in accents that would pronounce the r in 'farm'. Prevocalic l features in accents that include a schwa in 'film' – 'filum'.
- **Elision:** Missing sounds or letters – 'appen'.

### Lexis/semantics
- **Lexical variation** is where different terms are used around the country. Variation is particularly common in semantic fields of food, in terms of address, relationships, places or features of geography.
- **Semantic variation:** Are familiar words used in an unfamiliar way?

### Grammar
- **Creation of the negative:** Double negatives – 'I don't know nothing' – or negatives created without the auxiliary 'do' – 'I know nobody who makes keys.'
- **Pronoun use:** Some dialects still retain 'thee/thou' for you or use the object pronoun in place of the subject pronoun – 'us were'.
- **Preposition** use may vary – 'not as I know on [of]' or 'I could of [have] done it'
- **Non-standard use of** connectives: For example, the connective 'as' in place of the pronoun 'who' or 'that' – 'anyone as'.
- **Ellipsis:** Words missed out – 'What's time?'
- **Agreement:** For example, subject/verb – 'I were' or 'we was'.
- **Irregular verb forms:** Using, for example, 'I knowed' to match the regular formation of verbs. Using the infinitive – 'I be late' – instead of the present – 'I am late.'
- **Object pronoun** used as a conversation marker/for emphasis – 'I don't drive a car, me.'

### Idioms
Specific phrases, particular to a region, such as
- 'our mam' as a term of address or 'our Connie' to identify a family member
- 'duck' – a non-gender-specific term of address in the Midlands
- 'It's dark over Bill's mother's' – in the Midlands means dark clouds suggests it is going to rain.

## What are urban dialects?

As well as variation across regions, there is also variation across social and ethnic groups. In some cases it is due to influence from a 'home' language, which may be reinforced by consumption of culture such as music or film. The use of dialect forms will be evident in all forms of non-standard language use. Studies have described these dialects as Black English Vernacular or BEV or Black English. Also the term Hinglish has been coined to describe language influenced by Hindi and other Indian languages such as Punjabi and Urdu.

| Activity 16 | **How is language variation presented in the media?** |
|---|---|
| Pair work | On the following page is an extract from the *Daily Mail* (December 2006).<br><br>Make a list of the language features Sarah Harris reports. Are they to do with lexis, grammar or use?<br><br>What issues about language use does she raise? |

This report notices several factors in dialect spread:
- that new language use and slang often originate with young people, as they are more likely to be flexible in their language use
- that convergence creates language variation
- a feature called covert prestige whereby non-standard forms are considered preferable or of higher status by some groups in society – downward convergence describes a preference for non-standard rather than standard forms.

# Schoolchildren now speak 'The Queen's Hinglish'

**by Sarah Harris,** *Education Correspondent*

Your brother thinks he's a bit of a ranjha, but to you he's a complete bevakoof.

In other words, the big head thinks he's a whiz with the ladies but in your opinion he's actually a fool.

This new terminology is known as Hinglish, a mixture of English and South Asian languages such as Hindi, Urdu and Punjabi.

It is being used increasingly throughout the United Kingdom, particularly in playgrounds where children are freely experimenting with phrases such as changa, meaning 'okay' and chi-chi which is 'yuck'.

A dictionary of the hybrid language called *The Queen's Hinglish – How to Speak Pukka* has now been gathered by Baljinder Mahal, a Derby-based primary school teacher. She reveals that the collision of languages has produced colourful phrases such as 'machi-chips' for fish and chips and 'ganja' for bald.

A hooligan is a 'badmash' and a 'kamla' is a silly person.

The 29-year-old believes that much of the language's development is happening in multi-cultural playgrounds across the country.

She has heard white pupils using Asian words such as 'kati', meaning 'I'm not your friend any more'.

'I find children's manipulation of language very exciting. They mix two words up in the bat of an eyelid,' she said.

'It's incorrect to mix it up but who says it's incorrect? English is a mongrel language anyway.'

However she does not believe that the language will find its way into the classroom, as pupils are aware of its difference from Standard English in formal lessons.

Describing the language's development, she added: 'Much of it comes from banter – the exchanges between the British white population and the Asians.' . . .

Another multicultural hybrid language taking hold in the UK is Jafaican which is based on Jamaican and has undertones of West African and Indian.

In some London boroughs it has taken over from Cockney, the prevailing accent for generations, as inner-city white youths pick up the speech patterns of their black and Asian classmates.

## What are pidgins and creoles?

Sarah Harris's article refers to English as a 'mongrel language' and also describes a 'hybrid language'. She is referring here to how English can borrow from other languages.

The term 'hybrid language' expresses the phenomena noted in the creation of pidgins and creoles. When people speaking two different languages have to communicate, two things happen. First a basic language (pidgin) develops, with simple grammar and limited vocabulary. Second, a generation later, this simplified language gains the normal complexity of every human language, and then becomes a creole language.

As more and more contact with the dominant (European) community became inevitable, these pidgin languages developed and became drawn towards the European language, though never becoming identical with it because of the influence of the original African languages and dialects. This process of development is known as creolisation and the languages that develop into the mother-tongues of a community are known as creoles. The creole languages spoken by Afro-Caribbeans are sometimes called patois (or patwa) even when people who were born in Britain and whose parents were born in Britain speak them. Many creole-speaking people in Britain today can switch readily between patois and other varieties of English.

## Activity 17 — How do urban or patois-influenced varieties differ from Standard English?

Here is part of a conversation recorded between two friends in their school in London. Both girls were seventeen.

Study the conversation carefully and list any features, together with examples, which seem to differ from Standard English. You might find it helpful to list them under the separate headings of grammar, lexis and accent.

¿ indicates a glottal stop     | indicates overlapping speech

B   anyway Amy(.) | choh (.) Karen tol' me (.) yes
A                 | Karen
B   this is Karen to me now (.) she goes to me (.) well (.) about I mus' come to 'er par¿y right
A   | 'cause she told you init?
B   | yeah mhm 'course 'n' that (.) yeah right well anyway I went down there (.) me bring my sister-dem all me sister-dem come wid me y'know (.) come all the way down the (.) ah (.) party there she goes to me abou¿ i¿ now when we ge¿ there (.) we walk pas' the door to number fifty-nine – no lights
A   mhm
B   righ¿ (.) so w' walk up the top of the road (.) couldn't 'ear no music at all so my sister-dem start cussin' me like any-thing you know (.) 'bout me bomboklaat | an' all dis business
A                                                                                        | mhhhm
B   dere (.) well anyway (.) go back down dere right (.) an' we look 'pon now we see Jerry but dem come tell us | 'bout um aks us where de | party de (.) right?
A              | mhm                        | party is
B   so we say well definitely we come up 'ere 'cause Karen say it was 'ere right?
A   yeah
B   couldn' fin' not'in' so (.) we went back down dere lookin' at de gates (.) we find a letter there so f' say 'bout (.) party cancel
A   mhm

## Activity 18 — Representation in literature of 'Black English'

The two examples of Black English on page 80 are taken from literary sources. Text A is an extract from by *The Lonely Londoners* by Samuel Selvon. Text B is a poem by James Berry, who was born in Jamaica in 1924, and has lived in Britain since 1948.

In what ways do these writers depart from Standard English?

Why are they representing their non-standard language?

## Text A

Galahad, a West Indian living in London, has been unable to get employment and resorts to unusual methods to provide a meal for himself.

Galahad used to go walking in Kensington Gardens, the fog never clear enough for him to see down to High Street Ken. That particular winter, things was so bad with him that he had was to try and catch a pigeon in the park to eat. It does have a lot of them flying about, and the people does feed them with bits of bread. Sometimes they get so much bread that they pick and choosing, and Galahad watching them with envy. In this country, people prefer to see man starve than a cat or dog want something to eat.

Watching these fat pigeons strut about the park, the idea come to Galahad to snatch one and take it home and roast it. When he was a little fellar his father had a work in High Street in San Fernando, a town about forty miles from Port of Spain. It used to have pigeons like stupidness all about the street I nobody know where they come from, and Galahad father used to snatch and send them home to cook.

## Text B

### Words of a Jamaican Laas Moment Them

When I dead
mek rain fall.
Mek the air wash.
Mek the lan wash good-good.
Mek dry course them run, and run.
As laas breath gone
mek rain burst –
hilltop them work
waterfall, and all
the gully them gargle fresh.
Mek breadfruit limb them drip,
mango limb them drip. Cow, hog, fowl
stan still, in the burst of clouds.
Poinciana bloom them soak off, clean-clean.
Grass go unda water.
Instant I gone
mek all the Island wash – wash away
the mess of my shortcomings –
all the brok-up things I did start.
Mi doings did fall short too much.
Mi ways did hurt mi wife too oftn.

## Activity 19

Individual
Exam preparation

# Studying urban dialect

Analyse and comment on the following two texts. They are part of an investigation by a student into her own language and that of her friends entitled *Black and White talk: do they exist?* She describes herself as 'a young black girl in a predominantly white college'. She chooses the terms 'black' and 'white' to describe her friends and 'youths' for both males and females. G and D in this transcript are female; K is male.

### Transcript

K    wargwarn man wargwarn

G    wargwarn man | wargwarn

K                              | [laughs] WARGWARN

D    safe

G    hello Kendy

K    wargwarn

D    shut up man (.) why you so black?

K    dunno man

G    he can't help it

K    [inaudible]

G    not really he's a pub man at heart (.) | don't watch him

D                                                          | init man

[teasing Kendy]

D    Y'alright | mate

G                    | aayyyy wohaayy

D    [laughs]

G    init ken (2) ] [laughs] (2)   | aww babes

K                                        | no you're not funny |

D    yano what he did year (.) | he sed he could play the guitar

K                                                    | nar nar nar

K    don't get it don't get it twisted

G    s'alright ken

K    did I really tho?

G    wait what did he say |

D                                    | cuz like when fingy was playin the  | drums

G                                                                                      | yeah

D    he jus like (.) tai (.) taiwo sed he sed he | could play the guitar

K                                                          | arr ye ye ye I sed (.) ye

G    awww

D    you see him (.) he felt left out bless him | [laughs]

G                                                          | [laughs]

G    I dint know you lied like that

K    I don't lie man

### Text messages

Wa'apn Gee u kl?im jus lisnin 2 sum sizla bunin my chalice…lol txbk if u cn. Kb

Yo star hpe unuh gt hme ok n dat. Sz 4 disturbin u if u wer cachin zedz. Newayz im gna cum find u 1day soon yh k loln u lukd nice 2dat still. Nytnytx

yes yes…cnt wait to get home man the coach is smellin lyk lemon merang mixed with dutty bad bret man its RAW TING!! Errxxx

This is a comment the student made in her investigation:

'I noticed that some of the white people at college change how they speak when talking to me or deliberately bring up specific ethnicity centred topics as if in attempt to fit in or impress. So it seems even before I had learnt about Accommodation theory in English language I was already displaying it and witnessing others doing the same.'

These are some of the differences she noted between black and white originated texts and speech.

- Non-standard spellings were used for emphasis in the texts from black friends. Spelling may represent pronunciation – dutty.
- The effect of non-standard texting is to personalise and create comic effects. Texts from white friends conformed more to text-message conventions of abbreviating to save space.
- Grammatical structures were different: black youths used present tense copula deletion – 'why you so black' is missing the 'are' of Standard English. She also found examples of the double negative elsewhere in her data.

She noted influences from urban music such as hip-hop and R'n'B in the use of 'star' as a term of address. She also drew attention to the use of 'mate' in the transcript:

'Mate is another address term, which was used by youths of both ethnicities. However, in the context of the transcript, it clearly shows that the black youth has chosen this particular word to tease another black youth about sounding white. This may well mean that this is not actually a neutral word and that its presence in the transcript from three black youths is only for comic effect due to mimicking white speech.'

She noticed the following dialect lexis in the texts she collected:

- wa'apn is patois for *what's happening*
- bunin is patois for *burning*
- unuh is patois for *you lot*
- dutty is patois for *dirty*
- bret is patois for *breath*
- raw ting is patois for *something horrible*
- Sf is a *greeting*
- safe is a greeting
- sz means *sorry*
- wargwarn means *what's going on*
- pub man means *white.*

---

## Activity 20

**Pair work**

# Investigating and presenting differences between Standard English and British Black English

You now have a considerable amount of data available in British Black English: two conversations and two literary pieces.

Working in pairs, one of you should be responsible for grammar (morphology and syntax) and the other for lexis. Your task is to produce a wall chart for display in secondary-school classrooms that illustrates the differences between Standard English and British Black English. Make sure that you present the results of your investigation into this data in as lively and interesting a way as possible.

If you can find other examples of British Black English to aid your investigation, so much the better. Of course, you may use Black English yourself, in which case you'll have a plethora of material available!

If you can make recordings of speech, then you will be able to investigate pronunciation and prosody, which are only hinted at in the examples here.

If you can research something of the history of Black English, this will add an extra dimension to your wall chart.

## Review

This section has covered a range of issues connected with regional variation. You should now have a clear understanding of

- what dialect means
- the technical terms used to describe dialects
- how dialects vary from Standard English
- how dialects are represented in written texts
- attitudes and issues connected with dialect variation
- how to analyse and comment on texts that show dialect variation.

## Revision

1 Give a definition of dialect, regional, urban, social. What features does it include?
2 What is dialect levelling? What factors influence dialect preservation or dialect levelling?
3 Which language features tend to vary in different dialects?

# Changing technology and language use

In this section you will be learning to

- understand and analyse the discourses related to new technology using appropriate terminology
- understand and analyse how new technology creates different contexts for the production and reception of language
- analyse how these new contextual factors influence language variation and how technology influences language change.

New technology is developing all the time and any discussion of the language use in new technologies will quickly become dated. However, there are key concepts and ideas that are common across different types of new technology:

- public and individual language use, including ease of access
- interactivity
- the nature of spoken and written texts and mixed modes
- the creation of new discourses.

This is a topic area of which you will no doubt have much experience, therefore you will very quickly be able to relate the relevant concepts and ideas to texts and modes of communication that are familiar to you.

# Questions to ask about technology texts

### Is it public or personal? How does the technology influence access to the text?

New technology allows access to a mass audience, through e-mails, web pages, radio and TV. It also allows different private/personal communication, using texting, mobile phones and e-mails. Individuals can easily gain access to a range of information through the internet. It allows individuals in a domestic context to gain access to a wide audience – through message boards, blogs and sites like 'My space' or 'Youtube'. This audience may be known or unknown.

### How does the text use interactivity?

Many technologies are interactive, for example computers or TV. This often allows the consumer more control. It might be argued that new technologies are democratising – that they allow ordinary people to access and control public discourses in a way that was not possible in the past. Interactivity may be through manipulating the discourse as in a web page or through turn taking in e-mail and text messages, or through phone-ins.

### How does technology use modes?

Speech is usually

- spontaneous
- interactive
- can be adapted to the context and the responses of the listener
- ephemeral.

Writing is usually

- planned
- one sided rather than interactive
- doesn't adapt to the audience and is usually read away from the context of production
- permanent.

Whereas technology-related texts can be

- written and interactive – text messages, web pages, MSN, message boards, e-mails
- speech texts can be available to an unknown, distanced mass audience in TV or radio phone-ins and commentaries on sports or other events
- phone messages can be recorded so they are not necessarily interactive, spontaneous or ephemeral.

### How does technology influence discourse?

Because new technology is different from paper-based writing it has produced different discourse forms. For example, web pages, e-mails and text messages all have specific structures and layout. They are often 'read' differently from other written texts: not necessarily from top to bottom and from left to right. These texts might use graphology, images or animation differently from paper-based written discourses.

These forms often have different levels or concepts of correctness. It is quite common to find non-standard spelling and punctuation in e-mails or text messages. In part this may be because the message is interpersonal and the reader/writer know each other well or may be because the discourse does not entail the same level of correctness of other written texts. Non-standard grammar or incomplete sentences are common, noun phrases, ellipsis and other speech features are often found in these written texts, even if they are public and formal.

### How does technology influence lexis?

New technology requires new words – neologisms – to describe it. There are different types of neologisms. Word creation follows specific patterns, for example compounding, where two words are put together to describe a new object – motherboard, keyboard, mouse mat. Initialisms are common in computer terms – URL, FAQ, RAM, CD ROM. Analogy is also used – mouse, window, icon – where a similarity is noted between a new object and an existing one.

When looking at a technology text you should ask

- is it spontaneous
- is there turn taking
- is it interactive
- is it written, spoken, or does it have elements of both
- does it adapt to the audience
- is the audience participating (e.g. as in a phone-in)
- is it personal, private or to a mass audience, and does it intentionally blur the differences?

As many technology texts are linked to spoken texts they tend to develop aspects of speech such as sociolect, idiolect and the creation of identity. A group of people who often send texts to each other will develop a common sociolect that might be difficult for others to understand (as in the example on page 81). Or you might find that you converge to different texters, if you text in a different way to your parents and your friends. You might feel different groups have different levels of competency in text discourse and therefore use different styles of communication.

---

**Activity 21**

**Individual**

## Analysing a technology text

Write an analysis of the text on the following page. You should give particular attention to the aspects of the web page as a technology text.

- Is it spontaneous?
- Is there turn taking?
- Is it interactive?
- Is it written, spoken, or does it have elements of both?
- Does it adapt to the audience?

- Is the audience participating (e.g. as in a phone-in)?
- Is it personal, private or to a mass audience, and does it intentionally blur the differences?

Comment on the relationship it creates with the reader.

Describe how BookCrossing represents itself as a 'company' albeit one that doesn't make any money.

Visit the site yourself.

*more like giving, less like keeping*

members: 636,692
books registered: 4,529,917
good karma: *priceless*

**bookcrossing.com**™

email [ ]  password [ ]  [ log in ]

▷ catch/release map

home

join bookcrossing

▷ books

▷ people

▷ go hunting

▷ community

▷ the buzz

▷ support bc

**JOIN NOW** It's FREE! It's FAST! It's FUN!

Welcome to BookCrossing, where 636,692 people in over 130 countries come to share their passion for books with the world. How? It's easy.

Simply click on the link below and sign up for free in less than 1 minute-- that's it!

At BookCrossing, you can register any book you have on the site, and then set the book free to travel the world and find new readers.

Leave it on a park bench, at a coffee shop, at a hotel on vacation. Share it with a friend or tuck it onto a bookshelf at the gym -- anywhere it might find a new reader! What happens next is up to fate, and we never know where our books might travel next. Track the book's journey around the world as it is passed on from person to person.

Join hundreds of thousands of active BookCrossers daily in our many forums to discuss your favorite authors, characters and books in every genre throughout history right up through current releases.

Help make the whole world a library and **Sign up ≫** share the joy of literacy. Reading becomes an adventure when you BookCross!

Help spread the word and bookmark us at StumbleUpon, Del.icio.us, Digg and more!  BOOKMARK

Found a BookCrossing book?

Enter the BCID# here

BCID: [ ]-[ ]  [ Go! ]

**School Program:**

BookCrossing goes to School! (read more)

**Member Comments:**

When I discovered this site, it was like coming home. Exchanging books with people who also love the books they are exchanging and releasing--well, what more could you ask for.

**bookcrossing:**

n. the practice of leaving a book in a public place to be picked up and read by others, who then do likewise.

(added to the Concise Oxford English Dictionary in August 2004)

**recently released**

Marco Polo, Bali, Lombok
Released by Schmusefluse in Germany

Es fängt damit an, daß am Ende der ...
Released by Schmusefluse in Germany

The Terracotta Dog
Released by CaterinaAnna in Controlled Releases

More: (list) (map)

Visit the Supply Store

Shop online at our secure Supply Store. Every purchase supports BookCrossing, plus earns you *Members Plus!*

**international sites**

Japanese Mirror
Portugal Support
Spanish Mirror
European Support
European Support Sites
German Support
Dutch Support
French Mirror
French Support
Italian Mirror 1
Italian Mirror 2
Mexican Mirror

▷ catch/release map

## About BookCrossing

BookCrossing.com is a labor of love that was conceived and is maintained by Humankind Systems, Inc., a software and internet development company with offices in Kansas City, Missouri, and Sandpoint, Idaho. Looking for a break from the doldrums of creating yet another e-commerce website (that's just what the world needs), or email server application (oooh, those are doubly exciting), Humankind partner Ron Hornbaker sought to create a community site that would be the first of its kind, that would give back to the world at large, and that would provide warm fuzzy feelings whenever he worked on it. BookCrossing.com was the result.

The idea came to Ron back in March of 2001, as he and his wife Kaori were admiring the PhotoTag.org site, which tracks disposable cameras loosed into the wild. He already knew about the popularity of WheresGeorge.com (which tracks U.S. currency by serial number), and that got him thinking: what other physical object might people enjoy tracking? A few minutes later, after a glance at his full bookshelf, the idea of tracking books occurred to him. After two hours of research on the internet, Ron realized, to his surprise, that nothing like BookCrossing had been done on any significant scale. And so they went to work. By 3 A.M. that night, they had decided on the name (zero hits for "bookcrossing" on Google), registered the domain, and Kaori had sketched the running book logo on a crossing sign. The rest was merely execution.

After getting the green light from his partners in the software company, Ron went to work programming the site from scratch the next day, and about four mostly sleepless weeks later, on April 17, 2001, BookCrossing.com was launched with a simple $500 press release, the last time money has been spent promoting the site. Members trickled in at the rate of 100 or so per month until March of 2002 when the Book magazine article was published. Since then, BookCrossing has been the focus of countless TV, radio, and newspaper features around the world, gets about 300 new members every day, has its own category in the human-edited Google Directory, and has been added to the Concise Oxford English Dictionary as a new word. The fact that it has captured the passion and imagination of around 636,692 people worldwide, so quickly, has been a welcome surprise for everyone involved.

**recently released**

Bed Rest
Released by CaterinaAnna in Controlled Releases

Jacke wie Hose.
Released by Rosenfrau in Germany

Marco Polo, Bali, Lombok
Released by Schmusefluse in Germany

More: (list) (map)

**JOIN NOW** It's FREE! It's FAST! It's FUN!

Visit the Supply Store

Shop online at our secure Supply Store. Every purchase supports BookCrossing, plus earns you *Members Plus!*

**international sites**

Japanese Mirror
Portugal Support
Spanish Mirror
European Support
European Support Sites
German Support
Dutch Support
French Mirror
French Support
Italian Mirror 1
Italian Mirror 2
Mexican Mirror

About | News | FAQs | Privacy Policy | Contact & Support | Press & Media | Link To Us | Team | Jobs

## Activity 22 — New technology and discourse

**Pair work**

Technology is widely used in business or occupational contexts and therefore has aspects of occupational language. This text demonstrates many of the aspects of how language use is influenced by both the context of new technologies and occupation. It is a policy document giving advice on good practice for internet users.

- Check e-mail in-trays frequently and respond promptly.
- Think before you e-mail. E-mails should never be sent rashly or in anger.
- Don't type e-mails in capital letters IT LOOKS LIKE SHOUTING!
- Make sure e-mails are clear and are not open to misunderstanding. Humour and irony can easily be misinterpreted when read by another.
- If the contents of your e-mail are sensitive make sure it is only sent to the person you intend.
- Do not send too many copies of e-mails. Unsolicited, or 'junk', e-mail is unpopular and a burden to all users of the internet.
- Don't over quote previous e-mail messages when using the 'Reply' facility within e-mail.
- Don't send very large attached documents or files to large distribution lists.
- Virus check documents, spreadsheets, etc. that are sent and received by e-mail.
- Never include defamatory or offensive comments in e-mails.
- Internet e-mail is not secure. Internet e-mail should not be used for sensitive or confidential information and its use for personal data could constitute a breach of the eighth principle of the Data Protection Act (1998) that personal data should be kept secure.

Examine this policy document in terms of

- advice related to the new facilities available with e-mail
- the content of e-mails
- discourse conventions/how e-mails are written
- occupation-specific features.

Explain the issues raised by this document and how new technology changes the way people communicate. Turn to page 111 for a commentary.

## Review

You have now had a brief look at how new technology has influenced language use.

- You have been introduced to the key issues in analysing and considering technology texts and have had practice analysing a typical text.
- You have learned a range of technical terms to describe and analyse technology texts.
- You can consider the different contexts created by technology texts.
- You have looked at the issues raised by new technology in a work context.

**Revision**

1 What is the significance of a mixed mode?

2 How are technology texts spontaneous and interactive?

3 What new discourses are connected with technology?

4 What does 'concepts of correctness' mean and why are they significant in technology texts?

# Language and occupation

In this section you will examining how occupational contexts can influence language use. The key features you will look at are

- how occupations use lexis in a specialised way
- how occupational language uses specific discourses
- how an occupational setting influences the particular functions of language.

Do you have a part-time job? Are you familiar with any particular occupation? Do you belong to a group such as a music group or scouts who use language in a particular way?

## Lexis

You might use the terms 'specialist lexis', 'technical terms', 'semantic fields' or jargon. All these terms would describe lexis specific to an occupation. 'Technical terms' might be used to refer to terms that are not used in other fields or have different meanings in other fields. Jargon is a term that is usually used pejoratively, describing terms that unnecessarily exclude other people. One person's technical terms could be another person's jargon – it has a lot to do with attitude!

**Activity 23**

**Pair work**

## Can you identify specialist lexis?

The following words come from semantic/lexical fields linked with a particular occupation or group. Try to identify the occupation/group which uses each one.

- double toe-loop combination jump
- anabolic steroid
- e-commerce
- conveyance
- customers
- pirouette
- dressage
- torque
- mulch
- BSE
- gig
- conditioning treatment
- reverse thrust
- focus group
- milk quota
- statement

- turnover
- diocese
- NASA
- SATs
- scan
- ace
- design specifications
- silver service
- spreadsheet
- zoom lens
- footlights
- editorial
- shuttle
- striker
- whisk
- tort

## Specific discourses

Occupations have discourses or discourse structures that are typical of the workplace – agenda for meetings, minutes of meetings, policy documents, contracts.

Some occupations have specific structures to their spoken interactions. For example, classroom language has a very particular structure. Sinclair and Coultard recognised that there are three main functions for teacher talk:

- informative – 'Dictionaries are mainly used to look up meanings.'
- **directive** – 'REECE tell me one thing it's used for.'
- elicitation – 'You can also use it to look up the …?'

Directives can be delivered as imperatives, interrogatives or declaratives. Sinclair and Coultard also identified that classroom talk has a three-part structure:

- **elicitation** – T: You don't know what kind of book that is?(.) what book is it, Lewis?
- **response** – C: A dictionary
- **feedback** – T: A dictionary

This is also referred to as the IRF structure – initiation, response and feedback – and is sometimes found in other situations, not just the classroom.

Service encounters have specific structures – for example, an opening or greeting, a sequence of asking questions and gaining responses and a closing. You probably notice that every time you go to a particular shop or restaurant or cinema or even when you go to the doctor, the same exchange pattern is repeated. Workers are often specifically trained to repeat exact phrases with each customer. Politeness strategies may be central to service encounters. You can refer to these established exchanges as scripts, whether they are written down and read, remembered or simply repeated verbatim for each exchange.

## Functions

Some occupation interactions can be interpersonal, whether they are between workers or worker to client. Occupation interactions could be meetings which are highly structured and intended either to give instructions or to make decisions. They could be negotiations involving workers, possibly at different levels of the organisation. The aim of the negotiations would usually be to find some common, agreed plan fulfilling the different needs of those taking part. There may also be problem-solving discourse functions and instructive or training discourses.

When analysing occupation texts, you should consider these points.

- The context of the exchange – is it 'behind the scenes' or 'front of house'?
- The discourse – conversation, advert, web page, e-mail, letter, minutes, agenda, lesson, leaflet?
- Are there any set phrases or expressions that are typical of the occupation?
- The purpose, the goals and intentions of the participants – persuade, inform, negotiate, instruct, reprimand, praise?
- The structure: set openings, closings and scripts?
- The participants: between experts or between a member of the occupation and the public?
- Is it representing the occupation?
- Is there evidence of accommodation or convergence?

---

**Activity 24** | **That's a good idea**

The following transcript is an excerpt from a longer conversation taken from Deborah Tannen's *Talking from 9 to 5* (1994), a study of the different ways in which men and women talk to each other at work. A manager, Sid, is discussing with his secretary, Rita, preparations for an impending visit by several high-level managers from a regional office.

Read the transcript and describe the style of the conversation. Is, for example, Rita's role entirely subordinate? Note down any feature of language that reflects the influence of context. Clearly issues of power, occupation and gender will be operating in this exchange.

| Sid | Oh and I was meaning to ask you about that. When I meet them Sunday. I'll have the invi-invitation for Sunday night's activities, and also I'll have an agenda, for the following day? In fact an agenda for the following week, for them – to give them, is that right? |
| --- | --- |
| Rita | Well, we can – we can do that. |
| Sid | So that – so that that night they can plan on, they can just look down through the agenda and see where they're going the next day, and we don't just present it to them Monday morning first thing. |
| Rita | That's a very good idea, I'll uh – |
| Sid | and, uh, if it could just be in an envelope or something for each of them and when I give them the invitation I can give them also the agenda showing them what the – what is going to happen for not only Monday but Tuesday and Wednesday, they've got the whole three days laid out. |
| Rita | That's a very good idea. Okay we'll see if we can have a whole lot of things for you to present to them. |
| Sid | Okay. All right, yep, that's a good idea. |

Turn to page 112 for a commentary.

## Representation

Occupations work hard to present a positive image of themselves to the public. This is often revealed in advertising, but also in the language they use to the public. For example they may convey professionalism through technical lexis. They may choose semantic fields and lexis to show concern or caring. Lexis or grammar may convey customer choices. What are the attitudes and values of the occupation? These may be conveyed in the lexis, choice of modifiers, or through pragmatics or even through issues that are avoided, such as armed-forces adverts that don't mention killing or defence.

| **Activity 25** | **Investigating business advertising** |
| --- | --- |
| Individual<br>Group work | Collect a selection of advertisements or brochures produced by businesses. They could be printed or computer-mediated texts. Perhaps you could include the promotional material produced by your school or college.<br><br>In groups or individually, examine the techniques the organisations use to present a positive image of themselves. |

There is often a clear difference in status between the participants in an occupation text. We will examine the influence of power on language in the next section. All these aspects may be relevant to an occupational text.

| **Review** | In this section you have considered how occupation influences language use and the particular features of teacher talk and service encounters. You have looked at the types of discourse you might find in an occupational context and how occupations often have a very particular use of or type of lexis. |
| --- | --- |

**Revision**

1 What range of discourses is specific to occupational contexts?

2 What terms are used to describe lexical choices?

3 What is a script?

4 What do the terms 'behind the scenes' and 'front of house' mean and how would they influence language use?

# Power relationships and language

In this section you will be learning to

- describe and analyse texts relating to power, using appropriate terminology
- demonstrate critical understanding of the concepts and issues related to the exercise of power in language
- analyse and evaluate how the context of production influences language use
- understand how texts are read and understood in a power context, using the key constituents of language.

The previous sections have been about language variation, that is, how language varies according to the social context. This section considers how power relations influence the way language is used. Power relations are always socially based and may be linked to other aspects already discussed.

Power may be obvious, for example the instrumental power of a police officer or the government or teachers or in an occupational context where there is a hierarchy. It might also be influential power in newspapers or advertising, which seeks to influence opinions.

Language analysis looks at the discourses of powerful institutions and how language is used for such purposes as giving instructions or negotiating. In·some circumstances language is used to make things happen. These are referred to as perlocutionary acts or speech acts. For example, saying the words 'I now pronounce you husband and wife' or 'I sentence you to three years in prison' means that the action is accomplished.

## Instrumental power

In this subsection you will

- consider what is meant by power in language situations
- learn the key concepts, theories and terms related to how language demonstrates power
- investigate examples of instrumental power.

There is a range of institutions that wield instrumental power, all of which have their own discourses and lexis – government, religion, the law, education, for example. In many cases they rely on discourses to create their functions and operate. They may depend on ritualised use of language, as in a courtroom or a church. All these contexts use similar features of powerful language.

Language and Social Contexts



## Activity 26 — Analysing classroom language

**Individual**
**Exam preparation**

Here is an example of instrumental power you are familiar with: the language of education. This transcript is taken from a student's investigation into the language of a Year 3 junior-school classroom. It is followed by his findings, which are typical of many situations where power relations operate.

Examine how the features of classroom language (see 'Language and occupation' on page 88) are used in this extract.

- How does the teacher exercise power?
- How does she convey new information?
- How does she indicate that answers are right, or wrong?
- In what way is the conversation similar to or different from your current or recent experience of classroom discourse?

### Notation
T   teacher
C   pupil
a:  phonological stress through elongating the vowel sound.

T   Lewis you don't know what kind of book that is? (.) what book is it Lewis?
C   a dictionary
T   a: di:ctionary and who can tell me what a dictionary is used for? (.) wha:t's a dictionary used for? (.) it's got two ma:in uses (.) REECE tell me one thing it's used for
C   e:rm it's like (.) used for (.) to find out what things are about (.) or what they're for
T   THI:NGS (.) what thi:ngs are for (.) o:r
C   Like (2) erm |
C              | what things mean
T   Wha:t (1.5) can we have a be:tter (1) word for thi:ngs?(.) Wha:t? (1) I'll ask (.) Shanon
C   E:rm not sure what a wo:rd [inaudible]
T   Not sure in what way? (3) Not sure (2) sorry?
C   [inaudible]
T   Yes (.) you know e:xactly what I I I do agree with you but I was trying to get you to use one particular word. You look up the:
C   Ooh ooh [sticking hand up]
T:  Shanon
C   The index
T   The?
C   The index
T   Well (.) you can use the dictionary to look up the mea:ning (.) Ben (1) but you can also use it to look up the:?
C   The index
T   The:?
C   [inaudible]
T   Spellings (.) dictionaries are mainly used to look up meanings spellings of words BE:Njamin (.) THAT'S right i:sn't it? a:nd I don't want anybody to not know what a dictionary is again(.) OK what can anyone tell me about how the words are arranged in a dictionary? (.) How (.) are (.) they arra:nged? (.) in what o:rder? Be:njamin (.) has it ever occurred to you to join i:n this lesson in any way shape or form?

92

This summary of the student's findings indicates the features you should look for in a text demonstrating power.

**Discourse:** Participants can demonstrate power by their control of discourse and by choosing powerful discourses.

**Standard/non-standard language:** Generally the use of Standard English will create prestige; therefore public texts usually use Standard English. In more specific interpersonal contexts non-standard terms may be used to create convergence and because spontaneous speech often includes non-standard forms.

**Phonology** may be used to exercise power, by stressing words or drawing attention to them through elongating sounds – 'THI:NGS (.) what things are for (.) o:r'

**Specialist lexis:** The author can convey expertise through specialist lexis.

**Terms of address**: Participants may be addressed by professional terms or titles – Dr, Mr, Miss, Sir, Your Honour. They may be addressed in generic terms – people, class, pupils – or by personal names or terms of endearment – Shanon, Lewis, Reece, sweetheart, darling. Pronoun choice in address also indicates relationships. For example, 'you' (either singular or plural) creates a personal address and 'we' suggests a sense of inclusion.

**Directives** can be delivered in a range of ways – as imperatives, interrogatives, declaratives. They can be mitigated by politeness forms. For example, in 'Would you open your books' the use of both a question form and the modal 'would' makes the directive more mitigated. Choice of directives may be in response to face wants (face was examined in the gender section, see page 64).

| **Activity 27** | **Investigating classroom language** |
| --- | --- |
| Individual | There are many possible ways in which the language used in classrooms can be studied. The language used reflects very clearly the role that the participants adopt and this may be constantly changing. It is also very dependent on the age of the children in the class. |

Investigate one or more of the following topics (you may wish to add others to this list):

- the language teachers use to maintain order
- the role of questions
- address terms: teacher to pupil, pupil to teacher, teacher to teacher, pupil to pupil
- how language is used in problem-solving discussions between pupils
- a day in the language life of one pupil
- language differences between subjects
- use of standard and non-standard language
- language performance of ESL pupils.

## Activity 28 — Examining power language in a legal context

Individual

The next text comes from the context of legal power. It is a transcript of part of a hearing in the maintenance and arrears section of a magistrates' court. Note the power implication of the word 'hearing'. Who is authorised to 'listen'? Note how the Court is placed in the receptive role and the defendant in the productive. As you will see, the defendant has to give an account of himself.

Read the transcript and make notes on the following:

- the use of questions (who asks them?)
- other types of utterance from the magistrate
- any signs of a shift in who is controlling the hearing
- the direct exercise of power and how it is enacted
- the response of the defendant to how power is exercised over him.

Turn to page 112 for a commentary.

Numbers in brackets indicate the lengths of pauses in seconds.

| | |
|---|---|
| Magistrate | do you understand (6) |
| Mr A | yeh |
| Magistrate | you understand |
| Mr A | yeh |
| Magistrate | – that's good – now you've given us your number and you've given us your firm – and the office will be in touch with – the office will be in touch with them |
| Mr A | I'm going to leave there |
| Magistrate | pardon |
| Mr A | I'm leaving there |
| Magistrate | why are you leaving there (4) |
| Mr A | cause I don't want to pay that |
| Magistrate | – why not (2) Mr A. what do you mean you don't want to pay – don't you realize you've got an order to pay |
| Mr A | yeh – well if I'd have wanted to pay I'd have paid before wouldn't I |
| Magistrate | I don't know – at all |
| Mr A | yeh |
| Magistrate | there's lots of reasons why people don't pay |
| Mr A | I just don't want to – I'll pay to me children – yes – but not to her |
| Magistrate | – well if you flatly refuse to accept the order of the court there's only one alternative – then you'll go to prison |
| Mr A | yeh |
| Magistrate | is that what you're saying |
| Mr A | yes |
| Magistrate | will you fetch a policeman [to the usher] |
| Mr A | you can't do it now (2) I'm still uh under psychiatric treatment |
| Magistrate | you can receive that in prison Mr–uh A |
| Mr A | oh thank you [with ironic intonation] (5) |
| Magistrate | – you can't tell – you can't refuse to do something and tell us what we can do at the same time you know |
| Mr A | that's the system in't it |

## Activity 29

### Examining a range of power texts

For this activity you will benefit from working with two or three other students in order to collect a variety of examples. Look for examples of documents that embody formal rules and authority. Here are some examples:

- GCSE certificate
- hire-purchase agreement
- bus pass
- five pound note
- college/student contract
- birth certificate
- any legal document
- doctor's note
- coursework cover sheet.

Look at the language first and identify the words and phrases that signify the power or authority of the text. Authority may be signalled by a verb ('This certifies that …'), a signature, a promise or any combination of such things. Note too that documents of this kind possess an instrumental power: they prove something, enable you to do something, go somewhere or get in. Lose them, fail to sign them, let them get out of date, and if not actually in trouble, you will be in for a certain amount of inconvenience.

The combination of authority, force, formal laws and social conventions binds society together. It keeps us secure, in a state of 'law and order' to which, by and large, we assent and conform. It structures the way in which we think as well as behave. It constructs in our minds a value system and it does this through language, and particularly through different kinds of discourse. The possession of wealth, specialist knowledge and control of, or strong influence in, media and communications, make it possible to manipulate and exploit conformity.

## Activity 30

### Analysing a contract

Instrumental power is not always exercised between people of very different status. The student directors of a stage show at a sixth form college wrote the text on the following page. They were writing to an audience of their peers: other students in the show.

Refer to the terms and concepts on page 93 and comment on how they have used techniques of power. Comment particularly on the use of mitigation and recognition of face wants in their audience.

Turn to page 113 for a commentary.

**Bilborough College presents**

## Congratulations!

With all the auditions over – it's time to start the hard work! These 2 words will own you – for the next 7 months! (You'll understand soon enough...)

We'd like you to fill in this form – making a declaration of your commitment to the show and agreeing to what we expect of you. (But of course we'll be supporting and working with every one of you all the way, because without the cast – we don't have a show!)

| Please read this next bit carefully, fill the boxes and sign at the end. | |
|---|---|
| Name: | Tutor Group: |
| Email address:<br>(the one you check most regularly) | |
| Mobile number:<br>(we will chase you if you miss rehearsals!) | |

I agree to attend all Wednesday lunchtime rehearsals promptly (12–1:30pm) and will give prior notice of anticipated absence.

I agree to learn lines by the first rehearsal in September.

I am available for performances 1st, 2nd and 3rd December, plus the evenings of 30th and 29th. Some after-college rehearsals may be required in November.

I understand that the librettos MUST be returned in good condition, with all markings (that must be made in pencil) rubbed out. If the libretto is lost I agree to pay the replacement cost of £20.

I understand the commitment expected of me and agree to join the company of Fame The Musical at Bilborough College.

Signed _____     Date _____

## Activity 31  Communicating official information

**Individual**

Below are two texts for you to compare. The context, being under police arrest, is one in which power is only too evident. The law requires the police to inform arrested persons of the powers invested in the police and of the rights to which an arrested person is entitled. Text A is an early draft by the police who then consulted with the Campaign for Plain English, a pressure group which aims to clarify the language of official documents. Text B on page 98 is a revised version of the first draft.

Read the first text, imagining, if you like, that you have just been arrested! Make notes on your reactions as you read the document. Identify specific words and phrases that puzzle or worry you.

Now read the second text, noting what seem to you significant changes. What seems to be the point of the changes? Does improvement in communication lessen in any way the powers expressed in the document?

Turn to page 114 for a commentary.

**Text A**

DELAY OF RIGHTS
If you are in police detention suspected of having committed a serious arrestable offence and have not been charged, the rights at paragraphs 1 and 2 (over) may be conditionally delayed for up to 36 hours, if authorised by a police officer of the rank of superintendent or above.

FACILITIES PURSUANT TO PRISONERS' RIGHTS
1. If you are in police detention and your rights at paragraphs 1 and 2 (over) are not subject to delay you must be afforded the following facilities:
    a. If the person you want to be informed of your whereabouts cannot be contacted, you may choose up to two alternatives to be so informed.
    b. You may receive visits from friends or relatives at the discretion of the custody officer.
    c. You will be supplied, on request, with writing materials, your letters will be sent and you will be allowed to make one telephone call. Whether or not letters or telephone calls are at public expense shall be at the discretion of the custody officer.
2. Irrespective of whether your rights at paragraphs 1 and 2 (over) have been delayed or not, if you are a citizen of an independent Commonwealth country or a national of a foreign country you may communicate, at any time, with your High Commission, Embassy or Consulate.

FACILITIES FOR LEGAL ADVICE
If you are in police detention and your rights at paragraphs 1 and 2 (over) have not been delayed you may at any time consult and communicate privately, whether in person, in writing or on the telephone:
    a. With a solicitor of your own choice
    b. With the duty solicitor (where a Duty Solicitor Scheme is in operation).
    c. With a solicitor selected by you from a list of solicitors who have indicated that they are available for the purpose of providing legal advice at police stations.
Please note:
    Option b. above is always free.
    Options a. and c. are free unless you agree otherwise with the solicitor.

FINGERPRINTS
As a general rule, your fingerprints may not be taken by the police without your consent and such consent must be in writing if you are at a police station.
Your fingerprints may be taken by the police, without consent, in the following circumstances:
    a. If you are in police detention and
        i an officer of at least the rank of superintendent authorises them to be taken, such an officer having reasonable grounds for suspecting your involvement in a criminal offence and that he believes the fingerprints will tend to confirm or disprove your involvement in the offence; or
        ii you have been charged with a recordable offence and have not had your fingerprints taken in the course of the investigation of the offence.
    b. If you have been convicted of a recordable offence.

**Text B**

## Your four rights

1   The right to have someone told where you are.
2   The right to seek legal advice.
3   The right to read the Codes of Practice made under the Police and Criminal Evidence Act, 1984.
4   The right to receive, on request, a copy of your custody record on release. This right lasts for 12 months after release.

## Can the police delay my rights?

It is lawful for an officer of at least the rank of superintendent to delay Rights 1 and 2 for up to 36 hours if:
- you are suspected of a serious arrestable offence*, and
- you have not been charged.

But the officer must also have good reason to believe that to allow Rights 1 and 2 would:
- interfere with evidence or interfere with or harm another person, or
- lead to the alerting of other people suspected of an offence, or
- hinder the recovery of property obtained by crime.

If you are a citizen of an independent Commonwealth country or you are a national of a foreign country you always have the right to communicate with your High Commission, Embassy or Consulate. This right cannot be delayed or stopped.

## What must the police allow me to do?

*(This section only applies if Rights 1 and 2 have not been delayed)*

Right 1 says you may ask for someone to be told where you are. If this person cannot be contacted, you may choose up to two other people to be told.

You may receive visits from friends or relatives if the custody officer agrees.

If you ask for writing materials you will be given them. Your letters will be sent and you will be allowed to make one phone call. The custody officer will decide whether you will have to pay for postage and phone calls.

## How can I get legal advice?

The custody officer will give you a leaflet which explains:
- how to get legal advice,
- whether it will be free or not.

## When may the police take my fingerprints?

Normally the police may not take your fingerprints without your agreement. And if you are at a police station your agreement must be in writing.

However, the police may take your fingerprints without your agreement if you are in police detention and *either:*

- an officer of at least the rank of superintendent says they may be taken. Such an officer must have good reason for suspecting you are involved in a criminal offence and that he believes the fingerprints may confirm or disprove it, *or*

- you have been charged with a recordable offence* and have not had your fingerprints taken during the investigation of the offence.

The police may also take your fingerprints without your agreement if you have been convicted of a recordable offence.

*Please ask the custody officer if you are not sure what these terms mean.
The information on this side of the form is only a summary of the law to help you understand your rights. It is not a full statement of the law.

Power is a significant factor in a range of different situations. In this section on instrumental power you have learnt how to describe and analyse texts that demonstrate power. You are able to recognise how power is exercised through language choices and how power can be mitigated through language.

**Revision**

1   What is instrumental power?

2   How does discourse reflect power relations?

3   How might the following features convey power – directives, terms of address, lexical choices, phonology and grammar choices?

4   How is power mitigated through language choices?

# Influential power

The examples in the previous section looked at how power is conveyed by language when one person is clearly in a position of power over the other person: there is an asymmetry in their exchange. There are many other contexts where institutions or individuals exercise power by influencing others to change or form their opinions, persuading them or framing the debate on contentious subjects through their use of language.

The aim in this section is not to paint a picture of a greedy society, locked in a malignant, conspiratorial struggle of winners and losers, the powerful and the powerless, the exploiting profiteers and politicians and the exploited, duped general public. The main concern is to help you investigate the society in which you live through the texts it generates, and to concentrate particularly on expressions and reflections of social power in and behind those texts.

Norman Fairclough described a phenomenon typically found in influential power texts called synthetic personalisation. This is when public bodies, either commercial companies or bodies such as the government, create a personal tone in addressing consumers or the public. They may aim to give the impression that they are addressing an individual person rather than the mass audience that is, in fact, being addressed. This blurring happens particularly in technology texts, which can be personal or public texts. It might be achieved through

- pronoun choice (we/you or even I)
- colloquial lexis
- discourse markers of speech (well, so)
- personal details or references to break down the barriers between their public persona and the private person
- semantic fields that are personal rather than commercial or public
- presuppositions which also create a feeling of shared personal values.

# How do slogans influence the reader?

**Activity 32**

**Pair work**

## You know it makes sense – analysing slogans

Slogans are phrases devised to promote a product, a cause or an idea. Advertisers can make fortunes out of slogans, political parties have always depended on them, consumer products can sell in millions because of them. Large sums of money are invested in their invention and their hoped-for memorability, but slogans are relatively short lived in the media though they often linger in the mind.

Two examples are 'Because I'm Worth It' (L'Oreal) and the linked slogan 'Because he's worth it too' for products aimed at men. There are lots of discourse implications in this one.

- What role does each slogan assign to the reader? (Identification? Approval of self-worth?)
- What values or worldview lie behind it? What is taken for granted?
- What are the key words and grammatical points?

These are important questions to ask for any text.

Look at some modern commercial and political slogans. Try McDonalds, Coca Cola, Calvin Klein and the political parties.
For each example

- note if a verb is used
- examine the sentence type (e.g. imperative, statement)
- ask yourself what are the values lying behind it and what assumption is made about you, the reader.

**Activity 33**

**Individual**

## Analysing style

The following text illustrates very well a recurring language and society topic – attitudes towards uses of language. Disapproval can often be ferocious, as is evident in this *Sunday Express* article (from 1995).

1 Examine how the style of reporting attempts to influence opinion through the following features:
- the choice of lexis and semantic fields, e.g. semantic field of war '*fight/targeted/crusade*'
- the choice of adjectives and adverbs, e.g. '*dismayed*', '*properly*', '*clearly*'
- use of modals and hedges, e.g. '*many youngsters/could be affected*'.

2 Identify in clear statements of your own the language and society issues raised by this news item.

# FIGHT TO SAVE THE QUEEN'S ENGLISH

**TEENAGERS** who cannot speak or write English properly are to be targeted in a major "get the grunt" campaign.

Education Secretary Gillian Shephard has warned senior civil servants that Britain cannot afford to carry on producing inarticulate school leavers who rely on "communication by grunt".

Standards of spoken English have plummeted in the last two decades. Many youngsters are simply unable to express themselves clearly, concisely and courteously.

Dismayed employers have warned that our status as a major trading nation could be seriously affected unless future generations are taught basic communication skills.

Now Mrs Shephard is planning a new initiative, expected to be unveiled at next month's Tory party conference, to revive the use of the English language – which is one of her personal crusades.

School pupils will be graded to show potential employers how well they express themselves when dealing with colleagues or future customers.

The scheme, which has taken more than 12 months to formulate, is aimed at eradicating sloppy use of language by emphasising the need for clear expression.

Ministers believe this will be complemented by changes already made to the national curriculum, stressing the basics of grammar, spelling and punctuation. But a new system of assessing how articulate youngsters are is seen as vital.

Details are still being discussed by a special working party at the Department for Education and Employment.

The problem was highlighted last week when the National Association of Head Teachers wrote to Mrs Shephard listing concerns about pupil discipline and parental responsibility.

Among major worries it raised were the increased use of foul language by children as young as five and the problem of pupils starting school with few or no social skills.

Academics are concerned at the way British pupils lag behind youngsters from competitor countries, such as America, in communication skills. The problem is even apparent among brighter pupils who go on to university.

Two-thirds of firms and public bodies quizzed by the Association of Graduate Recruiters claim that graduates lack communication skills.

The Confederation of British Industry has been campaigning for five years for good communication skills to be developed in schools.

Mrs Margaret Murray, CBI head of training policy, said: "Communication skills are essential for all jobs.

"Employers need people who are articulate and good at listening, as well as good at reading and writing.

"Jobs now involve so much time on the phone and working in teams that good oral and listening skills are incredibly important."

Mrs Shephard told last year's Tory party conference: "Why should anyone expect to get a job if he or she can't speak or write clearly in our marvellous language?

"For too long we have been slack in our treatment of English. And we have impoverished our children in the process."

## Activity 34 How language creates social ideas

This is a recruitment advertisement for the newly formed Bath and North-East Somerset District Council. Read it three or four times. Don't be put off if you find it difficult to understand.

> The new authority will be: Member led, Officer driven, Customer focused; a team environment where the whole is greater than the sum of the parts; a flat management structure where employees and managers are fully empowered and decisions are devolved close to the customer; a culture of learning rather than blame; a clear sense of direction and purpose. A firm commitment to delivering high-quality public service through a combination of direct provision and effective partnerships.

This advert is, in modern terms, a mission statement (an interesting metaphor, by the way) seriously attempting to do something worthwhile for the society the Council is intended to serve. It is written in the language of management theory. Rewrite it so that it would make some sense to Aunty Flo and Uncle Jack, or your favourite down-to-earth members of the family.

What comes through very clearly in the recruitment advertisement is a vision of modern social management expressed in abstract language. It is interesting to replace abstract noun phrases by a mixture of concrete nouns and verbs just to explore what they could mean. Does 'a culture of learning' mean that the councillors will learn from their mistakes, or that customers must not blame them for mistakes? A 'flat management structure' could mean more equality among Council staff but it could also mean sacking middle managers, reducing promotion incentives and making the managers more powerful than ever over the employees.

Society is not just people living together in physical, economic circumstances; it also consists of ideas that are no less powerful and significant for being abstract. Language generates ideas and puts people's minds in tune with these ideas, for good or ill, by providing the means for talking, thinking and believing in them. Those who lived under the Nazi and Stalinist regimes bear witness to how new words, phrases and ideas took over even critical minds. Terms frequently used to describe these processes are propaganda and ideology.

This aspect of the relationship between language and society is not always, or even mostly, sinister. It just is. Idioms, metaphors, proverbs, sayings, folklore, all become part of our language 'common sense' without our even noticing. Changing attitudes toward aspects of society frequently show in a change of language, which is why investigating language change is so much more important as a linguistic study than just a historical study. The feminist movement, the multicultural nature of the English vocabulary and its spellings, and cultural changes in sexual behaviour have all brought about changes in the language through changed perceptions of social reality.

## Activity 35 How to analyse a political speech

Pair work
Exam preparation

This text is the final section of Tony Blair's speech when he resigned as Prime Minister in 2007. It was delivered as a speech to his constituency party but clearly the audience was the whole country and the international news companies.

Tony Blair, as Prime Minister, had a significant amount of instrumental power as he effectively ran the country, but much of politics is based on influential power – politicians aim to influence our opinions, our perspectives on debate.

In pairs, analyse this text, looking at how Tony Blair aims to influence opinion, how he aims to 'position the reader' and the attitudes and values that underlie his use of language. Do you notice any examples of synthetic personalisation?

Use these headings to help you.

- Generic nouns – everyone, people, nation, British
- Pronouns and who they refer to
- Colloquial idiomatic language
- Abstract nouns – instinct, decision, conviction
- How he refers to the professional and the personal
- Syntactic patterning particularly to present opposites
- How he refers to Britain
- Use of imperatives and who the imperative is directed at

Turn to page 114 for a commentary.

Decision-making is hard. Everyone always says: 'Listen to the people.' The trouble is they don't always agree.

When you are in opposition, you meet this group and they say: 'Why can't you do this?' And you say: 'It's really a good question. Thank you.' And they go away and say: 'It's great, he really listened.'

You meet that other group and they say: 'Why can't you do that?' And you say: 'It's a really good question. Thank you.' And they go away happy you listened.

In government, you have to give the answer – not an answer, *the* answer.

And, in time, you realise putting the country first doesn't mean doing the right thing according to conventional wisdom or the prevailing consensus or the latest snapshot of opinion.

It means doing what you genuinely believe to be right.

Your duty is to act according to your conviction.

All of that can get contorted so that people think you act according to some messianic zeal.

Doubt, hesitation, reflection, consideration and re-consideration, these are all the good companions of proper decision-making. But the ultimate obligation is to decide.

Sometimes the decisions are accepted quite quickly. Bank of England independence was one, which gave us our economic stability.

Sometimes, like tuition fees or trying to break up old monolithic public services, they are deeply controversial, hellish hard to do, but you can see you are moving with the grain of change round the world.

Sometimes, like with Europe, where I believe Britain should keep its position strong, you know you are fighting opinion, but you are content with doing so.

Sometimes, as with the completely unexpected, you are alone with your own instinct.

In Sierra Leone and to stop ethnic cleansing in Kosovo, I took the decision to make our country one that intervened, that did not pass by, or keep out of the thick of it.

Then came the utterly unanticipated and dramatic – September 11th 2001 and the death of 3000 or more on the streets of New York.

I decided we should stand shoulder to shoulder with our oldest ally. I did so out of belief.

So Afghanistan and then Iraq – the latter, bitterly controversial.

Removing Saddam and his sons from power, as with removing the Taliban, was over with relative ease.

But the blowback since, from global terrorism and those elements that support it, has been fierce and unrelenting and costly. For many, it simply isn't and can't be worth it.

For me, I think we must see it through. They, the terrorists, who threaten us here and round the world, will never give up if we give up.

It is a test of will and of belief. And we can't fail it.

So, some things I knew I would be dealing with. Some I thought I might be. Some never occurred to me on that morning of 2 May 1997 when I came into Downing Street for the first time.

Great expectations not fulfilled in every part, for sure.

Occasionally people say, as I said earlier: 'They were too high, you should have lowered them.'

But, to be frank, I would not have wanted it any other way. I was, and remain, as a person and as a prime minister, an optimist. Politics may be the art of the possible – but at least in life, give the impossible a go.

So of course the vision is painted in the colours of the rainbow, and the reality is sketched in the duller tones of black, white and grey.

But I ask you to accept one thing. Hand on heart, I did what I thought was right.

I may have been wrong. That is your call. But believe one thing if nothing else. I did what I thought was right for our country.

I came into office with high hopes for Britain's future. I leave it with even higher hopes for Britain's future.

This is a country that can, today, be excited by the opportunities, not constantly fretful of the dangers.

People often say to me: 'It's a tough job' – not really.

A tough life is the life the young severely disabled children have and their parents, who visited me in Parliament the other week.

Tough is the life my dad had, his whole career cut short at the age of 40 by a stroke. I have been very lucky and very blessed. This country is a blessed nation.

The British are special. The world knows it. In our innermost thoughts, we know it. This is the greatest nation on earth.

It has been an honour to serve it. I give my thanks to you, the British people, for the times I have succeeded, and my apologies to you for the times I have fallen short. Good luck.

# Discourse and charities

As well as businesses, who are trying to sell you something, and politicians, who are trying to influence you, there are charities. The purpose of charity texts is sometimes to persuade you to donate money and therefore their purpose is a little like a business, but also they may aim to influence your opinions. They may be campaigning adverts or be aiming to change the values and attitudes of society to eradicate the need for charity.

**Activity 36** ## Analysing charity adverts

Below is a Christian Aid advert which appeared in newspapers and magazines. Before you read it, turn to page 106 for some notes on the language used to influence in another charity poster.

Comment on all the features of language in social context that you think are relevant. Use of politeness techniques and discourse are particularly interesting. What is the purpose of the advert, aside from raising money?

Compare your notes with the commentary on page 115.

Sorry to bother you. Any chance of turning that thermostat down a degree?

Climate change isn't some threat to the future. It's today's reality. Environmental disasters, such as droughts in Niger, are wrecking people's lives with more and more frequency. And it's going to get worse. Want to do something about it? Good, we need people like you. Visit our website to see how the actions of you and your workplace can change the world for the better. Or text CLIMATE1 to 84880 for an 'Actions' poster.* Climate changed. Let's get to work. www.climatechanged.org

> ### The Children's Society: a billboard poster
>
> Image:  Picture of a young boy looking straight to camera
> Text:  (In large print) **What I need is a good listening to**
> Support the The Children's Society appeal 24th March–4th April / The Children's Society /
> Making lives worth living / We give young people a voice in society. To find out more phone...

Commentary

- The organisation is trying to change an attitude of mind.
- It is using a familiar aspect of habitual language use or idiom. 'They need a good talking to,' is often said of children.
- The advertisement reverses expectations: want/need, talking to/listening to.
- The society represents itself as spokepersons: 'We give young people a voice.'
- The use of 'What I need....' as a sentence opener is worth looking at. Other forms are: 'What we need...', 'What I think is...' Politicians frequently use similar constructions: 'What I would say to you is...'. This is sometimes referred to as metadiscourse, where the writer or speaker is directing the attention of the listener.

## Review

In this section on influential power you have examined in detail how different bodies use language to influence your ideas and your perception of the world, linking back to the start of the chapter, where we discussed how language influences thought (see page 55).

Power is a significant feature in any text. Many of the social contexts we have looked at involve aspects of power: some dialects have higher status than others; much of the early analysis of gender language was about power relations; representation of gender also conveys power relations; occupational contexts will involve power asymmetry either within the occupation or between a member of the occupation and a customer or client.

Having looked at the texts in detail you should be able to analyse any text that is trying to influence your ideas. You should also be able to make intelligent judgements about the techniques that are being used to influence you so that you can make informed judgements about what you are being told.

## In summary

These are the features you should look for in texts, especially when the focus of the analysis is the social context and the social values of the text.

- What is the worldview, ideology, belief and value system lying behind the text? This is often implied or taken for granted, for example, the party political allegiance of newspapers.
- Are there any contradictory ideas or values behind or underlying the text? A censorious moral attitude mixed with sensationalist enjoyment, for example, can be seen in many front-page newspaper stories.
- What point of view, ideology, beliefs do you, the reader, bring to the text?

**These are all macro-level questions.**

- What 'key words' are there in the text? These might be distinctive lexical choices, semantic fields, specialist vocabulary, euphemisms, antonyms/synonyms and metaphors.

- What grammatical choices have been made? Look at sentence function, modality, passivisation, pronoun reference.
- What graphic elements (pictures, typography) contribute to the meaning of the text?

**These are all micro-level approaches that help to explain the macro ideas.**

### Context and intertext
- What is the immediate situational context? Think about overt purpose, intended audience, point of writer/reader contact.

### In the text
- What historical factors contribute to the text? These might include prior knowledge and experience, connotations in words, interpretative slant on events, people and 'things' in the text, age of the text.
- What references are made to other texts in the culture? These need not be written texts; they could be film, song, TV.

**These are a mixture of micro- and macro-level observations.**

### Social roles and power relations
- What is the status and assumed or adopted role of the writer(s)? Authoritative/authoritarian? Egalitarian? Legal?
- What role is assigned to the reader? This is sometimes explicit, but is often implicit. It may be welcomed or resented but is frequently unnoticed and, therefore, complied with.
- What roles are assigned to persons in the text itself? Who is proactive, reactive, inert, passively acquiescent?

**These are macro-level questions but, again, the answers will lie in the micro-level evidence.**

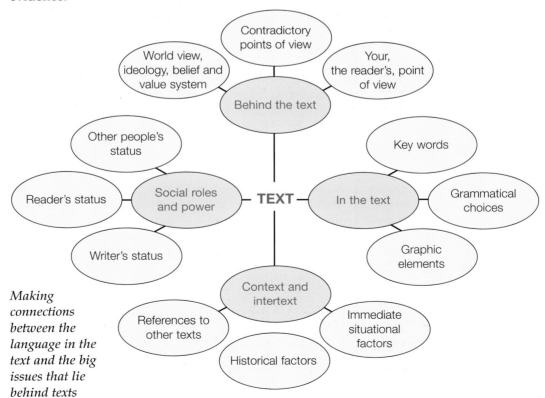

*Making connections between the language in the text and the big issues that lie behind texts*

1  What is influential power?

2  How is abstract language used to create effects?

3  How are techniques of synthetic personalisation used to persuade and influence an audience?

4  What kind of techniques would you expect to find in political rhetoric in order to persuade and influence an audience?

5  What does the term 'position the reader' mean?

**Commentary**

**Activity 6**

Otto Jespersen is the earliest commentator on this debate. He collected quantifiable evidence about reading speed and recall. Despite this evidence, his findings do not challenge the socially accepted norm that the 'highly distinguished men' in the test must have more intellectual power than the women. So his explanation finds a way of explaining their relative performance. The style in which he writes would strike most readers as being old fashioned, as well as his attitudes.

Peter Trudgill's findings are that, in general, women choose to speak more standard forms than men. He supports this by statistics from a range of surveys, across different societies. He tends to use sociological terms such as 'gender differences', 'urban dialect', 'sets of data'. He refers to the 'standard variety' and the 'prestige accent' and when he uses a value judgement he places it in inverted commas – 'better' indicating that he is aware that ways of speaking may be placed in a hierarchy, but he does not do this.

Dale Spender states that men control the language in terms of what it can express, what is said and who has the ability to talk, to the point where women are silenced. She uses emotive language such as 'debases', 'denigrates' and 'excludes' to describe the effects of language on women. She starts by discussing women in the third person then moves to using pronouns 'us' and 'we' for women and 'they' to describe men. This is a summary statement giving her opinions rather than evidence to prove it.

Jennifer Coates and Deborah Cameron describe the different views of women's language as being either about the differences in status between men and women or about different sociolinguistic groups. They use sociolinguistic terms such as 'communicative competence' and 'subcultures'.

Deborah Tannen places the debate into the context of relationships and strongly avoids value judgements about 'dominance'. She is primarily describing differences between the habits men and women have when they talk. Her focus is on concepts of 'communication' and 'relationships'. She also uses the term 'genderlect'. This is a summary of opinions rather than data.

The later texts tend to draw on and develop from the findings of the earlier texts, and assume that the earlier findings are well known.

**Commentary**

**Activity 8**

You should comment on the use of turn taking. Look at the interruptions or simultaneous speech and compare it to back-channel, rather than treating it as interruption or dominance of the original speaker. Take note of how all speakers participate, and are actively listening to the main speaker. You should also comment on the use of pronouns and the focus on emotional/personal/domestic topics, which is often considered as typical of women-only speech.

In her analysis Jennifer Coates points out that this doesn't follow the usual interaction of one speaker speaking at a time. In this example more than one speaker speaks at a time. The speakers use minimal responses and simultaneous speech. They seem to have joint sense that the topic has been dealt with. She describes this as showing 'the right to speak and the duty to support'.

**Commentary**

**Activity 10**

Text A

| Feature | Male and female | Female | Male |
| --- | --- | --- | --- |
| Nouns referring to character or associated with character | the prison, the chemistry sizzled, circumstances | A war-torn country, her heart, the wounded | prince, A royal request ..., dangerous secret, his child, the future of his kingdom |
| Verbs (as subject) | | tending, kept, stumbled, wished, have his child, fulfilling his request, save the country, save Nick, make a sacrifice | hiding, rescue his kingdom, find, asked |
| Verbs (as object) | asked, cost Katy | | |
| Adjectives/adjectival phrases | | Aid worker | the king of Baraq, Lost Prince, the cause of conflict, enigmatic |
| Adverbs | in the confines | | among prisoners |

This question is about representation, so you should make sure you phrase all your points in terms of how the text represents male and female. Your comments should not be phrased in a way that sounds as if you agree with them. For example, 'In this text, the female character is represented as being brave, resourceful and skilful as she is an aid worker, knows something about medicine and works in a war zone. Some of the terms associated with her show the character in a more passive or traditional representation of women: "make a sacrifice, wished, stumbled, and tended"; this is achieved through the verb choices that refer to the female character.'

As well as the pragmatic or discourse roles of gender, look also at the verbs that are associated with them and how active they are (at a grammatical level) in the text.

A question that focuses on this text's appeal to its target readers might draw on different features. You might comment on how the front cover, an attractive but dominant female, appeals to a female target readership. The name 'Mills & Boon' itself attracts and defines a specific audience, as do the descriptive terms 'breathtaking, romance, adventure, intrigue'.

### Text B

| Feature | Male and female | Female | Male |
|---------|-----------------|--------|------|
| Nouns/pronouns associated with ... | we | human being, women, unknown, vulnerability | dude, the jerk, a stranger, guys, harasser, over-the-top stallion, someone, partner |
| Verbs as subject | referring, communicating, tackle this | believe, feel hopeless, struggled, shouted back, stare, pointing, remarking, be yourself, decide | shouted, know, get used to it |
| Adjectives | | annoying, frightening, young, old, ugly, beautiful, thin, fat | intimidating |

**Pragmatics:** Assumes shared experience of 'catcalls'. Seems to assume a female relationship in the derogatory terms used about males and phrases such as 'You can't be yourself with a partner who writes off your feelings' address a woman in a relationship with a man. Uses humour through exaggeration and taboo/demotic language to gain audience interest and empathy. Uses opposites to put point across: 'ugly/beautiful', etc. Uses a range of direct address: 'you' (other women) and 'we' (men and women).

**Discourse:** The structure follows an argument: she explains the situation, establishes her qualification for addressing it and gives a range of solutions to the problem.

**Grammar:** She primarily makes statements to give her opinions status although she does quote questions and exclamations in the section of direct speech and finishes with a rhetorical question. Her choice of nouns, verbs, and adjectives shows her presentation of women as sometimes powerless and sometimes powerful. Men are almost always presented in a negative light.

**Lexis:** Her lexis is generally informal, colloquial, although she does use some less everyday lexis – 'exempted', 'harassment', 'appropriate',' the master plan of sexism'.

**Graphology:** Her picture reinforces the presentation of the advice as coming from a person who is known in a different sphere – she is also known as a singer.

| Text | Accent features | Lexical items | Grammar forms |
|------|-----------------|---------------|---------------|
| *Lady Chatterley's Lover* | yer, nob'dy, ma'es, ere, Ah, ther' isna, 'ud | appen, canna | nob'dy as, not as Ah know on, Ah know nob'dy as |
| *The Killing Jar* | | Mam, my mommar, All's, right mardy, a right clout, in a mardy | It were that year, I should of, My mommar wasn't having none of that, All's I really knew about it were, It were autumn, there was brown leaves, where they'd fell off the big trees, she'd took me away, I was well impressed, wouldn't move nowhere, They couldn't ring my mam or my mommar ner nowt in them days |

| | |
|---|---|
| The new facilities of the mode | Check e-mail in-trays frequently and respond promptly. Internet e-mail is not secure. |
| | Do not send too many copies of e-mails. Unsolicited, or 'junk', e-mail is unpopular and a burden to all users of the internet. |
| | Don't over quote previous e-mail messages when using the 'Reply' facility within e-mail. |
| | Virus check documents, spreadsheets, etc. that are sent and received by e-mail. |
| | Don't send very large attached documents or files to large distribution lists. |
| What is communicated/the content | Think before you e-mail. E-mails should never be sent rashly or in anger. |
| | Internet e-mail should not be used for sensitive or confidential information and its use for personal data could constitute a breach of the eighth principle of the Data Protection Act (1998) that personal data should be kept secure. |
| | If the contents of your e-mail are sensitive make sure it is only sent to the person you intend. |
| How it is communicated/ Discourse conventions or features | Don't type e-mails in capital letters IT LOOKS LIKE SHOUTING! |
| | Make sure e-mails are clear and are not open to misunderstanding. Humour and irony can easily be misinterpreted when read by another. |
| | Never include defamatory or offensive comments in e-mails. |
| Occupation-specific features | The discourse features of this policy document: use of imperatives, bullet-pointed items, unambiguous lexis, legal references, technical terms. |

**Commentary**

**Activity 24**

This is a text from an occupational context, but it also has issues of power and gender.

Sid uses mitigation through:

- questions at the start
- using 'ask' instead of 'tell'
- using 'if…' to give instructions.

Although Sid speaks the most, his role is to initiate discussion and decision-making. Rita reassures him and he confirms that he has been reassured and that they have agreed at the end. There is more of a role of 'thinking aloud' and reaching joint decisions than a boss using instrumental power over his secretary.

**Commentary**

**Activity 28**

From the context you know that power and authority reside in the magistrate (look up the meaning of the alternative name, Justice of the Peace; check also the etymology of 'magistrate' to see what power meaning is encoded there).

Mr A would have found himself under arrest if he had not attended the hearing and indeed faces the possibility of arrest anyway, for his resistance.

Notice that the magistrate is concerned that Mr A understands what is going on.

His second utterance confers approval on Mr A's answer – 'that's good', a sure sign of authority. It's an example of a conversational triple in which the normal pattern of paired exchanges (see the opening question paired with an answer) is broken by the addition of an underlining, evaluative remark – similar to the IRF structure noticed by Sinclair and Coultard as being typical of teacher talk.

Frequently, a word such as 'good', 'okay', 'right', 'fine' is used. 'That's good' can also mean, 'We can get on with the matter in hand'. From that point on, however, it becomes clear that the magistrate is not going to get the answers he would prefer.

Notice the pattern of Mr A's utterances after his first 'yeh': contradiction, repeated contradiction, negative statement, rhetorical question, affirmative, negative statement, including a positive alternative, confirmation, confirmation, negative protest, ironic thank you, rhetorical question.

If the magistrate's order to the usher to fetch a policeman is a threat, it has a powerful effect on Mr A. Note, though, how the magistrate uses a polite form to the usher: 'will you fetch …'.

Mr A's final remark wonderfully encapsulates his awareness of impotence in the face of legal power: 'that's the system in't it'. He remains resistant to the bitter end.

**Terms that convey different status:** congratulations

**Generic terms:** the cast

**Lexis to convey status/professionalism:** declaration of your commitment, join the company

**Politeness terms:** please, we'd like you to

**Use of modals**
- Of certainty: will
- Of obligation: must
- Of possibility: may
- To mitigate requests: would

**Use of pronouns**
- 'You' creates direct personal address. In this case the personalisation is not synthetic, as they do know each other as fellow students.
- 'You' is used interchangeably with 'I' to refer to the reader.
- 'We' creates a sense of a team rather than an individual person addressing the reader, which seems more mitigated.

**Semantic fields chosen to position the reader:** agree, am available, understand, commitment

**Positive lexis:** commitment, supporting, working with every one of you

**Discourse** has the form of a contract, supported by the graphology.

This is how the student analysed his text.

Therefore in this text where the initial relationship between team members and director is instigated it is important to exercise power minimally in language use (such as grammar) as power is established through discourse and lexis (*'With all auditions over'* … minimal power in grammar – exclamative sentence function, no directives; *'hard work'* and *'auditions'* specialist lexis-power).

It is interesting to note that the text requires a signature stating the 'commitment' involved in the show. This could be seen as a signature submitting to the power that the directors have, as they have composed the rules that the cast members agree to adhere to and are the main focus and agent present within them. *'I agree to attend'* – the text makes it seem that the reader is composing the contract in their own minds and then signing to adhere to it, as the first person focuses the text directly at the reader. The contract interestingly omits the object of the structure – which is the writer – in a lot of the contract points (*'I will give prior notice [to the directors]'*). The signature pragmatically works as submission of power and personality (*'join the company of Fame the musical'* ) by agreeing to be identified as just another part of the 'company of Fame the Musical' rather than a student of equal power level. This serves to establish the power relationship, not least in the use of the specialist nominal address of 'company of Fame The Musical' but also as the reader recognises that agreeing to being part of the company puts them in a submission of power to the directors, who constructed this text and indeed lead the company.

## Commentary

### Activity 31

None of the comments below invalidate your own observations. They illustrate a linguistic approach to the texts and should be included with your own.

Notice the use of the second person (you, your) throughout Text A, which makes the text entirely confrontational. In Text B not only are questions introduced, but there is also use of the first person (I, me, my), which offsets the directive use of the second person.

Whereas the opening sentences of Text A contain four conditionals (statements/declaratives beginning with 'if'), Text B begins with a list of rights. In other words, Text A states conditions including the unexplained term 'conditionally delayed', while Text B establishes immediately what the arrested person's rights are.

There is a further recognition in Text B that the term 'recordable offence' may not be understood. It is interesting, though, that because it is a specific legal term it has to be retained and cannot be paraphrased, hence the asterisked note (*Please ask …)

Notice that in both documents there are important anaphoric references (references to earlier parts). In Text A, however, the references to Rights 1 and 2 are inconveniently over the page, whereas Text B incorporates them on the same page.

The purpose of the text is to inform an audience that is literally a captive one. Information is often a form of power; keeping it secret creates unjust power; making information freely available shares the power. In this instance the authority and power to arrest a citizen carries with it the responsibility to maintain all the other democratic laws that govern both the police and those under arrest. Note that the Plain English Campaign has added a final note informing readers that the text 'is not a full statement of the law'.

## Commentary

### Activity 35

Commentators such as Stephen Poole and Norman Fairclough draw attention to how figures such as Blair use particular techniques to influence their listeners. Here are some examples.

- Centring debate and discussion on abstractions is very common in political and other influential power texts, many of them being used to give positive connotations without expressing any concrete ideas: opportunities, dangers, high hopes, Britain's future, vision, expectation, global terrorism, those elements, instinct, decision, duty, conviction.
- Passivisation/nominalisation: 'Decision-making is hard' does not refer specifically to his decision-making.
- Blurring the difference between I, you, we. In places 'you' is used to mean 'I': 'you know you are fighting opinion, but you are content with doing so'.
- Decision-making is framed in terms of thoughts, beliefs, ideas, rather than, for example, evidence or research: ' Hand on heart, I did what I thought was right.'

Modern media also often depend upon the sound bite and spin to formulate opinions and represent the speeches and ideas of politicians.

**Commentary**

**Activity 36**

The text and image require a fairly complex pragmatic understanding by the reader. The text uses negative politeness features and recognises face wants in starting with an apology 'sorry to bother you'. The direct address creates a familiar tone. The mitigated request and use of deictic reference 'that thermostat' creates familiarity with the reader, as if they were co-present and having a conversation. The text is presented as a quotation from the person although it is idiomatic British English to create a contrast with the image and make the message more striking. The idiomatic politeness sounds as if the reader is being asked to do something trivial, again this is contradicted by the image. the main text clarifies the message, through the recognisable logo and the references to 'climate change/threat/environmental disasters'. It continues the conversational discourse 'want to do something about it?/Good...'

This is sometimes referred to as metadiscourse, where the writer or speaker is directing the attention of the listener.

# Investigating Language

3

## At the end of this chapter you should be able to

- select and apply a range of linguistic methods, to communicate relevant knowledge using appropriate terminology and coherent, accurate written expression (AO1)

- demonstrate critical understanding of a range of concepts and issues relating to the construction and analysis of meanings in spoken and written language, using knowledge of linguistic approaches (AO2)

- analyse and evaluate the influence of contextual factors on the production and reception of spoken and written language, showing knowledge of the key constituents of language (AO3)

- demonstrate expertise and creativity in the use of English in a range of different contexts informed by linguistic study (AO4).

For a more student-friendly version of these Assessment Objectives, turn to page vii in the Introduction.

# What is a language investigation?

A language investigation can be a small research project or an essay. Its exact form and length will depend on the requirements of your exam board. Check with your teacher about what is expected and use the guidance in this chapter appropriately. One of the A-level specifications asks for an article accompanying the investigation; this is covered in the final section of this chapter (page 148).

Whatever the exact format used to investigate language, you must

- choose a topic that is both suitable and interesting to you
- ask one or more questions about this aspect of language
- collect data that will enable you to answer your question(s)
- analyse the data using appropriate linguistic methods
- evaluate your analysis once you have completed it.

And, of course, you must

- produce a report or an essay on an what you have discovered.

It is this report that is the end-product of your language investigation and which, naturally, you want to be good enough to gain high marks.

We'll be looking at each one of these aspects in this chapter, but remember, to be a successful language investigator, you must be

- open minded – don't have fixed ideas about what you are going to discover, or assume you know the answers already
- honest – don't twist the evidence to make it fit what you expected or wanted to find
- flexible – don't be frightened of having to change your approach if something unexpected turns up in the course of your investigation

- clear – don't confuse the reader (teacher or moderator) by presenting your findings in a perplexing or muddled way.

# Choosing a topic

This is absolutely crucial. Get it wrong and you're likely to have a very frustrating time working on something that doesn't interest you and in the end won't earn you very many marks. Remember, if it's to be a successful investigation, you will have to live and breathe it over quite a long time. Investigations that are worked on only as the deadline looms are invariably poor.

So what are the ground rules for choosing a topic?

## Reviewing your interests and resources

Language is everywhere, so finding material to work on shouldn't be a problem for you. Where do your interests lie? What resources are available to you?

Here are some questions to consider.

- Do you want to work with spoken or written data?
- Do you have an interest in child language?
- If so, can you access child language data?
- Do you have a part-time job or are you involved in extra-curricular activities like team sports, dance classes?
- Is there anyone amongst your family or friends who speaks with a distinctive accent or uses a particular dialect?
- Do you e-mail or text to a range of people?
- Have you an interest in the effect of gender in language?

## Four other considerations

- Get the focus right. That is, work on the right amount of data and choose a focused question you can address in the recommended word count.
- Don't demonstrate the obvious. For example, there are differences between magazines aimed at women and men but so obvious as not to be worth pointing out. This means there will be few significant points of comparison to be made.
- Is there any relevant theory you should research? If you're working with gender, child language, accent, dialect then there are theorists you should be aware of and read up on. Some of the research might be quite old and you should consider whether the ideas still hold today.
- Don't worry, though, if there seems to be no theory to draw on. The important thing is to get the right linguistic methods in place to analyse your data.

## The starting keys

These, then, are the keys to the start of a successful language investigation.

- Choose a topic you are interested in.
- Choose a topic for which you are able to collect data.
- Have a clear and specified focus for your investigation.
- Be realistic about the question(s) you are asking of the data.
- Work on only a modest amount of data.

To sum up: a good starting-point is when you have noticed something particular about language, in whatever context, and you decide to explore this further.

## Activity 1 · The right idea

Here are twenty titles of language projects that students recently completed. Ten of them are very good and led to successful investigations; ten of them are weak and led to predictable results.

Decide which category each title falls into.

Say what the strengths of the good titles are.

Suggest the advice that you would give the students who submitted the weak titles.

Turn to page 155 for a commentary.

1. The use of naming as a persuasive device in the *Sun* and the *Independent*
2. How do speakers adapt their language when speaking to an adult with learning difficulties?
3. The language of metaphor in spoken football commentaries
4. Perceptions of the English language
5. The use of questions in a classroom context
6. The language of *Big Brother*
7. An investigation into the child language acquisition of a two-year-old and a five-year-old
8. A comparison of teletext subtitles with the original dialogue in *Coronation Street*
9. A comparison of the language of the *Daily Telegraph* and the *Sun*
10. The use of euphemism for male and female body parts in Mills & Boon
11. Language change in the Bible
12. French influences on English vocabulary
13. The differences between British Black English compared to Standard English and American Black English
14. How is language used in university websites to persuade students to apply?
15. The language abilities of my three-year-old sister
16. Attitudes of London teenagers to a Yorkshire dialect
17. The language of health leaflets
18. A comparison of the song lyrics of Dolly Parton and The Beatles
19. Greetings and closures on radio phone-in programmes
20. A comparison of Coca-Cola adverts 1920–2000

# Collecting data

Here we will be looking at the best ways of collecting data to ensure that your project is both manageable and focused.

## Collecting spoken data

There are five main methods.

1. Making notes: you listen to what is being said by the participants and take notes.
2. Questionnaires: you ask people to tell you about the way that they use language. You can do this either by interviewing them or by asking them to fill in a questionnaire that you have devised beforehand.
3. Making a recording with the speakers' knowledge: you ask the participants to agree to being recorded, though you might not tell them exactly what it is about their speech that

interests you. They might be involved in a variety of tasks from reading a passage aloud to taking part in a conversation, or from reminiscing about their past to being interviewed.

4  Making a recording without the speakers' knowledge: the speakers are unaware that they are being recorded. This method can be used in a variety of speech situations, but you **must** ask their permission to use what you have recorded. You **must not** use it if they do not agree.

5  Making a recording from TV, film, radio, the internet, podcasts: obviously one of the simplest methods of obtaining spoken data.

## Activity 2 — Assessing methods of collecting spoken data

Discuss each of the methods of collecting spoken data. For each method write down its strengths and its weaknesses. Do there seem to be any common strengths or weaknesses? Can you think of any other appropriate methods of collecting data?

Perhaps the commonest danger in collecting spoken data is what is known as the observer's paradox. Obviously, for your investigation to be as effective as possible, you want the language data you collect to be both natural and spontaneous. Sitting your friends round a tape-recorder and asking them to have a conversation is not likely to be very productive! If you thrust a microphone in someone's face, if you place a tape recorder in the middle of a group of people or even if you just tell them they are being recorded, then people are frequently embarrassed and don't act normally. The very act of observation produces the exact opposite of what you want. Hence the paradox.

There are a number of ways of overcoming this. You must try to make the recorder and the whole recording process as unobtrusive as possible. You can divert the speakers' attention from your real language interests or from their embarrassment by asking interesting or challenging questions that focus their attention on what they are saying rather than on how they are saying it. You could surreptitiously switch on the recorder only when the conversation has been under way for some time and people have got used to your presence, or you could ignore the early parts of any recording you make. It's best if people don't know the real reason they are being recorded. For instance, if you tell them that you are investigating local accents, speakers may well consciously exaggerate (or play down) their own accent and the data you collect will be neither authentic nor useful.

## Activity 3 — Choosing methods of collecting chosen data

Here are six questions that could provide the focus for investigations of spoken language. For each one, discuss which of the five main methods on page 118 would be most useful for collecting appropriate data. The titles of the 'good' projects in Activity 1 would provide additional practice.

- Do women use more standard forms in their speech than men?
- What differences, if any, are there in the spoken language of three generations of the same family?
- Does the way children talk to each other differ from the way they talk to a teacher or parent?
- Do dialect terms survive in your area?
- What are the distinguishing features of the language used in magistrates' courts?
- Are girls better at learning a foreign language than boys?

# Collecting written data

It is easier to collect written texts for your investigation than spoken ones, as you will not encounter problems such as the observer's paradox. However, there are still a number of factors to bear in mind if you opt to investigate written data.

### How much will I need?

The exact amount will vary from topic to topic, but it's important not to fall into one of the two traps of collecting either too much or too little data. To conduct an investigation into graffiti based on only four examples, as one student did, is courting disaster. The more frequent mistake, though, is to have too great an amount of data to work on, with the result that either you can't find a clear path through the morass or what you have to say remains at a very superficial level. Don't think that an examiner will be impressed by the sheer amount of material you have managed to amass. In the end, it's the quality of your investigation that counts and by having too much material you will make it very difficult to succeed. It's better, for example, to investigate the language of newspaper editorials by concentrating on one red-top tabloid, one mid-range tabloid and one broadsheet – the *Mirror*, the *Daily Express* and *The Times*, say – rather than looking at examples from every national daily.

### What should I keep constant?

A mistake to avoid is having too many variables in the data you collect, as this is likely to lead to unreliable results. For example, suppose you wanted to investigate whether there are any differences between boys' and girls' writing abilities at the age of eight (already you would have removed the age-related variables). Then you would need to ensure that the data you collected came from children of roughly the same ability and that it was the same type of writing (story, diary, reportage, for instance) and had, ideally, been produced under the same conditions and with the same stimulus (probably in class). To look at writing from children of different ages, of different abilities and at different types of writing, however, would not be practicable within the confines of a short project.

You should always ask yourself or your teacher just how great your range of material needs to be and how to eliminate the unproductive variables.

### Questionnaires

These can be a very useful way of collecting data, both written and spoken, but they need to be approached with caution, as there are a number of pitfalls lurking for the unwary. Here are some ways to create an effective questionnaire.

- Ensure that the data you need for your topic can best be collected by questionnaire.
- Design your questions carefully and always trial them to iron out any mistakes, potential confusions or ambiguities before you distribute the questionnaire. Questions should always be simple and unambiguous. Don't have too many or too few and begin with simpler ones to put your respondents at ease.
- Decide whether you want spoken or written answers from your informants.
- Follow the basic structure of
  - introduction (who is asking the questions, why they are being asked, what will be done with the answers)
  - questions about the informant (ask only questions to which you really need the answers – age or occupation may or may not be relevant)
  - questions about the data.

| Activity 4 | **Asking questions** |
|---|---|

Here are three questions that would be unsuitable for a questionnaire together with three reasons for their unsuitability. Match the question with the appropriate reason.

**Questions**
1  Why do people think the Birmingham accent is so ugly?
2  Do you think that men interrupt in conversation more than women?
3  Do you ever use these words for the police: rozzers, the Bill, pigs, bizzies, cops?

**Reasons**
1  Influences the answer by suggesting what might be the case.
2  Loaded question. You have to accept that the proposition is true to be able to answer this question.
3  Question too vague. It restricts the answer you would receive.

**Review**

In this section you have been given the opportunity to

- take an overview of a language investigation
- consider its content
- consider its scope
- consider its potential
- be aware of some of the pitfalls.

# How to structure a language investigation

Here is the best way to structure an investigation. It needs these sections:

- **Introduction**
- **Hypothesis**[*]
- **Methodology**
- **Analysis**
- **Conclusion**
- **Evaluation**[*]
- **Bibliography**
- **Appendices**

*Optional

We shall look at each of these in turn.

## Introduction

The introduction sets the scene for what is to come and a good, clear and focused introduction will always put the moderator in a positive frame of mind. In a short piece an opening paragraph will suffice; in a longer project you should aim to write about 250 words.

**121**

The following points, therefore, need to be adjusted according to the length in mind. In your introduction, you should

- clearly identify the topic you intend to investigate
- explain your reasons for choosing the topic
- establish what the focus of your investigation is
- put your investigation into its wider context
- make brief references to any relevant research.

You do not need to

- discuss in great detail the historical background to your chosen topic
- give detailed accounts and explanations of relevant research or theories.

## Activity 5 — Introductions 1

Here is a good introduction written for an investigation into the language used in a children's Saturday morning television programme. Read it and note how it reflects the points made above about what an introduction should have.

Turn to page 155 for a commentary.

*Dick & Dom in da Bung-low*, a popular children's show, has been criticised for its use of bad grammar, fast indiscernible speech and 'lavatorial content'. In this investigation I am going to look at the language used by Dick and Dom in the show to see if there is any truth in these claims.

*Dick & Dom in da Bung-low*, is shown on Saturday morning between 9am and 11am on BBC2. Presented by Richard McCourt (Dick) and Dominic Wood (Dom) it is aimed at an audience of eight to twelve year olds. However, like many Saturday morning TV shows aimed at children (for example: ITV's *sm:TV Live!* and the 70s classic *Tiswas*) the use of slang, 'youth' language and risqué jokes has attracted a cult following, particularly from students and young adults.

Since it was first broadcast in 2002 the show has undergone several format and network changes. This investigation is based on the format of the current series (the fifth series), using data from the show broadcast on Saturday 11th February 2006. The show has a basic framework involving games, cartoons and short pre-recorded clips; the rest of the show is unscripted and is broadcast live. At least that is the impression given by the show though how much is really improvised is difficult to be clear about. The programme is probably not actually 'live' in real time but this doesn't take away from its very informal appearance. The basic format of the show is as follows:

Dick and Dom invite five children (usually between the ages of eight and twelve) and a celebrity to the Bungalow to play a series of games. These six contestants are called 'Bungalow Heads', and they compete to win 'Bungalow Points' which in turn win them 'Bungalow Prizes'. Games played in the episode I collected my data from include:

| | |
|---|---|
| Dick and Domtionary | Don't Go Daddy |
| Euuhhh…Yum Yum | Baby Race |
| Get Your Pants On | DC Harry Batt's Interrogation Game |
| Babba Poorly Mama | Creamy Muck Muck. |
| Bungalow Translation Game | |

In between the games cartoon programmes are shown. These include *Krypton The Superdog* and *The Wrong Von*. The pre-recorded clips 'Diddy Dick and Diddy Dom', which features miniature puppet versions of the hosts acting out an amusing scenario, and 'Raymond News Reader', a spoof news update, are also shown. Additionally, there are two games played out of the studio by Dick and Dom and a celebrity contestant: 'Bogies' and 'Eeny Meeny Macka Racka Rari Dominacka Shickapappa Dickiwoppa Rom Pom Stick'. The games and pre-recorded clips may vary from week to week, but the overall format stays the same.

Despite criticisms received from Parliament and media watchdog Ofcom, the show was awarded two children's BAFTAs in November 2004. Its popularity led to a week's worth of *Comic Relief in da Bung-low* celebrity specials in March 2005, which is when I first noticed it. I have chosen this investigation as I find the debates surrounding the way language is used on the show interesting, and I would like to find out if the criticism the show receives is legitimate.

The 'da' in the title suggests to me an aspect of BE (Black Vernacular English) and I expect there may be other examples of 'youth' contemporary language in the show. The young target audience suggests that the overall language will be very informal, too, but other than this I do not know what language features to expect. I want to conduct this investigation with an open mind and adjust my focus as my research develops.

**Activity 6** | ## Introductions 2

Now read two more introductions. Both are concerned with exploring spoken language and gender. One is good and one is problematic. Decide which is which and note the pluses and minuses that each has.

Turn to page 155 for a commentary.

### Introduction A

Are women seen as 'bitchy' if they swear a lot? Are men more focused on logical things as opposed to emotions? I decided to find out if what many other people before me had discovered was still true in this day and age.

According to Lakoff, females are more polite, less direct in commands and in that way use pragmatics frequently. Males, in contrast, compare females to machines and are more vulgar in speech. I decided to use wider reading to form my own study into language and gender. Gender is an important area within the study of language. It is difficult to find examples of gender in writing as it is planned, however because speech is spontaneous, there are clear features that can be looked into that define male and female speech.

I chose to study language and gender in spoken language because I found the topic very interesting, especially the way that previous researchers have assumed that males are the most dominant in conversation. I decided to see if this was true by studying one same sex conversation from both males and females and then putting some of the same individuals into a mixed conversation. Due to background reading, I was expecting males to interrupt more than females in a mixed context and to control the conversation. I also decided to look at the kind of topics that come up in the same sex conversations and the type of language used, and how that changed in a mixed gender environment.

### Introduction B

Does gender affect language? According to linguistic research there is a difference in language used by men and women. Each gender is said to have socially characteristic expectations when involved in talk. I have become very interested in this aspect of language and have decided to investigate further.

Some of the differences between men and women in speech include:

A difference in phonological and grammatical tendencies. Both Dale Spender and Peter Trudgill suggest that men tend to use non-standard forms with covert prestige while women, in particular lower class, move towards the prestige form within formal situations.

A difference in interruption usage and techniques. For example, linguists such as West and Zimmerman suggest that males are more likely to interrupt than females. As well as introducing different styles of interruptions, co-operative and competitive, they suggest that women are more likely to interrupt co-operatively, opposing men who are seen most likely to interrupt competitively.

A difference in supportive and non-supportive features. Strodbeck and Mann suggest that females take a more supportive approach to a conversation using politeness forms, such as modal auxiliaries, while males opt towards a more aggressive side, using directives.

This information interests me hugely, encouraging me to investigate whether these different styles apply. My focus for my investigation will be whether these differences between male and female speech can still be traced today.

# Hypothesis

Check the specifications of your exam board to see if you need to include one. A good hypothesis will reflect the thinking behind your investigation, indicate some of the linguistic features you have noticed about your focused area and suggest some of your aims. Try not to have a rigid list of things you expect to find; keep it fairly open minded.

If a hypothesis is not specifically demanded then you don't have to include one. Better to just have an idea of what you want to explore and mention this in your introduction.

Keep an open mind about your findings.

Be honest; analyse what's there.

# Methodology

There are two things to cover in this section. First, you should explain how you collected your data and the reasons for the approach you took. For example, it is here that you would discuss the design of your questionnaire (if you used one) or the way that you set about making a recording of a conversation. It would not, for instance, be very satisfactory merely to say 'I sat my mates down and told them to have a conversation'. If your project is concerned with written rather than spoken data, then you should explain on what basis you chose those particular texts to investigate.

The second thing that the methodology should include is an explanation of the analytical frameworks you have adopted for your investigation. Provide answers to questions that a moderator would be looking for: questions such as

- What will the investigation be about?
- If selections from the data are being made, why?
- What linguistic methods will be used?
- If theorists are being used, who (unless covered in the introduction)?

## Activity 7 — Methodologies

Read these two methodologies. They are from the same investigations as Activity 6 about spoken language and gender. Match the methodologies to the introductions and note the pluses and minuses that each has.

Turn to page 155 for a commentary.

### Methodology C

I have recorded and transcribed data from a group of four Year 9 boys and four Year 9 girls, of the ages thirteen-fourteen. These students answered a series of questions on gender issues, as a group, firstly of all boys, then of all girls, moving on to a final collection of two mixed groups answering the same questions each time. All data was recorded within the same formal school context in a classroom containing only the four students involved within each group as well as myself, the interviewer and a tape recorder.

I intend to analyse these transcripts and find out whether differences between male and female language usage appeared in my data.

My linguistic methods will focus on:

- interruptions
- supportive and non-supportive features
- convergence and divergence.

I obtained permission slips from every student involved so that this material could be used for analysis in my investigation.

### Methodology D

I got together five of my friends to take part in same-sex conversations for an hour in our study periods. I conducted the boys' conversation first, sitting three of my friends in a room with the tape recorder and leaving them to it. I recorded for an hour because I thought that at least I might get some real data if I did it for that long. I then did the same with the girls. For the mixed conversation I took two from each of the conversations and sat them in a room together with an extra girl.

I did have a problem with parts of the girls' conversation because at the beginning one of the girls kept talking to the tape recorder, which polluted my data. However, it occurred less later on and therefore allowed me to use the later data for my transcript.

After recording the data I took a three-minute segment about forty minutes in because I thought that they might be speaking naturally by this point. I then transcribed it as best I could and analysed the language used in all three conversations.

These examples tell us that a weak methodology is actually more than that. It reveals flaws in the thinking behind an investigation and the planning of the data collection. Well-thought-out ideas should lead to well-thought-out ways to collect the data. Therefore a good methodology is simply the writing-up of a good investigation. Methodologies reveal the underlying thinking and focus.

Problems collecting data can lead to a rethink of the focus of the investigation. Problems can especially occur with 'live' informants. If you plan to use friends or family then careful thought needs to go into what exactly you want to collect and then how best to do it. Children's spoken data can also be awkward. If you want to explore children's spoken language then think very carefully about the situation. For example, setting children a task to work on would give a structure to an investigation focusing on gender and co-operation. Even then things won't always work out first time. A famous film star once said, 'I never work with children or animals', and for good reason.

## Analysis

This is the important one. This is the heart of your investigation. This is where you will get your marks and this is where your approach is crucial. Remember you are not writing an essay and in order to explore the language thoroughly you need to think carefully about the structure of your analysis and the linguistic methods most appropriate for your data.

The ideas section later in this chapter (page 130) will give you some ideas and some linguistic methods to use to help explore the language of your data.

---

| **Activity 8** | ## Analyses |
| --- | --- |
| Pair work | |
| Group work | |

In twos or threes read these openings to analyses from four different investigations. Then rank them from best to worst. Give reasons for your decisions.

Turn to page 156 for a commentary.

### Analysis A
**Boys will be boys**

There is no mention of anything remotely interesting to me in the boys' conversation. Quite frankly, half of the time I can't even understand what they're saying. Most of their conversation is filled with technical jargon about computers and how they work which progresses to maths. Unfortunately, this is what we have to put up with nearly everyday from one of the boys and he is also extremely hard to understand because he talks fast and mumbles. Their conversation is mainly Boy One explaining something with Boy Two desperately trying to steer the conversation onto a different subject and failing. There are a total of five interruptions mainly by Boy Two. There is general cooperation on attempting to solve a mathematical equation with paralinguistic features, such as drawing diagrams on the board.

Little can be said for the pragmatics in this extract. It is all fairly straight forward, perhaps adhering to the male stereotype of not having much emotional involvement. However, there are a few utterances by Boy Two that can be read into. 'I'm going to take refuge in my art', for example, could actually mean that the boy isn't interested in the topic that is being covered and hopes that his evident disinterest will help to change the topic. He then later says, 'Therefore it is (inaudible) and proves you are crap', which indicates that he thinks the topic should be over by now and he is very bored.

## Analysis B
### Interruptions

Linguistic research, such as that by West and Zimmerman, has shown that there are commonly two types of interruptions: a competitive style and a cooperative style.

The competitive style applies when a speaker intends to hijack the conversation with determination to put their point across. The cooperative style differs from this and applies when the speaker wishes to show that they agree with the statement in question and would like to show their supportive point.

This past linguistic research from French and Local also claimed that men are generally more likely to take on the competitive style of interruption while women take the more cooperative approach.

I have decided to look into this when analysing my data.

The table below shows the recorded interruptions and their context within the transcripts that I collected.

| Gender | Number of interruptions overall | Number of interruptions – cooperative | Number of interruptions – competitive |
|---|---|---|---|
| Boys (in same sex group) | 19 | 15 | 4 |
| Girls (in same sex group) | 12 | 7 | 5 |
| Boys (in mixed sex group) | 6 | 3 | 3 |
| Girls (in mixed sex group) | 7 | 5 | 2 |

As shown in the table the transcripts I have analysed question this past research.

As expected I found that the males of the group interrupted more times than the females did at a ratio of 25:19.

Although boys did interrupt in a competitive style so did the girls. Both sexes tended to use this competitive style around the same number of times, with neither widely outstanding.

## Analysis C
### Lexis

As well as there being considerable change in the lexis of the advertisements there are also many similarities. One of these similarities is the abundance of adjectives in each advertisement. An example of this are the adjectives 'delicious' and 'refreshing'; 'refreshing' is repeated in all the advertisements. One of the explanations for this could be they have used the repetition as a marketing ploy so that it is ingrained in the minds of those who have read the advertisements. So that when they feel like a 'delicious' or 'refreshing' beverage they automatically think of Coca-Cola.

Other adjectives such as 'wholesome', 'invigorating' and 'un-matched goodness' are also used in the adverts. These like the aforementioned adjectives convey an entirely positive image to the reader. The use of such descriptive language also allows the reader to visualize the product.

As the advertisements progress with time the lexis is more monosyllabic. Reasons for this could be that with time people have tended to be busier, therefore they may have less time and patience to stop and read advertisements. Potentially this could be why in 1943 the company shortened Coca-Cola into 'Coke'.

### Analysis D
#### The Sex Pistols
The Sex Pistols were one of the very first punk bands, originating from the 1970s, and are still remembered today for iconic songs such as 'God Save the Queen'.

'God Save the Queen' acts as a rebellious, controversial message and was widely regarded as an attack on the British monarchy, criticising the queen and the way in which the band they feel England is treated as a result of her empowerment. The record was subsequently banned by the BBC, whose Radio 1 station was one of the most popular at the time. The song proves to be a national anthem for punks who share the shocking views portrayed 'she ain't no human being', and the repetition of the word England is therefore very personal and direct, ensuring that their audience takes notice of the message. The song's title 'God Save the Queen' is also repeated a total of six times throughout the song, emphasising the song's irony, as the message is controversially about antiestablishment. The connotations that are drawn from the word England are that of royalty and England as a society. However, this is again ironic as the hidden message found behind the line 'we love our Queen' is about how the royal family exploit and abuse England.

## Conclusion

Having completed the analysis of your data, you need to draw some conclusions from your work. In a short piece a concluding paragraph will suffice; in a longer project you should aim to write about 250 words.

It's clearly important that your conclusion should relate to the focus of the investigation that you outlined in your introduction and that it answers the question(s) you posed there. It should stem directly from your analysis of the data, but if your analysis doesn't show what you expected it to, then your conclusion should reflect this. Don't be tempted to manipulate your data, your analysis or your conclusion to make them fit with what you expected to find. A language investigation should be like a rigorous scientific experiment: scientists start with an open mind about the phenomena they have observed and if unexpected findings occur, they record these and ask further questions.

Finish with a short evaluation of your investigation. Did it work? Would you have done anything differently?

## Activity 9 — Conclusions

Read these two conclusions. One is clearly better than the other and reflects a better approach, a better focus and a better idea.

### Conclusion A
My data has produced potential evidence for and against many of the theories that I researched. My findings potentially support Goodwin's argument whereby in single sex male groups the facilitators tend to acquire an order of hierarchical status, thus agreeing with Coates' theory that men tend to base their language on competition. This may be, however,

because they have hierarchical job positions. Thus, the chefs lower down the job status hierarchy may not have spoken as much for fear that they would be accused of not working hard enough. Similarly, the transcripts contain possible evidence that would conclude that men try to show off their masculinity by self-aggrandizement and the use of expletives. In addition, the analysis could be seen as evidence supporting Milroy's theory that a high density and multiplex social network acts as a 'norm-enforcing mechanism'. This is because it could be said that the chefs' language was informal, because it contained many similarities with Bernstein's Restricted Code, which he argued was less prestigious than the Elaborated Code.

It is not possible to say, however, that the data analysis has produced strong evidence that either supported or contradicted these theories because the analysis was based on a small amount of data. In order to produce evidence that was more accurate and reliable I would have to analyse a larger amount of raw data.

To keep within the word limit I have included the results from the questionnaire in appendix four. If I was to do this project again, instead of analysing issues of power and gender in the transcripts, I would make the focus of the project much narrower by only studying how the chefs' language was affected by their high density and multiplex social network

Overall my project was successful because I did reveal some interesting details about language use within the workplace. However, if I used a larger collection of transcripts then perhaps the conclusions about the chefs' language use would have greater accuracy and reliability.

## Conclusion B

My hypothesis was that over time what and how artists write lyrics for their songs. I looked at a band that was around in the 1960s and 1970s to a band that has been around since the early 1990s. This study is a comparative study as I am comparing two different artists together on language features.

I was hoping to find that artists nowadays write songs about different things that might have been taboo and something people couldn't talk about back in the 1960s and 1970s. I was also hoping to find that artists nowadays use a lot more non-standard English and colloquial language.

What I found was that artists back in the 1960s and 1970s used to write songs more about love and emotional warmth found in relationships. Their songs were very simple and very repetitive, for example in 'Love Me Do' the first song by The Beatles there are three verses which are very similar with only one or two words changed and a chorus with only three lines. Artists these days seem to write their songs about more different things and their songs are not repetitive. They also seem to be longer and have a faster rhythm. Songs written in the 1960s and 1970s seem to be more 'feel good music' whereas songs written nowadays can be more depressing and written about more serious matters, for example in the Oasis song 'Cigarettes and Alcohol' there are hints at the singer's drug problems and his broken relationships.

# Evaluation

Check to see if your exam board asks for any evaluation of your investigation. This is where you reflect on the overall scope of your work. Don't feel you have to force an evaluation along the lines of 'if I had had more time I would have added this data or that data'. Many students successfully incorporate some evaluation into their conclusion and this is often the best option.

## Bibliography

You should always include a list of the primary sources you have read, drawn from or quoted. These might be books, articles, websites. To make this bibliography as scholarly as possible, you should always include the complete details. For books there is a convention that you should follow: author(s), date of publication, title, place of publication, publisher. For example:

- Carter, R. and McCarthy, M. (2006) *Cambridge Grammar of English*, Cambridge: Cambridge University Press.

Song lyrics should be shown like this:

- Imagine, lyrics John Lennon, (1971) Apple.

Websites used should be sourced like this:

- www.telegraph.co.uk  Map that shows Northerners have the last laff, Fenton, B. , 28.3.07.

You should list the references in your bibliography in alphabetical order.

If you refer to a book in your investigation, you should write, for example, 'Carter and McCarthy (2006: 77–8)', including the page numbers, if appropriate. Similar conventions apply if you refer to an article from a journal or from a collection of articles in a book.

## Appendices

Your language investigation project should end with appendices. Basically, there are two types of appendix. In one you should include any relevant documentation that you used to collect your data. In most cases, this is likely to be a copy of your questionnaire. In the other appendix you should include the data that you have been investigating. This would be either written data or transcripts of spoken data. If you have used a questionnaire, you do not need to include a copy of every person's response. It is sufficient to provide a summary chart. Appendices do not count towards your word total for the project.

---

**Review**

In this section you have been given the opportunity to

- work with the best structure for a language investigation
- look in more detail at its various sections
- assess different examples of student writing.

---

# Ideas for language investigations

The investigation ideas in this section are divided into the different categories of spoken data (spontaneous and crafted) and written data.

## Spoken data

### Conversation: spontaneous

In this section you will be learning about

- the features of spontaneous conversation.

Conventional ways of analysing language come from written language. When we analyse written language we can talk about sentences and punctuation and we can also talk about spelling mistakes and fluency.

Spoken language is quite different. It has its own particular features and needs to be analysed in quite different ways. Here are some common features of spoken language and terms used to describe them, with examples.

- **Utterances:** label for a person's speech; better than using the term 'sentence'.
- **Interruptions:** when someone else wants to butt in.
- **Overlaps:** like an interruption but intended to support the speaker rather than interrupt.
- **Response tokens:** short utterances which signal that a speaker is being listened to and also encourages them to continue. Response tokens can be minimal – 'mm', 'yeah' or even just supportive laughter; or they can be more positive – 'right', 'excellent', 'cool'. They are sometimes called back-channel behaviour. They may also be overlaps.
- **Fillers/pauses:** these can be silent or unvoiced, or voiced – 'er', 'um'.
- **Hedges:** terms which soften what someone says – 'I think', 'I guess', 'sort of'. They can also seek support from the listener – 'know what I mean?'.
- **Vague language:** a bit like hedges. This can be quite common in some people's speech – terms such as 'like', 'whatever', 'kind of' (normally transcribed as 'kinda').
- **Discourse markers:** words which start off a new topic – 'okay', 'now', 'right'.
- **False starts:** starting to say something, stopping, then starting again.

## Activity 10 · Analysing a transcript

Here is a transcript of three students in conversation on an adventure holiday in Costa Rica. In order to see how conversation works and to record it faithfully we need to use different punctuation from written language. The key shows the notation used for different features of spoken language. How many of these features can you find?

**Key**
(.) is a normal pause of about half a second.
(1), (2), etc. are pauses of 1 second, 2 seconds, and so on.
+ indicates an interruption, with the speaker's turn continuing at the next + sign.
= indicates an utterance which is cut short.
Capital letters indicate emphasis (and are also used for proper nouns).
Square brackets are used to indicate non-verbal sounds – [laughter].
Apostrophes are used where necessary – I'm, you're.
Otherwise other punctuation marks are excluded.
Non-standard spellings are sometimes used to suggest pronunciation – gotta.

C   okay so we're dangling our legs off the edge of Luna Lodge in Costa Rica and it=
E   it's so good
H   it's amazing
C   we are virtually falling into the rainforest
H   yeah the view is fantastic

E  it's dark (1) even though it's+
C  even though it's dark
E  +it's dark and like=
H  dark (1.5) dark but it will be great when it in the morning
E  yeah
C  I can't=
E  wait to wake up in the morning
C  oh yeah no we're gonna you know we're right positioned in you know in front of the edge
H  on the edge
C  well not on the edge but+
E  and look at our little+
C  +near the edge
E  +feet dangling [all laugh]
H  ehh
C  but right we were trying to find out whether the sun rises er in the view cos it's it's basic virtually a view just like right in front of us
E  mm
C  we're wondering
E  a 180 degree view
H  it is
E  yeah we've got a 180 degree view
H  view
C  but then we were told that actually this is the Pacific and erm yeah we're in the west [all laugh]

## Activity 11 — Spoken-language investigations

Look at this list of ideas for spoken-language investigations. Which have the best potential?

1  Recording friends talking in a social setting – for example, when eating
2  Recording a driving instructor with their pupil
3  Recording a teacher giving a lesson
4  Recording a parent talking to their 36-month-old child

Turn to page 156 for a commentary.

## Activity 12 — Try it yourself

Practise recording some real conversation and transcribe it using the key in Activity 10 on page 131.

# Conversation: theories

In this section you will be exploring ideas about

- the social nature of conversation
- the effect of social class on accent
- the effect of social class on dialect.

**Conversation** has been defined as

- the use of speech for informal exchange of views or ideas or information, etc.
- talk between people – 'I very much enjoyed our conversation yesterday.'

**Accent** can be defined as

- the way we pronounce words.

The prestige accent in the United Kingdom is called Received Pronunciation (RP). Many people think of it as the 'BBC accent'. In some ways everyone has their own individual accent; this is called idiolect.

**Dialect** can be defined as

- the use of particular lexis – lass, snicket, ginnel
- the use of non-standard grammar – I were, you was.

Standard English is the dialect that has prestige. It is the norm for writing books and teaching to non-native English speakers. Anything other than Standard English is termed a non-standard dialect.

We often adapt our language in different situations. This is pragmatic – different in different situations. The opposite is dogmatic – the same in different situations. We probably all like to think of ourselves as being pragmatic.

Our accent and dialect give us our identity and are a part of belonging, or not belonging, to groups.

Here are some theories which might be useful for linguistic methods.

H.P. Grice (1975) suggested four 'rules' we unconsciously follow to help make conversation effective. He called this the co-operative principle. These rules are very much to do with the fact that we are social animals.

1 The maxim of quality: speakers try to tell the truth.
2 The maxim of quantity: speakers give the right amount of information.
3 The maxim of relevance: speakers try to stick to the point.
4 The maxim of manner: speakers try to present their material in an orderly way.

Conversational implicatures are inferences based on the normal assumption that these maxims are being followed. So if someone says, 'I'm hungry', a reply might be 'There's the Carleton Hotel.' The inference (or implicature) here is that the Carleton Hotel sells food, is nearby and is open, fulfilling the maxims of quality and relevance.

Robin Lakoff (1975) has suggested three other 'rules' which she calls the politeness principle. They are

1 don't impose
2 give options
3 make your receiver feel good.

Her research found that women are better at using these rules than men.

Lesley Milroy (1970s) investigated three working-class communities in Belfast. Her research highlighted some of the effects of language as social bonding and also how the tightness of a social network can be influential. For example, a closed network is when an individual's personal contacts all know each other. This can occur with groupings made up of relatives, neighbours or work colleagues. The effect is often that individuals use language closer to the local or social vernacular – that is, informal, colloquial language which may also reflect local dialect.

Basil Bernstein (1971) has carried out work examining social groupings and suggests two types of language: the restricted code and the elaborated code. The elaborated code is more complex than the restricted code but also more explicit and therefore more comprehensible to an outsider. On the other hand the restricted code is more implicit and context dependent. Utterances are more likely to be informal and in non-standard English. Participants are also very aware of the context so that even implied meanings are understood.

Bernstein argues that working-class students have access to their restricted code but middle-class students have access to both restricted and elaborated codes.

Peter Trudgill (1970s) studied speech in Norwich to find out how and why people's ways of speaking varied. One of the variables he studied was the final consonant in words like 'walking' and 'running'. In Standard English, the sound spelled -ng is a velar nasal. In Norwich, however, the pronunciation 'walkin' and 'talkin' is frequently heard, as if there was simply 'n' on the end. Trudgill notes that this feature is not unique to Norwich.

Trudgill's study discovered the following.

- In all social classes, the more careful the speech, the more likely people were to say 'walking' rather than 'walkin'.
- The proportion of -in' (walkin' type) forms was higher in lower social classes.
- The non-standard -in' forms occurred much more often in men's speech than in women's, and this was true for all social classes.
- When women were questioned about what they thought they were saying, they tended to say they used the standard -ing forms more often than they really did.
- When men were questioned about what they thought they were saying, they tended to say they used the non-standard -in' forms more often than they really did.

Trudgill's figures for social class and gender differences in the use of the standard, prestige -ing form in Norwich when people used a formal style of speaking are as follows.

|  | Male | Female |
| --- | --- | --- |
| middle middle class | 96 | 100 |
| lower middle class | 73 | 97 |
| upper working class | 19 | 32 |
| middle working class | 9 | 19 |
| lower working class | 0 | 3 |

Jenny Cheshire (1982) studied dialect in Reading amongst adolescent boys and girls. She focused on their use of the following non-standard dialect terms.

- Non-standard -s – They calls me all the names under the sun.
- Non-standard has – You just has to do what the teachers tell you.
- Non-standard was – You was with me, wasn't you?
- Negative concord – It ain't got no pedigree or nothing.
- Non-standard never – I never went to school today.
- Non-standard what – Are you the little bastards what hit my son over the head?
- Non-standard do – She cadges, she do.
- Non-standard come – I come down here yesterday.
- Ain't = auxiliary have – I ain't seen my Nan for nearly seven years.
- Ain't = auxiliary be – Course I ain't going to the Avenue.
- Ain't = copula – You ain't no boss.

She found that the non-standard forms were all used less often by the girls than the boys, apart from the non-standard do. Her findings conformed to the pattern that female speakers adhere more closely to standard forms, while male speakers use non-standard forms more consistently.

## Activity 13 | Research

**Group work**

In twos or threes suggest three investigations which could draw on these ideas/research.

**Homework**

For homework research

- the work of William Labov
- the terms convergence and divergence
- the terms covert and overt prestige.

## Conversation: power

In this section you will be exploring

- power in spoken language.

How can power be exercised in spoken language? Three important ways are control by

- the amount actually said – which can be calculated as a mean length of utterance, or MLU
- control of topic
- response mechanisms.

### MLU

In a conversation involving two or more people, counting the number of words each uses can give a useful indication of who is controlling the floor. A simple scientific way of doing this (always useful in a research piece like a language investigation) is to count the total number of words each person says and divide by the number of utterances. This gives the average number of words for each utterance or mean length of utterance – MLU.

Try calculating the MLU for this transcript of a short excerpt from a conversation between two chefs in a restaurant kitchen.

> C1 [singing] get into the groove (.) girl you've gotta prove your love for me (.) like that bitch
> C2 this time next week Josie's on her hen night
> C1 yeah (5) somebody will be trying to give it to her
> C2 yeah probably
> C1 but you would wouldn't ya mate (.) yeah try and get the bride (.) whenever there's a hen party (6) I went on one when I was in Newcastle (.) on a hen (.) on a stag night
> C2 I was goin' to say what a hen night

Here each chef speaks three times, so there are three utterances. If you do a word count for Chef 1 you should get 58 words; divide this by 3 and you get an MLU of 19.3. If you do the same for Chef 2 then 20 words divided by 3 gives an MLU of 6.6. This numerical comparison clearly shows that each time Chef 1 speaks he says more than Chef 2, on average 13 words more.

### Control of topic

Who controls the topics in the conversation and how they are controlled is also a good indicator of power. These controls can be

- first introduction of a new topic
- control of that topic.

### Response mechanisms

These involve

- ignoring attempts by others in the conversation to change direction
- interruptions of others' utterances.

## Activity 14   Write your own conversation

**Pair work**

In pairs, create and write two conversations between two or more people where

1 each participant is trying to dominate
2 the participants are quite happy for one person to dominate.

About a page should be enough for each conversation.

Do an MLU count for each of the participants and analyse how control is maintained.

The counterparts of controlling response mechanisms are supportive response tokens given by the other participants happy to support the topic. They can be minimal – 'mm', 'yeah 'or even just supportive laughter; or they can be more positive – 'right', 'brilliant', 'cool'.

## Activity 15   Chefs transcript

Read the full transcript of the conversation between the two chefs which follows.

Do an MLU count for each chef and comment on the responses from Chef 2. Remember that a + sign indicates an interrupted turn which continues at the next + sign.

Turn to page 157 for a commentary.

C1 [singing] get into the groove (.) girl you've gotta prove your love for me (.) like that bitch

C2 this time next week Josie's on her hen night

C1 yeah (5) somebody will be trying to give it to her

C2 yeah probably

C1 but you would wouldn't ya mate (.) yeah try and get the bride (.) whenever there's a hen party (6) I went on one when I was in Newcastle (.) on a hen (.) on a stag night+

C2 I was goin' to say what a hen night

C1 +stag party (.) I went to Teddy's Nightclub in South Shields (.) and we were in there with the groom (.) I don't know how we knew him (.) I think (.) erm and one little (.) and one of the lads we knew erm it was his brother+

C2 yeah

C1 +in-law to be kind of thing (.) and an American guy (.) oh man what a spanner (.) he didn't drink (.) or he couldn't drink much (2) so he was going round with a bunch of wild drinkin' Geordie lads and he couldn't drink (.) and I mean he didn't last five minutes (.) he was really sort of wasted away by the time we got to the nightclub (.) anyway there was a hen party in there (.) so me and the lads sort of (.) he sat down in the corner and we got over and were dancing away (.) anyway this lad came over and said I can't believe it (.) of all the nightclubs we have to pick my sister's in with her erm hen party (.) er anyway I'd been dancing around with this little blonde girl (.) and giving her a bit (.) of the you know bump 'n' grind and all that kind of stuff (.) lambada (.) badly badly lambadaing erm who only turned out to be his fiancé (.) he got the right hump with me+

C2 ohh

C1 +I wasn't supposed to know (.) I mean I told him it wasn't (.) and I went into defensive mode and sort of said hey she's a slapper mate (.) it probably the best way of dealing with the situation (.) I was only about eighteen nineteen or something (.) young gun

## Activity 16  Analysing media data

Take this further by researching and analysing different kinds of 'live' media data:

- competitive game shows
- chat shows
- reality TV shows.

Depending on the pragmatics there are often extra factors at work in this kind of data. Also, there can be several audiences: other participants, studio audience, home audience. You will find

- spontaneous features
- power mechanisms
- entertainment factors
- concerns about presentation of self.

An extra dimension when there is a live studio audience is to use the key xXXXXxx to indicate the rise and fall in volume and the duration of applause.

Practise your analytical skills on this transcript of the *X Factor* game show.

| | |
|---|---|
| Audience | xXXXXxx |
| Louis | hey (.) guys you have improved one hundred per cent (.) in one week (.) you're already looking like you're a slick (1) sophisticated pop band (.) I think you could be like (1) er (.) the new boyband (.) the new Take That (.) you know+ |
| Audience | XXXxx |
| Louis | +and everybody's singing great (.) and (.) I know you could do better (1) boys (.) fan (.) tastic I hope you get the votes |
| Eton Road | thank you |
| Audience | XXxx |
| Sharon | I tell you guys (1) just when you know you say boybands are so passé (.) are so done to death (.) you come up (.) you are so unique (.) you each have your own individual style (.) you're so much fun (1) and you know I love you |
| Eton Road | [laugh] |
| Audience | xXXXXxx+ |
| Sharon | [laughs] I do I can't help it |
| Audience | XXxxx |
| Sharon | Antony+ |
| Louis | Antony |
| Sharon | +I just can't help it (.) you know (.) Kelly has already proposed to you this afternoon |
| Antony | [laughs] |
| Sharon | and we just adore you (1) I really do adore you |
| Antony | thank you |
| Sharon | you can do no wrong for me |
| Audience | xXXXXXxx |

## Conversation: script

In this section you will be considering

- the features of a script
- spontaneous features in certain scripted data/drama.

---

**Activity 17**

**Group work**

## Script 1

In twos or threes brainstorm and note down how you think a script of a popular drama differs from spontaneous conversation.

---

**Activity 18**

## Script 2

In simple terms a script will have none of the non-fluency features of spontaneous conversation. Look at this list of features. Which are non-fluency terms and which are just general terms to describe conversation? Which would you expect in a script?

- Utterances
- False starts
- Discourse markers
- Hedges
- Vague language

- Adjacency pairs
- Headers
- Tails
- Interruptions
- Overlaps

- Fillers/pauses
- Response tokens
- Repetition

Turn to page 157 for a commentary.

## Activity 19 Script 3

Group work

Homework

Class work

In twos or threes discuss and choose two different TV soaps.

For homework transcribe short sections of about 4–5 minutes, sharing out the work.

In class, work on your transcripts, looking for any features of script and any features to suggest spontaneous conversation.

**Further ideas to explore in investigations**
- Non-fluency features in play scripts – for example, *Fen* (Caryl Churchill)
- Representation of accent/dialect in play scripts – for example, *Road* (Jim Cartwright), *Saved* (Edward Bond)
- Representation of accent/dialect in film scripts
- Representation of accent/dialect in novels – for example, *Trainspotting* (Irvine Welsh)
- Power in *Desperate Housewives* (ABC TV Network)

## Speeches

## Activity 20 Speeches 1

Here is the opening of a speech given by President Bush on the day of the Twin Towers attack. It was his third and last 9/11 speech. Read it and list any persuasive devices. Note that this speech is presented here like a written piece. When you research other speeches you will mostly find them in this format.

Today, our fellow citizens, our way of life, our very freedom came under attack in a series of deliberate and deadly terrorist acts. The victims were in airplanes or in their offices: secretaries, business men and women, military and federal workers, moms and dads, friends and neighbors. Thousands of lives were suddenly ended by evil, despicable acts of terror. The pictures of airplanes flying into buildings, fires burning, huge structures collapsing have filled us with disbelief, terrible sadness, and a quiet, unyielding anger. These acts of mass murder were intended to frighten our nation into chaos and retreat. But they have failed. Our country is strong. A great people has been moved to defend a great nation.

This speech employs a lot of repetition. This helps to add weight to what is being said. Lists of three can be particularly effective:

- 'our fellow citizens, our way of life, our very freedom'
- 'airplanes flying into buildings, fires burning, huge structures collapsing'.

The final statement – 'A great people has been moved to defend a great nation' – has a parallel syntactic structure where 'great people' is balanced against 'great nation'. When there are two balanced elements like this then you can also refer to it as a contrasting pair. There is also deliberate use of pronouns, with 'our' and 'us' being set against 'they'.

Here is a list of some of the linguistic methods you could apply to your own speech data:

- repetition and three-part lists
- repetition and syntactic parallelism
- contrasting pairs
- pronoun use
- metaphor.

**Extension activity:** To extend this idea collect the three Bush speeches given on the day of the Twin Towers attack. Analyse each one and compare their developing ideas.

The full effect of a speech, though, can really be understood only when it is heard. Investigations which rely only on the printed word may be successful but an investigation can be much more rewarding and thorough when a speech's 'heard' features are taken into account.

## Activity 21    Speeches 2

Advanced ways of analysing speeches draw on an exploration of prosodic effects – sound features. A good investigation would comment on how sound features add to the qualities of a speech. The main things to note would be

- pace – fast, slow delivery
- emphasis
- rising/falling intonation.

Adopt your own key to show these features. For example:

- for pace, colons can indicate drawn-out vowels – toma::to'
- for emphasis, use upper case
- for rising/falling intonation, use arrows.

Listen to a speech and transcribe it. Many speeches can be accessed through the internet. Focus on the sound and use your key to highlight these features.

A speaker's handling of a live audience can add an extra dimension to a speech analysis. Use the key xxXXxxx to indicate audience response.

## Activity 22    Speeches 3

Media speeches can prove another interesting area for speech analysis. The following is a transcription of a speech from the film *Legally Blonde*. Try to get a DVD of the film so that you can listen to it too. Can you add any more indications of sound: for example, stress and intonation? Then analyse it.

on our very first day at Harvard (.) a very wise Professor quoted Aristotle (.) the law is reason free from passion (.) well, no offence to Aristotle (.) but in my three years at Harvard I have come to find that passion is a key ingredient to the study and practice of law (3) and of life (.) it is with passion (.) courage of conviction (.) and strong sense of self that we take our next steps into the world (1) remembering that first impressions are not always correct (2) you must always have faith in people (1) and most importantly (.) you must always have faith in yourself

**Note:** (.) means a normal pause and (1), (2) or (3) indicate how long a pause is in seconds.

## Investigation practice: scaffolding

Doing some scaffolding exercises will help you get started with your investigations. Let's assume you have an idea, a focus and you have collected some good data. We will look at scaffolding for investigations of

- text messaging with regard to gender
- language use in the *Jeremy Kyle Show*.

### Text messaging with regard to gender

A good starting-point would be to focus on the openings of the text messages and classify them. It's often a good idea to present findings in a table; then you can comment on the more interesting features.

| | **Openings** | | | |
|---|---|---|---|---|
| | Adaptations of hello | Formal | Colloquialisms | First name |
| Male | M2 hey<br>M6 hi<br>M11 hi<br>M13 hey hey<br>M15 hey<br>M16 hey<br>M18 hey<br>M19 hello<br>M20 hey | M1 gud morning | M4 ahoy<br>M5 yo<br>M9 yo<br>M12 weeyy<br>M14 aye aye | M1 gud morning raj<br>M15 hey raj<br>M16 hey stace |
| | 9 | 1 | 5 | 3 |
| Female | F1 hello<br>F5 hey<br>F6 hey<br>F7 heya<br>F9 hey<br>F10 hey<br>F11 hey<br>F14 hey<br>F15 hi<br>F18 hey<br>F20 hey | F2 gd day | | F3 stacie stacie stacie<br>F4 raj<br>F8 raj<br>F10 hey raj<br>F12 raj<br>F16 raj<br>F18 hey raj<br>F19 katy<br>F20 hey raj |
| | 11 | 1 | 0 | 9 |

This investigation has a sensible balance of data: 20 male and 20 female messages, labelled M1–M20 and F1–F20. A good comment on the openings could read:

'The table shows some interesting results regarding the different openings used by males and females. The most commonly used openings by both genders are the standard variations of 'hello', which is conventional of text messaging. Colloquialisms are only used by the males, which shows that they use text messaging more informally and humorously. However, there are still only a small number of colloquial openings, making it difficult to reach a firm conclusion. Only three of the males' messages use first names in their openings while the females' openings show they make more use of proper nouns, making their messages more personal.'

## Activity 23  Analysing text messages

The same investigation classified the text message endings. Write a comment on what you notice about these endings – about a couple of paragraphs.

Now list at least three other areas of text messaging which you think might be relevant and interesting in a gender-based text messaging investigation. These areas will help give you appropriate linguistic methods to follow.

Turn to page 157 for a commentary.

| | Endings | | | | |
|---|---|---|---|---|---|
| | First name | Full name | Nickname | Phrasal | Endearing |
| Male | M15 rob | | M3 the robatron<br>M7 deano | M13 tb | M3 love |
| | 1 | 0 | 2 | 1 | 1 |
| Female | F3 lucy | F2 stacey hilary carey<br>F10 stacey hope cole<br>F20 stacey cole | F4 luscious<br>F5 nee<br>F6 magz<br>F7 laur | F2 rsvp<br>F4 tb<br>F6 tb<br>F9 holla back youngin<br>F10 tb<br>F18 tb<br>F20 tb | F2 lurve<br>F3 love love love<br>F4 love<br>F5 lv<br>F8 luv u<br>F9 love love<br>F10 lv<br>F11 love u 4eva<br>F18 love u<br>F20 lv |
| | 1 | 3 | 4 | 7 | 10 |

### Language use in the Jeremy Kyle Show

The *Jeremy Kyle Show* is a daytime TV show presented by Jeremy Kyle and usually involves couples or family members who appear on the show with problems they want resolved. DNA and lie detector tests are frequently used when one guest is suspected of lying. Jeremy Kyle himself talks through the problem, offering his own help and guidance and often offering after-show support such as counselling.

The show runs for 65 minutes and is normally broken down into three mini-episodes, three different problems to be resolved. A good focus for an investigation would be to analyse 3–4 minutes of each mini-episode, apply the same linguistic methods to each transcript and then draw conclusions.

Here is one initial way into exploring the data, which just deals with the first problem presented in the show entitled 'Should I dump my girlfriend if my ex passes the lie detector?' The speakers are Jeremy Kyle, Wayne and Elaine (Wayne's ex-girlfriend).

| **Mean length of utterance (MLU)** | | | |
|---|---|---|---|
| | Wayne | Elaine | Jeremy Kyle |
| Total number of words spoken | 188 | 286 | 245 |
| Total number of utterances | 23 | 24 | 22 |
| Mean length of utterance | 8 | 12 | 11 |

A good comment on this data could start in the following way.

From this table it can be seen that although a lot of words are spoken, the mean length of utterance (MLU) is very short in comparison. This could be because in the situation of the chat show the pace is very fast and there are a lot of interruptions as the guests are attempting to grab floorspace in order to put their point across. Most of Jeremy Kyle's utterances are also short and they tend to be questions or to confirm a point.

As the host of the show it might be expected that he would have a larger MLU than his guests. However, Elaine has the greater MLU and holds the most floorspace.

There is a studio audience and a TV audience and the show does revolve around entertaining the audience. By having a studio audience present there is always feedback as to what is happening and being said on the show. During some of Elaine's utterances the studio audience laugh and find her entertaining. This may be why Jeremy Kyle allows her to have dominance in the conversation. Ultimately he has the power to control the conversation but he allows guests to hold floorspace if it is to the amusement of the audience.

As well as adding things like audience response, a full analysis here would also include some quotes from the data to support comments being made.

## Activity 24  Analysing media talk

**Pair work**

Suppose your focus for an investigation is to chart and explore how Jeremy Kyle controls the conversation, while ensuring an entertaining, even dramatic show. Which of the following areas do you think should be part of your linguistic methods? Discuss this in pairs.

- Discourse structure – looking at how Jeremy Kyle uses the background, problem, solution, evaluation (bpse) structure to prompt guests to tell their story

- Jeremy Kyle's guest introductions

- Pragmatics – looking at Jeremy Kyle's different use of language depending on the stance he adopts or whether he takes sides in the problem
- Jeremy Kyle's use of questions: open, closed, rhetorical, tag
- Jeremy Kyle's intonation
- Interruptions
- Use of humour, sarcasm
- Jeremy Kyle's handling of the audience.

Suggest other TV shows which would be good to analyse in terms of power and entertainment.

Turn to page 157 for a commentary.

# Written data

## Written language over time

In this section you will be exploring

- ideas for language-over-time investigations
- some linguistic methods useful for data analysis.

| **Activity 25** | ### Comparative studies |
|---|---|
| Group work | |

A comparative study is a good idea for a language-over-time investigation. It helps focus on what changes have taken place and helps give a framework of linguistic methods.

Working in twos or threes, for each of these single items of data suggest at least one other piece of data which would extend the investigation.

- The obituary of Princess Diana – from *The Times,* 1998
- A letter from a soldier serving in Iraq – 2003
- An extract from Dorothy Wordsworth's diary – published 1750
- An advert for Ovaltine – 1920

Turn to page 158 for a commentary.

| **Activity 26** | ### Dorothy Wordsworth's diary |
|---|---|

Here is an extract from Dorothy Wordsworth's diary. She is describing travelling through parts of northern England. What would be some of the language features you could comment on here? Sometimes it's helpful to rewrite some of the data in modern English.

> July 16th, Friday Evening. The weather bad, almost all the time. Sara, Tom, and I rode up Bedale. Wm., Mary, Sara, and I went to Scarborough, and we walked in the Abbey pasture, and to Wykeham; and on Monday, the 26th, we went off with Mary in a post-chaise. We had

an interesting ride over the Wolds, though it rained all the way. Single thorn bushes were scattered about on the turf, sheep-sheds here and there, and now and then a little hut. Swelling grounds, and sometimes a single tree or a clump of trees. Mary was very sick, and every time we stopped to open a gate she felt the motion in her whole body – indeed I was sick too, and perhaps the smooth gliding of the chaise over the turf made us worse. We passed through one or two little villages, embosomed in tall trees. After we had parted from Mary, there were gleams of sunshine, but with showers. We saw Beverley in a heavy rain, and yet were much pleased with the beauty of the town. Saw the Minster – a pretty, clean building, but injured very much with Grecian architecture. The country between Beverley and Hull very rich, but miserably flat – brick houses, windmills, houses again – dull and endless. Hull a frightful, dirty, brick-housey, tradesmanlike, rich, vulgar place; yet the river, though the shores are so low that they can hardly be seen, looked beautiful with the evening lights upon it, and boats moving about. We walked a long time, and returned to our dull day-room but quiet evening one, quiet and our own, to supper.

## Activity 27

**Pair work**

## Advertisements

In pairs research adverts over time. Make sure they have a common theme – for example, adverts for

- beauty or health products
- food, but focused – Bisto gravy, sweet bars
- drink, but focused – Coca Cola, Guinness for women
- household appliances
- cars.

Collect six to eight adverts. Try to establish a sequence, for example adverts from 1920, 1935, 1950. Make sure each advert has enough written data.

Give an illustrated presentation to the class and get feedback on how good your adverts would be for an investigation.

Here is a list of linguistic methods for language-over-time investigations:

- spelling changes
- semantic changes
- punctuation
- sentence length/complexity
- formality of register
- archaic syntax.

## Activity 28

**Group work**

## Adding data

Here are two more questions to discuss in twos or threes.

- What data could you add to extend an investigation involving the lyrics of 'Imagine' by John Lennon – released 1988?
- What data could you add to extend an investigation involving *Pride and Prejudice* by Jane Austen – first published 1813?

Turn to page 158 for a commentary.

## Imagine

Imagine there's no Heaven
It's easy if you try
No hell below us
Above us only sky
Imagine all the people
Living for today

Imagine there's no countries
It isn't hard to do
Nothing to kill or die for
And no religion too
Imagine all the people
Living life in peace

You may say that I'm a dreamer
But I'm not the only one
I hope someday you'll join us
And the world will be as one

Imagine no possessions
I wonder if you can
No need for greed or hunger
A brotherhood of man
Imagine all the people
Sharing all the world

You may say that I'm a dreamer
But I'm not the only one
I hope someday you'll join us
And the world will live as one

## *Pride and Prejudice*: the opening of Chapter 1

It is a truth universally acknowledged, that a single man in possession of a good fortune must be in want of a wife.

However little known the feelings or views of such a man may be on his first entering a neighbourhood, this truth is so well fixed in the minds of the surrounding families, that he is considered as the rightful property of some one or other of their daughters.

'My dear Mr. Bennet,' said his lady to him one day, 'have you heard that Netherfield Park is let at last?'

Mr. Bennet replied that he had not.

'But it is,' returned she; 'for Mrs. Long has just been here, and she told me all about it.'

Mr. Bennet made no answer.

'Do not you want to know who has taken it?' cried his wife impatiently.

'You want to tell me, and I have no objection to hearing it.'

This was invitation enough.

# Other ideas for written data

## Activity 29 — Ideas for investigations

Brainstorm ideas for written investigations using as starting-points

- university websites
- sports reports
- text messages, e-mails, MSN texting
- newspaper articles.

What would be your focus?

How would you select the data?

What questions would you ask of the data?

## Activity 30 — Sports writing

Read this article which was printed in various newspapers in April 2007. What opportunities does it offer for a language investigation? What other data would extend it?

# Reeling Fulham in dogfight

## Cottagers suffering relegation fears

**Fulham boss Chris Coleman is facing up to a dogfight for survival in the English Premiership – with the Cottagers fans turning their fire on his troops.**

Coleman told his charges to get ready for the battle of their lives if they want to stay in the big time and keep the boo-boys off their backs.

'When you are in a dogfight you have to fight like dogs. If it is a gunfight you can't afford to go in with just a knife,' the 36-year-old Welshman said.

'It is only results that are important now and it doesn't matter how we get them. I will take being booed for being boring or whatever but we know we have good players. Now they have all got to become scrappers as well.

'We've got to believe we can stay in the Premiership this season. We've got to get the points we need and the players know full well the position we are in.'

Fulham lost 3–1 to visitors Manchester City at Craven Cottage on Monday, their fifth defeat in a winless eight-match streak that left them four points above the relegation zone.

Coleman and the Cottagers were booed as the players trudged off.

Fulham visit Reading on Sunday, and must also face Champions League spot chasers Arsenal and Liverpool in their remaining five games.

'I don't think I have seen the players like this before. They are devastated, gutted. They are only

human and so are the supporters,' Coleman told reporters afterwards.

'You could see the loss of belief in the players' faces.

'They were edgy and nervous but we need somebody to step forward and come up with something to get us a result. We can't just moan about bad luck. Every team which has struggled has had their bad luck and it is up to us to get over it.'

Monday's third straight away win eased resurgent Manchester City's relegation fears. The result left City in 12th place and nine points clear of the drop zone with six games remaining.

'I can't have sympathy for "Cookie" Coleman even though he is a great lad,' Blues boss Stuart Pearce told reporters.

'We are in a competitive business and everyone is desperate to win games down at the bottom.

'We need to finish the season strongly and I want the players to ask themselves if they can improve.'

**Postscript:** A week later the Fulham manager Chris Coleman was sacked and the team survived relegation – just. At the end of the season Stuart Pearce was also sacked.

In this section you have been given the opportunity to

- evaluate potential for successful language investigations

- work with various linguistic methods

- practise transcription

- practise working with spoken and written data

- practise scaffolding with data.

# The creative element

In this section you will be

- exploring and practising the creative element.

This part of the investigation coursework covers the Assessment Objective

- demonstrate expertise and creativity in the use of English in a range of different contexts, informed by linguistic study (AO4).

You may have already worked with these ideas (or will be doing so) in Chapter 4, on creative and original writing. For the investigation coursework this means writing a media article

- for a non-specialist audience
- about the issues and/or language debates surrounding your chosen investigation topic.

If you have set about your investigation successfully you will have done some background reading and research around your topic. Your article is

- not dependent on the success of your investigation
- not a commentary.

## Activity 31 The importance of context

**Pair work**

It is always important to know where your article is going and to read examples – style models. Working in pairs rank the following in what you think would be good contexts to aim for/write for.

- *The Times* newspaper
- *Sun* newspaper
- *Daily Mail* newspaper
- *Modern English Teacher* magazine
- *Times Educational Supplement* newspaper
- *Cosmopolitan* magazine
- Thai Airways in-flight magazine
- BBC website

Turn to page 158 for a commentary.

# The article itself

A good article will need to have your own findings and research incorporated into it. Look at your analysis, decide what is most interesting and then work on how to present it in a user-friendly way. Newspaper articles often have a 'What if?' angle to their stories. That is, they aim to get the reader to think along the lines of: 'What if this happened to me?' They aim to get the reader to connect with the content of the story. Can you do this with your findings? Can you do this with your article?

Approach your article from two angles:

- structure
- content

## Structure

A good structure makes for a better read and an effective way to present your knowledge. A good structure in many ways mirrors that of the investigation itself with these sections:

- **Introduction** – this could be the background to the topic or a summary of findings of your own analysis
- **Development** – this is the expansion of your findings, facts and perhaps statistics but presented in a user-friendly way
- **Conclusion** – this is a summary and comment on your main findings or an evaluation which poses new questions.

## Content

This is where you balance your presentation of facts with a level of register and lexis appropriate for a non-specialist audience.

The rest of this section explores these areas with examples and activities to practise appropriate writing.

## Activity 32 Register 1

**Pair work**

Read this opening of an article based on an investigation into chef conversation in a restaurant.

This text opts for a background introduction but is not suitable for a non-specialist audience. In pairs, rewrite it so that it's more comprehensible – and more interesting – for the general public. Here are some tips.

- Rewrite or omit some of the jargon.
- Aim for a catchier opening.
- Create an angle for the content.
- Leave out some of the theorists and flesh out the ones you do leave in.

Language is a vital part of our personal and social standing and our language habits and idiolect reflect our experiences and individual biographies. Individual speakers do not always speak the same way. The pragmatics of the situation or the 'felicity conditions' (Finch 2003) affect the style of the speaker. The register a speaker may use depends on a variety of sociolinguistic features, such as the gender of the group, the difference in status between the speakers, or 'facilitators' (Holmes 1984), and the purpose of the conversation. Facilitators are the participants in a conversation who are responsible for ensuring that the interaction flows smoothly and fluently.

Research carried out, by among others Milroy and Coates, highlights some of the effects of language as social bonding and also how the tightness of a social network can be influential. For example, a closed network is when an individual's personal contacts all know each other. This can occur with groupings made up of relatives, neighbours or work colleagues. The effect here is that it often results in individuals using language closer to the local or social vernacular, that is informal, colloquial language which may also reflect local dialect.

Language used in the workplace – occupational dialect – is often multi-purposed because it can fulfil several functions depending on context. Bernstein has carried out work examining social groupings and he suggests two types of language: the restricted code and the elaborated code. The elaborated code is more complex than the restricted code but also more explicit and therefore more comprehensible to an outsider. On the other hand the restricted code is more implicit and context-dependent. Utterances are more likely to be informal and in non-standard English. Participants are also very aware of the context so that even implied meanings are understood.

## Activity 33  Register 2

Read this article from the *Telegraph* (March 2007) about accent. It opens with a summary-of-findings introduction. What makes it interesting and therefore successful? What kind of conclusion does it have?

Turn to page 159 for a commentary.

# Northerners have the last laff

The grarse spreading out from its London roots is gradually stifling the graaas, but one of Britain's leading accent experts said yesterday that a larf will never drown out a laff.

Students of the voices that make up a patchwork quilt of spoken English across the country have drawn up a map of the way in which the long 'a' of received pronunciation has followed the exodus of Londoners into the rest of southern England. But a sort of linguistic Hahdrian's Wall just south of Birmingham is keeping the long grass out of northern England and the rest of Britain.

Not so long ago people in counties such as Suffolk, Cambridgeshire, Oxfordshire, Hampshire and Wiltshire would pronounce 'grass', 'bath' and 'after' as if they were spelled with a double 'a'.

Today, younger generations will say those words as the Queen does, or indeed as they do in the Queen Vic on EastEnders, as if the 'a' was lengthened with an 'h'.

The old, extended 'aa' is restricted to southern England west of a line from Cheltenham through Bristol and Bath to the south coast and in a redoubt around Norfolk.

But the curt northern 'bath', 'staff' and 'laff', sorry 'laugh', has stood resolute against southern invasion. A line drawn from

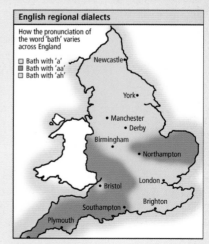

**English regional dialects**

How the pronunciation of the word 'bath' varies across England

☐ Bath with 'a'
■ Bath with 'aa'
☐ Bath with 'ah'

the Severn, just south of Birmingham and up to the Wash delineates larf from laff and it looks like it always will.

## Activity 34 The rewrite 1

Text A is a report of a study into male and female talk in its 'pure' form as presented in the American journal *Science* in July 2007. Text B is a version of these findings presented for the general reader in *The Times* (also in July 2007).

This was a study with potential interest for many but needed the right level of facts and a user-friendly register. Other media such as the *Telegraph* and the BBC website also produced user-friendly versions.

In pairs, match the original facts to their transformation in *The Times*. Note also the more friendly register adopted in *The Times*. Where in the article is this most apparent? Also, what facts of its own does *The Times* add to sustain interest?

Turn to page 159 for a commentary.

**Text A**

# Are Women Really More Talkative Than Men?

Women are generally assumed to be more talkative than men. Data were analyzed from 396 participants who wore a voice recorder that sampled ambient sounds for several days. Participants' daily word use was extrapolated from the number of recorded words. Women and men both spoke about 16,000 words per day.

Sex differences in conversational behavior have long been a topic of public and scientific interest [1, 2]. The stereotype of female talkativeness is deeply engrained in Western folklore and often considered a scientific fact. In the first printing of her book, neuropsychiatrist Brizendine reported, 'A woman uses about 20,000 words per day while a man uses about 7,000' [3]. These numbers have since circulated throughout television, radio, and print media (e.g., CBS, CNN, National Public Radio, *Newsweek*, the *New York Times*, and the *Washington Post*). Indeed, the 20,000-versus-7000 word estimates appear to have achieved the status of a cultural myth in that comparable differences have been cited in the media for the past 15 years [4].

In reality, no study has systematically recorded the natural conversations of large groups of people for extended periods of time. Consequently, there have not been the necessary data for reliably estimating differences in daily word usage among women and men [5]. Extrapolating from a reanalysis of tape-recorded daily conversations from 153 participants from the British National Corpus [6], Liberman recently estimated that women speak 8805 words and men 6073 words per day. However, he acknowledged that these estimates may be problematic because no information was available regarding when participants decided to turn off their manual tape recorders [4].

Over the past 8 years, we have developed a method for recording natural language using the electronically activated recorder (EAR) [7]. The EAR is a digital voice recorder that unobtrusively tracks people's real-world moment-to-moment interactions. It operates by periodically recording snippets of ambient sounds, including conversations, while participants go about their daily lives. Because of the covert digital recording, it is impossible for participants to control or even to sense when the EAR is on or off. For the purpose of this study, the EAR can be used to track naturally spoken words and to estimate how many words women and men use over the course of a day.

In the default paradigm, participants wear the EAR for several days during their waking hours. The device is programmed to record for 30 s every 12.5 min. All captured words spoken by the participant are transcribed. The number of spoken words per day can then be estimated by extrapolating from a simple word count, the number of sampled sound files, and the recording time per sound file.

We addressed the question about sex differences in daily word use with data from six samples based on 396 participants (210 women and 186 men) that were conducted between 1998 and 2004. Five of the samples were composed of university students in the United States, and the sixth, university students in Mexico. Table 1 provides background information on the samples along with estimates for the number of words that female and male participants spoke per day [8].

The data suggest that women spoke on average 16,215 (SD = 7301) words and men 15,669 (SD = 8633) words over an assumed period of, on average, 17 waking hours. Expressed in a common effect-size metric (Cohen's $d = 0.07$), this sex difference in daily word use (546 words) is equal to only 7% of the standardized variability among women and men. Further, the difference does not meet conventional thresholds for statistical significance ($P = 0.248$, onesided test). Thus, the data fail to reveal a reliable sex difference in daily word use. Women and men both use on average about 16,000 words per day, with very large individual differences around this mean.

A potential limitation of our analysis is that all participants were university students. The resulting homogeneity in the samples with regard to sociodemographic characteristics may have affected our estimates of daily word usage. However, none of the samples provided support for the idea that women have substantially larger lexical budgets than men. Further, to the extent that sex differences in daily word use are assumed to be biologically based, evolved adaptations [3], they should be detectable among university students as much as in more diverse samples. We therefore conclude, on the basis of available empirical evidence, that the widespread and highly publicized stereotype about female talkativeness is unfounded.

**Text B**

# Female Chatterbox?
## It's a myth and we can put a lid on it, say scientists

She is one of the loudest stereotypes of popular culture, famous for dominating conversation with what Chas and Dave described as 'more rabbit than Sainsbury's'.

The female chatterbox who never lets men get a word in edgeways, however, is nothing more than a myth, according to research. Contrary to common belief and even to scientific assertion, women do not talk more than men.

The first rigorous study exploring the verbosity of men and women has found both sexes equally capable of irritating jabber. The typical woman speaks an average of 16,215 words a day, while an average of 15,669 words pass the lips of men, a difference so small it is not statistically significant.

The most loquacious people of all, indeed, tend to be men, but men are also the most taciturn. All three of the biggest talkers who took part in the research were male, the most prolific of whom yakked his way through 47,000 words in a day. The most effusive woman managed a mere 40,000.

At the other end of the spectrum, one man spoke an average of just over 500 words each day. There were nine men who spoke fewer than 2,000 a day, compared with only four women.

As an average of 16,000 words are spoken each day, people who talk at 120 words per minute – the speed at which the BBC's Huw Edwards reads the news – would end up speaking for a little more than two hours of the 17 they typically spend awake.

The *Little Britain* character Vicky Pollard, by contrast, speaks at 330 words per minute, and would get through the average daily word allocation in just 49 minutes.

The findings, from a team at the University of Arizona, overturn a notion that is not only popular with the public, but which has also found its way into scientific research.

A book published last year, *The Female Brain*, by Louann Brizendine, a neuroscientist at the University of California, San Francisco, claimed that women use 20,000 words a day compared with just 7,000 for men, and the same statistics have been quoted widely by the media and even by marriage-guidance counsellors.

Some of these reports were seen by Jamie Pennebaker, Professor of Psychology at the University of Texas, who was surprised by the figures. He researches language use among men and women, and was sure that he would have been aware of so large a difference.

Professor Pennebaker already had the evidence he needed to investigate the matter, in the form of recordings of almost 400 students he had accumulated between 1998 and 2004. He then teamed up with a former student, Matthias Mehl, of the University of Arizona, to pore over the data.

In their previous work, Professor Pennebaker and Dr Mehl had asked five groups of students in the US and one in Mexico to wear microphones that recorded snatches of their conversations throughout the day. Although they were told that the devices recorded at random, they actually operated for 30 seconds every 12.5 minutes. The results showed no significant differences between men and women. 'Whatever people might think, the stereotype is wrong,' Professor Pennebaker said. 'What is interesting about this study is that we found nothing at all. It's unusual in science for a study that finds nothing to generate such interest. It overturns a notion that has become part of the cultural mainstream.'

He said that, as all the participants were college students, it was possible that older age groups would behave differently, though he thought it unlikely. 'It might be that once guys get to 30 or 40 they run out of things to say,' he said. 'But I don't think so.'

The stereotype, Professor Pennebaker said, might result from differences in what men and women said, and when they said it. 'We do have evidence that women use many more personal pronouns, such as he, she and I, while men use more articles – a, an and the,' he said. 'That suggests women are talking about people and men are talking about things.

'There's also literature that suggests when there is marital conflict men tend to clam up and women tend to talk a lot.'

**Activity 35** | ## The rewrite 2

Now try something similar yourself. Text A is an original report of a study into doctor-patient communication. Its starting-point was the value of doctors sharing their own personal information with patients. The focus was the amount of time in a consultation spent on talking about the doctor or the patient. The report uses 'MD-SD' to mean self-disclosure by the doctor.

Read the report then produce a user-friendly article based on it. Remember to think about your structure. What sort of introduction are you going to choose? What sort of conclusion? Be inventive with colloquial lexis. Can you add any new issues?

Text B is a personal blog about patient rights. Try to incorporate at least two ideas from this data in your own article.

Turn to page 159 for a link to an article for comparison with your own.

**Text A**

# Physician Self-disclosure in Primary Care Visits
## Enough About You, What About Me?

Susan H. McDaniel, PhD; Howard B. Beckman, MD; Diane S. Morse, MD; Jordan Silberman, MAPP; David B. Seaburn, PhD; Ronald M. Epstein, MD

*Arch Intern Med.* 2007;167:1321–1326.

**Background:** The value of physician self-disclosure (MD-SD) in creating successful patient-physician partnerships has not been demonstrated.

**Methods:** To describe antecedents, delivery, and effects of MD-SD in primary care visits, we conducted a descriptive study using sequence analysis of transcripts of 113 unannounced, undetected, standardized patient visits to primary care physicians. Our main outcome measures were the number of MD-SDs per visit; number of visits with MD-SDs; word count; antecedents, timing, and effect of MD-SD on subsequent physician and patient communication; content and focus of MD-SD.

**Results:** The MD-SDs included discussion of personal emotions and experiences, families and/or relationships, professional descriptions, and personal experiences with the patient's diagnosis. Seventy-three MD-SDs were identified in 38 (34%) of 113 visits. Ten MD-SDs (14%) were a response to a patient question. Forty-four (60%) followed patient symptoms, family, or feelings; 29 (40%) were unrelated. Only 29 encounters (21%) returned to the patient topic preceding the disclosure. Most MD-SDs (n = 62; 85%) were not considered useful to the patient by the research team. Eight MD-SDs (11%) were coded as disruptive.

**Conclusions:** Practicing primary care physicians disclosed information about themselves or their families in 34% of new visits with unannounced, undetected, standardized patients. There was no evidence of positive effect of MD-SDs; some appeared disruptive. Primary care physicians should consider when self-disclosing whether other behaviors such as empathy might accomplish their goals more effectively.

**Text B**

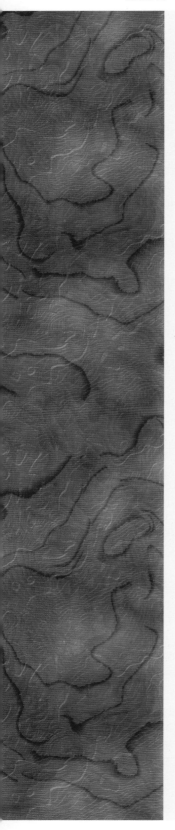

# Yackety Yak: It's all about the doctors
so said the doctors in a study conducted in Rochester, NY and reported in the Archives of Internal Medicine …

It seems that 100 doctors were studied over the span of a year to see how they communicated with patients. Mystery patients made appointments, visited the doctors, then recorded their conversations. Even though the doctors had given permission for that to happen, they didn't know for sure which patients were the fake patients.

In one-third of the conversations, the doctors talked about themselves, likely in an effort to create a rapport with the patient.

But when that happened, 80% of the time the conversation never returned to where it began –  meaning – the conversation never turned back to whatever the patient was saying or asking. Meaning – patients didn't get their full service, nor did they have the opportunity to get answers to all their questions.

The interesting commentary shows that the doctors who did the research were, in a word, appalled at themselves. I give credit to Dr Susan H. McDaniel and Dr Howard Beckman, who led the research, for owning up to their own befuddlement at the results.

Hey – at least give them a pat on the back for trying!

But, give them a swat for being clueless, too.

I see a few different aspects here for sharp patienting:

First – doctors hear that their patients want to establish a rapport, or that patients want a doctor with good 'bedside' manner... BUT... nobody teaches those doctors just how to accomplish that. So what happens? Because they don't know any better, they talk about themselves. (And, OK, sorry, can't resist, remember that in way too many cases, we ARE talking about a group of superegos. not always. but certainly a majority of the time.)

Hey medical schools – do you hear that? There's been a cry to teach doctors some bedside manner for years... do you hear this?   huh?

Second – if doctors talk about themselves and still try to stick to their 6 or 7 insurance-alloted minutes? Well then – that's definitely wrong! If they want to spend the patient's precious time talking about themselves, so be it, but either discount the visit, or make sure the patient gets what s/he is paying for.

Third – we are empowered patients. We are free, intelligent and have questions. The tenets of smart patienting tell us to get the conversation back on track ourselves! We don't have to converse at the doctor's direction – we can direct the conversation ourselves, can't we? Ask those questions. Don't allow yourself to be derailed!

Kudos to the primary care doctors who were willing to be studied. Kudos to those doctors who analyzed and published the results. Kudos to the doctors who 'get' the results and wish to move their patient interaction into a more positive direction.

And mega-kudos to those patients who can establish a rapport with their doctors, without allowing it to detract from their care.

**Review**

In this section you have been given the opportunity to

- consider the content, structure and audience for your article

- read articles of differing content and register

- write articles yourself.

Remember, this has been practice and your final article may need to be a different length so check the recommended word count.

**Commentary**

**Activity 1**

Good investigation titles: 1, 2, 3, 5, 8, 10, 14, 16, 19, 20.
Weak investigation titles: 4, 6, 7, 9, 11, 12, 13, 15, 17, 18.

**Commentary**

**Activity 5**

First, this reads well, is fluent and clearly reflects a thoughtful approach to the topic. Second, the writer mentions her interest in the language of the programme, what others – the press – have said about it, and what she intends to explore in the language. She gives a good summary of the programme, what it contains, and gives notice of which areas she will focus on. There is also some very nice background information on the programme's reaction from others. This is enough to put everything in context. Anyone coming to this completely new will have no doubt about what the writer first noticed, about her interest and about her intentions.

**Commentary**

**Activity 6**

Introduction B is the more helpful of the two. It summarises some guiding theories which will set the linguistic methods for the investigation and help give it a focus. Anyone reading this will have a fairly clear idea of what the student intends and what areas in particular will be explored. This introduction promises a thoughtful investigation to follow.

Introduction A, on the other hand, is vague and general. Its premise is one of stereotypes and assertions; its language is equally imprecise. For example, what does she mean by 'females are more polite, less direct in commands and in that way use pragmatics frequently'? Her comments also reveal some very simple generalisations: 'Males, in contrast, compare females to machines and are more vulgar in speech.' The moderator is not really sure what to expect, what linguistic methods the writer will use. Initial impressions suggest a vague and highly subjective investigation.

**Commentary**

**Activity 7**

Methodology C goes with Introduction B, and Methodology D with Introduction A.

Methodology C continues the thoughtful explanation behind the investigation. We are given a clear idea about how the data is being collected and who is involved. We are told that the informants will answer a series of questions, so we know that there is a control mechanism at work, and the linguistic methods are summarised. The writer has been right to get permission too. It would have been even better to have a list of the questions with some rationale for these choices.

Methodology D continues the muddled thinking shown in its introduction. The make-up of the informants is unclear – just 'friends' – and a random section of data is being used without any clear justification. Of more consequence for the success of the investigation is the fact that there is no structure to the conversations. It might be, of course, that the 'friends' produce some good data to analyse but, equally, it might be so random as to be very difficult to make any sensible comment possible.

## Commentary
### Activity 8

Analysis B is the best, then comes Analysis C, then Analysis D, with Analysis A the worst.

Analysis B starts with a clearly appropriate heading – 'Interruptions' – which gives the initial exploration of the data focus and meaning. It draws on relevant theory – and not too much – then presents the findings in a sensible tabulated form. Having done this the student can go on to discuss some of these features. This has the rigour of a report, of a research piece. It gets to the heart of the data and enables the student to demonstrate good knowledge of linguistic terminology.

Analysis C certainly has some strengths. It uses some linguistic terminology and comments on relevant language use in adverts. But with more focused linguistic methods it could be even better. The approach adopted by the student in this investigation is to use four broad headings under which to discuss the data: 'Lexis', followed later in the analysis by 'Grammar', 'Discourse', 'Pragmatics'. These headings are fine as an initial starting-point but if they are not further refined – into positive lexis, sentence type, spoken register, etc – then they will serve only to encourage mini-essay-type responses.

Analysis D is a very general response – in fact the title of the investigation is very general too: 'The Language of Punk Music'. Sometimes if you are too 'close' to your data – and this is a common problem with lyrics – you end up writing a sociological piece rather than a language investigation.

Analysis A is far too informal in its approach. The writing is very personal and lacking in any linguistic comment.

## Commentary
### Activity 11

Actually they all have good potential.

1    To make this work at its best it would need to use a focus such as gender issues. What do theorists on gender lead you to expect in the way that language is used?

2 & 3  A good focus here would be on power and/or teaching strategy. Exchange structure theory developed by Coulthard, Sinclair and Brazil (1975 onwards) would help with linguistic methods.

4    Child language acquisition theory would help with this idea, with the main focus on child-directed language.

**Commentary Activity 15**

Chef 1 is the chef with the higher status. He dominates the conversation and holds the floor. He tells the main story and Chef 2's function here is to support him. Chef 2 clearly signals the fact that he's listening to what Chef1 has to say with response tokens like 'yeah probably', 'yeah', 'ohh'.

**Commentary Activity 19**

A script is written. It will be thoughtfully planned. There will be a cohesion and a structure to the dialogue. By and large questions will get answers, there will be no false starts, there will be no repetition.

But to help suggest spontaneous conversation there may be interruptions and overlaps. There may also be fillers, hedges and vague language.

Some comedies or situation comedies may also include spontaneous features, for example *The Royle Family* (BBC) – indeed this gives it its main comedic thrust.

**Commentary Activity 23**

There are several things you could comment on here. One is the fact that only four of the male messages actually bother with an ending. Another is the variety, and length, of the female endings. Some opt for name, phrasal and endearing endings – F2 has 'lurve stacey hilary carey rsvp'.

Also 50% of the female endings use 'love' or variations of the word. Females are also keen to maintain contact and seven messages end with a request to text back.

Other areas that might be explored in these text messages are

- other uses of names and terms of endearment
- spelling difference and abbreviated forms
- punctuation differences
- use of humour
- mlt – the mean length of text.

**Commentary Activity 24**

All these areas are very useful linguistic methods under which to analyse your data. Which ones you use more will depend on your data. As for other TV shows good for analysis, there are, of course, many linguistic methods and which you might choose will depend on current TV schedules. Here are some tips.

- Adding a gender slant might be interesting, especially where there are two show presenters, one male, one female.
- Choosing a show which is currently courting publicity or controversy might give you extra ammunition for any creative element your exam board demands.

**Commentary**

**Activity 25**

The obituary of Princess Diana would compare well with an obituary of another well-known person from an earlier period – for example, Queen Victoria or John F. Kennedy or Lord Nelson. Similarly a letter from a soldier serving in Iraq would compare well with a letter from a soldier from an earlier period – for example, the Crimean War or the war in Vietnam.

An extract from Dorothy Wordsworth's diary would compare well with a more modern diary – for example, Bridget Jones'. Bear in mind, though, that Bridget Jones' diary is a piece of fiction and Dorothy Wordsworth's, though literary in style, is not.

The 1920 advert for Ovaltine would compare well with other Ovaltine adverts over time. Alternatively the focus could be adverts for similar products over time.

**Commentary**

**Activity 28**

Lyrics can be tricky. Although mainly meant to be heard rather than read they need to be analysed on the page. The obvious thing to do with 'Imagine' is to take another three or four lyrics by John Lennon and chart his development in what he writes and how he writes. Comparisons could also be made between his early work with Paul McCartney and his later solo work. Another idea is to chart the change in the work of John Lennon and Paul McCartney with the Beatles. So, for example you could take one lyric from their first album, one from their second, and so on. You still need to find a focus and a pattern and avoid random selections.

Other ideas on lyrics:

- development in other artists, for example Madonna or Morrissey
- pop songs over time
- 'protest' songs over time.

The Jane Austen data has two issues. First the selection of the data from the novel. You can't do the whole novel. So for good ideas consider one or more of the following:

- the opening of the novel
- descriptions of the main character(s)
- descriptions of key moments, for example proposals of marriage
- dialogue.

The second issue is the other data. The obvious choice is to compare the Jane Austen data with a more modern romance novel. Other comparison ideas are

- *Pride and Prejudice* the novel and the film (any version)
- different *Pride and Prejudice* film versions
- Jane Austen's novel *Emma* and the film *Clueless*.

It's important to think carefully about your selection of material. Too much difference and it's hard to know what to say. Too little difference and you have the same problem. Only you will know if you have enough to write about.

**Commentary**

**Activity 31**

1= *The Times* newspaper, *Daily Mail* newspaper, BBC website
4= *Times Educational Supplement* newspaper, *Modern English Teacher* magazine

6= *Sun* newspaper, *Cosmopolitan* magazine
8= Thai Airways in-flight magazine

The first three would be ideal places for which to pitch your article and good places to research. Of course other newspapers and general websites for a similar audience should also be looked at.

The next two might be suitable but as their audience is more specialist the demands for the writing would also be of a higher register.

The two in sixth place are probably unsuitable – but for different reasons.

The last one is more likely to want to publish articles about holidays, duty-free goods or Thailand than articles about issues in the English language.

**Commentary**
**Activity 33**

The title and opening sentence immediately gain attention as well as nicely summarising the main findings of this research. The facts are helpfully illustrated by the map, which enables readers to plot their own position in the country.

Facts about the 'a' vowel are developed, references to *EastEnders* help make the information user friendly and explanations of accents, as you would expect here, are given in eye dialect rather than IPA versions.

The article ends with a summary conclusion which echoes the opening sentence.

This, of course, is from a newspaper and follows a typical structure of a good newspaper story. Reading and analysing newspaper articles is always good preparation.

**Commentary**
**Activity 34**

The writers of *The Times* article have taken a limited number of facts and statistics from the original research and used these to underpin the main gist of the piece – that women do not speak much more than men. This is contrary to earlier research but, more important, contrary to the popularly held stereotype of the talkative female.

There are many deliberate attempts to achieve a more colloquial register, for example

- more rabbit than Sainsbury's
- irritating jabber
- yakked his way through 47,000 words.

Interestingly this lexis comes early in the piece and helps set the tone. As the piece develops the lexis remains more neutral.

*The Times* article develops by introducing the notion of how long each day we might speak according to the speed at which we speak.

Its conclusion is not a summary of the original findings but an evaluative one and opens up issues to do with male and female relationships.

**Commentary**
**Activity 35**

Follow this link for another version of the doctor–patient research, from the *New York Times*. How does it compare with yours?

http://www.nytimes.com/2007/06/26/health/26doctors.html?_r=1&ref=health&oref=slogin

# Creating Your
# Own Texts

4

## At the end of this chapter you should be able to

- select and apply a range of linguistic methods, to communicate relevant knowledge using appropriate terminology and coherent, accurate written expression (AO1)

- demonstrate critical understanding of a range of concepts and issues relating to the construction and analysis of meanings in spoken and written language, using knowledge of linguistic approaches (AO2)

- analyse and evaluate the influence of contextual factors on the production and reception of spoken and written language, showing knowledge of the key constituents of language (AO3)

- demonstrate expertise and creativity in the use of English in a range of different contexts informed by linguistic study (AO4).

For a more student-friendly version of these Assessment Objectives, turn to page vii in the Introduction.

## Introduction

Judging from the opinions voiced by successive generations of English Language students, the chance to produce and submit pieces of personal writing in a variety of formats is probably one of the major reasons why you have chosen to follow the subject at A level. You will have followed GCSE courses which gave you some opportunities to try out different types of writing both for coursework and under the more restrictive conditions of an exam, but you may well be of the opinion that there was just not the chance to write, at a personal level, at sufficient length or depth.

Whichever exam-board specification you are following, you will have a chance to build on and extend favourite styles of writing and to reflect on how and why you have created these new texts. The aim of this chapter is not to teach you to write, because you are well able to do that already. You wouldn't be following an A-level English Language course if you hadn't demonstrated some proficiency in writing. It is hoped, however, that the chapter will help you to become a better writer and, specifically, to write in a way that will bring you success in your coursework submission. That does not mean, of course, that every activity you use from this chapter must end up as a piece of coursework – the idea is that you try a variety of tasks and styles of writing in order to discover your favourites and your strengths within the requirements of the exam specification you are working to.

There are so many different types or modes of writing. Throughout your English course, you will have opportunities to study some of them, but the vast majority you just come up against in your everyday life. All of us write frequently and have been doing so since we first learnt. You may feel driven to write and gain considerable enjoyment from writing short stories, poems, articles for a school or college newspaper, lyrics for the band you play in, slogans for competitions, letters to friends, a diary or a blog. Sometimes you may write because you have to: taking the minutes of a meeting, writing a letter of complaint, writing up a science experiment or an essay in sociology or even an examination answer. Sometimes our writing is simply concerned with helping us organise ourselves, ranging from writing shopping lists or notes of things to remember to filling in a UCAS form and producing a personal statement or applying for a job. You already possess a broad range of writing skills – now the challenge is to harness and hone these in order to produce a winning submission by the end of the course.

In addition to advice on possible approaches, this chapter includes examples of actual candidates' work at different levels (both texts and their associated commentaries) which should prove helpful to you in all aspects of the production and presentation of a coursework folder. It should be emphasised, however, that these are provided not as templates to be followed slavishly, but more as a series of exemplars which illustrate aspects of good practice and proven successful approaches. No two folders are going to be identical – even if the subject-matter of the texts is similar, the approaches to the content will be as different as the writers!

# Getting started

It is often suggested that much of the best writing is likely to come from your own personal experience, so this first activity is designed to demonstrate just how much 'writing potential' is contained in everyone's everyday life.

## Activity 1 | Daily record

Keep a brief journal for the next seven days. Make sure there is at least one entry for each day which could lead to at least one writing suggestion for each day.

There is no need to invent specific 'writing opportunities' to put into your journal – just make a note of the everyday happenings involving the people, the places and the events you come into contact with. A couple of sentences for each event should be enough.

In order to give you an idea of how this works, here is a real-life example of a journal. Use it as a model.

### TUESDAY

A group of us sat in the common room, talking about the books we read in our spare time – it's amazing that virtually none of us have read any 'real' books since we were forced into studying texts for GCSE – so it wasn't much of a conversation. We then discussed the range of terrible part-time jobs we have between us – it's amazing the tricks some employers will try to pull on us innocent students!

I've arranged to go shopping with Mark tomorrow – the first time ever – should be interesting!

### WEDNESDAY

I was amazed Mark was so easy to shop with, I know it's important in a relationship to enjoy doing things together – but there are some things that you just don't expect to go so well. He does have some strange tastes in music though – he claims that no decent bands have emerged recently and that all the best songs were written at least fifteen years ago – where has he been?

**THURSDAY**

Not a very interesting day I sat around reading. Dad had a go at me for not doing my homework. I know what he means but it's his tone of voice that puts me off.

**FRIDAY**

Big brother Simon brought a laptop home from work and showed me how to operate it. Coursework looks distinctly possible all of a sudden. I might actually pass English Language now. Technology to the rescue!

**SATURDAY**

Laura left for Germany last night (Saturday – I'm writing this on Sunday). She was really upset about forgetting to say goodbye to Benjie (the dog) and she started crying at the airport, which started me off.

**SUNDAY**

Arrived late at Richard's surprise party and missed his reaction. I left early. I was tired and Laura had wanted to be there. It just felt odd that all her friends were there and she wasn't

**MONDAY**

Sat around all through my free morning trying to do homework. I didn't write anything for a few hours. I don't know what I was thinking about but I do remember watching two pigeons on the fence. They seemed to be practising synchronised movement. One would fly further along the fence and the other would follow and they'd bob their heads down one after the other. Is that how all relationships work? REMINDER Little bro' David accidentally opened my letter from Luke. I won't forget that one.

**TUESDAY**

My Birthday and I was stuck inside doing homework, but at least Mum and Dad turned the telly off and kept bringing me drinks and biscuits. Perhaps they do understand about coursework deadlines! Family! What would we do without them?

Hardly the most exciting week of her life, but it provided the student with a wide variety of suggestions for writing, as you will soon be able to see!

## Activity 2 | Writing outcomes

Produce a table of outcomes based on the events in your journal in which you suggest the following for each day:

- a topic about which you could write
- the purpose for which the piece would be written
- the medium/channel in which the text would be presented (also known as the text type)
- the audience for which the text would be prepared.

As an example to give you a start, here is a table of outcomes associated with the journal extract in Activity 1.

| Day | Topic | Purpose | Medium/Channel | Audience |
|---|---|---|---|---|
| Tuesday | Reading can be fun | To persuade | Magazine article or talk on children's TV or radio programme | Top junior/early secondary school pupils (just boys?) |
| | Problems associated with part-time employment | To inform | Letter to local newspaper or article in school newspaper | Local newspaper readers or school pupils/students |
| Wednesday | Taking the boyfriend shopping | To entertain | Magazine article or Item for radio programme (Radio 1 or Local Radio) | Teenage girls or young radio listeners |
| | The day the music died | To inform and entertain | Article for a part-work on the history of pop music | '30-something' music fans |
| Thursday | Family problems | To entertain | Short story | Teenage readers |
| Friday | Using ICT to improve standards | To instruct | 'How to...' article or leaflet | Students |
| Saturday | Travel article about cheap flight destinations | To inform | Newspaper or magazine feature article | Anyone interested in travel |
| Sunday | Organising a surprise party | To instruct | Lifestyle magazine article | Dependent on selected magazine |
| Monday | Descriptive, atmospheric piece, including personal responses to surroundings | To entertain | Extract from autobiography, or extract from novel or short story | Mature adult readership |
| Tuesday | Study skills for A level – coursework advice | To instruct/ advise | Section of student handbook or leaflet | A-level students |

# Choosing a subject

Much of the writing you will have done up to now, say, for GCSE, will have been in the form of an essay on a subject unlikely to have been of your own choosing. 'Write me an essay on … and have it finished by Tuesday' will probably sound familiar to you. By contrast, it is very important that your piece of writing for A-level English Language coursework should have, wherever possible, a real equivalent.

As you work your way through this chapter you will notice that all the activities are geared towards production of

- specific text types, with identifiable purposes or modes and recognisable audiences.

The four most familiar modes, and the ones in which you will most frequently be asked to write for A-level English Language, are

- writing which entertains (the entertainment mode)
- writing which persuades (the persuasive/argumentative mode)
- writing which informs (the informative mode)
- writing which instructs or advises (the instructional/advisory mode).

Whichever exam board you have been entered for, there will be restrictions imposed about how long your pieces should be and about the purpose or mode of your writing. There are also usually stipulations about the audience and sometimes about the genre or text type. For these reasons, the approach taken towards the activities will be a consistent one, as follows.

1 Identify a preferred topic for writing.
2 Choose a suitable style model. 'Suitable' is the key word here – make sure your model provides you with positive aspects of language use to imitate or adapt. If you choose a substandard or weak piece as a model, then the outcomes are likely to unsatisfactory. As the computer boffins sometimes observe, 'Garbage in, garbage out (GIGO).'
3 Examine the style model closely to gain insights into the sort of language techniques professional and/or experienced writers use in their production of the text.
4 Adapt or adopt some of the techniques for the new piece of writing.
5 Produce a first draft.

**Review**

In this section you have been given the opportunity to

- identify the many different opportunities for writing derived from everyday life
- recognise the four major purposes for writing
- familiarise yourself with a basic strategy or approach towards the production of your own texts.

# Writing to entertain

This is a very wide category. Don't be misled by the word 'entertain'. You don't have to make your audience laugh out loud – the term is used to describe any kind of writing that provides enjoyment to readers or even just holds their attention in a positive way. Some examples are

- travel writing
- extract from an autobiography
- dramatic monologue
- article for a magazine
- short story
- comedy sketch
- chapter from a novel
- drama script
- letter to a magazine
- story for a younger audience
- collection of verse.

How many different examples can you add to the list?

Many of these text types lend themselves easily to the A-level requirements for text production or original writing or whatever your exam board has entitled their unit. We will concentrate on and examine more closely a selection of these that will enable you to choose a writing assignment which

- is from a clearly identifiable genre or text type
- is clearly either literary or non-literary
- has a recognisable place in real life
- is for an identifiable target audience
- is capable of being produced convincingly within suggested word limits.

# Travel writing

If travel writing is to qualify as writing to entertain, then it must do more than just list where a place is, how to get there, what buildings can be seen, how visitors can be entertained and where they might stay. That may well be usefully informative, but it is hardly likely to provide enjoyment or hold readers' attention in a positive way. What is needed is a strong personal viewpoint on the place in question, with carefully chosen detail and if possible some lively comments to help the reader share some of the writer's opinions or at least to provoke a response. (If you feel more comfortable writing in a more specifically informative mode, you might like to try Activities 32–36, also related to travel and visiting different locations, in the Writing to Inform section – see page 200.)

American author Bill Bryson is a widely accepted master of this particular brand of travel writing and his well-known publications – including *Notes from a Small Island* (travels around the UK), *Neither Here nor There* (travels in Europe), *The Lost Continent* (travels in small-town America) – all contain wry observations about the many places he has visited throughout his life.

---

**Activity 3** | ## Travel writing – style model analysis

Read through the following extract from Bill Bryson's *Notes from a Small Island.* Write notes about the sorts of techniques that he is using in order to engage and entertain his readers. To make this process more straightforward, the paragraphs have been numbered, and some words and phrases have been underlined to draw your attention to them.

What effect do you think the author is trying to achieve?

A commentary is included on page 227, but you should complete your own version before consulting it. The commentary is not supposed to be a definitive list of techniques, and you may very well be able to spot further examples.

1 Bournemouth is a very fine place <u>in a lot of ways.</u> For one thing it has the sea, which will be handy if global warming ever reaches its full potential, though <u>I can't see much use for it at present,</u> and there are the <u>sinuous</u> parks, collectively known as the Pleasure Gardens, that neatly divide the two halves of the town centre and provide shoppers with <u>a tranquil green place</u> to rest on their long slog from one side of the centre to the other – though, of course, if <u>it weren't for the parks there wouldn't be the long slog.</u> Such is life.

2 The parks used to be described on maps as the Upper Pleasure Gardens and Lower Pleasure Gardens, but some councillor or other force for good realised the profound and unhealthy implications of placing Lower and Pleasure in such immediate proximity and

successfully lobbied to have Lower removed from the title, so now you have the Upper Pleasure Gardens and the mere Pleasure Gardens, and <u>lexical perverts</u> have been banished to the beaches where they must find such gratification as they can by rubbing themselves on the <u>groynes</u>. Anyway, that's the kind of place Bournemouth is – genteel to a fault and proud of it.

3    Knowing already of the town's carefully nurtured reputation for gentility, I moved there in 1977 with the idea that this was going to be a kind of English answer to Bad Ems or Baden-Baden – manicured parks, palm courts with orchestras, swank hotels where men in white gloves kept the brass gleaming, bosomy elderly ladies in mink coats walking those little dogs you ache to kick (not out of cruelty, you understand, but from a simple, honest desire to see how far you can make them fly). Sadly, I have to report that almost none of this awaited me. The parks were very fine, but instead of opulent casinos and handsome kursaals, they offered a small bandstand occupied on occasional Sundays by brass bands of mixed talent dressed like bus conductors, and small wooden erections – if you will excuse the term in the context of the Lower Pleasure Gardens – bedecked with coloured glass pots with a candle inside, which I was assured were sometimes lit on calm summer evenings and thus were transformed into glowing depictions of butterflies, fairies and other magical visions guaranteed to provide hours of healthy nocturnal enjoyment. I couldn't say because I never saw them lit, and in any case, a shortage of funds and the unconscionable tendency of youths to yank the pots from their frames and smash them at each other's feet for purposes of amusement meant that the structures were soon dismantled and taken away.

4    I strolled through the (Lower) Pleasure Gardens and on to the tourist information centre on Westover Road to see what alternative entertainments were on offer, and couldn't find out on account of you now had to pay for every piece of printed information that wasn't nailed to the wall. I laughed in their faces, of course.

5    At first glance, the town centre looked largely unchanged, but in fact progress and the borough council had been at work everywhere. Christchurch Road, the main thoroughfare through the centre, had been extensively pedestrianised and decorated with a curious glass and tubular steel edifice that looked like a bus shelter for giants. Two of the shopping arcades had been nicely tarted up and there was now a McDonald's, a Waterstone's and a Dillons, as well as one or two other establishments less directly connected to my personal requirements. Mostly, however, things had been subtracted. Beale's department store had closed its excellent book department, Dingle's had intemperately got rid of its food hall, and Bealeson's, yet another department store, had gone altogether. The International Store had likewise vanished, as had, more distressingly, an elegant little bakery, taking the world's best sugar doughnuts with it, alas, alas. On the plus side, there wasn't a scrap of litter to be found, whereas in my day Christchurch Road was an open-air litter bin.

6    Around the corner from the old vanished bakery on Richmond Hill were the splendid, vaguely art deco offices of the *Bournemouth Evening Echo,* where I worked for two years as a sub-editor in a room borrowed from a Dickens novel – untidy stacks of paper, gloomy lighting, two rows of hunched figures sitting at desks, and all of it bathed in a portentous, exhausting silence, the only noises the fretful scratchings of pencils and a soft but echoing *tunk* sound each time the minute hand on the wall clock clicked forward a notch.

Discuss Bryson's techniques and note down a few choice examples.

Throughout this piece, Bill Bryson produces a lively, humorous but critical view of an area of the country that he knows well. In order to do this, he uses a number of language techniques to create his account, including

- first-person narrative – he is there, observing, commenting
- mixed register – a combination of educated words and phrases and everyday conversational English
- selective detail – concentrating on the unusual, the nostalgic, the 'shared experiences', producing the impression of a guided tour
- *double entrendre* and innuendo – seeking approval through laddish humour
- extensive use of contrast – then/now, old/new
- suggesting approval or disapproval without explicitly stating his point of view.

## Activity 4    Your turn now

Now choose a place that you know well. It could be the town where you live, or where you go to school or college, or a familiar holiday resort. Imagine that you are revisiting this place in order to produce a 'Bill Bryson style' account. Describe your visit in such a way as to make sure that your readers will be able to share your opinions (positive or negative). You might like to make use some of the techniques identified above.

You could start off by simply outlining the basics of your visit.

- How did you get there?
- What was the first thing you saw?
- Where did you go next?
- Who did you see/meet?
- What else did you see?
- How did the visit end?

You could then pick up on some or all incidents and embroider them using your favourite techniques. The framework suggested by being a visitor or a tourist should allow you to adopt a logical structure of arrival – looking around – making observations – moving on, etc.

Although Bill Bryson uses some exaggerations, some quite pointed criticisms and some ironic observations in his views on the various places he visits, the underlying feeling his readers receive about these places is one of good-humoured comment with drawbacks and advantages of each location both mentioned. It is possible that the place you want to write about has few or even a complete lack of redeeming features! If this is the case, you could consider producing a text for a different audience in a different mode.

One such alternative would be to write a piece for a magazine such as the *Idler,* a bi-yearly British magazine 'devoted to promoting its ethos of "idle living" and all that entails'. It was founded in 1993 with the intention of exploring alternative ways of working and living – as a counter to the idea of the 'work ethic'. A regular column within the magazine is a semi-serious attempt to find Britain's worst places to live, called 'Crap Towns'. The audience for a piece like this can be judged by the editor's description of the magazine: 'The intention of the magazine is to return dignity to the art of loafing, to make idling into something to aspire towards rather than reject.' As well as providing a radical and thought-provoking read, the *Idler* is also very funny. Here is part of a 'Crap Towns' column that appeared in the *Idler* in 2003.

# CRAP TOWNS

Grimy Cleator Moor, grim Grantham and snobby Thorpeness come under fire. Go to www.idler.co.uk for the latest entries

### CLEATOR MOOR
**Population: 2,000**

THIS wild west Cumbrian town is a forgotten outcrop on a forgotten part of England, neglected since the Great Depression destroyed it almost 100 years ago. It most closely resembles the town in *Pale Rider* – after Clint Eastwood's killed nearly everyone, painted the houses red and renamed it Hell.

There is one long, infinitely desolate main street full of dangerous pubs, smashed up cars and heavily fortified shops. The few bored inhabitants drift around like tumbleweeds, looking for someone like YOU to hit. They're so hard that when they die they use them to hold up bridges. When they're alive they're more dangerous than sarin gas. And they have generations of anger to expend,

HELL

rightfully pissed off at the way no one has ever done anything to help them or their unhappy home.

The closest "outsiders" ever get to Cleator Moor is when they tramp within a mile of its boundaries on Wainwright's Coast To Coast walk. The famously straight talking creator of the walk advised anyone thinking of taking a diversion into the town to "abandon hope".   **"Billy Badmatches"**

### GRANTHAM
**Population: 33,000**

GRANTHAM, Oh Dear God, Grantham.

Truly there has never existed before such a heady concoction of boredom and inertia, such a malevolent mix of dilapidation

and depravity. When Milton wrote about about the crushing despair and misery of hell – it was clear that the poor man had heard of Grantham. It's true it has produced a clutch of famous characters; Margaret Thatcher, Isaac Newton, the first female police officer (already there is the distinctive sound of a barrel being scraped) but in the main, Grantham is fetid pile of dung.

The Earlsfield Estate has apparently got (or at least had) the highest crime rate per capita of any

| NOTES FROM THE COUCH |

council estate in the country. Some accolade. This is because of Grantham's oppresive boredom; there is nothing to do but go drinking under-age and commit violent crime. On a Friday night, large herds of 14 and 15 year olds roam the streets, trying to get served in the towns' numerous pubs. When they don't achieve this exorbitant goal, they turn on each other, which usually results in either hospitalisation, or another teenage pregnancy.

It is a town somewhat devoid of morals, but what truly defines its sense of worthlessness is the eagerness with which its inhabitants continuously talk of leaving. It was voted the most boring town in Britain on a poll conducted by a national radio station, and, despite the afore-mentioned luminaries, the best thing to come out of Grantham (as revealed in another poll) is apparently the A1.

Save yourselves: Don't Go There.     **David Finch**

### CRAP TOWN TRIVIA

Outside Grantham's Beehive pub, in Castlegate, is what's referred to by the tourist blurb as "The Living Sign". It's mentioned on a series of brown signposts dotted around the town. But it isn't a living sign. It's just a beehive stuck in tree. It's a real anti-climax when you find it.

IS THIS THE MOST BORING TOWN IN BRITAIN?

| Activity 5 | To produce a negative outlook on a familiar place |

Read through the 'Crap Towns' column carefully, focusing on the section about Grantham, and make notes on the techniques used by the writer to emphasise the negative aspects of Grantham. Give the paragraphs numbers, as for the Bill Bryson piece, to make the task more straightforward.

Choose a place familiar to you and use the same structures and techniques to construct a critical piece in the same style and of about the same length (250–300 words).

# Autobiography

Moderators and examiners often say that the most convincing writing from A-level students comes when they write about something that they know well and that is in their own sphere of experience – so the next activity should fit this bill admirably. The subject you know most about is you, especially your early life – you were there!

There are literally hundreds of autobiographies available for you to read – about sports and music stars, actors and politicians, broadcasters and charity workers, to name but a few. Hopefully you will be able to find a suitable style model. Remember the advice given earlier (GIGO!) and choose one which will act as a **good** example with techniques that are worth noting and adapting.

When you select an episode to write about, it is often helpful if the incident has a structure of its own, with an introduction, a central or main part, and a natural conclusion. The events of a day, or a journey, or a visit, for example, have their own internal structure which helps give shape to your writing.

It is also worth considering the sorts of experiences that your reading audience may also have been through themselves. There's nothing like shared laughter or pain to create empathy.

| Activity 6 | Producing a chapter from your autobiography |

First make a list of some memories from your life that come to mind easily – they're the ones that you will be able to recall in the level of detail required to entertain your readers. Put this list aside for later.

As in Activity 5, before you start constructing your chapter, you are going to look at a style model to see how it works, so that you can use it as a basis for your piece of writing. The subject-matter is something that we are all familiar with – 'First Day at School', from *Cider with Rosie* by Laurie Lee.

> One morning, out of the blue, my sisters wrapped me up in scarves, tied up my shoelaces, thrust a cap on my head and stuffed a baked potato into my pocket.
>
> 'What's going on?' I asked.
>
> 'You're starting school today, Loll.'

'Oh no I'm not! I'm staying at home!'

I burst into loud tears but my sisters picked me up, kicking and screaming, and carried me up the road towards the school.

I arrived at school. I was three feet tall and fatly wrapped in all my scarves. The potato was burning my thigh. The playground was like a war zone. Old boots, ragged stockings, torn trousers and skirts were skating and skidding around me.

Suddenly, the rabble closed in. Tall girls with frizzy hair and huge boys with sharp elbows surrounded me and began to poke and prod me. They plucked at my scarves, spun me round, screwed my nose and stole my potato.

Eventually, I was rescued by a teacher who led me off to the Infants' classroom. The room was filled with toys such as I had never seen before – coloured shapes and rolls of clay, stuffed birds, train sets and dolls for painting.

At the end of that first day, I went home in a smouldering temper.

'What's wrong with you then, Loll? Didn't you like school?'

'They never gave me the present!' I stormed.

'Present? What present?'

'They said they'd give me a present!'

'I'm sure they didn't. You must have made a mistake.'

'They did. They did. They said: "You're Laurie Lee, aren't you? Well you just sit there for the present." So I sat there all day but they never gave me the present! I'm not going back there again!'

It's quite obvious that this was written some time ago – the book was published in the late 1950s, and this extract refers to the author's early childhood round about the time of the First World War (1914–1918). In spite of the rather quaint and old-fashioned details (socks referred to as 'stockings' and having a baked potato as packed lunch), the types of experiences don't really seem to have changed that much in nearly a hundred years. So, you can use this as a style model for producing a chapter from your own autobiography.

Refer to your list of memories and select one which has left a really lasting impression. Make a copy of the template and fill in the details of your memorable day or occasion trying to use some of techniques suggested by the author.

| Laurie Lee's text | Your memorable occasion |
| --- | --- |
| The first and earliest thing that he remembered about his first day at school | |
| Conversation with family members. Makes his feelings clear? | |
| Journey to school – most vivid memories? Eager anticipation or impending doom? | |

Arrival. First impressions. Description of physical surroundings including similes, metaphors. Effects on senses, what he saw heard, smelled felt, etc.

First contacts with strangers. Positive or negative?

The 'official' day begins. Description of activities. Selective use of detail

End of day – reporting his feelings and attitudes to family members – more use of dialogue

Summing up – overview looking back at day

After you have completed your template, you can then produce a first draft, full of your own details and memories. It is generally helpful at this stage if you can share your writing with other members of the group or even someone who was there at the time. Feedback like this can help you refine and improve both the level of detail and the impact your writing has.

# Writing dramatic monologues

The next style model is an extract from 'Her Big Chance' – a dramatic monologue by Alan Bennett, from his collection *Talking Heads*.

The main feature of a dramatic monologue is that it tells a story entirely from the side of and in the voice of the narrator, and generally the narrator is unreliable. He or she doesn't always fully understand what is going on in the story, and there is often a great deal going on that he or she is not totally aware of. In 'Her Big Chance', Lesley, the narrator, mistakenly thinks she has a great deal to offer both as an actress and as a person, but the audience quickly sees that she is shallow, has very limited dramatic ability, and doesn't realise that she is constantly being taken advantage of.

## Activity 7 | Dramatic monologue – style model analysis

Read the extract and see if you can identify techniques that Alan Bennett is using to achieve his dramatic effects. Make a note of these techniques. The paragraphs have been numbered to provide easy reference points.

Compare your notes with the commentary on page 228.

> **Lesley is in her early thirties. She is in her flat. Morning.**
>
> 1  I shot a man last week. In the back. I miss it now, it was really interesting. Still, I'm not going to get depressed about it. You have to look to the future. To have something like that under your belt can be quite useful, you never know when you might be called on to repeat the experience.
>
> 2  It wasn't in the line of duty. I wasn't a policewoman or someone who takes violence in their stride. It was with a harpoon gun actually, but it definitely wasn't an accident. My decision to kill was arrived at only after a visible tussle with my conscience. I had to make

it plain that once I'd pulled the trigger things were never going to be the same again: this was a woman at the crossroads.

3 It wasn't Crossroads, of course. They don't shoot people in Crossroads, at any rate not with harpoon guns. If anybody did get shot it would be with a weapon more suited to the motel ambience. I have been in Crossroads though, actually. I was in an episode involving a fork lunch. At least I was told it was a fork lunch, the script said it was a finger buffet. I said to the floor manager, I said, 'Rex. Are you on cans because I'd like some direction on this point. Are we toying or are we tucking in?' He said, 'Forget it. We're losing the food anyway.' I was playing Woman in a Musquash Coat, a guest at a wedding reception, and I was scheduled just to be in that one episode. However in my performance I tried to suggest I'd taken a fancy to the hotel in the hope I might catch the director's eye and he'd have me stay on after the fork lunch for the following episode which involved a full-blown weekend. So I acted an interest in the soft furnishings, running my fingers over the formica and admiring the carpet on the walls. Only Rex came over to say that they'd put me in a musquash coat to suggest I was a sophisticated woman, could I try and look as if I was more at home in a three star motel. I wasn't at home in that sort of motel I can tell you. I said to the man I'd been put next to, who I took to be my husband, I said, 'Curtains in orange nylon and no place mats, there's not even the veneer of civilisation.' He said, 'Don't talk to me about orange nylon. I was on a jury once that sentenced Richard Attenborough to death.' We'd been told to indulge in simulated cocktail chit-chat so we weren't being unprofessional, talking. That is something I pride myself on, actually: I am professional to my fingertips.

4 Whatever it is I'm doing, even if it's just a walk-on, I must, must, <u>must</u> get involved, right up to the hilt. I can't help it. People who know me tell me I'm a very serious person, only it's funny, I never get to do serious parts. The parts I get offered tend to be fun-loving girls who take life as it comes and aren't afraid of a good time should the opportunity arise-type-thing. I'd call them vivacious if that didn't carry overtones of the outdoor life. In a nutshell I play the kind of girl who's very much at home on a bar stool and who seldom has to light her own cigarette. That couldn't be more different from me because for a start I'm not a smoker. I mean, I can smoke if a part requires it. I'm a professional and you need as many strings to your bow as you can in this game. But, having said that, I'm not a natural smoker and what's more I surprise my friends by not being much of a party-goer either. (Rather curl up with a book quite frankly.) *However,* this particular party I'd made an exception. Thing was I'd met this ex-graphic designer who was quitting the rat race and going off to Zimbabwe and he was having a little farewell do in the flat of an air hostess friend of his in Mitcham, would I go? I thought, well it's not every day you get somebody going off to Zimbabwe, so I said 'Yes' and I'm glad I did because that's how I got the audition.

To be able to produce a dramatic monologue of your own, you need to provide two basic ingredients:

● a character (to tell the story)
● a story for the character to tell.

Working though the three following activities will help you construct a dramatic monologue of your own.

## Activity 8

**Group work**

# Constructing a character

This activity can be adapted to match however many students there are in the group. Each participant should make or be given a copy of the template.

| | |
|---|---|
| What is the character's name? | |
| What is his/her age? | |
| Where does he/she come from? | |
| Trade/profession/occupation? | |
| Describe his/her clothing. | |
| Where do we meet this character? | |
| How does he/she speak? Accent? | |
| Level of education? | |
| What items of equipment/props are associated with this character? | |
| How does he/she spend his/her time? | |
| Name one thing he/she is particularly keen on. | |
| Name one thing he/she absolutely hates. | |

To work effectively, this activity must be carried out at a rapid pace.

1. Each person starts by filling in the top row of their template.
2. On a signal they pass it to the next person in the group.
3. The next person fills in the second row and passes the template on.
4. The process continues until the grid has been completely filled.
5. Each completed grid is passed back to the person who wrote in the character's name.

Furnished with all the background information on your grid, you should be able to form a picture of a central character. Obviously, with all the different contributors, you may not be able to incorporate all the suggestions, but you should have plenty of material to work on. Put this aside for later – you will need it for Activity 9.

When you are working out the story that your character is going to tell, remember that the dramatic monologue has its own particular characteristics.

- The reader takes the part of the silent listener.
- The speaker uses an authoritative, often argumentative tone, putting forward exclusively his/her side of the story. There is no-one there to argue with him or her, so the viewpoint is essentially one sided.
- The reader completes the dramatic scene from within, by means of inference and imagination, often seeing more than the speaker appears to be offering.

| Activity 9 | Constructing a story |

Choose one of the following openings (or one of your own) and write a paragraph, in the voice of your chosen character, incorporating as much information suggested by your completed grid from Activity 8 as you can.

- We had a spot of excitement yesterday …
- Once upon a time I thought I had my life planned out, but …
- Thinking about it afterwards, I realised …
- I felt such a fool …
- You'll never believe what happened today …

By the time you have written a paragraph, you should know if it is working. If possible, read your paragraph aloud to other members of the group – they should be able to tell you if it is on the right lines.

Once you have firmed up the details of the character and the subject-matter, it might help to make a brief bullet-pointed summary of the main events of the story. This should help you to

- make sure that you tell the whole story – and not just record the random thoughts of the narrator
- make sure that there is a proper ending and that the monologue doesn't just fade out purposelessly!

| Activity 10 | Analysing a student monologue |

Here is an example of a student's monologue, submitted as a part of a coursework folder. Read it through a couple of times, then jot down a bullet-pointed summary of the story.

Compare the original and the bullet-pointed summary. You should be able to see how, by presenting the incidents solely from the point of view of the narrator, the student has produced a totally one-sided version.

### Just Another Conquest

*Sylvia is a brisk woman in her early seventies. She is wearing a smart black twin set and pearls. She is sitting in a chintz armchair, a hat on an occasional table next to her. It is late afternoon.*

SYLVIA

An odd time, three o'clock. I've always thought so. Too early for tea and too late for lunch, but I suppose if it's there you feel obliged to eat it. They'd put on a nice enough spread, though: Quiche Lorraine, salads, you know the type of thing. Buffet. Bit plain, perhaps. Mind you, they'd put a trifle at the end of the table. I mean, I ask you, trifle at a wake? Rather vulgar, I thought. Poor sod didn't even like the stuff, so God knows why it was there. Needless to say, there wasn't much of it gone when I'd left. Didn't stay too long. Thought it best to make a swift retreat, otherwise I'd have been spotted by Valerie and have never escaped.

The service was nice enough. Didn't go on too long. I've been to some funerals that went on for what seemed like hours. It's probably the hymns. We had the usual fare today; 'I vow to thee my country' and 'Jerusalem', except you could barely hear them over the wailing in the front pew. Honestly, the way she was going on, you'd think you were in India. Funerals go on for days there. Lots of crying and boo-hooing and all that carry on. It's not for me. Grief ought to be something private and dignified, not a public display. When my Leonard died, God rest him, I barely wept at the funeral. I couldn't, not with all them people watching me. *(Pause)* I wouldn't have minded today except for the fact that he'd only been married to this one for barely two months. She's a good fifty years his junior. Bet he's left her a substantial amount in the will, if not all of it. That's all she is, a gold digger. Mind you, he might surprise us yet. We'll see in the morning. I got told today he left me a little something, so I'm to go along to the house and listen to it being read out. Bet they serve up left-over trifle.

*Go to black*

*Come up on Sylvia sitting at the kitchen table, a cigarette in her hand, a statuette and a cameo brooch placed in front of her on the table. Lunchtime.*

The filthy bugger. 'The Ecstasy of St. Ethelburga' it's called, according to the solicitor, who couldn't have been more than twelve by my reckoning. Apparently, it's to remind me of our 'fun times'. I got some funny looks. I can tell you. Trust Brendan to leave me something that I won't be able to find a place for. I mean, look at it. It's not at all fit to sit next to my Beswickware. If I wanted pornographic figurines, I would have bought some a long time ago.

*She examines the figurine closely.*

I didn't know people could bend that way. At any rate, I certainly won't be able to now. Not at my age. Pity.

I'm surprised he remembered, actually. I was just one of his many conquests. He could barely keep it in his trousers, the randy old sod. Mind you, I didn't exactly say no. Too many Vodka Gimlets. Of course, I hadn't had anything the next time or the next for that matter. I suppose you could say we had an affair. We didn't think so at the time. It was just something that happened. Leonard never found out, mind. *(Pause)* Over thirty years ago, now. It was all rather thrilling.

That still doesn't excuse this thing *(indicating the ornament)*. I'll have to hide it in the airing cupboard or something. The brooch is nice enough though. You don't often see cameo brooches nowadays. Mother-of-Pearl casing by my reckoning. Pretty little thing.

Turns out that he hadn't left all the money to Chantelle, or whatever her name is. She got the house, but the money wasn't really mentioned. Perhaps he got rid of it before he died, one last joke to the world. He was always one for a joke was Brendan. And a bit of slap and tickle.

*Go to black*

*Come up on Sylvia, seated in the chintz armchair as before. She is wearing a smart dress with the cameo brooch. She is surrounded by storage boxes. She has a glass, possibly containing a Vodka Gimlet. It is early evening.*

I don't usually watch *Antiques Roadshow*. I came across it by chance, as it happened. Anyway, this man came on with a similar figurine to mine. Of course, they didn't show it at the correct angle, or full frontal, as it were, but this is the BBC we're talking about, not Channel 4. The excitement wasn't poking into the camera, shall we say, but I'd have known it anywhere. You don't forget about a thing like that in a hurry. The valuer, Tim Wonnacott I think he was called, funny little man, said that he never thought he would ever see one of these things in his career. Apparently, they're a set of three, so there's two more to mine knocking around. Commissioned by the Duke of Marchpane, whoever he was, who apparently was quite fond of erotica in art. Some obscure Italian sculptor made them for him, but the set was broken up and lost around eighty years ago. Worth quite a pretty penny, too. £500,000. Half a million pounds for each of the filthy things. So, of course, I get myself down to Sotheby's and they were all quite excited over Ethelburga's excitement, and she certainly realised her potential at the sale. I don't know what Mother would have thought; she was in the Salvation Army.

I've always wanted a bungalow. Leonard never did, though. Always said 'what's wrong with this place?' What was right with it, more like. The draughts, I used to tell him. And the amount of dust it collects. I'm forever dusting. Of course, I shan't have to now. This house is far too big for me on my own, and I shan't have to take the ashes out of the grate anymore, either. I'm going to have central heating. This time tomorrow, I'll be Mrs. Sylvia Bennett of The Grove, with central heating throughout and a fully automated Jacuzzi hot tub.

Went past Brendan's house today on my way to the Post Office. 'For Sale' sign out front. I looked over the privet and saw two men shifting furniture into a transit van. According to Valerie, Brendan had squandered all of his money before he passed on. Just left Chantelle with a pile of debts, apparently. I almost felt sorry for her, but her type just carry on. They always do. She's one of those who's into `OIL': 'Old, Ill and Loaded'. She'll find somebody new to bleed dry, somebody a bit more gullible than Brendan. But not too soon, hopefully.

If I'm having a hot tub, I'm going to need a bikini. Give Brendan something to stare down at, the dirty so and so.

*Fade out*

## Activity 11 · Writing a monologue

Now write your own monologue, using the information you have gained from Activities 8–10.

# Writing a magazine feature

This section looks at how to produce a piece suited to a particular magazine. Every Sunday, an article entitled 'A Life in the Day of…' appears in the colour supplement magazine of the *Sunday Times*.

It is a deceptively simple idea; people from all walks of life – male or female, old or young, famous or unheard of, rich or poor – give an account of what they get up to on a single day in their life. If it was just a simple list of events, a piece like this would be neither demanding enough to allow you to show how good your writing skills are, nor interesting enough to keep your audience engaged.

In fact, what the best of these articles do is to use the frame or structure of a typical day to allow the writer to express and explain their thoughts and feelings about a number of issues suggested by the events and occurrences that make up the day. For example, we might find out more about the writer's

- dreams, hopes and ambitions
- likes and dislikes and the reasons for them
- family and friends and how important they are
- interests in and attitudes towards wider issues.

It is by commenting on the incidents and occurrences of everyday life that the writer engages with the audience.

## Activity 12 — Analysing a style model

Read through the following style model and see if you can identify which parts are narrative (storytelling) and which parts are comments on the issues suggested by the events of the day. It is 'A Life in the Day of Frank Lampard' that appeared in the *Sunday Times* in October 2005. The paragraphs have been numbered to provide reference points.

Next, copy the grid and fill it in with the details of the article. Note the balance between events and comments. Some of the boxes have been filled to give you a start.

| Paragraph | Time | Event | Issue /Comment |
|---|---|---|---|
| 1 | Before 8 | | |
| 2 | 8 am | | |
| 3 | | | |
| 4 | 8.45 | | |
| 5 | 10.30 | Training | |
| 6 | | | Relationships with wife and baby |
| 7 | Afternoon | | Relationships with parents |
| 8 | Afternoon | | |
| 9 | Evening | | |
| 10 | Bedtime | Bedtime routine | |

*The Chelsea and England footballer lives in Chelsea with his Spanish fiancée, Elen, their baby daughter, Luna, and their French mastiff, Daphne.*

1 The alarm on my mobile is set for 8, but with the baby I'm often already awake. At the moment we've got a maternity nurse helping Elen, but once she goes, I'm sure things

will get a lot earlier, a lot more hectic. Right now I've got about three-quarters of an hour before I leave for training. I don't bother showering. I just freshen up, stick on jeans and trainers, let the dog out and get her food. Daphne's a french mastiff – like the one in that movie *Turner & Hooch*. She slobbers a bit, but she's got a beautiful face.

2  Breakfast is usually a mug of strong English-breakfast tea and a bowl of Coco Pops. If I get bored, the Frosties come out. But I always go back to Coco Pops – I've been having them since I was a kid. We get the *Sun*, *Mirror* and *Daily Mail* delivered, so I usually have a quick flick through and then set off in the car – a blue Aston Martin – for the training ground in Cobham.

3  I'll turn on the radio or listen to music. I like U2 and Coldplay, but James Blunt's single 'You're Beautiful' has really stuck in my head of late. Being in the middle of a season, the sessions aren't too heavy. There are days when it's harder to motivate yourself – you're tired or have things on your mind, but on the whole I enjoy it. I'm a bit of a fitness fanatic, anyway. I got that from my father. He played for West Ham.

4  I wanted to be a footballer for as long as I can remember. It was all I thought about. But right from the start, Dad drummed it into me that as well as practice you had to be fit. So from quite a young age I'd go off with him on his two- or three-mile runs around Romford, Essex, where we lived. It paid off. By 13, I was good enough to train with two or three different professional clubs after school. I was a day pupil at a private school in Brentwood and I was determined to do well there too. I got nine O-levels, including two As and an A-star, and my teachers wanted me to go on and do A-levels. But if I was going to make a real go of the football, I knew I couldn't. Sometimes I think that if I hadn't made it as a footballer, I'd quite like to have been a lawyer.

5  Training lasts about an hour and a half, then it's in the shower and lunch. I eat at the grounds, where they do things like pastas, salads, meat, chicken and fish. There's not much I don't like when it comes to food, and there aren't too many rules about what we should and shouldn't eat. But obviously, for extra energy, I tend to load up with more carbs a couple of days before a game. After lunch I try to keep my days clear, so I can head back home to Elen and the baby. But I do a bit of charity work and I'm currently involved in the Tesco Sport for Schools & Clubs scheme, which is aimed at inspiring kids to take up a sport.

6  Luna's still only two months old, but I've already bought her first Chelsea outfit. I even got her a shirt with No 8 on the back – the full works. When I got it I didn't show Elen, I just rushed upstairs and put it on Luna. When I came down and Elen saw her, she said: 'She's not going out of the house dressed like that!' I love singing nursery rhymes to Luna. The only thing is, I can't remember most of the words, so I have to make them up.

7  In the afternoon, Mum often pops round for a cup of tea. Her and Dad have bought a place in London, which is great, and also means they're at all the games. I'm very close to Mum – a real mummy's boy, to be honest. We're very similar. Quite sensitive, quite shy. Whereas Dad's been the big influence on my career, Mum's been the one who shaped me as a person: you know, how to treat people, manners, that kind of thing. These days she juggles a lot of her time between me and my two older sisters, as they've also got little girls.

8   I'll usually take Daphne out for a walk or a run. Or sometimes I'll go out shopping. Occasionally I'll have a blast. The other day I bought a couple of lovely Yves Saint Laurent suits in Sloane Street, and this belt is from Dolce & Gabbana. I'm not really into buying the latest gadgets, but I do appreciate something like a good watch. The one I'm wearing is an Audemars Piguet – a limited-edition Montoya. Sometimes we'll all drive out to a country village, maybe go looking for antiques – I love old furniture. We've only been in our house about six months, so we're still looking for things. One of my favourite pieces is a study table from eastern Europe.

9   Elen and I go out for a meal a couple of times a week, but we eat in the rest of the time. I've got a thing for M&S's chicken in breadcrumbs at the minute. So it'll be something like that with jacket potato and salad. Elen mainly does the cooking, but occasionally I'll throw a few bits together – maybe a pasta with tomato, chilli and garlic. Normally it comes out okay – not always. Then we might relax in front of the telly. I love things like *The Sopranos* and I confess to getting addicted to things like *Big Brother* and *The X Factor*. But if it's something like *Question Time*, I just end up shouting at the box.

10  Before bed I'll let the dog out, do the lights, the alarm and then I might read for a while. I recently finished *The Da Vinci Code*, and Roy Keane's autobiography, which was a great insight into the footballer. Sometimes, when I think about all those dreams I had as a kid and where I am now, I have to pinch myself. The hard work, the determination, the sacrifices – they all paid off. Life right now couldn't be sweeter.

## Activity 13    Your turn now

Draw up a grid as in Activity 12 and fill in the time and the event columns with the details of one of your days. Select some of the events which will allow you to reflect on the kinds of issues listed at the beginning of this subsection.

Use your grid to write up a full-length draft. Try to maintain a balance between just outlining what you do, and commenting on its wider significance. Your piece should then fit the requirement of writing for a particular publication at a suitable length and in a suitable register. If you decide that it is worth submitting, you could investigate an edition of the *Sunday Times* magazine and imitate the exact layout, complete with title, introduction and picture.

# Narrative writing

The longest standing and most enduring type of imaginative writing is storytelling. We are all very familiar with novels, short stories, all the various types of plays and quite a few poems. The vast majority of literature amounts to narrative writing, so it is hardly surprising that many students choose to include a short story in their coursework folder and some exam specifications insist on one.

If you are considering writing a short story, be warned – it sounds a great deal easier than it often turns out to be in reality! There are so many different types that can be used as style models, so many possible outlets for the end result and so many different possible target audiences that it is a well-nigh-impossible task to present a universal template for successful short-story writing. There are, however, some general pointers that can be used to encourage you to make the most of your ventures into this genre.

First of all, let's take a look at what makes a good story. We'll try the by now familiar process of dissecting a specimen of what we're studying to see what makes it work.

## Activity 14  The features of a story

Read through this miniature story from *Cider with Rosie*, by Laurie Lee, and make notes on what its essentials really boil down to. What exactly makes it into a story?

> Once there lived a lovelorn blacksmith. For years he had loved a local spinster, but he was shy, as most blacksmiths are. The spinster, who eked out a poor existence by boiling and selling toffee, was also lonely, in fact desperate for a husband, but too modest and proud to seek one. With the years the spinster's desperation grew, as did the blacksmith's speechless passion.
>
> Then one day the spinster stole into the church and threw herself down on her knees. 'O Lord!' she prayed, 'please be mindful of me, and send me a man to marry!' Now the blacksmith by chance was up in the belfry, mending the old church clock. Every breathless word of the spinster's entreaties rose clearly to where he was. When he heard her praying, 'Please send me a man!' he nearly fell off the roof with excitement. But he kept his head, tuned his voice to Jehovah's, and boomed 'Will a blacksmith do?'
>
> 'Ern a man's better than nern, dear Lord!' cried the spinster gratefully.
>
> At which the blacksmith ran home, changed into his best, and caught the spinster on her way out of church. He proposed, and they married, and lived forever contented, and used his forge for boiling their toffee.

Once you have established some basic considerations, it is time to try your hand at some exercises designed to sharpen some of your story-writing skills.

## Activity 15  Serial writing

**Class work**

This is a class exercise designed to produce awareness of the importance of the 'what happens next' element in storytelling.

Work in groups of four and give each member a number – 1, 2, 3 or 4. Each of you takes a starter sentence below corresponding to their allocated number, and writes it down.

1  Steve/Steph raced to the rescue, but would he/she be in time? …
2  There it was again. She/He got up to investigate and …
3  George/Georgia struggled wildly, but it was no good …
4  If I had known what was going to happen, I would never have gone there in the first place …

For exactly 5 minutes, you each write a melodramatic narrative episode based on your starter sentence. The primary object is to keep the reader guessing about what will happen next. Towards the end of the 5 minutes, you should manoeuvre their character(s) into a climactic, 'cliffhanging' predicament, the more seemingly impossible the better. The first episode thus ends with the suspenseful problem.

Next number 1 passes their episode to number 2 in their group, 2 passes theirs to number 3, 3 passes theirs to 4, and 4 passes theirs to number 1 in the next group, and so on round the class.

Each writer reads the first episode they have been given then writes for another 5 minutes, adding a second episode to the previous one. Once again, the aim is suspense, and the new episode should once again end with a 'cliffhanger'.

When the 5 minutes is up, all stories are passed on again, and the procedure is repeated.

Finally, the fourth episode is written. This time, each writer takes the story before them to the final climax, and ends the story by resolving the essential problem one way or the other. A surprise ending, or at least a very dramatic finale, is invaluable.

Now, all stories are returned to the initial writers, and the results are discussed. Thoughtful analysis in this exercise will yield very useful insights into the basic problems of story-writing.

## Activity 16

**Individual**
**Group work**

## Story writing – it's a problem!

As either an individual or a group exercise one or more of these improvised stories could be drafted more fully.

- Decide upon a character or characters (keep the number down).
- Invent a problem which is plausible in terms of the character, and set up a series of events which move away from, then towards, resolution of the problem.

## Activity 17

## Short story writing – style model analysis

Find a short story you consider to be successful and analyse it in terms of

- character and motivation
- plot
- structural qualities/unities.

This should provide a fertile basis for class or group discussion.

## The big problem of story-writing

We have defined in a simple way what we are talking about in discussing stories. But how do you 'make up' one? Where do you get it from?

Writers draw their material from real life. People they have known (or just seen in the street), situations or relationships they have witnessed or heard of, intensely felt themes, places or events which suggest possibilities for fictional invention: these are the starting-points of fictional storytelling. Of course, they are no more than starting-points. The successful story-writer creates his/her story by inventing other characters, events, themes and so on which give structure and meaning to the original idea. What starts as an observation of life becomes 'art'.

A very significant feature which ultimately governs this process of fictional 'growth' is credibility. That is to say, if readers can accept and/or identify with the characters or setting or sequence of actions then they should be able to believe that whatever occurrence suggested by you – the writer – *might* well have happened. Even quite exotic imaginings (the stories of Roald Dahl, for example) become fictionally 'true', if what happens is believable within the framework of expectations set up by character and situation. On the other hand, even quite ordinary happenings seem phoney and unconvincing if they violate the readers' expectations. In storytelling, lie as hard as you like – invent what you want provided that within the world of the characters' situation, it *might* have happened.

Real life and experience are the starting-points and the yardstick for the fictional storyteller. If you lose sight of this and invent too wildly or invent plots that are too convoluted and complicated, your story will become so blatantly unlike 'reality' that the reader will stop 'believing'; when this happens the story is dead. All the clever tricks that good writers can use to 'improve' on real life do not affect this basic truth – stories, above all other forms of creative writing, must appear to imitate reality.

## Further activities to encourage story-writing

### Activity 18 | Story writing based on character

Take a real person whom you know or have met or have seen and who has made a real impression on you. Invent or adapt a situation, action or relationship which is somehow typical of this character's nature – for example, rivalry, disagreement, attraction.

Develop some sort of expectation based on this situation – a conflict to be resolved, for instance – and satisfy it one way or another, again in line with the character's essential nature.

Write this up in conventional story form.

### Activity 19 | Story writing based on conflict situations

Take a real person you know and place them in an invented but not improbable situation, such as

- having a different spouse
- facing a situation in which their fears/prejudices are confronted
- losing their job
- having an accident which radically alters their lifestyle
- winning the lottery jackpot
- becoming involved in some extremist or activist cause – animal rights, religious extremism, eco-warrior.

Develop a story which arises out of the inevitable conflict between the person's nature and the situation you have created.

# Important ingredients of successful stories

### Conflict

Conflicts are very good subject-matter for stories. The conflict may be

- between two or more people
- between people and natural forces
- between individuals and groups/society
- between different aspects of one person's nature.

Regardless of their form, conflicts generate dramatic interest: they not only arouse the reader's interest, but are invaluable for bringing out character and setting off action. Indeed conflict is one of the fascinating aspects of the human condition. It is at the heart of most people's problems, and of nearly all good stories!

### Plot

The author E. M. Forster wrote

'A plot is ... a narrative of events, the emphasis falling on causality. "The king died and then the queen died," is a story. "The king died, and then the queen died of grief," is a plot. The time-sequence is preserved, but the sense of causality overshadows it.'

A plot explains why the story develops in the way it does. In Laurie Lee's story in Activity 13, the blacksmith gained the heart of the spinster because he was a fast thinker and a good mimic. Stories which have no plot (stories in which events happen without apparent reason) fail to satisfy because they go against one of the basic assumptions that we all make about experience – that things happen for a reason.

In real life, experience can be a bit like a maze; we often don't know why or how something has happened. But a good story can clarify experience. A good story acts as a guide through the maze so that the pattern is clear.

Of course, the plot does not constitute the whole story. But in general it is like a body's skeleton shaping and supporting the story. Plots aren't always simple and they don't have to be blatant. But they should be there.

## Activity 20 | Resolving complications

Consider a character (preferably based on someone you know, perhaps the person you used in Activity 18 or 19) in a specific setting. Create for the character some sort of complication, such as

- being wrongly accused of something
- not being able to find something on which they rely
- meeting interference from someone else
- being prevented from doing something by some difficulty or disaster such as an accident.

Have the character struggle in vain against the complication, until a moment of crisis is reached, then invent a solution.

Repeat this sequence once or twice more, then finish the story by resolving once and for all the series of complications.

## Conclusions on story-writing

Do not underestimate the difficulties associated with writing short stories. Before undertaking this genre, you need to able to

- create or re-create experience, primarily through the power of your imagination
- adopt suitable means of expression – description, narrative, dramatisation, dialogue, etc.
- engage and maintain the interest of your selected audience
- bring the piece to a satisfying conclusion.

None of this is likely to just happen when you pick up your pen or switch on your computer, so in addition to following the advice in this section, you will probably need to

- read plenty of examples of short stories (especially those aimed at the same sort of audience that you are aiming at)
- 'road test' your writing by allowing others (especially those who might be in your chosen target audience) to read and respond to it
- be prepared to draft and redraft in response to reader feedback.

# Writing poetry

Poetry is arguably the most complex and is almost certainly the most dreaded area of imaginative writing – at least by markers and moderators of original or creative writing coursework! Why should this be?

The answer is probably something to do with the fact that writing poetry is an elusive and intensely private creative act. Inspiration (the spontaneous overflow of powerful feelings) is widely regarded as the starting-point for poetry – a claim less frequently made for prose and dramatic writing, and almost never for formal non-fiction writing. Poetry has had over the centuries, and still retains, an aura of creative mystery. Poetry is the most precisely concentrated of all literary forms.

This all makes poetry a difficult form to include in a coursework folder. Most people recognise that poetry has its special ways of picturing reality. Most people can respond to these qualities in the same way as many respond to good music, but poetry is often such an intensely personal means of expression that it is difficult to judge in the same way as other forms of writing.

So, how can we use what we already know or have picked up from other forms of writing to begin to master this complex form? First, by taking advice from US poet Robert Frost and starting to write poetry straight away. Secondly, by working, one by one, through the areas which make poetry special.

## Inspiration

We are going to take an emotional response, write it down, see what it looks like, clarify, extend or contract it, then rework it until we're happy with it.

What do we write about? What inspires us? In general, we are inspired by things which carry a considerable amount of emotion, such as

- strong feelings – love, hate, fear, disgust, admiration, or the things that inspire them
- strong beliefs – religious, political, social and/or personal
- personal interests – music, children, sports, hobbies, special causes
- favourite objects or places
- special experiences – holidays, bereavement, forming new or breaking old relationships, struggles, discoveries, understandings.

## Activity 21 — Poetry writing – personal feelings

Think very carefully about a place or person or object that means a great deal to you. Then try to find words to express that feeling. Begin where you like and just write down your impressions as they come to you, in any order. Gradually build up a picture of the subject that you can share with others.

When you have recorded all your thoughts and impressions, leave it for a while – at least a day, possibly up to a week.

Then go back to your writing. Refine it and articulate it until you feel you have an entire poem. Then share it with one or more people – listen to their impressions, take note of their questions, and if necessary redraft your piece.

## Activity 22 — Committee poem

**Group work**

Form groups of between three and five students. Each group then chooses a topic that appeals to all (or most) members. This could be a person, a place, a feeling.

As a joint brainstorming exercise, work up a list of all the feelings, images, qualities you attach to the topic. Divide a page into two columns and write your list in the first column. Now find words and phrases to describe each of these, and write them in the second column.

Rough out your poem, using appropriate words/phrases from your lists. Discuss improvements, restructure it, refine the details, etc.

Type up a fair copy and discuss the product with the rest of the class. Take note of feedback and redraft if necessary.

This process can also be used by an individual to construct a poem.

## Imagery – the pictures a poem makes

What makes poetry different from most other forms of writing is its striking ability to recreate experiences or feelings; to paint a picture in words as fresh and tangible as the real thing. Poetry works primarily through images. The following activity can help to support this.

## Activity 23 — By association

Words have built-in suggestions of approval or otherwise (connotations) which the writer can use to create an image.

Make a table with two columns, headed 'Positive' and 'Negative', and use it to sort the following adjectives according to the associations they suggest to you. Add further words of your own.

- thunderous
- wispy
- callous
- slithering
- imperious

- radiant
- knife-like
- slimy
- sensuous
- glint-eyed

- honeyed
- spongy
- tyrannous
- rumbling
- passionate

- velvet
- blue-eyed
- magical

Apply each word to an object, a thought, a feeling or a person, a place, etc., with which you would not normally associate it. Then try to assess the impact that it now has.

This is a technique that many poets use to great effect. The best way to appreciate it and many other poetic techniques is to read for yourself the work of outstanding poets. There are far too many to name in a book of this sort – just look in anthologies and find out what makes an impression on you.

## Activity 24

**Individual**
**Group work**

## Use your senses

This can work as either an individual or a group exercise. Each person or group selects a topic rich in sight, sound, scent or touch potential, such as

- The sea
- Rush hour
- A summer evening

- Children at play
- The fight
- Hard at work.

Try to visualise the scene in as much detail as possible. Write down words and phrases that come into your head as you 'observe' it, especially how it affects each of your senses. Set a time limit for visualising each theme – say 5 minutes in the first instance.

Next, re-order and revise the words and phrases – perhaps combining them or adding unexpected or unusual descriptive words and phrases (see Activity 22). Try them out on other members of the group and receive and act on feedback.

Retain copies of all the stages of production to act as evidence, just in case you produce something that impresses you enough to constitute a viable piece of coursework.

# The range of poetry

We have looked at why people write poetry, and we have studied some of its special qualities. Finally, what can you write poetry about? There used to be a well-entrenched belief that you should write poetry only about 'pretty' subjects, like flowers, sunsets and children. But is that true?

D.H. Lawrence considered that 'the essence of poetry … is stark directness'. For the Romantics (Wordsworth, Shelley, Keats and the others), poetry was tied up in the beauty of nature, while for T.S. Eliot, it was about the soullessness of modern life. Poetry is a literary tool, endowed with very special power, by which virtually any vision of the world can be expressed.

So you can write poetry about virtually anything. For every identifiable category of writing in general, there is a poetic equivalent: narrative, descriptive, expository, autobiographical, assertive, analytical, instructive, dramatic, documentary, satirical, gently humorous, etc. Look through a few good anthologies and you'll find them all there.

That's a good piece of advice to end on. Probably more than most other branches of literature, poetry repays close study. Such is its conciseness and precision of expression that you can learn a great deal very quickly.

Read it, write it, and watch yourself improve.

---

**Activity 25** | ## Experiment with the poetic 'voice'

Pick a subject, preferably one you know and care about, then write about it in verse using 'voices' from any two of these five categories

1  impersonal, neutral
2  impassioned, pleading
3  ritualistic
4  intimate, personal, emotional
5  ironic, witty, mocking

When you have finished, compare the different effects that can be achieved by varying the poetic voice.

---

### Postscript: poetic forms

If you are interested in the more formal patterning conventions of poetry (haiku, blank verse, quatrains, couplets, sonnets, and all the rest), look them up in a literary companion, ask a teacher to go into detail or turn to page 18 for a short introduction to rhyme and metre. This section does not attempt to cover them, because there are so many, and because they are of doubtful use to most student writers.

Indeed, a word of warning needs to be sounded: until you are very experienced in the writing of verse, even seemingly simple conventions like rhyme can be quite unexpectedly treacherous – rhyme could lead you into using words that completely derail your meaning, or reduce it to anticlimax and/or unintended hilarity. Just read the following verse by Scottish 'poet' William Topaz McGonagal.

> Torquay lies in a very deep and well-sheltered spot,
> And at first sight by strangers it won't be forgot;
> 'Tis said to be the mildest place in all England,
> And surrounded by lofty hills most beautiful and grand.

Don't try to paint a masterpiece (poetically speaking) before you have mastered basic drawing and painting!

---

**Review** | In this section on writing to entertain you have been given the opportunity to participate in activities which allow you to demonstrate expertise and creativity in the use of English in a range of different contexts informed by linguistic study (AO4).

The expertise is demonstrated by the specific genre awareness shown by your basing your piece(s) on the text types provided by the style models used.

The creativity is shown by the originality of the content that you have brought to your versions.

The various A-level specifications make slightly different demands about the exact requirements of the submission, but by following the guidance and approach to the activities in this section, you should have no difficulty in

- meeting any word-count requirements
- identifying the specific purpose, audience and genre of your final piece
- providing explicitly referenced sources
- providing annotated style models
- showing evidence of early planning and preparation.

# Writing to persuade

You cannot go very far in this life without coming across texts, both written and spoken, whose main purpose is to influence you in some way or another – buy this, join that, donate some cash – in other words, to persuade.

Many of these types of texts use a variety of sophisticated techniques to get us to change our minds or to accept another point of view. Throughout this section we will be looking closely at a number of successful persuasive texts to identify the following key factors.

- What is the author of the text trying to achieve?
- Who is the author of the text trying to persuade?
- What is the best format or text type for the particular purpose?
- How, in terms of persuasive techniques, does the author of the text effectively target the audience?

So that examining the style models will help you to produce a successful piece of writing, we have also tried to ensure that

- the context of the persuasive text under examination is likely to be familiar to you
- the perceived target audience is so far as possible a real one and the members of the target audience are genuinely open to persuasion
- the genre/format of the piece is suited to both purpose and audience.

| Activity 26 | Select a suitable text type and identify the target audience |
|---|---|

**Group work**

This activity could alternatively be carried out as individual work throughout.

1  Each student makes a list of different texts designed to persuade that they have come across recently. These could have been encountered at home, in school or college or out in the big wide world. They could be written or spoken. Students should list as many as they can.

2  Group members share their lists and create a master list. (This master list can be on a large sheet of paper, or on a whiteboard.)

3  Each group member is given the same number of different text types from the master list and decides who might be the typical audiences for such a text. Ideas are then fed back to the group and recorded on the master list.

The outcome might look something like this – though probably will contain many more examples!

| Text types | Possible audiences |
|---|---|
| Magazine advertisements | Special-interest groups (depending on subject-matter of magazine), age-related audiences (depending on title of magazine), gender-related audiences (depending on title of magazine) |
| Newspaper editorials | Depends on selected newspaper (tabloid/broadsheet) and political stance of newspaper/journalist |
| Letters to the editor | Depends on selected newspaper (tabloid/broadsheet) or magazine and perceived views of readership |
| Political speeches | 'Fellow believers' or don't knows. Councillors, MPs, audience at public or political meeting |
| Assembly presentations | Age-group specific. Could be gender specific |
| Leaflets | Special-interest group (level of prior knowledge might be significant), age- or gender-related audiences |
| Brochures | Special-interest group (level of prior knowledge might be significant), age- or gender-related audiences |
| TV or cinema commercials | Depends when/where commercial is broadcast |
| Articles in magazines/newspapers | Depends on selected newspaper (tabloid/broadsheet) or magazine and perceived views of readership |
| Charity appeal letters | Audience selected by charity. Often depends on socio-economic status and probably perceived liberal tendencies |

## Activity 27
**Group work**

## Select a suitable topic and some of the arguments that might be used

This activity is ideally suited to groups of five, though it can be adapted quite easily for smaller or larger numbers. Each person will need a copy of the 'I believe' template.

1  Each group member completes the central 'I believe' section on their template with any statement that represents an opinion. It really doesn't matter if the statement is a heartfelt belief (such as 'I believe that war can never be justified') or totally trivial or facetious ('I believe that life is improved beyond measure by Marmite', for example).

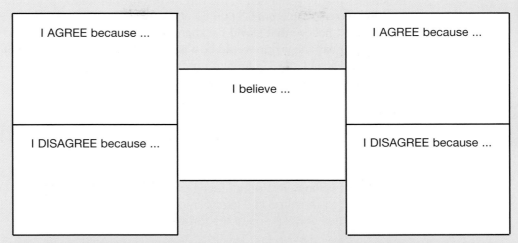

2   Each template is passed to another member of the group, who completes one of the 'I AGREE because' or 'I DISAGREE because' boxes. They can choose between agreeing or disagreeing with the original statement but must include a reason or example to support whatever they write.

3   Each template is then passed to a third member of the group, who completes one of the remaining incomplete boxes. This student can also choose whether to support or oppose the original statement.

4   Another box is completed by a fourth member of the group, who might have to express an opinion which does not match their real opinion, as both the 'I AGREE' boxes or both the 'I DISAGREE' boxes may already be complete.

5   The last incomplete box is completed by a fifth member of the group, who will have no choice between agreeing or disagreeing. Thinking about and justifying an opinion which is not entirely in sympathy with your own is good practice for when you create your own persuasive text. It gives you experience of presenting a counter-argument – a useful and often effective persuasive technique in itself.

6   The completed template is returned to its original 'owner', who now has a selection of responses which provide the basis of a persuasive text – namely, a subject about which to write and a discussion of some of the issues surrounding it.

Here is an example of a completed template.

| I AGREE because ... | | I AGREE because ... |
|---|---|---|
| People who smoke know that it is bad for them, and so it is the smoker's own fault if she or he gets ill. | I believe ... | Cosmetic surgery is about vanity in personal appearance, and the taxpayer shouldn't have to pay for other people's vanity |
| I DISAGREE because ... | ... that the NHS should not pay for non-essential treatment. | I DISAGREE because ... |
| Free health care is a basic human right and should be available to all. | | It is impossible to say with certainty what is non-essential. Psychological well-being is often as important as physical health! |

The subject-matter contained in the central box of your template should give you an idea about the most suitable publication for a persuasive letter on this topic. For example, if you have stated, 'I believe that David Beckham should still be in the England team', then a specialist football magazine would be a sensible place to send it, while if you stated, 'I believe that present-day US foreign policy is a serious threat to world peace' then the letters pages of a reputable broadsheet newspaper might be more suitable.

## Activity 28 — Writing a persuasive letter based on a style model

The style model here is a letter written by Charles Dickens to the Editor of *The Times* newspaper in 1849. Some devices or techniques used by the writer are listed in the right-hand column. (Note that techniques identified for a particular paragraph may be developed or repeated in a later paragraph.) Read both the letter and the comments carefully, then choose one of the following activities.

*Either:* Draft a letter addressed to the editor of a suitable publication in which you attempt to persuade the readership of the strength of your views on the topic in the middle box of your template from Activity 27. Before you start drafting your letter, look back at the style model and try to identify some examples of techniques that can be adapted for your purposes. Use a suitable selection of persuasive techniques to support your viewpoint.

*Or:* If the subject-matter/topic on your template is not really suited to a letter to a newspaper, or a public figure such as the Prime Minister or a local politician, choose a suitable text type and target audience from the list of outcomes from Activity 26. You can then produce a first draft of a persuasive text.

| Style model | Techniques used |
| --- | --- |
| Sir | |
| I was a witness of the execution at Horsemonger Lane this morning. I went there with the intention of observing the crowd gathered to behold it, and I had excellent opportunities of doing so, at intervals all through the night, and continuously from day-break until after the spectacle was over. | Stating the subject-matter/topic. Saying why the writer has a particular interest/qualification in commenting on the topic. |
| I believe that a sight so inconceivably awful as the wickedness and levity of the immense crowd collected at that execution this morning could be imagined by no man and could be presented in no heathen land under the sun. The horrors of the gibbet and of the crime which brought the wretched murderers to it faded in my mind before the atrocious bearing | Use of powerful emotive vocabulary, especially adjectives. Use of hyperbole (exaggeration) to emphasise points. |
| When I came upon the scene at midnight, the *shrillness* of the cries and howls that were raised from time to time, denoting that they came from a concourse of boys and girls already assembled in the best places, made my blood run cold. As the night went on, screeching, and laughing, and yelling in strong chorus of parodies on negro melodies, with substitutions of 'Mrs. Manning' for 'Susannah', and the like, were added to these. When the day dawned, thieves, low prostitutes, ruffians, and vagabonds of every kind, flocked on to the ground, with every variety of offensive and foul behaviour. | Appealing to the senses (especially sight and hearing). Use of groups of three. Use of direct reference or quotation. Use of powerful verbs with specific connotations. |

Fightings, faintings, whistlings, imitations of Punch, brutal jokes, tumultuous demonstrations of indecent delight when swooning women were dragged out of the crowd by the police, with their dresses disordered, gave a new zest to the general entertainment. When the sun rose brightly – as it did – it gilded thousands upon thousands of upturned faces, so inexpressibly odious in their brutal mirth or callousness, that a man had cause to feel ashamed of the shape he wore, and to shrink from himself, as fashioned in the image of the Devil.

When the two miserable creatures who attracted all this ghastly sight about them were turned quivering into the air, there was no more emotion, no more pity, no more thought that two immortal souls had gone to judgement, no more restraint in any of the previous obscenities, than if the name of Christ had never been heard in this world, and there were no belief among men but that they perished like the beasts.

Use of sound patterning (phonology), especially alliteration.

Use of sophisticated/educated register to give an air of authority.

Use of contrasts (Devil/Christ – see next paragraph).

Use of powerful metaphor

Use of specific semantic field (e.g. religion)

The outcome of either of these tasks may provide the first draft of a persuasive text that can be developed into a strong piece for submission as part of your coursework folder. But it may turn out to be unsatisfactory because either the text type or the chosen audience or the methods chosen to persuade do not quite work. If that happens, retain the first draft as evidence of preliminary work, and think about modifying one, some or all of text type, tone or audience.

If your topic does not really seem important enough to rate a letter to the 'quality' press, there is another alternative which would allow you to express your opinions in an influential way – a newspaper or magazine column. Most newspapers and many magazines provide a regular opportunity for writers – sometimes regular journalists but often 'personalities' in other fields of popular culture – to put across their views in a powerful way that may be entertaining or irritating, depending on your viewpoint.

One such personality is Jeremy Clarkson – primarily known as a motoring expert – who has written a regular column in a broadsheet newspaper for many years. In this column he has given the reading public the benefit of his strongly held views on a variety of subjects, expressed in such a way as to leave you in no doubt that you are expected to agree with him!

## Activity 29 Writing a newspaper column

Here is one of Jeremy Clarkson's columns from the *Sunday Times* (February 2007). Read through the column and try to identify the persuasive devices or techniques he uses. Make a note of some examples. The paragraphs have been numbered to help you.

There is an annotated version of the column in the commentary on page 229.

## Drip-drip-drip of a revolution

1 The news last week that olive oil, Marmite and porridge cannot now be advertised during television programmes aimed at children confirms something I've suspected for a few months. There's a revolution going on in Britain and no one seems to have noticed.

2 When the French and Russian proletariat rose up against the middle and upper classes, they made a lot of noise and used pitchforks. Whereas here the revolutionaries are using stealth and a drip-drip-drip policy of never-ending legislation.

3 It started when they let ramblers trample all over your flowerbeds and then, of course, there was hunting. We know that the antis couldn't really have cared less about the wellbeing of foxy woxy, but they hated, with a passion, the well-heeled country folk who charged about on their horses shouting tally ho.

4 Then came the attack on four-wheel-drive cars. 'It's the environment,' they smiled, but it's no such thing. Otherwise they'd be up north taxing people with clapped out Ford Orions and telling fat people in council houses to get out of the chip shop and lag their bloody lofts.

5 No, they go after Chelsea Tractors because these are symbols of middle-class success. You have to remember that trade unionists and antinuclear campaigners didn't go away. They just morphed into eco-mentalists because they realised that global warming was a better weapon than striking, or doing lesbionics for mother Russia in Berkshire.

6 Think about it. They tell you not to go to Tuscany this summer, and they throw withering looks at the Ryanair flights to Gascony. But when Kentucky Fried Chicken starts advertising a bucket of supper with disposable plates and nonbiodegradable plastic cutlery so you don't have to get your fat arse out of your DFS sofa and wash up, do we hear a murmur? You can cup your ears as much as you like but the answer is no.

7 Instead we get Ofcom listing what it considers to be junk food and therefore unsuitable for children. Chicken nuggets? Plain white bread? Oven chips? Diet drinks? Nope, along with a lot of oven ready 'meals', these are all fine apparently.

8 But Marmite, porridge, raisins, cheese and manuka honey? 'Fraid not. This is what middle-class kids eat so it's all wrong, and now it can't be advertised on television in the afternoon.

9 Meanwhile you have John Prescott insisting that each new housing development can only get a planning green light if it 'spoils some Tory bastard's view'.

10 It gets worse. Ken Livingstone has not extended the congestion charge into Tower Hamlets or Newham. Nope. He's gone for Kensington and Chelsea. And we learnt last week of plans to turn Sloane Square, the epicentre of middle-class shopping and conviviality, into a tree-free crossroads.

11 I've checked and strangely there are no plans to build a new road through the statue of Harold Wilson in the north's equivalent of Sloane Square – George Square in Huddersfield.

12 There are, however, plans afoot to give Janet Street-Porter and others of a Gore-Tex disposition access to a 10-yard-wide corridor around all of Britain's 2,500 mile coastline. So you worked hard all your life and saved up enough to buy a bit of seclusion by the sea? Well sorry, but Natural England, a sinister sounding bunch, has advised Defra, which sounds like something the Nazis might have dreamt up, that your garden should be confiscated and that there should be a 'presumption against' giving you any compensation.

13 You see what I mean. On its own, that's no big deal. But lob everything else into the mix and it becomes clear that traditional Britain is under attack. It's porridge and Jonathan Ross's back garden today, but tomorrow Mrs Queen will be transported to Scotland and summarily shot. You mark my words.

14 I bet the chief executive of Barclays agrees. He announced last week that the bank had made record profits, and was probably feeling pretty chuffed, right up to the moment he was summoned to a television studio and presented as the unacceptable face of capitalism who goes round the countryside at weekends stamping on puppies.

15 I felt it too on Thursday, because for reasons I can't be bothered to explain I was in London with a Rolls-Royce and no one ever let me out of a side turning.

16 Why? As I've said before, Simon Cowell, who is a rich man, gives the exchequer more each year than is generated by all the speed cameras put together. If you combined the tax contributions of all those who have Rollers, I bet you'd have enough to pay for Britain's air traffic control system.

17 And that's before you start on how much Britain's rich do for charity. Last year a bunch of hedge fund managers raised £18m in a single night to help Romanian orphans. At one party Lady Bamford's mates stumped up £3m for the NSPCC. And I had lunch on Thursday with a chap who, so far as I could tell, single-handedly looks after every disadvantaged child in the land.

18 And yet, when he climbs into his Bentley to go home at night, a bunch of communists and hippies, egged on by faceless former Greenham lesbos in government think tanks, makes sure he can never pull into the traffic flow.

19 Not that he's going anywhere anyway, because Ken Livingstone has taken £8 a day from middle-class Londoners and given it to a crackpot South American lunatic in exchange for cheap oil, which means the capital is choked with buses full of Bulgarian pickpockets fleeing from the police.

20 I notice this morning that the blossom is out on my trees. And yet, somehow, it doesn't feel like summer's coming.

## Activity 30 — Your views welcome!

Produce a similar column, with a strong personal voice, based around a topic that you feel strongly about. Use techniques similar to those used by Jeremy Clarkson where appropriate.

# Spoken persuasive texts

Ever since the time of the Ancient Greeks, possibly even before, speaking persuasively in formal situations has been an important part of society. For that reason there are thousands of examples of impressive speeches made by public figures on all kinds of significant topics, using a wide selection of persuasive techniques, available for all to study. That would seem to suggest that writing a speech, based on one of these marvellous style models, would be a sensible and straightforward choice for a coursework submission. But before you throw yourself into researching some great Greek or Roman orator, or looking for the collected speeches of Winston Churchill, consider this advice from a senior moderator from an exam board reporting on this exact subject.

> 'If you, quite appropriately, study the best rhetorical speeches including Martin Luther King, etc. make sure you do not go too far in trying to incorporate **all** the features of such speeches into your writing. If you do, you run the risk of ending up with speeches which are inappropriate to a large extent for the more modern and "lesser" topics being dealt with, where the heavy rhetorical flourishes are quite inappropriate.'

This is not to say that looking at great speeches is a waste of time – far from it. By all means study 'Friends, Romans, countrymen …', 'I have a dream …' and 'We will fight them on the beaches …' to see how various effects can be achieved, or turn to pages 42–47 for an introduction to rhetorical devices. However, always remember the golden rules for the production of successful coursework pieces.

- Know your audience – who am I writing for?
- Know your subject-matter – what am I writing about?
- Know your purpose – what am I trying to achieve?
- Know your situation – when and where would this piece appear in real life?

Then

- Choose your genre – what is the best text type or format to choose?
- Choose your content – how will I select the most appropriate and effective material?
- Choose your tone – what will be the best way of presenting/expressing the material?

When all these questions have been answered, you can make a start on your own speech.

## Activity 31 — Preparation for the production of a persuasive speech

1   Construct and fill in a grid like the one below. (A grid like this can also be used in the early stages of planning for other types of texts and other purposes for writing.)

| Question | Notes | Example answers |
|---|---|---|
| What am I writing about? | This should be something you are familiar with and feel strongly about. | The Buddy reading scheme in the school |
| Who is the 'author' of this text? | This could be you, or it could be a persona you create for the specific situation. | Year 13 student |
| Who is it aimed at? | The audience should be identified as specifically as possible in terms of age, gender, level of knowledge and understanding, etc. | New Year 12 students, male and female, some of whom have been in the school for five years and some who have only joined for sixth form |
| Where and when will they encounter the text? | This, again, should be as specific as you can make it, and as realistic as possible. | At a Year 12 assembly, early in the new school year. |

| | | |
|---|---|---|
| What is my desired outcome? | To change minds? To alter behaviour or actions? To encourage participation or donation? | To encourage a large number of students to participate in the scheme. |
| What is the best format/ text type for this piece? | Be realistic – select something that would have a chance of working in real life! | Presentation (speech) with slide show and or visual aids/props. |
| What tone will be most effective for this purpose and audience? | Decide how you as the author of the piece want to appear to the audience. Are you a highly qualified expert? Do you want to sound friendly and approachable? Formal? Conversational? | Friendly but authoritative. Fellow student, experienced and enthusiastic. Use of interpersonal language and anecdotes, but formal enough to be taken seriously. |

2   Study the following style model and identify examples of some of the persuasive techniques that are flagged up in the right-hand column. The text is the address by the ninth Earl Spencer at the funeral of his sister Princess Diana.

| Style model | Persuasive techniques |
|---|---|
| I stand before you today the representative of a family in grief, in a country in mourning before a world in shock. | Identifying who you are, and introducing the topic. |
| We are all united not only in our desire to pay our respects to Diana but rather in our need to do so. | Use of first person plural (we) to suggest solidarity. Stating specific purpose. |
| For such was her extraordinary appeal that the tens of millions of people taking part in this service all over the world via television and radio who never actually met her, feel that they, too, lost someone close to them in the early hours of Sunday morning. It is a more remarkable tribute to Diana than I can ever hope to offer her today. | Identifying first 'selling point'. Suggesting audience's likely agreement/response. |
| Diana was the very essence of compassion, of duty, of style, of beauty. All over the world she was a symbol of selfless humanity, a standard-bearer for the rights of the truly downtrodden, a truly British girl who transcended nationality, someone with a natural nobility who was classless, who proved in the last year that she needed no royal title to continue to generate her particular brand of magic. | Use of groups of three. Use of positively marked lexical choices. |
| Today is our chance to say 'thank you' for the way you brightened our lives, even though God granted you but half a life. We will all feel cheated that you were taken from us so young, and yet we must learn to be grateful that you came along at all. | Suggesting the required response from the audience. |

Only now you are gone do we truly appreciate what we are now without, and we want you to know that life without you is very, very difficult.

*Talking directly to someone outside the audience – to show them that they are dealing with real people.*

We have all despaired at our loss over the past week, and only the strength of the message you gave us through your years of giving has afforded us the strength to move forward.

*Use of shared values.*

There is a temptation to rush to canonise your memory. There is no need to do so. You stand tall enough as a human being of unique qualities not to need to be seen as a saint. Indeed, to sanctify your memory would be to miss out on the very core of your being, your wonderfully mischievous sense of humour with the laugh that bent you double, your joy for life transmitted wherever you took your smile, and the sparkle in those unforgettable eyes, your boundless energy which you could barely contain.

*Introducing second selling point.*

*Extensive use of powerfully positive adjectives to describe key features.*

But your greatest gift was your intuition, and it was a gift you used wisely. This is what underpinned all your wonderful attributes. And if we look to analyse what it was about you that had such a wide appeal, we find it in your instinctive feel for what was really important in all our lives.

Without your God-given sensitivity, we would be immersed in greater ignorance at the anguish of AIDS and HIV sufferers, the plight of the homeless, the isolation of lepers, the random destruction of landmines. Diana explained to me once that it was her innermost feelings of suffering that made it possible for her to connect with her constituency of the rejected.

*Use of direct quotation or close reference to words of someone closely involved.*

And here we come to another truth about her. For all the status, the glamour, the applause, Diana remained throughout a very insecure person at heart, almost childlike in her desire to do good for others so she could release herself from deep feelings of unworthiness, of which her eating disorders were merely a symptom.

*Stating an interim conclusion – what we have achieved so far.*

The world sensed this part of her character and cherished her for her vulnerability, whilst admiring her for her honesty. The last time I saw Diana was on July the first, her birthday, in London, when typically she was not taking time to celebrate her special day with friends but was guest of honour at a charity fund-raising evening.

*Developing next point.*

She sparkled, of course, but I would rather cherish the days I spent with her in March when she came to me and my children in our home in South Africa. I am proud of the fact that apart from when she was on public display meeting President Mandela, we managed to contrive to stop the ever-present paparazzi from getting a single picture of her.

That meant a lot to her.

Use of very short sentence for emphasis.

These are days I will always treasure. It was as if we'd been transported back to our childhood, when we spent such an enormous amount of time together, the two youngest in the family.

Emphasising personal involvement of speaker.

Fundamentally she hadn't changed at all from the big sister who mothered me as a baby, fought with me and endured those long train journeys between our parents' homes with me at weekends. It is a tribute to her level-headedness and strength that despite the most bizarre life imaginable after her childhood, she remained intact, true to herself.

Stating opinions authoritatively as if they were facts.

There is no doubt that she was looking for a new direction in her life at this time. She talked endlessly of getting away from England, mainly because of the treatment she received at the hands of the newspapers.

I don't think she ever understood why her genuinely good intentions were sneered at by the media, why there appeared to be a permanent quest on their behalf to bring her down. It is baffling. My own, and only explanation is that genuine goodness is threatening to those at the opposite end of the moral spectrum.

Stating and rejecting opposing points of view.

It is a point to remember that of all the ironies about Diana, perhaps the greatest is this: That a girl given the name of the ancient goddess of hunting was, in the end, the most hunted person of the modern age.

She would want us today to pledge ourselves to protecting her beloved boys, William and Harry, from a similar fate. And I do this here, Diana, on your behalf. We will not allow them to suffer the anguish that used regularly to drive you to tearful despair.

Exerting 'moral pressure' – implying it's the sort of thing you ought to do.

Speaker sounding more definite and like an authority figure.

Beyond that, on behalf of your mother and sisters, I pledge that we, your blood family, will do all we can to continue the imaginative and loving way in which you were steering these two exceptional young men so that their souls are not simply immersed by duty and tradition but can sing openly as you planned.

Starting to sum up – pulling together the ideas mentioned above.

We fully respect the heritage into which they have both been born, and will always respect and encourage them in their royal role. But we, like you, recognise the need for them to experience as many different aspects of life as possible, to arm them spiritually and emotionally for the years ahead. I know you would have expected nothing less from us.

Back to using 'we' – emphasising shared values.

William and Harry, we all care desperately for you today. We are all chewed up with sadness at the loss of a woman who wasn't even our mother. How great your suffering is we cannot even imagine.

I would like to end by thanking God for the small mercies he has shown us at this dreadful time; for taking Diana at her most beautiful and radiant and when she had so much joy in her private life.

*Initiating closing sequence – re-stating purpose of speech in different words.*

Above all, we give thanks for the life of a woman I am so proud to be able to call my sister: the unique, the complex, the extraordinary and irreplaceable Diana, whose beauty, both internal and external will never be extinguished from our minds.

*Final powerful concluding statement in a single complex and carefully balanced sentence.*

3   Produce a draft version of a speech/talk on your chosen subject. Keep in mind, at all times, who the target audience is and when and where they might be listening to the piece.

4   Perform the speech (or at least read it out loud) to an audience (ideally one similar in some way to your identified target audience). Take feedback, particularly about how effectively the arguments come over. This will help you find out whether your speech works as a spoken piece.

5   Make any adjustments necessary to make it more effective and convincing.

## Review

In this section you have been given the opportunity to

- consider the wide variety of persuasive texts that exists in society
- examine a variety of relevant persuasive texts that could act as style models
- identify a variety of persuasive techniques
- consider the suitability of certain genres or text types for different purposes and audiences
- practise composing a variety of persuasive texts – a persuasive letter, a newspaper/magazine column, a persuasive speech.

# Writing to inform

One of the most basic functions of human language is, and always has been, the transmission of information. Most speech – from casual gossip right through to formal discussion – serves this purpose, as does much of writing. Newspapers, magazines and non-fiction books in particular owe their very existence to the need to transmit information to their readers.

So if recording and reporting information is such an important function of writing, how can we make sure that we manage this function successfully?

# Basic requirements for effective information texts

- You must have something to say – the *what* of informative writing.
- You must have a specific audience who want to know – the *who* of informative writing.
- You must connect the above by the best means you can – the *how* of informative writing.

Now consider the following example of informative writing. It is taken from a free magazine available to travellers on the Virgin Trains Inter-City Network, so it is clearly aimed at informing travellers and potential visitors to localities served by that network.

ROCK 'N' ROLL

## LIVERPOOL

"THE CAVERN – WHERE THE BEATLES PLAYED 292 TIMES – CELEBRATES ITS 50TH ANNIVERSARY THIS YEAR"

**(Clockwise from top left)** Local band Ladytron – they're quite friendly once you get to know them; start work on your hangover at Korova; oh, now what's the name of these boys again? Don't tell me, I'll have it in a minute...; get some Scouse hospitality at Hope Street Hotel

**THE BEATLES LOOM LARGE OVER** LIVERPOOL, **BUT DON'T GET TOO HUNG UP ON THE FAB FOUR. A LOT HAS HAPPENED SINCE THE 60s, AND THE CITY STILL PRODUCES TOP BANDS, FROM THE TEARDROP EXPLODES TO THE CORAL...**

### Korova
Named after both the Milk Bar in *A Clockwork Orange* and Echo & The Bunnymen's old label, Korova opened with the aim of recreating the feverish creative atmosphere of famous Scouse post-punk clubs such as Eric's. Eighteen months later, this bar-kitchen-club – a joint venture between owner Rob Gutmann and local electro-pop band Ladytron – is doing just that, its roster of club nights and gigs providing a forum and haven for all sorts of renegade music makers and restless clubbers.

### Wall Of Fame
Liverpool has produced more chart-topping acts than any other UK city. You'll find over 50 years of No1s remembered on Mathew Street's wall of fame, which is a bank of

commemorative discs bringing together legends such as Gerry & The Pacemakers, Frankie Goes To Hollywood and, erm, Atomic Kitten.

### The Beatles
In Liverpool, there are Beatles links around every corner, from cafés and pubs, such as the Jacaranda and the White Star – where the band played and socialised – to areas such as Strawberry Fields that inspired their songs. Many tours are available, such as a two-hour Magical Mystery bus tour (see www.visitliverpool.com for more details). The Beatles Story museum tells exactly that, in 18 chronological features with an audio tour that features many of the main players in the Beatles' evolution. Out of town, accessible only by pre-booking a tour, you'll find Mendips and Forthlin Road, Lennon and McCartney's childhood homes.

### The Cavern's 50th
The Beatles played here 292 times, cementing the club's reputation as the epicentre of Merseybeat, if not British rock 'n' roll. Rebuilt, brick-by-brick, on the original site in the early 80s, The Cavern celebrates its 50th

anniversary this year. Events to celebrate this include a week of concerts, from 16 January. On 21 February, the club remembers The Beatles' first 1961 show.

### Divine vinyl
Liverpool's equivalent of Rough Trade, Probe Records has been servicing local refuseniks with quality indie/underground sounds since 1971. Club kids, meanwhile, should try dance specialists 3 Beat, a few feet down Slater Street.

### Club hopping
Locals recommend Le Bateau and, in particular, its discerning Saturday night indie club, Liquidation. The Zanzibar is another hotbed of diverse activity, while Barfly has gigs and local club nights such as the excellent Chibuku Shake Shake.

### FACT
Fed up with the Fab Four? Then visit the Foundation for Art and Creative Technology. Primarily an art-house cinema and gallery space, FACT also hosts suitably esoteric music events, such as Hive Collective's regular electronica sessions.

## CONTACTS
**Korova** 39 Fleet Street Tel: 0151 709 7097 **Beatles Story** Britannia Vaults, Albert Dock Tel: 0151 709 1963 **Cavern Club** 10 Mathew Street Tel: 0151 236 1965, www.cavern-liverpool. co.uk **Probe** 9 Slater Street Tel: 0151 708 8815 **3 Beat** 5 Slater Street Tel: 0151 709 3355 **Le Bateau** 62 Duke Street Tel: 0151 709 6508 **Zanzibar Club** 43 Seel Street Tel: 0151 707 0633 **Barfly** 90 Seel Street Tel: 0870 9070999 **FACT** 88 Wood Street 0151 707 4450 **Alma De Santiago** Dovedale Towers, Penny Lane Tel: 0151 709 7097 **Magnet** 45 Hardman Street Tel: 0151 709 6969 **Hope Street Hotel** 40 Hope Street Tel: 0151 709 3000

## BASICS
**EAT** Alma De Santiago
This new 'bar, bodega and grill' – a sister venue to the well-received Alma de Cuba – is housed in an iconic local building, Dovedale Towers. And, as you might hope, it has a few Beatles connections – it's on Penny Lane for a start, and John Lennon's Quarrymen played here in 1957.

**DRINK** The Magnet
A cool, dimly-lit bar and club, rocking a modernised take on the 50s-diner style. Central to Liverpool's musical life, it offers a nutritious diet of indie, sophisticated hip-hop, funk and house and, at the legendary Go-Go Cage night, you can lose yourself in a storm of savage rock 'n' roll.

**STAY** Hope Street Hotel
It's not cheap, but the rooms at this ultra-chic boutique hotel are a real treat. Moreover, downstairs you'll find the Residents' Lounge bar and some truly impressive original cocktails. A pianist often serenades drinkers with a twist, reworking Kylie and The Killers hits in the club style.

## Activity 32

**Individual**

# Questioning an informational text

Look at the text about Liverpool and answer these questions. The same questions can be asked of any informational text. Your answers will help you build up guidelines for constructing your own informational text.

- How does this writer attempt to interest the reader in the subject-matter of the piece? To what extent is this successful?
- How does the writer organise the subject-matter? How is the material organised and sequenced? How much is generalisation, how much specific detail? Can you spot introduction, conclusion, etc.?
- How successfully has the writer assessed the needs of the audience? Are assumptions about levels of previous knowledge correct? Has the writer anticipated perceptively the type and level of information that the audience requires?
- Is the information provided straightforward and accessible, accurate and comprehensive?

**Group work**

This activity can be carried out by small groups, who can discuss the questions and then report back to the full class. If a number of similar informational texts are found and a different one allocated to each small group, then when they report back to the full class, an overview about various techniques used in informational writing can be built up.

## Activity 33

**Individual**

# Informative writing about a place

Choose a place you know well – because you live there, or because you are a regular visitor. Decide what sort of potential visitors to this place you are trying to inform, and what publication would carry an article about it.

Divide a blank sheet of paper into sections for pictures and sections for text in the same or a similar way to the sample text. Fill in the picture sections with brief descriptions of pictures you would put in the relevant places. Write headings in the spaces for text and outline the sort of information you would include.

**Pair work**

Exchange your outline with another student for feedback, which should be focused on the questions:

- Would this be suited to its suggested target audience in terms of how it is presented?
- Would this be suited to its suggested target audience in terms of what it contains?

If, as a result of this exercise, you feel that this early draft has potential you might want to develop it further as a possible informational coursework piece.

## Where does information come from?

There are five distinct ways of acquiring the information you need to build your own informational text. Every informational text will consist of at least one of the following, though most likely a combination of two or more. The success – or otherwise – of any text depends on achieving the best balance between your chosen text type and audience.

1 **Personal experience:** When you write about the job you do, your special hobby, your favourite sport, people you have met, or experiences you have been through, you are automatically an expert, owing to your direct first-hand experience.

2 **Personal observation:** If you make a specific effort to observe people, places and things to form part of your text you are doing what journalists have traditionally done over the years – acting as a trained observer – and your version of what you saw can be regarded as more or less trustworthy.

3 **Second-hand experience:** If you talk to people who are directly involved with your subject-matter and record what they have to say, either in writing or on tape, then you can say your information comes from witnesses or primary sources.

4 **Research:** If you consult reliable written or internet sources of information, then write up your own version, you can say that your information is based on secondary sources or documentary evidence.

5 **Visual or graphic data:** 'One picture is worth a thousand words' – cartoons, photographs, maps, charts, tables, diagrams are all valid alternative means of passing on information.

These ways of acquiring and presenting information have deliberately been put in the order in which they appear above.

● The most reliable basis for writing is direct knowledge.
● The further away the writer is from the source of information, the greater the chance of inaccuracy or unreliability.
● Use of indirect knowledge (from research or second-hand experience) increases problems relating to reliability and also problems of readability if information is passed on without being processed and prepared for audience and purpose.

So, seeing it, experiencing it, doing it, or watching it are the only really effective ways of knowing a subject well enough to tell others about it.

## Activity 34 Informative writing – analysis

What means of conveying information have been used in the text on Liverpool? Put each section into one of the five categories. What is the balance? How reliable do you think that this makes the article?

Try the same test on other information texts. This should give you a clearer idea of how to make your own attempts more reliable and authoritative.

Don't forget – if you do not acknowledge that information that you have included is from secondary or documentary sources, but allow the impression to be given that it is direct first-hand experience and this becomes obvious, then you are risking the trustworthiness of your text and casting doubt on your attempts to be authoritative.

## Know your audience

This boils down to three basic and fairly obvious factors.

● **What are they interested in?** In general your audience will only want to read about things which they are already personally familiar with, or have a strong motive for finding out more about.

- **How much do they already know?** In general a high level of factual and technical content is not appropriate when a complicated process is being presented to an audience composed of people without specialised knowledge. On the other hand, if the topic is one that is particularly well known, then generalisations alone are unlikely to prove truly informative.
  - Don't tell your audience what they know already.
  - Don't keep them in the dark.
  - Don't assume knowledge that they are not likely to have.
- **How can you gain and keep their attention?** Even though the above factors will to some extent limit your room for manoeuvre, you still have a variety of linguistic shots in your locker! Humour, graphic detail, using everyday language to explain technicalities can all help make material which normally would have a limited audience much more widely accessible. But
  - some subjects will never have any appeal outside their natural target audience
  - some subjects demand a neutral, objective stance which puts writer's 'tricks' out of the question – you can't imagine, for example, a serious magazine such as *Which?* filling its reviews of digital cameras or computer monitors with witty one-liners!

> To sum up this section so far, the *how* must not be in conflict with the *what* and the *who* – there must be a suitable balance.

If you have completed Activities 32–34, you should be ready to consider writing a major piece which would be suited to submission as a polished informational text. We shall look at two alternatives:

- a piece of travel journalism suitable for the holiday section of a weekend broadsheet newspaper
- a feature article about a popular personality suitable for an entertainment-based glossy magazine aimed at a 20– 30-something reasonably affluent and educated audience.

In both cases the approach will be the same:

- discover a style model
- discuss/analyse the features of the style model
- select a topic of your own
- adapt or incorporate the relevant features of the style model
- produce a draft version of a text of your own.

# Travel journalism

Most major broadsheet newspapers produce sections or supplements relating entirely to holidays or tourism. Their general purpose is to inform the readership about trips and vacations available throughout the world. They differ from the kind of persuasive texts produced by travel agents, airlines, etc., in that they do not view the destinations as a package to be sold. Instead they try to provide potential travellers with enough background and information about relevant factors to allow them to make up their own minds.

Providing a lengthy list of places, prices and average temperatures would not be very likely to keep the average broadsheet reader engaged for very long, so it is important that such articles are presented in an interesting and original fashion. This means that they can provide ideal style models for you, and that your piece should easily meet the assessment requirements for the higher mark bands.

It should not prove difficult for you to find your own examples. Any copy of the *Sunday Times*, *Observer*, *Sunday Telegraph* or *Independent on Sunday* will provide you with instant examples, and a quick exploration of any of their website archives will more than likely furnish you with an article relating to the sort of area or the type of holiday that you would feel competent to describe.

Before you find one of your own, let's take a closer look at this example based on an article which first appeared in the *Observer*. It fits into the category of 'personal' reporting, where there is as much emphasis on the writer's feelings and experiences as there is on conveying facts. In its best forms, it combines a respect for the facts with a novelist's flair for telling a good story, and the borders between reporting and entertaining become really quite blurred.

# The pirate queen's retreat
## Once a haven for Irish buccaneers, Clare Island has plenty to offer treasure-seekers today, says Catherine Mack

You couldn't make it up. A 16th-century Irish chieftain and pirate who headed a fleet of 20 ships, fought against Queen Elizabeth I's forces, and, oh yes, was a woman. Luckily for the producers of *Riverdance*, whose swashbuckling rendition of *The Pirate Queen* has just opened on Broadway, it's all true. The real pirate queen, Grace O'Malley, took refuge from her foes on Clare Island, County Mayo, and is thought to have died in nearby Newport in around 1603. I chose to forgo the Broadway treatment of Irish history and embarked on a journey to find out why this island offered her the perfect hideaway.

Although Clare Island is only three miles from the coast, it feels like a world away from the rest of booming Ireland. My fellow passengers on the O'Malley family-owned passenger ferry, the *Island Princess*, leaving from Roonagh, 20 miles outside Westport, are two burly fishermen, a priest and a sheepdog. Local community camaraderie hits you the minute you step

*I prayed for storms and one more day in this rainy paradise*

on board, but, quick to include the stranger, they inquired about my visit. I was just about to launch into my pirate queen story when

my land legs kicked me in the stomach. Discovering the parrot rather than the pirate within, I was immediately as sick as one, and managed to spray the Princess's deck repeatedly. An O'Malley gent offered me tissues and water, saying, 'Bit lumpy today, isn't it?' I looked down to inspect the damage and realised he was describing the swell of the sea not the former contents of my stomach.

Twenty minutes later I was met at Clare Island quay by the daughter of the B&B owner, Mrs O'Malley, who insisted on giving me a lift up the hill, although it is only a few minutes' walk. We drove past Grace's original stronghold, now a derelict fort on a hill overlooking the harbour and sandy coves below. We took one of the two island roads: this one marked 'To the lighthouse', and the other 'All other routes', which should make for easy orientation. If you haven't left all notions of traditional tourist trimmings behind on deck, then now is the time. Mrs O'Malley was out, the key was in the door, so I was to help myself to tea, sit by the peat fire and make myself at home.

I struggled to leave the roaring fires, but eventually continued up the road to the lighthouse. The three-mile road is tucked in at a safe distance from the rugged cliffs along the island's north coast, with views of the towering heights of Croagh Patrick on the mainland. I passed only one car and a couple of cottages on this walk. When it finally came into view, I realised it was no ordinary lighthouse. I had also heard it was vacant and for sale, so I took a peek. It comprises two apartments, a main house and the original round tower. This beauty has been used as a private home since it was decommissioned in 1965 and with its painted wooden floors, seven bedrooms and designer light fittings, I imagine it will make an amusing purchase for one of Ireland's many millionaires. The islanders desperately want to keep it in local hands and convert it into a hotel or tourist centre. Not enough money in the heritage pot, they are told. I can't help wondering where the plundering warrior is when they most need her.

On my way back to the quay I stop at Ballytoughey Loom, where Beth, the weaver, shows me her workshop and, indeed, the fruits of her loom. I want to buy everything. The multicoloured yarns adorning the shelves of her cottage are spun so skilfully into scarves, bags and tablecloths, that I too am spun into some sort of Celtic craft overdrive. This work would not be out of place in Liberty's, but mass production is of no interest to Beth. How right she is, and how smug am I, sporting a new designer scarf.

Next door, Ciara runs residential yoga and cookery courses. I was welcomed into the beautiful wooden house with a cup of nettle tea, proudly presented (and picked) by the vegetarian cookery course visitors. The date and apricot biscuits were enough to sell the course for my next visit. I strolled back, watching the sunset, pondering the creative and entrepreneurial skills of these women. The 16th-century warrior has definitely left her feminist mark here.

Back at my O'Malley stronghold, Kathleen apologised for not having a hot dinner, but set out a salad big enough to feed a fleet, washed down with tea, bread and butter. Waves of nostalgia rushed over me, but it was only when apple pie was presented that I realised I was reliving a weekend in my favourite auntie's house. I even dared to ask her if I could wash my jeans, as they were still recovering from the 'lumpy' conditions. 'I'll take care of that for you, no bother,' she said, and they were washed, ironed and placed on my pillow at bedtime, along with a packet of

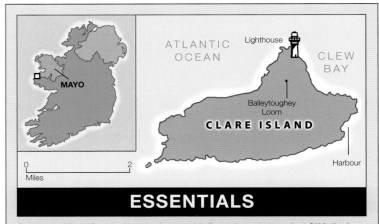

## ESSENTIALS

Catherine Mack flew to Knock airport with Ryanair and stayed at O'Malley's B&B. Rooms from €30pp, including full Irish breakfast. For ferries to Clare Island see www.omalleyferries.com. Return €15 adults €5 children. For more details on Clare Island, see www.clareisland.org and discoverireland.com. For Ballytoughey weaving workshops see www.clareisland.info/loom. For yoga retreats and courses see www.yogaretreats.ie

Sea-Legs. This must be the Clare Island answer to the chocolate on the pillow, I thought – and smiled at this act of quiet unassuming kindness.

After Auntie Kathleen's fuller-than-full Irish breakfast the next morning, I set out to explore 'all other routes'. The starting point was Grace's fort down at the quay, from where she commanded her private army and fleet. It is hard to accept that this scene of feminist politics and battle tactics is now a neglected ruin. I walked for a few miles along the south coast's rugged, undulating landscape, which rises to heights of 400 metres along the inland ridge. I stuck to the lowland and aimed for the O'Malley shop before rain hit. And, boy, does it hit. I reached the shop just in time, only to be told by a local farmer, 'The shop only opens for 10 minutes after Mass on a Saturday'. I battled on to the medieval abbey nearby, famous for Grace's tomb. But this was locked, and the only sign of O'Malleys was on the headstones all around.

It was time to leave the dead O'Malleys behind and realise that Clare Island is a living monument. If there are no tourist facilities, this is the choice of these private people. It is enough that they choose to share their precious island and lives with visitors. I returned to the B&B after a few hours' exhilarating walk through sunshine, wind, sleet, rain (and sun again) to find a note telling me to help myself to tea and a sandwich and that dinner would be at about seven. There is no going hungry on this island, that's for sure.

The ferry O'Malleys phoned with bad and good news. 'There are storms coming in tomorrow, so it's not looking good for the crossing. The good news is that you are invited to "the party" later.' Kathleen handed me a torch, warning me to watch out for potholes if I was going to be taking to the roads after dark. Strengthened by a roast dinner, and with the party not starting until 10pm, I went in search of my own personal warrior within. Back on the dark lighthouse road, it took a couple of miles for me to shed my city jumpiness, expecting hooded muggers to pop out from behind rocks at any minute. Finally I perched on a rock and switched off the torch. The only noise was the wind, a cacophony to score this scene of star-studded perfection. Grace was right. This is the perfect hideaway.

Back at the quay, I was welcomed into the warmth of 'the party', where almost a hundred people of all generations sang 'Happy Birthday' to another O'Malley. Hot whiskey in hand, I was told, 'Looks like the ferry might go after all.' I accepted another whiskey and prayed for storms, and one more day in this rainy paradise. But these warrior O'Malleys don't break their word, and we took on the rising swell at midday. Any romantic notions about having found my own warrior within were shattered in minutes, as history repeated itself, all over the poor deck of the Island Princess.

These white horses of Clew Bay might be wild, but they will never stop me from returning.

## Activity 35 — Preparation for writing

The following process is aimed at the style model provided. If you have found a style model of your own to match your own style and interests, the same process can be applied to that piece.

1   Divide a sheet of paper into two columns. Head one column 'Information' and the other 'Personal reactions'. Read through the article, paragraph by paragraph, and note down how each function is represented. For example:

| Information | Personal reactions |
| --- | --- |
| Clare Island is three miles from the Irish coast off County Mayo. | The author chose to visit Clare Island in preference to viewing the Broadway treatment of Irish history. |
| Grace O'Malley was a 16th-century Irish female chieftain and pirate who took refuge from her enemies on Clare Island. | She thought Clare Island was totally different from the rest of Ireland. |
| A Broadway musical based on her true story has just opened. | |

When you have completed that, you should have a clear idea about the balance between information (fact) and personal reaction (opinion) that is acceptable and effective in an article of this sort.

2   Look more closely at the way in which the article is set out. What use does the writer make of items other than continuous writing in order to increase the impact of the text? Use a table like this to note down your findings. A pull-quote is an interesting or provocative phrase 'pulled' from the text and displayed in a central position to interest or entice readers.

| Item | Purpose |
| --- | --- |
| Title | |
| Subheading | |
| Picture of author | |
| Other picture(s) | |
| Pull-quote | |
| Boxed text | |

3   Look at the opening sentence of each paragraph. How many of them either start with or contain 'I' or 'my'. Why do you think that might be?

4   Select some words and phrases which the writer uses to imply her approval of the island, its inhabitants and the way of life it represents.

When you have worked your way through these tasks, you should have formed an impression of the combination of techniques that go to make up an interesting and successful article for the travel supplement of a weekend broadsheet newspaper.

## Activity 36 — Writing your article

Think of a place with which you are very familiar. It could be somewhere you have recently been on holiday, or even somewhere close to where you live, but which you think you could make sound very attractive.

Draw up a grid like the one in Activity 34 which divides content into information and personal reaction. In the information column write down the factual background to your visit to your chosen place. Use a phrase or two to describe each location or other information. Use one row for each paragraph.

In the second column, identify how you are going to put yourself into the article – what incidents occurred at each location? Whom did you meet?

You should now be ready to construct your account, by combining the story of your visit with the factual information you want to convey to your readers.

When you have done this, and you are happy with the content, consider some layout decisions.

- What title are you going to give this piece?
- Does it need a subheading (with or without a by-line – writer's name)? If so, what?
- Is a picture of the writer (you!) needed?
- Can you think of a pull-quote? If so, where should it go?
- Do you need a boxed section to vary the visual impact of the text and to present significant information in a prominent position. If so, where should it go?

Now you should have all you need to produce a completed piece, with evidence of early planning, and an annotated style model.

At this stage, it should be noted that it is rarely if ever a requirement that texts submitted for coursework must be presented in a professional-looking layout. After all, you are studying for an English Language qualification, not taking a graphics or design course. However, if you have the time, the inclination and the necessary technical expertise to present your work like this, it is an additional way of demonstrating to your teachers and external moderators that you have an understanding of how this particular genre works – something which is more difficult to do effectively just by using words.

## Feature articles

The main characteristic of this type of article is that it is a combination of factual information about the personality who is the main subject of the piece, together with quotations or reported speech derived from an interview between the subject and the writer. Feature articles also usually contain many of the characteristics of the type of travel journalism dealt with in the previous section.

The process to produce an article like this should be, by now, a familiar one:

- examine a style model closely, identifying the significant and effective techniques used in terms of both layout and content
- decide upon the subject for your article
- carry out the research
- produce a draft version of the text
- apply suitable layout techniques.

# A word of warning

If you want to hunt down your own style model, that is of course a very good idea, especially if the one you find is a closer match to the sort of piece that you are hoping to produce at the end of the process. You should, however, be careful about your choice. In magazines, interviews are often presented in the form of a question forming the heading to each paragraph followed by a direct quotation from the interview providing the answer. This happens especially in magazines designed for a younger reading audience, or those aimed at the end of the market where instant impact and entertainment are more important than a detailed and in-depth examination of the subject. Although this is a widely accepted and popular form of presentation in certain circumstances, that particular style is unlikely to allow you to demonstrate the highest level of writing skills required for the best marks. There is a higher level of complexity associated with converting interview answers to a mixture of narrative, reporting and direct quotation, and it is this process that we will be attempting to reproduce.

## Activity 37 — Close examination of a model feature article

The Russell Brand feature on pages 210 and 211 is from *Hotline* magazine. Read through the article then complete the tasks that follow. If you have chosen your own style model, you can use the same approach.

Look closely at the way in which this article is set out. What use does the writer make of items other than the continuous writing in order to increase the impact of the text? Use a copy of this template to answer the question.

| Item | Purpose |
| --- | --- |
| Title | |
| Subheading | |
| Pictures | |
| Pull-quote | |
| Boxed text | |

Draw up a grid with these headings.

- Paragraph number
- R or Q or O?
- If Q, then what was the question?

Number the paragraphs of the text and fill in the grid as follows.

- Fill in the paragraph number.
- If you think the content of the paragraph is based on **research** by the interviewer then write 'R' in the 'R or Q or O?' column.
- If you think the content is the answer to a **question** asked by the interviewer, write 'Q' in the 'R or Q or O?' column, then try to work out what the question was and write it in the third column. Remember, interviewers' questions are likely to be open questions (looking for a detailed answer), rather than closed questions (able to be answered by a single word, often yes or no).
- If you think the content is just an expression of the writer's/ interviewer's opinion, write 'O' in the 'R or Q or O?' **column**.

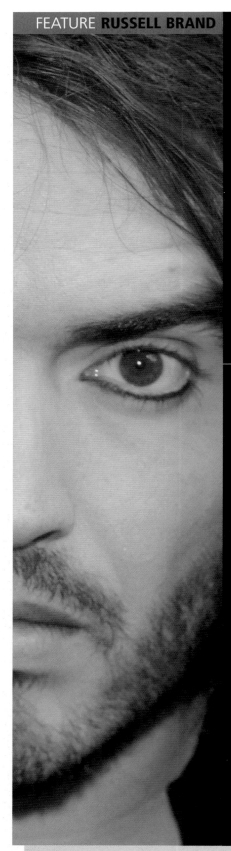

# DON'T STOP ME NOW

RUSSELL BRAND'S NEW-FOUND SOBRIETY IS NOT ONLY GOOD NEWS FOR HIS SANITY, BUT ALSO FOR BRITISH COMEDY IN GENERAL, SAYS DOMINIC MIDGLEY

RUSSELL BRAND won two major awards last year: *Loaded* magazine gave him its Lafta award for Funniest Man of the Year, while *GQ* magazine named him Most Stylish Man of the Year. These prizes neatly encapsulate the challenge facing Brand, as he vies to become a serious cultural icon rather than just a TV star. The presenter of *Big Brother's Big Mouth* is funny, but is his style threatening to eclipse his content?

Style is certainly something Brand has in spades. With his shock of long, dark, curly hair, beanpole figure and fondness for parties and beautiful women, over the past year he has been a gift to the gossip columnists. Last summer, hardly a day went by when he wasn't pictured above a story recounting the tale of one sexual conquest or another, most notably Kate Moss. The danger was that he would become more famous for having sex and taking crack than cracking jokes.

All that appeared to have changed recently, however, amid reports that Brand had met a 'lovely girl' and was going steady – and it wasn't a celebrity of any sort, but a blonde art-school student. While, given his track record, there is plenty of scope for a relapse, Brand may never have a better opportunity than right now to consolidate his position as one of the biggest names in British comedy and

achieve his aim of making it in Hollywood. Whether he calms down to do so remains to be seen.

Today Brand, who was once sacked by MTV for turning up for work dressed as Osama bin Laden the day after 9/11 with his heroin dealer and dealer's son in tow, is shaping up to become one of the biggest forces in British entertainment – up there with names such as Jonathan Ross, Jarvis Cocker and even the late, great Peter Sellers.

Brand first made his name in stand-up comedy but reached a broader audience hosting the Channel 4 spin-off show, *Big Brother's Big Mouth* (originally *Big Brother's EFourum*) and is now a household name.

In addition to his *Big Mouth* gig, he has hosted anarchic chat show *1 Leicester Square* on MTV and *Russell Brand's Got Issues* on E4. He also found time to complete a nationwide stand-up tour in the second half of 2006, released a DVD and most recently has landed a new Saturday night show on BBC Radio 2.

It's all been something of a dream come true for a man whose boyhood heroes were all comedians. Particular favourites of his included Tony Hancock, Richard Pryor, Peter Cook and Billy Connolly, and all four of these, like Brand, had – shall we say – *issues*.

## FEATURE RUSSELL BRAND

Hancock spent years battling alcoholism and depression before committing suicide in Sydney. Pryor was heavily into drugs – once famously setting himself on fire while freebasing cocaine – and only finally went clean when he was diagnosed with multiple sclerosis.

Cook spent much of his life as an alcoholic, and while he moderated his intake, and sometimes stopped entirely (under the influence of his third wife), he still died at the relatively young age of 57. Billy Connolly was sexually abused by his father between the ages of 10 and 14, became addicted to alcohol and cocaine, and says his relationship with his second wife Pamela Stephenson 'didn't change me, it saved me'.

Brand's background is equally troubled. He says he was 'a desperately unhappy wheezing little twerp' as a child,

*NO ONE BECOMES A DRUG ADDICT BY CHOICE. FROM THE HIGHEST COKED-UP EXECUTIVE TO THE LOWEST BIG ISSUE SELLER, THEY DESERVE COMPASSION*

a bulimic and self-cutter in adolescence and a serious drug addict by the time he was in his teens.

His problems can be traced to a bitterly unhappy home life. His parents split up when he was a baby, and his mother – who he has always adored – went on to marry a man he hated.

Things only got worse when his mother contracted the first of three bouts of cancer and Brand was farmed out to stay with his father or friends whenever she was in hospital.

He was badly behaved and disruptive at school but found redemption of sorts in acting, and his performance in a school production of *Bugsy Malone* earned him a place at the Italia Conti stage school, and then the Camden Drama Centre. By this point he had effectively left home, spending nights on friends' sofas or in girls' beds.

'At one point I lived in a room above a pub,' he says. 'Despite this life of stealth and frugality, I managed to find enough money to fund a drug habit.

'Other than performing, drugs were the first thing that made me feel happy and relaxed.

'People generally do them for comfort or escape. No one becomes a drug addict by choice. From the highest coked-up executive to the lowest *Big Issue* seller, they deserve compassion.'

He adds: 'I would smash things and cut myself, do incredible things but they were tolerant and persevered with me because I was a good little actor.' There came a point where the tolerance of his tutors was stretched too far, however, and Brand ended up being expelled from both his drama schools. In the circumstances, the role of stand-up comedian was about all he was fit for.

'I started doing stand-up because it gave me control and autonomy,' he explains, 'and I was dead good at it. There were lots of talent shows at the time and I got to the final of one at the Hackney Empire. Then I went to the Edinburgh Festival and got good reviews.'

This success attracted the attention of MTV and he was given a slot interviewing stars such as Kylie Minogue. But his addiction to heroin and crack was only made worse by the fact that his new job gave him more money to feed his habit, eventually leading to his dismissal.

The man to thank for Brand's return is John Noel, the agent who persuaded him to go into rehab.

'The right word is "forced",' says Brand. 'It was physical and psychological coercion. If a regime in the Third World had used the same tactics, Amnesty International would have been straight on to them.'

They decided that he would attend a day-release programme somewhere far away from the attractions of the capital. And so Brand moved to a bed and breakfast in Bury St. Edmunds and was put on a course of sleeping pills complemented by an opiate blocker called Subutext.

Unlike addicts who are treated in rehab clinics such as the Priory, as an outpatient Brand was forced to learn to steel himself against the temptations of the outside world from day one, and he remains a fan of that system to this day. Since his course of treatment three years ago, Brand has managed to stay completely off not only drugs, but also alcohol and even coffee.

'I try to avoid caffeine because my blood is now so toxin-free that I might as well have crystal meth as a cup of tea,' he says.

Given that he is a big fan of yoga too, these days he comes across as more Gwyneth Paltrow than Oliver Reed. And that could be good news for British comedy.

## ON BRAND: GREAT RUSSELL QUOTES

'I just go into a ladies' jeans shop, loom around the door, freak people out a bit, and go, "I'm here to buy some attire if you don't mind. Dress me up all right nice!" *On his shopping habits*

'I don't take drugs or drink anymore, or smoke cigarettes or drink coffee. I do yoga every day. I'm much happier. I think you have to treat it as an allergy. I do have a lunatic fringe to my character, or an element of decay – as I suppose a lot of performers do – but I'm not a toxic, malicious pain in the arse. Normally.' *On his new-found sobriety*

'A smutty Lewis Carroll labyrinth following a white rabbit of filth.' *On internet porn*

'She had a great arse but a horrible personality. She was like this beautiful bum's really annoying best friend.' *On one of his ex-girlfriends*

'...an inability to kick a ball was akin to having a My Little Pony in lieu of testicles.' *On his family's view of his own, meagre football skills.*

Russell Brand appears in *The Secret Policeman's Ball* available now on DVD. Dominic Midgley is associate editor (features) of thelondonpaper

In the grid below (which also includes the text of the paragraphs), the first few have been done, to give you a start. Some of the paragraphs contain more than one source of information, and sometimes there is more than one way in which the end result could have been achieved.

When you have done this you should be able see how the balance between research, opinion and questioning works in the production of a feature article, and you should be able to use this to inform the way you construct your article.

| Paragraph number and text | R or Q or O? | If Q, then what was the question? |
| --- | --- | --- |
| 1   Russell Brand won two major awards last year: *Loaded* magazine gave him its Lafta award for funniest Man of the Year, while *GQ* magazine named him Most Stylish Man of the Year. These prizes neatly encapsulate the challenge facing Brand, as he vies to become a serious Cultural icon rather than just a TV star. The presenter of Big Brother's *Big Mouth* is funny but is his style threatening to eclipse his content? Style is certainly something Brand has in spades. With his shock of long, dark, curly hair, beanpole figure – and fondness for parties and beautiful women, over the past year he has been a gift to the gossip columnists. Last summer, hardly a day went by when he wasn't pictured above a story recounting the tale of one sexual conquest or another, most notably Kate Moss. The danger was that he would become more famous for having sex and taking crack than cracking jokes. | R  O | |
| 2   All that appeared to have changed recently, however, amid reports that Brand had met a 'lovely girl' and was going steady – and it wasn't a celebrity of any sort, but a blonde art-school student. While given his track-record, there is plenty of scope for a relapse, Brand may never have a better opportunity than right now to consolidate his position as one of the biggest names In British comedy and achieve his aim of making it in Hollywood. Whether he calms down to do so remains to be seen. | Q  O | How's your love life? |
| 3   Today Brand, who was once sacked by MTV for turning up for work dressed as Osama bin Laden the day after 9/11 with his heroin dealer and dealer's son in tow, is shaping up to become one of the biggest forces in British entertainment, up there with names such as Jonathan Ross, Jarvis Cocker and even the late, great Peter Sellers. | O | |

4    Brand first made his name in stand-up comedy but                    R
     reached a broader audience hosting the Channel 4 spin-
     off show, *Big Brother's Big Mouth* (originally *Big Brother's
     EFourum*) and is now a household name.

5    In addition to his *Big Mouth* gig, he has hosted anarchic
     chat show *1 Leicester Square* on MTV and *Russell Brand's
     Got Issues* on E4. He also found time to complete a
     nationwide stand-up tour in the second half of 2006,               R
     released a DVD and most recently has landed a new
     Saturday night show on BBC Radio 2.

6    Brand's background is equally troubled. He says he was 'a
     desperately unhappy wheezing little twerp' as a child, a
     bulimic and self-cutter in adolescence and a serious drug          Q
     addict by the time he was in his teens. His problems can
     be traced to a bitterly unhappy home life. His parents
     split up when he was a baby, and his mother – who he
     has always adored – went on to marry a man he hated.
     Things only got worse when his mother contracted the
     first of three bouts of cancer and Brand was farmed out
     to stay with his father or friends whenever she was in
     hospital.

Now you have sorted out the balance between research, questions and opinion, you need to concentrate on who you are going to choose as the subject of your article. Essentially, there are two choices:

- an already established personality
- someone you know – a 'potential' personality.

If you choose the first option, there are instant difficulties. You are unlikely to be able to interview the person, and so the only way that you will be able to include 'interview data' is if you adapt it from another interview, in which case you will struggle to achieve any true originality. You could adapt research information to resemble interview data, but it would be difficult to make this sound convincing. If you were to invent anything to include, this would instantly make the article into fiction, and it would veer towards writing for entertainment rather than for information. So the second option – the potential personality – would seem favourite!

You need to think about where such an article could be published. A sixth-form or college magazine, profiling students, teachers or local personalities who have achieved something worth reading about in sport, drama, music or something similar, would seem a reasonable start. You never know, teachers or lecturers may have a story to tell! Sometimes local personalities may prove both interesting and accessible.

The same principle applies as mentioned before: people generally write more convincingly about subjects of which they have some experience. So go and find someone near to home with something interesting to report!

### What sorts of questions should subjects be asked?
To provide all the information necessary for an article such as the Russell Brand feature, the personality needs to be asked these three different types of questions.

- Purely factual questions – What's your name? Where were you born?
- Descriptive questions – What was it like when you …? What has been the best bit about …?
- Philosophical/theoretical questions – What do you think is a recipe for perfect happiness? If you ruled the world, what three changes would you make?

Factual questions can either replace or be replaced by research from external sources by the interviewer.

## Activity 38 — Preparing effective interview questions for the feature

Using these guidelines, draw up a list of around ten questions (perhaps five factual plus three descriptive plus two philosophical) to ask one of a wide variety of personalities who could be the topic of a feature article.

Here are a few possible questions.

| Factual questions | Descriptive questions | Philosophical questions |
| --- | --- | --- |
| When …? | What happened when …? | If you had one wish, what would it be? |
| What … ? | What is the best …? | If you won the jackpot on the Lotto, how would you spend it? |
| Who …? | Who has made the biggest impression on you in the field of …? | |
| Where …? | | |
| Why …? | | |

When you have made your list of questions, decided who to interview, interviewed them, and recorded the answers, it's time to write up the answers. Follow the pattern suggested by your analysis of the style model in Activity 36. Mix up the R, Q and O content in a similar proportion to the model.

Try to make sure that the register of your piece is suited to the audience that you had in mind. If you can, persuade someone who is reasonably representative of your target audience to read through your first draft and suggest any improvements. Make any adjustments necessary in the light of the feedback you receive and that's another piece of coursework sorted!

## Review

In this section you have been given the opportunity to

- look at the different types of information that constitute an informational text
- study suitable style models
- analyse/annotate style models
- find a suitable subject for your article and generate relevant information
- produce an informational text.

# Writing to instruct

Instructional writing is both the simplest and the most difficult style of writing to undertake. Why this seeming contradiction?

- On the one hand, it is clear that instructional writing should be straightforward, clear, logical and easy to follow.
- On the other hand, writing that is all those things is unlikely to be imaginative, varied, stylish and cultured: indeed showing little of all of those properties normally associated with high marks in English Language assessments.

So the challenge is to provide some approaches to instructional writing and some final outcomes that will give access to the highest mark bands and contribute positively to good quality coursework submissions.

Instructional writing can range from highly concrete 'nuts and bolts' technical explanations (such as 'How to organise a children's birthday party') through to quite abstract 'instructions for living' (such as 'How to be a cool dad'). No simple all-purpose technique exists. Instead, we must go back to the basics.

## What subject are you writing about?

Describing how to perform a trick on a skateboard, alter an article of clothing, or cook a steak successfully is going to involve you in problems quite different from those attached to giving advice on the successful handling of aged relatives or on how to cope with exam nerves.

Very technical subjects approximate to a highly scientific model: they automatically tend towards a high degree of structure (numbered steps, detailed diagrams, use of specialist vocabulary, for example) while omitting 'human interest' or background material altogether.

Very 'human' subjects approximate much more to a literary or philosophical style: they tend towards a more discursive structure, generalised vocabulary and illustrations, and a relaxed, almost conversational style.

## What audience are you writing for?

With a specialist audience, you can make more assumptions about levels of understanding, cover more complex aspects and make relatively little concession to the 'reader interest' factor. The general reader, however, will have to be convinced of the value or interest of the subject, then carefully helped along through a series of crystal-clear explanations in quite simple (non-specialist) language, and perhaps even shown a picture, diagram or a dummy run-through that no one could possibly misunderstand.

## How can you make sure subject and audience are synchronised?

All the conventional techniques of writing, including virtually all of those mentioned earlier in this chapter, are at your disposal here: everything from varieties of genre and style through to tricks of persuasion, dramatisation and analysis. The absolute essential, as ever, is to make sure that you select your task wisely.

Let's look at a short piece of instructional writing to try to gain a handle on some of the issues. It is taken from the advice column of the *Sydney Sun* newspaper.

---

**If you happen to be bitten, keep your cool. The first step in the treatment of all bites and stings (except snakebite) is to clean the wound.**

**Bees, ants and wasp bites can be serious.** People with allergic reaction to these stings should seek medical attention immediately. Otherwise, extract the sting and apply alkaline solution such as weak ammonia, baking soda, or blue bag. To remove the barb, edge it sideways with a fingernail.

**Ticks** can be dangerous if not removed quickly. Apply kerosene, turps, methylated or any other spirits to kill the animal. Then get the patient to a doctor to remove it. Don't try to get it out yourself.

## Spiders

All spiders have venom glands and many are capable of using them with painful results.

Only Funnel Web (found within a 160km radius of Sydney) and the Red Back spiders (found in all states) are potentially deadly.

Red Back spiders are found in quiet, dark areas, such as garden rubbish, under the house, and in seldom-used country toilets.

Only the female is harmful. She is larger than the male, with a pea-sized body.

**If you are bitten by a Red Back spider:**

- Send for medical help immediately.
- Apply a cold compress.
- If the bite is to a limb, apply a tight constrictive bandage to the upper limb, and an arterial tourniquet.
- Support the limb with a splint and a sling.
- Don't move the limb. Wait until medical help arrives.
- Try to retain the spider for identification.

---

## Activity 39   Writing to instruct – style model analysis

Read the advice column carefully. In what ways have these instructions been constructed according to the subject it is dealing with? You could comment on

- the type of detail/explanation used
- the structure
- the style and tone
- the vocabulary used.

What type of audience are these instructions aimed at? How can you tell?

When you were considering the answers to the questions in the activity you probably came across the secret of effective instructional writing.

- Include everything that is essential for the reader to know to complete the task or to reach the necessary level of knowledge.
- Express it in such a way that the reader can understand the process and carry out the suggested actions.

Easy to say – but much more difficult to achieve!

Before starting to construct a set of instructions you should ask yourself the following searching questions. If you can't answer a confident yes to all of them, do not continue until you are able to do so.

- Am I absolutely clear about my subject-matter?
- Do I have enough personal knowledge about the topic to ensure my instructions are accurate and reliable?
- Have I identified my audience as precisely as possible?
- Am I aware of the audience's present level of knowledge and understanding?
- Am I conscious of the level of technical or specialist language I may have to use? If some of it appears too complex, have I made plans to make sure it can be explained more simply within the text?
- Do I have a clear idea about my preferred format?
- Can I try out the finished product on someone representative of the target audience to gain feedback?
- Am I prepared to make changes in light of any such feedback?

If your answers to these questions are all yes then you are ready to go! If you are still a bit unsure about some of them then you could try these short trial exercises to help you clarify some of the points the questions raise.

## Activity 40 — Writing to instruct – differentiation

Choose a process that you know a fair bit about. It doesn't have to be complex or detailed – for example, you might choose how to take a corner in football or hockey or ordering a book or CD from Amazon. Write two brief sets of instructions for the process, one for a 'first timer' and the other for someone who already knows a bit about it. Compare the two texts and try to work out how you made them different.

## Activity 41 — Writing to instruct – suited to audience?

Consider the following piece, which is taken from a set of instructions for building a dog kennel. What do you think of them? Would they work if you tried to follow them? Would they work for anyone? If so, who? What would you have to do to make them more user friendly?

> When the half joints have been cut, screw the upright end frame members together, then attach the base piece in the same way. Prop up both end frames or get someone to help you. Nail the floorboards in position, butting them firmly. Now nail on the roof planks, overlapping them and remembering to start at the bottom and work upwards. Finally nail on a horizontal ridge plank.

# Selecting your own task

If, after working your way through this section, you decide that a piece of instructional writing will be a useful addition to your coursework submission, then you need to set yourself a suitable task. You could try completing a task analysis template like the example shown here. The right-hand column has been filled in to show how it works. You can adapt it to suit whatever topic you choose to write about.

Once the basic decision has been made – that is, what you are going to write about – then it is no longer necessary to fill in all the spaces in the alternatives column.

If, after you have chosen a particular topic, the answers to the later questions on the template suggest that the task will prove difficult, impossible or just impractical, then go back to the top and attempt the questions again but choose a different topic. Sooner or later you will find the right one!

| Prompt questions | Planning notes |
| --- | --- |
| *What do I know enough about to instruct others about?* | **Alternatives**<br>Having a good time on a Friday night<br>Working in a shop<br>Using my mobile to text<br>Changing a tyre on my car<br>Using the machines in the gym<br>Attracting members of the opposite sex<br>Texting |
| *What is my preferred choice of topic?* | Texting |
| *Who would need to know about this?* | Members of the 'pre-mobile' generation. Parents, grandparents, ageing relatives! |
| *How much would they already know?* | Varied – but probably not a great amount. Starting from scratch is probably the best bet. |
| *What would be the best format/text type for my instructions?* | Handy pocket/handbag-sized booklet/leaflet |
| *Where might my target audience encounter my instructions?* | Giveaway in suitable newspaper or magazine. Given to customers 'of a certain age' with the purchase of a phone. |
| *What level of technical/specialist language can I use?* | Some will be necessary – but explanation (not patronising or condescending) can be built in. |
| *What techniques relating to layout, illustrations, etc., can I use to make my instructions clearer?* | Pictures of keypads, shots of mobile screens with examples on, etc., will help illustrate the instructions. Short sections, subheadings to break the text up and avoid confusion. |
| *What preliminary research (if any) do I need to carry out?* | There are a number of websites – particularly from the various phone manufacturers and network providers – that provide some relevant information. The Millie Dowler Charitable Foundation also ran a campaign some years ago to persuade young people to show their parents how to text. |
| *Who can I use to 'road test' my ideas?* | Parents. Teachers. Other relatives |

## Activity 42 — Texting for the pre-mobile generation

Make your own copy of the task analysis template and fill it in with your own ideas.

You also might like to consider this student's piece, which is based on her responses to the template. It should give you an idea how the template works in practice.

**TEXT LIKE A TEENAGER**

A BEGINNER'S GUIDE

ITE PPL! HWS U? HPE U NJOY THS FAB GUIDE WHCH TELS U HW 2 TXT GD. TKE MI ADVICE N UL B TXTN LKE A TEENAGR IN NO TIME!

Didn't understand any of that? Don't worry, read on and all will become clear...

**1.** The first and most important thing is to open a new message and get to grips with what keys you have to press to get the right letters.

If you want to type for example "Hey" you have to press no.4 twice as 'h' is the second letter featured on the key. You then have to press the no.3 key twice to get an 'e'. Finally you press the no.9 key three times to get a 'y'.

If you want to type a number eg, 2 you have to keep your Finger on the 2 key until a number 2 appears on your screen.

**2. abc** Now we can really have some fun. The idea of SMS messages (texts) is to send the most amount of information using the fewest words or letters to save money. The average mobile phone company charges about 10-12p for a text message and so we have to try and send all the information we need in that one text. One way of making your text shorter is by deleting vowels and/or consonants from the words you wish to type. Here's how it is done...

Vowel deletion: take the word "sounds"
Remove the vowels– ' ' and ' '
sounds ──→ snds

Consonant deletion: take the word "going"
Remove the ' '
going ──→ goin

And if you're feeling really adventurous, you could remove both vowels and consonants.

Vowel and Consonant deletion: take the word 'what'
Remove the middle consonant and vowel– ' ' and ' '
what ──→ wt

See, its not that hard now is it?

**3. def** Now another way of shortening words is to use a number homophone (a number to replace letters) Here are the numbers most commonly used in texting:

1. can be used in words such as 'anyone' ──→ any
2. can be used to replace 'to' or 'too' ──→ I'm going
4. can be used to replace 'for' ──→ a card   my mum
8. can be used to replace 'ate' ──→ I'll be l   home

For example...
Is any1 going 2 Mark's house l8r 2nite 4 pizza and a movie.

**4. ghi** Another little trick that is often used in texting is shortening words into just one letter. Here's how it works...

can be used to replace 'be' or 'bee'
replaces 'see' or 'sea'
 is used locally to mean 'Dee' as in the river
can mean 'ok' or 'okay'
replaces 'queue'
can be used to replace 'are' or 'our'
replaces 'tea' or even 'tee'
 can replace 'you'
And finally...
 means 'why'

**5. jkl** Now lets practise, using everything we have learned so far...
Have a go at translating the following sentences into text talk...
(Answers below)

1. I'm going out tonight for tea with some mates.
2. Do you want to see the new Bond movie next week?
3. Are you going to that new bar on Saturday?
4. What is the weather going to be like?
5. Do you think Dave will be alright?
6. What are you going to wear tomorrow?

Think you've cracked it?
Check your answers below...

Answers...
1. Im goin out 2nite 4 t wit some m8s
2. Do u wnt 2 c th new Bond movie nxt wk?
3. R u goin 2 tht new bar on sat?
4. Do u think Dave will b alrite?
5. Wt r u goin 2 wear 2mrz?

## Example of successful instructional topics

To complete this section on instructive writing, here is a list of topics that have been undertaken recently under this heading, with varying degrees of success.

**Technical tasks**
- Setting up the school eco-garden
- Basic cooking for your first year at uni
- Beginners' guide to mountain biking
- Becoming a reading 'buddy'
- Learning a new skateboard stunt
- Wakeboarding
- Setting up your own website

**Instructions for living**
- How to achieve world domination [satire – obviously!]
- How to be a success in sixth form/college
- Getting your own way with your teachers
- How to be happy
- Getting to grips with the new technology

Remember that if you follow the guidelines in the section above, particularly with regard to content (topic choice), audience and text type, then you should be able to create a successful piece. Never forget, though, that ultimately you need to impress your assessors with the level of your writing skills to gain the higher grades – make the instructions too simple or basic and, however well they may work in practice, they may not provide enough evidence of your writing expertise. So set yourself a challenging task!

### Review

In this section you have been given the opportunity to

- look at the key indicators for successful instructional writing, in terms of topic, audience, content and text type
- recognise the two main subsets of instructional writing – technical and 'instructions for living'
- study suitable style models
- analyse style models
- find a suitable subject for a piece of instructional writing and consider various methods of producing it effectively
- produce an instructional text.

# Writing commentaries on your work

In addition to producing a number of pieces of your own writing for your coursework submission, you may be required to write a commentary on your work. In this section, you will be looking at

- what a commentary is
- why commentaries are needed
- a methodology for producing effective commentaries
- examples taken from both good and not so good commentaries.

# What is a commentary, and why may you have to write one?

A commentary is a genre of writing, and like any other it has a purpose, audience, form and content.

The purpose of a commentary is to record the process of your writing, reflect on it and thus, it is hoped, enable you to become a better writer. It should aim to explain all the choices you made as you were producing the piece of writing.

The audience for your commentary is quite a tricky one, because in a sense there are two, or maybe even three, audiences each with a different agenda. The first and most obvious audience is the assessor (your teacher and later perhaps the external moderator). You may consider either or both of these figures as some kind of ogre whose sole aim in life is to knock as many marks as possible off your work, taking great delight in doing so. Whether this is true or not, the fact remains that they can't do so if you have mastered the art of effective commentary writing.

It is probably more helpful when writing a commentary for you to think of teachers and moderators as part of an audience consisting of other writers. If you think of yourself as writing for other (apprentice) writers – explaining to them the processes you went through in composing your piece, the choices you had to make and the reasons you made them – then you are more likely to get both the tone and the content of your commentary absolutely spot on.

The third audience for your commentary may well be yourself. One way of thinking about your commentary is to see it as a log or journal of your writing whose purpose is to help you become a better writer. As in a diary, when you record events and reflect on them, so in a commentary you are reviewing and reflecting on the stages, processes and decisions you made during the process of composition.

# What form should a commentary take?

There is no set form for a commentary. If you are writing it on a piece of coursework, then there are many forms it could take. Here are some suggestions, but you should use any form that is suitable or comfortable for you and which fulfils the particular requirements of the exam specification that you are following, in terms of both length and content. You could write

- a log or journal of your writing in which you record your comments throughout the process of writing from planning to publication
- a pre-commentary, in which you write about what you hope to achieve, followed by a commentary at the end of the writing on whether your aims have been achieved
- an essay written after completing your piece in which you reflect on the stages of composition and the choices you have made.

# What should a commentary contain?

There no set content for a commentary either. You are free to choose what you wish to focus on, but, of course, much will depend on what you have written in your original piece and its drafts. For example, a commentary on a short story for six-year-olds is likely to focus on very different issues from one on a leaflet for senior citizens about the welfare and benefit rights available to them.

Nevertheless, you should focus on how you have composed your piece to suit its audience, purpose and context. Here are some possible questions your commentary could answer.

- Who is my intended audience?
- Where did I get my ideas from?
- What research or prior reading did I do?
- What help did I get from others (teachers, parents, fellow students)?
- Did I base my writing on any particular model?
- What did I change, omit, add, revise during the writing? Why?
- What was the response of people who read it in draft form?
- Did I adapt it in the light of these responses or comments?
- What particular language choices (lexis, tone, register, etc.) did I make and why?
- How did I organise and structure my material?

Here are some examples taken from some real students' commentaries, together with some moderators' comments.

| Student's commentary | Moderator's comments |
| --- | --- |
| I could have used better words. | 'Better' in what way? Explain what you mean. Give some examples. |
| I could have put more into it. | What? Be specific! More effort? More words? More humour? |
| My story is called 'The Haunted House'. It's about this girl and her boyfriend. They go away for the weekend. | I know all this – I've just had to read your very boring story! |
| The second draft is better ... I put 'stomach' instead of 'guts'. | Is this all you have to say about the changes you made?! |
| I decided to make my final piece of writing an instructional piece. I have written an instructional piece on 'How to throw a successful party' not only to help people organise a party but to write an instructional piece that was light-hearted. | Yes, I think we know you're writing an instructional piece by now! |

I'm sure that none of you reading this are likely to write such commentaries! However, it is possible to identify three DON'TS which you should try to avoid at all costs.

## Three don'ts: don't be anecdotal

An anecdote is a short narrative from one's private life and it can be quite easy to slip into one when writing a commentary. Anecdotes can be interesting and amusing when told in the right circumstances, say at a party or in a pub, but they are not really suitable for reflections on a piece of writing. The following extract demonstrates the dangers of an anecdotal commentary.

> The piece is based on a time when we went on our Duke of Edinburgh's Award expedition. We were camping in a field at the side of a small lake. In the middle of the night Amy woke up and said that she could hear someone outside the tent. No-one wanted to go outside, but then we heard a strange noise …

This might have been the germ of a piece of entertaining writing, but it is not commentary. It is clear that the writer was trying to explain the source of her ideas for her informational writing, but she has badly misjudged the purpose of a commentary.

## Don't just describe

> My healthy eating text is aimed at primary school children in years five and six. It could be given out at school or found in libraries or health centres.
>
> It contains many facts designed to be informative, because my own viewpoint on healthy eating should not be taken into consideration. I chose to present the information in a simple form, with sub-headings in upper case, underlined and numbered and the paragraphs separated by spaces. This gives the reader an idea of the contents and lets him/her easily find what they want to read.
>
> As it is an information text I have used short paragraphs, big headings. As my audience is junior school children I have put in plenty of pictures and put the writing in different colours to keep the reader's attention. For example, 'How many portions of Fruit and Vegetables should you eat every day?' is a heading and I have then put a short paragraph answering the question.

All this writer has done in this badly written commentary is to tell us what we have already read in her 'healthy eating text'. If we have read it carefully, we will have noticed that she has used 'short paragraphs', 'big headings' and 'plenty of pictures'. There is no need to tell us what we already know! We know that the writing is 'in different colours'. She is describing what she has written, not giving us any insight into the processes of thinking, planning and drafting that went into the creation of the piece. It is therefore not a commentary.

## Don't be superficial

In these extracts from a commentary, the writer is dealing with a leaflet on hip-hop music. He fails to illuminate any of the processes involved in its composition, merely observing that he had to change his first draft. For this commentary to be effective, there would need to be some detailed illustration and justification for the changes he refers to.

> I found my information leaflet really quite easy to write. I already knew a lot about the subject because I am a hip-hop fan so I only had to do one draft. Because of this the commentary is much more difficult to write, because there isn't all that much to say about it. … A leaflet is a straightforward type of text to produce and it was easy to fit all the information I wanted into it. About the only big change I made was to change it from an article into a leaflet because my teacher said a magazine article was too much like my first piece of coursework, which is a newspaper article.

## One do: do use good practice

In contrast, here is an extract from an excellent commentary. The writer had produced an instructional booklet entitled 'The Student Food Guide' for complete novices in the kitchen and wrote an extremely thorough and detailed commentary. There is not enough space to reproduce all of it, but here is the opening section, which shows how commentary can be done effectively!

'The Student Food Guide' is a guide aimed at students who are not familiar with the kitchen, written to instruct them how to prepare simple food. It is in the style of a booklet, and as it would come free in a fresher week pack, it can be aimed specifically at this select target audience. It is also non-gender-specific in order to widen the audience as much as possible.

In order for a food company to be willing to sponsor this leaflet, it seemed sensible to include at least one of their products in every recipe, so for this reason I have included many of that company's products in this leaflet and have printed the company's name in a large font before each product name. This advertises the company products to the readers, as does the logo on the front cover. I have also included colourful cartoon pictures on most pages, relating to the recipes to give the leaflet a 'fun' feel and to avoid the stereotypical serious recipe book image which could put off students who do not know how to cook. Text effects are also employed within the leaflet. This aids the reader in their understanding of the recipes and makes it easier to read as in each recipe the words 'Equipment' and 'Ingredients' are underlined, as well as products appearing in bold, with hints and suggestions in italic, bracketed or boxed. Also, the instructions for each recipe are in stages and each stage is numbered so that they are easy to follow, and each recipe begins on a new page making the booklet easier to read.

I have used alliteration in the text, e.g. 'Putting Off An Essay Pancakes'. This repetition of the letter 'P' makes the recipe sound more memorable to the reader. This device is also employed with 'Brown Sauce To Branston Pickle'. The alliteration also serves the purpose of keeping the tone informal. I have also made use of onomatopoeia in the crisp sandwiches recipe through use of the word 'crunch' which enables the reader to 'hear' the food, thus making it more appealing. Repetition of the same word three times in one sentence also helps make the key messages of the text more memorable, 'No fuss, no expensive ingredients and no skill required'.

I have intentionally not used any highly specialist terminology because the target audience has limited knowledge of the topic. However, there is some basic terminology from the semantic field of cookery, such as 'grill pan', 'batter' and 'beat the eggs', which are relatively well known terms. There are also a few terms from the semantic field of university life, for example 'fresher week' and 'Uni'. Apart from these terms, I have written most of the leaflet in Standard English to make it accessible to foreign students studying as well as native English speakers. The only non-standard terms which are also non-specialist are casual words such as 'ooze' and expressions like 'Popeye-like strength' and 'pluck up the courage', which also serve to make the text less formal.

As this text is written in the style of recipe book, some words are omitted for brevity e.g. 'cut sandwich'. Here the definite article is not needed to understand the instruction, so can be omitted. Imperatives are widely used as this is an instructional piece and also many declaratives because the text is also informing its audience. For example 'cheese on toast is great because it can be varied so much'. Simple and compound sentences (e.g. 'Empty beans into saucepan and cook on high power for 1 minute') are the most commonly used types to ensure it is easily understandable.

Although the register of this booklet is authoritative as the originator is more knowledgeable than the audience and is instructing them, the tone is also humorous as the text has a secondary purpose to entertain, and it does this through use of irony ('nice mess'), casual language ('heaps of essays') and humour ('For best results serve with an Italian accent').

I feel that my booklet is successful as it is explicit in its instructions and suited to the target audience.

# A five-question method for constructing a commentary

If you have followed all or even some of the advice about producing the various different types of writing earlier in this chapter then you should have at your disposal evidence of early planning, annotated style models, and possibly one or more draft versions. All of these provide valuable background for the construction of the commentary.

The bulk of the content can be chosen by following the process outlined in this template.

| | |
|---|---|
| **What is this text?** | |
| **Who is it by?** | |
| **Who is it for?** | |
| **What is it for?** | |
| **Language use?** | Graphology |
| | Phonetics/Phonology |
| | Lexis |
| | Grammar |
| | Discourse |
| | Pragmatics |

You should answer the first four questions in as much exact detail as possible, but the section dealing with language use should be completed selectively. Do not work mechanically through each of the six language concepts but choose the most significant ones which have contributed most to the impact of the piece.

## Activity 43

**Pair work**

### Writing a commentary – peer assessment

Choose a piece of writing that you have completed at least as far as a decent first draft. Use the five-question technique to produce a draft commentary for the piece.

Swap commentaries with another student. Give and receive feedback, taking into account the three don'ts and the one do from pages 222–223. Use this feedback to inform your next, improved version.

## Language concepts

Here is a brief outline of the language concepts which will allow you to write about your language use in your commentaries.

- Discourse relates to stretches of speech or conversation and how language is used to express the interests of a particular group or institution – for example, the discourse of law, politics, the media.
- Grammar relates to the fundamental structures and functions of English – the written word, spoken utterances, sentences and texts.

- Graphology relates to the contribution made to the meaning of a text by writing, printing and images as a system of signs.
- Lexis relates to vocabulary choices available to users of English.
- Phonetics/ Phonology relates to the contribution made by voice to the communication of meaning, including intonation, rhythm, pace, volume and word stress.
- Pragmatics relate to the ways in which social conventions and implied meanings are encoded in spoken and written language.

For more on each of these language concepts turn to pages 6–18 and 23–26.

Other useful additions to the commentary could be

- some reflections on the choice of style models, in particular those aspects that have been adapted, used or imitated
- some insight into how the piece has progressed through its various drafts.

# Commentary writing and Assessment Objectives

The following table summarises the relevant Assessment Objectives for A-level English Language for commentary writing and explains briefly what this means you have to include or show to score highly in each area.

| Assessment Objectives | | What this means for commentaries |
|---|---|---|
| AO1 | Select and apply a range of linguistic methods, to communicate relevant knowledge using appropriate terminology and coherent, accurate written expression | Systematic and evaluative exploration of data, selecting appropriate linguistic methods – suitably tentative conclusions drawn<br><br>Accurate and perceptive linguistic knowledge<br><br>Appropriate, controlled and accurate expression |
| AO2 | Demonstrate critical understanding of a range of concepts and issues relating to the construction and analysis of meanings in spoken and written language, using knowledge of linguistic approaches | Clear, perceptive understanding of the genre requirements considering a judicious range of concepts and ideas<br><br>Conceptualised discussion which illuminates writing and drafting process – integrated exemplification |
| AO3 | Analyse and evaluate the influence of contextual factors on the production and reception of spoken and written language, showing knowledge of the key constituents of language | Sensitive, consistently insightful awareness of purpose and audience – systematic reference to salient features from writing and style models<br><br>Analytical and systematic interpretation of context |
| AO4 | Demonstrate expertise and creativity in the use of English in a range of different contexts informed by linguistic study | This objective is tested in the texts you produce, not the commentaries. |

**Review**

In this section you have been given the opportunity to

- discover exactly what a commentary is

- appreciate why commentaries are needed

- examine examples taken from both good and not so good commentaries

- try out a methodology for the production of effective commentaries

- see how the writing of commentaries relates to the overall Assessment Objectives for A-level English Language.

That's about it. When you have learned all that textbooks and teachers can offer, the rest is up to you. Follow the advice of Roman philosopher Epictetus, who advised 2000 years ago

'If you want to be a good writer – write!'

**Commentary**

**Activity 3**

1   The paragraph starts with a simple sentence, seemingly praising Bournemouth in an unqualified way – until the sting in the tail, 'in a lot of ways'. This hints at Bryson's somewhat negative attitude right at the beginning. He soon builds on this by claiming not to be able to understand the 'use for' the sea. He uses an elevated register – 'sinuous parks' and 'tranquil green place' – only to contrast at times with some very colloquial language – 'the long slog'. This switching between sophisticated and conversational language is a characteristic way in which Bryson engages and entertains his audience.

2   This little anecdote about the naming of the Pleasure Gardens allows Bryson to make sarcastic references to the local 'busybody councillors' and also to make some thinly veiled sexual innuendos – playing on the double meanings of 'lower pleasure' and 'groynes/groins'. The final sentence once again emphasises the author's view of Bournemouth, which he describes as 'genteel', which the dictionary defines as *trying to* seem polite and refined'.

3   This is continued when Bryson talks about 'the town's carefully nurtured reputation for gentility' and builds a comparison (not entirely serious) with some of the Continent's most prestigious spa towns. He recites a list of the most impressive and luxurious features, 'manicured parks', 'palm courts with orchestras', etc., but brings us all down to earth by remarking that 'almost none of this awaited me'. This technique of seemingly building Bournemouth up with grand comparisons and then identifying the reality as being much less impressive is repeated to good effect. For example, the expected 'opulent casinos' are replaced by the anti-climactic 'a small bandstand' and the 'handsome kursaals' become 'small wooden erections' (more innuendo?).

4   A very brief paragraph underlining the unsatisfactory nature of a Tourist Information Office that sells information to tourists.

5   A detailed look at how the town centre has deteriorated over time. The present-day set-up (sarcastically referred to as 'progress') is described in largely negative terms ('a curious glass and tubular steel edifice that looked like a bus shelter for giants') compared to the older version ('elegant little bakery' and 'the world's best sugar doughnuts'). The most positive comment he can find for present-day Bournemouth is 'there wasn't a scrap of litter to be found'.

6   More nostalgia based on the writer's prior knowledge of the area – summoning up a picture (exaggerated) of Dickensian working conditions. Note the appeal to the reader's senses – 'old-fashioned bakery' (smell), 'untidy stacks of paper' and 'gloomy lighting' (sight), 'fretful scratchings of pencils' and 'echoing *tunk*' (hearing).

## Commentary

### Activity 7

1   The opening lines of the monologue provide a surprise – it sounds as though the speaker is a cold calculating killer. We need to read on to find out what's going on. Perhaps the speaker is unaware of the impact of what she is saying – unawareness is something we will come to associate her with.

2   The second paragraph continues in a similar vein – still we don't have enough information to work out what is going on. There is just a hint that a dramatic incident is being referred to in the phrase 'a visible tussle'.

3   The third paragraph finally reveals the set-up – the speaker is an actress, apparently involved in some fairly low-budget films. The way she talks gives the impression that she thinks she is something special – ' I'd like some direction on this point' – but her real priorities are revealed when she admits that she wants to 'stay on after the fork lunch for … [the] weekend'. Her lack of sophistication is apparent when she refers to the 'formica' and the 'carpet on the walls'. Her claim that she prides herself on being 'professional to [her] fingertips' just underlines how much her opinion of herself is different from the reality.

4   Paragraph 4 extends and emphasises the idea that Lesley's view of herself is mostly self-delusion. She says she is regarded as a serious person but that she never gets 'to do serious parts'. She says that she only ever gets to play 'the kind of girl who's very much at home on a bar stool and who seldom has to light her own cigarette', but she still claims that she is a professional, because she can 'smoke if a part requires it' (hardly a major dramatic ability). Her easy acceptance of an invitation to attend a party for someone she hardly knows thrown by someone she knows even less shows how desperate she is to make social and possibly professional contacts at any cost, while justifying it by saying 'well it's not every day you get somebody going off to Zimbabwe'.

Overall the writer uses the opening paragraphs of the monologue to establish the occupation of the speaker (third-rate actress desperate to grasp any part in any type of film) and also to establish her character (someone who can convince herself that she is some kind of highly skilled professional). Having established these important points, he can now relate the rest of the incident, knowing the audience have enough information to complete the dramatic scene.

Note that techniques identified in a particular section may well be developed or repeated in a later section.

### Drip-drip-drip of a revolution

1 The news last week that olive oil, Marmite and porridge cannot now be advertised during television programmes aimed at children confirms something I've suspected for a few months. There's a revolution going on in Britain and no one seems to have noticed.

*Selective choice of detail to support writer's viewpoint*

*Main thrust of the article identified in general terms*

2 When the French and Russian proletariat rose up against the middle and upper classes, they made a lot of noise and used pitchforks. Whereas here the revolutionaries are using stealth and a drip-drip-drip policy of never-ending legislation.

*Reference to historical precedent*

*Parallel structures in sentences to emphasise contrast*

3 It started when they let ramblers trample all over your flowerbeds and then, of course, there was hunting. We know that the antis couldn't really have cared less about the wellbeing of foxy woxy, but they hated, with a passion, the well-heeled country folk who charged about on their horses shouting tally ho.

*Writer's viewpoint made obvious by choice of detail*

*Use of child-like language to emphasise point*

4 Then came the attack on four-wheel-drive cars. 'It's the environment,' they smiled, but it's no such thing. Otherwise they'd be up north taxing people with clapped out Ford Orions and telling fat people in council houses to get out of the chip shop and lag their bloody lofts.

*Presenting weak version of opponents' argument*

*Countering it strongly*

5 No, they go after Chelsea Tractors because these are symbols of middle-class success. You have to remember that trade unionists and antinuclear campaigners didn't go away. They just morphed into eco-mentalists because they realised that global warming was a better weapon than striking, or doing lesbionics for mother Russia in Berkshire.

*Carefully selected vocabulary to emphasise writer's point of view*

*Personal attacks on opponents*

*Invented words for comic effect*

6 Think about it. They tell you not to go to Tuscany this summer, and they throw withering looks at the Ryanair flights to Gascony. But when Kentucky Fried Chicken starts advertising a bucket of supper with disposable plates and nonbiodegradable plastic cutlery so you don't have to get your fat arse out of your DFS sofa and wash up, do we hear a murmur? You can cup your ears as much as you like but the answer is no.

*References to popular culture to ensure audience can identify with viewpoint*

*Use of (mild) taboo language for effect*

*Use of rhetorical questions – suggested answers support writer's point of view*

7 Instead we get Ofcom listing what it considers to be junk food and therefore unsuitable for children. Chicken nuggets? Plain white bread? Oven chips? Diet drinks? Nope, along with a lot of oven ready 'meals', these are all fine apparently.

*Use of colloquial (conversational) language to build solidarity with audience*

*Use of short phrases to form a list*

8 But Marmite, porridge, raisins, cheese and manuka honey? 'Fraid not. This is what middle-class kids eat so it's all wrong, and now it can't be advertised on television in the afternoon.

Selective use of examples for effect

Opinion stated as though it were undoubted fact

9 Meanwhile you have John Prescott insisting that each new housing development can only get a planning green light if it 'spoils some Tory bastard's view'.

Personal attacks on opponents

Use of (unattributed) quotation

10 It gets worse. Ken Livingstone has not extended the congestion charge into Tower Hamlets or Newham. Nope. He's gone for Kensington and Chelsea. And we learnt last week of plans to turn Sloane Square, the epicentre of middle-class shopping and conviviality, into a tree-free crossroads.

Use of first person plural (we) to suggest shared values

Use of sophisticated register to impress

11 I've checked and strangely there are no plans to build a new road through the statue of Harold Wilson in the north's equivalent of Sloane Square – George Square in Huddersfield.

Use of the absurd or exaggeration to emphasise a point

Use of specific examples

12 There are, however, plans afoot to give Janet Street-Porter and others of a Gore-Tex disposition access to a 10-yard-wide corridor around all of Britain's 2,500 mile coastline. So you worked hard all your life and saved up enough to buy a bit of seclusion by the sea? Well sorry, but Natural England, a sinister sounding bunch, has advised Defra, which sounds like something the Nazis might have dreamt up, that your garden should be confiscated and that there should be a 'presumption against' giving you any compensation.

Exaggerated or totally one-sided expression of opponent's point of view to make it appear absurd

Use of highly emotive words or phrases, implying disapproval

13 You see what I mean. On its own, that's no big deal. But lob everything else into the mix and it becomes clear that traditional Britain is under attack. It's porridge and Jonathan Ross's back garden today, but tomorrow Mrs Queen will be transported to Scotland and summarily shot. You mark my words.

Direct address to readers

Use of 'loaded' words and phrases

Use of balanced structures

14 I bet the chief executive of Barclays agrees. He announced last week that the bank had made record profits, and was probably feeling pretty chuffed, right up to the moment he was summoned to a television studio and presented as the unacceptable face of capitalism who goes round the countryside at weekends stamping on puppies.

Introducing well-known and/or well-respected public figures to support arguments

15 I felt it too on Thursday, because for reasons I can't be bothered to explain I was in London with a Rolls-Royce and no one ever let me out of a side turning.

Use of personal experience by the writer

16  Why? As I've said before, Simon Cowell, who is a rich man, gives the exchequer more each year than is generated by all the speed cameras put together. If you combined the tax contributions of all those who have Rollers, I bet you'd have enough to pay for Britain's air traffic control system.

Asking questions and then answering them yourself

17  And that's before you start on how much Britain's rich do for charity. Last year a bunch of hedge fund managers raised £18m in a single night to help Romanian orphans. At one party Lady Bamford's mates stumped up £3m for the NSPCC. And I had lunch on Thursday with a chap who, so far as I could tell, single-handedly looks after every disadvantaged child in the land.

Listing supportive evidence

Use of selected statistics

18  And yet, when he climbs into his Bentley to go home at night, a bunch of communists and hippies, egged on by faceless former Greenham lesbos in government think tanks, makes sure he can never pull into the traffic flow.

Use of extreme/exaggerated contrasts to identify supporters as good and opponents as evil

19  Not that he's going anywhere anyway, because Ken Livingstone has taken £8 a day from middle-class Londoners and given it to a crackpot South American lunatic in exchange for cheap oil, which means the capital is choked with buses full of Bulgarian pickpockets fleeing from the police.

Vocabulary choices made using negative connotations for opponents

Barely concealed extreme (politically incorrect) points of view

20  I notice this morning that the blossom is out on my trees. And yet, somehow, it doesn't feel like summer's coming.

Final powerful summing-up of point of view or attitude

# How Language Develops

At the end of this chapter you should be able to

- select and apply a range of linguistic methods, to communicate relevant knowledge using appropriate terminology and coherent, accurate written expression (AO1)

- demonstrate critical understanding of a range of concepts and issues relating to the construction and analysis of meanings in spoken and written language, using knowledge of linguistic approaches (AO2)

- analyse and evaluate the influence of contextual factors on the production and reception of spoken and written language, showing knowledge of the key constituents of language (AO3)

- demonstrate expertise and creativity in the use of English in a range of different contexts informed by linguistic study (AO4).

For a more student-friendly version of these Assessment Objectives, turn to page vii in the Introduction.

## Introduction

For the purposes of your A-level studies this chapter on language development is divided into two sections: 'Language Acquisition' and 'Language Change'. The former deals with how we, as individuals, acquire language and become literate human beings. The latter introduces you to the concepts of language being always changing and of how and why this happens.

You already know how to analyse transcripts and texts in detail. Exam questions on language development will ask you to do this within the contexts of language acquisition and language change. The following sections explore these contexts and introduce you to new concepts and ideas from language study that will help you to develop your analytical skills within these areas. You will also be asked to think about language debates surrounding the processes of language acquisition and language change and to conduct research of your own.

# Language acquisition

## Child language development (CLD)

'Grown-ups never understand anything for themselves, and it's tiresome for children to be always explaining things to them.' (Antoine de Saint Exupéry)

Humans invented language by adapting their breathing and their ability to bite, taste and swallow food, in order to produce speech sounds. The American linguist Charlton Laird described language very succinctly as 'educated breath'.

Zoologists, psychologists and anthropologists have considered the significance of the arrival of language in the long story of human evolution. Here are some of the things they had to say.

> Humans in their modern form, *homo sapiens sapiens*, arose at least 40,000 years ago, and it is reasonable to assume that a refined and precise form of language was on their lips.
>
> (Richard Leakey)

> In order to produce speech you have to be able to stop your tongue at 50 different positions in your mouth … Think of what happens to your tongue when you are trying to do a tricky manipulative task, such as threading a needle: the tongue pops out and moves in sympathy. And young children almost always protrude their tongue when they're writing.
>
> I see language as a continuum stretching from the written word to the utterance of a single word between two people who know each other so well that it carries as much meaning as a paragraph.
>
> (Roger Fouts)

> … tool-making and language skills are similar, if not identical skills.
>
> (Ralph Holloway)

> Perhaps the most pervasive element of language is that, through communicating with others, not just about practical affairs, but about feelings, desires and fears, a 'shared consciousness' is created. Language is without doubt an enormously powerful force holding together the intense social network that characterises human existence.
>
> (Richard Leakey)

Using their own physical resources in much the same way as they used flints and wood as tools, humans appear to have invented language out of sheer necessity brought about by living together. Bound together by speech, early peoples developed cultures some of which in turn invented the writing systems that have come down to us today.

Learning to distinguish the systematic use of the 44 meaningful sounds of the English language is a prerequisite for language acquisition. Congenital deafness will seriously impair this learning process. The gradual acquisition of the ability to produce those meaningful sounds depends initially on breathing and healthy vocal cords, and then on a change from nasal to oral breathing, an increase in the size of the oral cavity in relation to the size of the tongue, the strengthening of the muscles of the mouth and the growth of teeth. It is not difficult to chronicle these stages of physical growth upon which speech depends.

There are however other aspects of language acquisition apart from the ability to speak and listen which need to be considered, not just because they are interesting in themselves but because of what they contribute to a better understanding of the functions and structures of language in adult life. Language acquisition is not just about listening, speaking and, later, reading and writing; it is also about the mental processes that go on behind all those activities.

Since the 1960s, researchers have built up an impressive statistical picture of the mental stages that begin with listening and speaking and continue long after a child has become a user of the spoken language. In particular researchers have concerned themselves with the acquisition of different grammatical functions and structures. If we accept that a normal child is programmed at birth to acquire a native language, or native languages, then what researchers are observing are the processes or stages of development that a child will undergo.

# A way in – context and features

The purpose of these initial activities is for you to explore what you already know or suspect about the way that human beings acquire language. Here you will

- demonstrate your understanding of a range of concepts and issues related to the construction and analysis of meanings in spoken language, using your knowledge of linguistic approaches
- analyse and evaluate the influence of contextual factors on the production and reception of spoken language, showing knowledge of the key constituents of language.

## Activity 1 — Learning a foreign language

Acquiring language is something that you have already done successfully, so successfully that you probably don't remember doing it. You will however have probably had some recent experience of trying to acquire a language different from your own. Think about your language learning experiences at school and write down your responses to the following questions.

- Which languages were you formally taught at school?
- Why were these languages taught as opposed to others?
- How successful was your acquisition of these languages?
- Why do you think this was the case?
- Are you still studying another language? Why? Why not?

Write down some things that you can remember learning about another language – words, phrases, grammatical points, types of lesson. What do you notice about your recollections?

How is learning a new language at school different from learning language as a young child?

Language acquisition at whatever age is a learning experience. As A-level students you are experts in the process of learning, you have been doing it for a very long time. The next activity is designed to explore how learning works and what circumstances make for successful learning.

## Activity 2 — How do we learn?

**Individual**

Individually, think of an example of a very positive learning experience you have had and then try to think of a negative one.

**Group work**

In groups, share and compare these experiences. You can go into as much or as little detail as you wish.

Under the headings 'Positive' and 'Negative', write down the things that contributed to your positive and negative learning experiences. You can do this individually or as a group. Each student or a representative from your group should then write your key findings on the board under the same two headings.

Class work

You have now created a map of key concepts of successful and unsuccessful learning. As a class, discuss the patterns that have emerged. How do you think these relate to the experience of a young child learning language for the first time?

# Stages of spoken language development

Observation of children's spoken language development shows that there are identifiable 'stages' in the process of early language learning. It is important to remember, as with any form of learning, that not everyone reaches the same stage at the same time. It is also important to remember the distinction between speech and communication – recent work with young children and forms of sign language, like Makaton, shows that they can 'communicate' through signs before they can physically speak.

This chart outlines the most significant stages in early child language development.

| Typical age | Spoken language development |
| --- | --- |
| 12 weeks | Cries less; squeals and gurgles; vowel-like cooing |
| 6 months | Cooing changes to babbling; consonants, repetitive consonant-vowel patterns |
| 1 year | Signs of understanding some words and simple commands; melodic utterance (intonation) |
| 18 months | Has between three and 50 words; uses single-word utterances, holophrastic stage, single open-class words or word stems |
| 2 years | Joins words together; creates own sayings; wants to communicate, the two-word stage, 'mini-sentences' with simple semantic relations |
| 24–30 months | Telegraphic sentence structures, fastest increase in vocabulary, new words every day, frustration if not understood by adults |
| 30 months + | Grammatical or functional structures emerge, vocabulary of some 1000 words, 80% utterances intelligible |
| 4 years | Language well established, differences from adult norms more to do with style than grammar, questioning is key feature of language |
| 5 years | Children have a wide vocabulary, sentences usually correctly structured, pronunciation may still be childlike, may use words and phrases from television or other sources |

**Exam tip:** In an exam you will not be expected to recount the stages of acquisition but you will need to be able to apply them to data where relevant.

Researching stages of development

Of course, speech is not the only thing that is happening at this time. Children's motor skills, cognitive skills and emotional intelligence are also developing. In groups, using the internet, research other milestones in child development between the ages 0 and 5. Start with www.bbc.co.uk/cbeebies/grownups/children_learn. Use your search engine to widen your research. Put together your own chart of other key stages of development (cognitive, physical, emotional, behavioural).

During your research make notes on the different ways this information is presented depending on the audience for each website – look especially at how it is presented to parents.

## Learning in isolation

Think back to your exploration of effective learning in Activity 2. How often did positive learning experiences involve other people? Interaction with others is essential to our development and never more so than when acquiring language. As far back as the sixteenth century it was established that babies isolated from human speech would not learn to talk. Children need to interact in order to learn how language works.

**Activity 4** Feral children

Using the internet and other resources available to you research what happens to children's language development when they do not interact normally with others. Start your research at www.feralchildren.com. Write a report that includes case studies of Genie and other 'feral' children. Your report should detail what impact they had on our knowledge of language acquisition and include an account of the Critical Period Hypothesis.

## Child directed speech (CDS)

As adults we seem to know the importance of interaction – mothers will talk to their babies as soon as they are born. A child's hearing is vital to language development, and hearing problems at an early age will often impact upon the development of speech. The language input that children experience at the start of their lives is often a quite distinct variety, referred to as child directed speech.

**Activity 5** How adults speak to children

Look at the following list from Wikipedia of words that adults use when talking to children. How many are familiar to you? What are the key features of these words in terms of sounds, structure and meaning?

- baba (bottle)
- beddy-bye (go to bed, sleeping, bedtime)
- ickle (little)
- icky (disgusting)

- binkie (blanket)
- blankie (blanket)
- boo-boo (wound or bruise)
- bubby (brother)
- oopsie-daisy (small accident)
- dada (dad, daddy)
- din-din (dinner)
- num nums( food/dinner)

- jammies (pyjamas)
- nana (grandmother)
- owie (wound)
- pee-pee (urinate)
- poo-poo (defecation)
- potty (toilet)
- sissy (sister)

## Activity 6 — Researching CDS

Research child directed speech. Were there any particular words that your family used when talking to you as a child? If you have any young children in your family, observe the way that adults talk to them. Watch some television programmes made especially for young children. How do the presenters talk to their audience? What, for example, are the key language features of an episode of *Teletubbies* or *In the Night Garden*?

When you have collected data on this topic, use each of the language concepts (covered in more detail on pages 6–18 and 23–26) to make your observations more specific. How does child directed speech work in terms of the different language levels?

Write up your findings as a poster or a handout to share with the rest of the class.

## One-sided conversations

Here is an example of a one-sided conversation (from David Crystal, *Cambridge Encyclopedia of Language*, 1987).

| | |
|---|---|
| Michael (3 months) | [Loud crying] |
| Mother | [ENTERS room] Oh my word, what a noise! What a noise! [picks up baby] |
| Michael | [sobs] |
| Mother | Oh dear, dear, dear. Didn't anybody come to see you? Let's have a look at you. [looks inside nappy] No, you're all right there, aren't you. |
| Michael | [spluttering noise] |
| Mother | Well, what is it, then? Are you hungry, is that it? It's a long time since dinner time? |
| Michael | [gurgles] |
| Mother | [nuzzles baby] Oh yes it is, a long, long time. |
| Michael | [cooing noise] |
| Mother | Yes, I know. Let's go and get some lovely grub, then …. |

During your research into child directed speech you will have probably noticed that adults have 'conversations' with children, even though the child cannot respond. At this stage the child is learning how interaction works. Eye contact, face-to-face exchange of expressions, turn taking and gesturing are all skills a child needs in order to be able to communicate effectively – they are all significant features of CDS.

| Activity 7 | Analysing CDS |
| --- | --- |

Write a short analysis of the one-sided conversation shown above. Make sure that you highlight as many significant features of CDS as you can.

| Activity 8 | Learning to sign |
| --- | --- |

**Pair work**

Read the following article about Makaton which appeared in the *Guardian* newspaper in March 2007. In pairs discuss the advantages of teaching children to sign whilst their spoken language is still developing. Can you think of situations where the ability to sign might have been helpful to you?

# Let your fingers do the talking

**Tim Dowling**

If you don't understand Makaton, you could soon be in the minority. Although created in the 1970s as a communications system for people with learning disabilities and speech disorders, Makaton's combination of signs, gestures and printed symbols is now taught in many primary schools to spur the development of language in children. It's official: talking with your hands is good for you.

A charity called the Makaton Vocabulary Development Project organises training and controls the trademark, but Makaton's foremost proponent at present is Mr

Tumble, the star of Something Special, a children's programme on the BBC channel CBeebies. Something Special is primarily aimed at children with learning disabilities, but its widespread popularity has made Makaton familiar to most of Britain's under-fives.

Margaret Walker, who devised Makaton with Kathy Johnston and Tony Cornforth (the name comes from the first syllables of their first names) is keen to stress that the system should not be described as a sign language. 'People in the deaf world would be very distressed,' she says. Although Makaton's signs are derived from British Sign Language

(or the local sign language of the nation in question – it's used in more than 40 countries), they are primarily intended to reinforce the spoken and written word. In the early years, only key words are signed (car, house, hello, food), but as a child develops, Makaton can stretch to all the words in a sentence, and even grammar.

Even if you have never heard of Makaton, you may have already seen it. The printed symbols – mostly simple cartoons featuring stick figures – are intuitive enough that they are now used in hospitals, law courts and historic buildings to help people who can't read English, or read at all, find their way.

# Spoken language development

As with all other varieties of language, developing speech can be analysed using the different areas of language study. As children we have to acquire not only the sounds of English but also its structures, meaning and discourses. Look back at the chart detailing the stages of spoken development (page 235). You will notice that in terms of spoken output different language features appear to emerge in turn. In terms of input, however, it is important to remember that children are exposed to language on all levels from the day they are born.

## Phonology

Here some nursery children are describing their walk to a local shop. How are they using phonological devices to enhance their meaning?

> R    And then you drive and you …
> J    Yep … broom broom …I'll drive … broom … nee … naw … nee … naw … broom [brake noises]
> T    But we didn't drive, when we went, we didn't drive did we, Robert …What did we do?
> R    We walked.
> J    [in a sing-song] Walk walk walk walk walk walk

---

**Activity 9**

**Individual**

## Making sounds

Say the alphabet slowly to yourself. Are there different ways of doing this? Focus your attention on your mouth. What do you notice about the physical production of sound?

Say the alphabet again a few times. Can you identify any difference between the production of vowel sounds and consonants? Are some sounds more difficult to pronounce than others?

**Class work**    Share your findings with the class.

---

Effective production of sound depends on quite complex manipulation of muscles, tongue and teeth. As children are developing these skills they will often use other ways of pronouncing words.

- **Deletion:** To simplify sounds children will delete more challenging sounds. These might include final consonants, unstressed syllables or consonant clusters (more than one consonant – br, sh).
- **Substitution:** Easier sounds may be used instead of more complex ones – 'handu' instead of 'handle'.
- **CVCVs:** Children will often use preferred word structures rather than adult norms. Consonant–vowel–consonant–vowel (CVCV) is a structure commonly used.

---

**Activity 10**

**Pair work**

## Analysing child utterances

In pairs, analyse the following child utterances. What strategies are the children employing in order to say these words?

- tak manana (banana)
- me not tit (sit)
- mummy gib (give)
- me lili (little)
- this not bi (blue)
- gu here (glue)
- it not lu off (flew)
- no me leep (sleep)
- lug icky (slug)
- it bitu me (bitten)
- give me ratu (rattle)
- more buread (bread)

**Activity 11** **Listen to the child**

Whenever you are analysing children's speech you should avoid deficit prescriptive evaluation (saying a child is 'wrong' or 'can't do' something). Children get very frustrated when adults try to correct their language.

Read the following transcript of a four-year-old talking about what he wants to be when he grows up. How would you evaluate the role of the adult here? What language strategies is the child employing?

| | |
|---|---|
| Adult | What do you want to be when you grow up? |
| Child | A dowboy. |
| Adult | So you want to be a dowboy, eh? |
| Child | [irritated] No! Not a dowboy, a dowboy! |

## Building a vocabulary (lexis)

Do you use all the words you know on a regular basis? The answer is probably 'no'. As adults we each have a large vocabulary (lexis), on average around 40,000 to 50,000 words. We have latent or passive vocabularies, words which we know but don't use. Children are the same, they understand more words than they can say. By the time they are 18 months old most children will have an active vocabulary of around 50 words.

**Activity 12** **First words**

**Pair work**

With a partner, draw up a list of words that you think might appear in a child's first fifty. What language observations can you make about your list?

Now look at the following list. How does yours compare?

| | | | | |
|---|---|---|---|---|
| • ball | • sit | • hi | • no | • that |
| • dog | • baby | • nice | • Daddy | • down |
| • give | • go | • yes | • milk | • put |
| • bye-bye | • allgone | • up | • car | • biscuit |
| • dirty | • juice | • stop | • more | |
| • cat | • Mummy | • shoe | • this | |

These words (from data in David Crystal, *Cambridge Encyclopedia of Language*, 1987) are typically found in a child's first fifty, although no two children are the same. Using your knowledge of language concepts and features, classify them in as many ways as you can. You may find it useful to write the words on separate cards in order to manipulate them more effectively.

What sorts of 'conversation' can you have using just these words? What conclusions can you draw about early vocabulary?

# Overextension and underextension

At first vocabulary is very limited but as it grows the child will employ overextension and underextension.

**Underextension** occurs when a child will use the term 'white' to refer to snow but will not refer to her socks as being white. Pyjamas are only pyjamas when the child is wearing them, not when they are in the washing machine or in the drawer.

**Overextension** occurs much more frequently. This is where a child associates a word with many more things than it actually applies to. The child may use the word 'moon' to refer to a slice of lemon, a crescent-shaped piece of paper, cows' horns, yellow and green chillies. The word 'kick' might refer to kicking a ball, can-can dancers, a cat playing with wool or a fluttering moth.

# Semantics

In 1973 an American researcher, Roger Brown, published *A First Language* where his team demonstrated how grammar and semantics worked together. He analysed utterances into different types of semantic or meaning relationship as follows.

| Semantic relation | Utterance | Context |
|---|---|---|
| agent + action | daddy kick | dad kicks ball |
| action + affected | throw stick | child throws stick |
| agent + affected | me ball | child kicks ball |
| action + location | sit chair | child sits on chair |
| entity + location | spoon table | spoon is on table |
| possessor + possession | daddy coat | points to dad's coat |
| entity + attribute | kitty big | sees a tiger at a zoo |
| nomination | that cake | that is a cake |
| recurrence | more ball | finds second ball |
| negation | no ball | has lost ball |

## Activity 13 — Semantic relationships

Try applying Brown's semantic relationships to the following utterances:

- take bikky
- mummy give
- clock ticking
- big hand
- me little
- eat crips

Did you find any of these hard to classify? What further information would you need to be sure of your analysis?

# Grammar

Much of the child language data you will be asked to analyse will comprise short extracts and incomplete utterances. In order to make your analysis as detailed as possible you will need to be very specific about how a child's grammar is working and employ the grammatical terminology you have learnt to good effect.

## Activity 14  Grammar in use

Read the following transcript. Kate (2 years 6 months) is sitting on the knee of a family friend.

> Adult  [pointing to one of Kate's feet ] What's that?
> Kate  A footsie.
> Adult  [pointing to both feet] What are these?
> Kate  Two footsies – no, two feetsies, I mean.

In as much detail as you can, write a paragraph explaining what this exchange tells us about Kate's grammatical development.

What you have just described is the process of overgeneralisation or grammatical overextension. Did your analysis include the following terms: noun, plural, regular, irregular, diminutive ending, child directed speech?

Another frequently occurring example of overgeneralisation is in the formation of the past tense:

- we wented
- it flied
- they runned.

Such examples can usefully be described as virtuous errors. Always look for the logic behind these when you come across them in transcripts.

There are various key features of early grammar development that you need to be aware of. The following stages are particularly significant.

## Holophrases

Holophrases are one-word utterances that are heavily dependent on context for interpretation. Intonation is important to distinguish questions (signalled by an upward intonation pattern) from statements (signalled by a downward intonation pattern).

Consider the one-word utterance 'Dada'. What different meanings could it have?

## Two-word stage

At about 18–20 months a child moves on from holophrases to using two words. This is known as the two-word stage and is important because it signals the beginning of grammatical competence. We can begin to analyse the child's language learning in terms of the grammar the child has understood and is able to use.

In the two-word stage, utterances are still heavily context dependent. The two words can be

- noun + noun – dolly chair
- noun + verb – teddy drop
- verb + noun – find mummy.

In the two-word stage some of the combinations a child uses begin to suggest adult syntax. The child says 'teddy kiss' when she has made her teddy kiss her doll. When she makes the doll kiss teddy she alters her word order and says 'kiss teddy'. The child seems to have a developing awareness of the position of the subject and object in relation to the position of the verb in a sentence.

Some researchers have referred to the connection between the two words a child uses in the two-word stage as pivot grammar. Children do not say two unrelated words. There is always a connection. Pivot markers can be seen in the following utterances:

- all-gone milk, all-gone teddy, all-gone daddy,

where the pivot is 'all-gone', and

- more milk, more daddy,

where the pivot is 'more'.

To analyse pivotal grammar and semantic grammar you have to understand and analyse the context of the utterance.

## Telegraphic stage

Telegraphic stage is the name given to the stage where only the most essential language features are used, as in a telegram or text message. The child will make the following exclusions:

- auxiliary verbs – especially the form of the verb 'to be'
- articles
- prepositions.

It is important to analyse the words omitted as well as the ones the child uses. Why do children omit the words 'the' and 'a'? Is it perhaps because we do not stress them in conversation?

---

**Activity 15** **Telegraphic texting**

Take five text messages you have received recently. What are the most common exclusions made by the senders? Why do you think this is the case?

---

### Pronouns – ME, ME, ME!!

Children are prone to egocentricity. Think of *Teletubbies* – how is the real baby represented in this programme? As a baby you are not only the centre of your own universe, things are done to you, you are an object. Children will often use the object pronoun 'me' where adults would use the subject pronoun 'I': for example, 'me want to read that.'

Children are also very concerned with the concept of possession. Look out for the use of possessive pronouns in transcripts.

### Prepositions

It has been suggested that children acquire the use of pronouns as they learn about position, location and place. Think about children's songs and rhymes – how many focus on movement and action? 'The hokey cokey' and 'Hickory dickory dock' are two examples. How many more can you think of?

### Verbs

It has been observed by researchers in the United States and several European countries that young children 'invent' verbs out of nouns they already know, and do it very effectively. Later, they do not need to be corrected; they automatically discontinue the strategy when it is no longer needed.

| **Activity 16** | **Creative verbs** |

Look at the following examples then write a short paragraph about the way children manipulate language to create new verbs.

| Utterance | Likely meaning |
| --- | --- |
| The man is keying the door. | The man is opening the door with a key. |
| I want to button it. | I want to turn it off by pressing the button. |
| I'm souping. | I'm eating soup. |
| They're teaing. | They're having tea. |
| Pillow me! | Throw a pillow at me! |
| I'm darking the letters. | I'm scribbling over the letters to make them dark. |
| She's rounding it. | She's making the skipping rope into a half-circle. |
| Can you higher that? | Can you make that higher? |

Look at the data below (from Eve Clark, *Strategies for Communicating*, 1980). The utterances were made by a two-year-old boy. The @ symbol indicates a vowel sound inserted between the words as in 'make-a-that'.

| Utterance | Context |
| --- | --- |
| I do it again | Said as S knocks over blocks |
| You doing that | Said as adult builds blocks into a tower |
| You do do it, OK? | Asking adult to unroll some tape, after trying unsuccessfully to do it himself |
| You do [@] that! | Indicating which toy the adult should take out of a box |
| Uh oh. I did | Said as S turned off tape recorder by pushing a knob |
| The clown do! | Asking adult to make the toy clown do what clowns do |
| Make name! | Telling adult to write his name |
| I make a little doggie | Said as S cuts a dog shape out of Play-Doh |
| Make it go in there | Asking adult to get a crayon back into its box |
| Make [@] that | Said as S pointed to the hand moving on a clock; seemed to be a request for the adult to move the hand on |
| It go there | Talking about a block lying on the floor |
| Red went boom | Talking about a red block that fell on the floor |
| They go in the car | Talking about two storybook characters |
| 'N turn [@] go up | Said as S turned a puzzle piece the right way up |
| 'N go like that | Said as S dropped puzzle pieces on the floor |

Write a paragraph on what you have observed about young children learning to use a familiar English verb.

Do not make the mistake of assuming that the children in these data samples are at a primitive stage of development. They are at an early stage, yes, but their uses of language are intelligent and effective. They have a purpose for using language and a competence to communicate what they mean. For example, they know how to fasten the present-tense participle '-ing' to the nouns in order to make them work as verbs. Nobody taught them to do that; they worked it out. Notice also the use of a comparative form – 'higher'– at the end of the first sample of data.

In the second sample of data, the following aspects of grammatical competence are apparent in the use of verbs:

- use of phrasal verbs – 'go in', 'go up'
- use of irregular past tense – do/did, go/went
- combined verb forms – 'make it go', 'turn go up' (unusual, but it works).

Note also 'go like' to describe manner and the emphasis in 'you do do it'.

The remarkable thing about young children's uses of the language is not deficiency or incorrectness but the efficiency and the logic of the language strategies they use in making meanings out of limited resources. The limitation is merely a factor of age and inexperience, not of ability.

**Exam tip:** Always look for the logic behind what a child is doing with their language, even if, at first, what they say may not seem to make sense.

## Negatives and questions

Here are some suggestions by George Yule (in *The Study of Language*, 1985) based on his observations of certain aspects of grammatical development in young children. He comments on ways of asking questions and ways of forming the negative. Notice how these are not just structural aspects of grammar, they are functions. This illustrates the point frequently made by researchers that children use language in purposeful ways to achieve ends and satisfy needs, not to practise structures.

|  | Questions | Negatives |
|---|---|---|
| 18–26 months | use any 'wh-' word or use rising intonation | begin an utterance with 'no' or 'not' |
| 22–30 months | more 'wh-' words; rising intonation still used | 'don't' and 'can't' in front of verb |
| 24–40 months | invert subject and verb – 'Can I eat it?' | 'didn't' and 'won't' appear; 'isn't' comes later |

The last grammatical structure to be learnt is the passive. When do you use the passive voice? Can you think of reasons why this grammatical structure is learnt later than others?

## Pragmatics

Understanding pragmatics depends on our understanding of social situations. We become familiar with a wide variety of social situations only through time and experience. Children often appear rude because of their lack of experience with different social contexts. In this example Janet, a neighbour, is talking in the living room to Anna's mother. Anna (two years) has walked between them.

> **Anna** [to her mum] Is she staying to tea?
> **Mum** Oh Anna, you shouldn't talk about Janet like that. It sounds rude. You say 'Is Janet staying to tea', don't you? [Anna sucks her thumb and hides her face in her mother's apron.]

How has the social context affected the language used by parent and child? What effect do you think this exchange had on Anna's language learning?

> A little girl answers the phone. The caller on the other end says, 'Hello, is your Daddy in?' The little girl replies, 'Yes!' and puts the phone down.

How is the girl's understanding of the social context different from the caller's?

Modal verbs and the passive voice are essential to our codes of politeness. Note that these are some of the last grammatical structures that children acquire. For more on modal verbs, turn to page 14.

## Activity 17

**Pair work**

## Why do we lie?

Read this article from the *Guardian* (April 2007).

# The truth about lying and laughing

**Richard Wiseman**

Other researchers have explored the development of deception in children. Some of the most interesting experiments have involved asking youngsters not to take a peek at their favourite toys. During these studies, a child is led into a laboratory and asked to face one of the walls. The experimenter then explains that he is going to set up an elaborate toy a few feet behind them. After setting up the toy, the experimenter says that he has to leave the laboratory, and asks the child not to turn around and peek at the toy. The child is secretly filmed by hidden cameras for a few minutes, and then the experimenter returns and asks them whether they peeked. Almost all three-year-olds do, and then half of them lie about it to the experimenter. By the time the children have reached the age of five, all of them peek and all of them lie. The results provide compelling evidence that lying starts to emerge the moment we learn to speak. Perhaps surprisingly, when adults are shown films of their children denying that they peeked at the toy, they are unable to detect whether their offspring are lying or telling the truth.

In pairs, discuss the function of lying. As adults, why do we do it? Why do you think the children in the experiment lied? To what extent is our ability to lie dependent on our understanding of social context?

Parents tend to correct truth conditions rather than grammar. If correction worked you'd expect children to grow up speaking the truth ungrammatically.

There is evidence to suggest that the correct use of grammar is more to do with maturity than simply imitating what adults say. What observations can you make on the following dialogue?

| | |
|---|---|
| Child | Nobody don't like me. |
| Mother | No, say 'Nobody likes me.' |
| Child | Nobody don't like me. |

[Eight repetitions of this dialogue.]

| | |
|---|---|
| Mother | No, now listen carefully: say 'Nobody likes me.' |
| Child | Oh! Nobody don't likes me. |

# Creativity

Children are linguistically creative because they haven't learnt the norms. Their language use is not restricted by social convention and sensitivity to social context.

Metaphor had a key role in the origins of language development. Consider how many metaphors involve parts of the body:

- Outward movement – the *foot* of the mountain, *ribs* of a ship, *head* of a school
- Inward movement – I *see* what she means, he *held* on to his point of view.

---

## Activity 18 — Playing with language

**Individual**

Write down as precisely as you can what Matthew and Kate are doing with language in these transcripts.

> Matthew (two years) is watching his mum spoon stewed rhubarb into a bowl.
> **Matthew**   Dis rubile looks like biscetti (spaghetti)
>
> **Kate**   Can I have a bit of cheese, please – cheese please – that's a rhyme.

**Group work**

Collect young children's jokes and rhymes. In small groups pool your data and classify it by lexis, grammar, semantics and pragmatics. Analyse your groupings and make some suggestions about how children like to play with language. What aspects of language appeal to children's creativity?

---

## Theories

Research into how we acquire language is extensive. The table summarises the most dominant theories that you should be aware of when you are analysing child language. Remember that theory can be supported or disputed by real data. In an exam you will be expected to show your awareness of theory as it may or may not apply to the data you are given. Your own analysis is more important than the rigid application of theory. Having studied child language development in practice, you are in a position to put forward your own ideas also.

| Theoretical approach | Summary | Things to consider |
|---|---|---|
| Imitation | Children copy the language that they hear and repeat it until they have got it right. | This approach does not take into account virtuous errors or original utterances. Do you use only sentences that you have heard before? |
| Behaviourism | Positive reinforcement of correct imitation will result in children acquiring good language habits. | |
| Innateness | The human brain is 'hardwired' to acquire language. It has what has been described as a Language Acquisition Device (LAD) that allows us to learn language. Children recognise patterns in language and experiment with them. This allows language to be learnt quickly and explains features such as overgeneralisation. | Think about the factors that prevent children from acquiring language successfully. Is language production simply an innate process? |

*continued overleaf*

| Cognition | Language is an integral part of a child's general development. It develops as the child's experience of the world grows. Children need to experience and understand concepts such as 'up' or 'bigger' before they can successfully apply language to them. | Although there are identifiable stages in language learning they are not necessarily 'universal'. Language acquisition is a rapid process on many levels. Can grammatical development be explained by a cognitive approach? |
|---|---|---|
| Input and interaction | Many adults adopt a particular variety of language when speaking to their children (motherese, caretaker language, child directed speech). This is important in establishing and maintaining meaningful communication with a child and is therefore significant in the process of language development. | Research into this area is still developing. The importance of input is taken very seriously but a direct relationship between CDS and child language output is hard to establish. |

## Activity 19    Look up a linguist

Pair work
Group work

There are many important personalities in the study of child language development. They are often associated with a particular theoretical approach.

You are going to produce a class booklet introducing some of these researchers and their ideas about language acquisition to an A-level audience. Work in pairs or small groups to research these linguists and their contribution to the study of language acquisition:

- Noam Chomsky
- Steven Pinker
- Jean Piaget
- Lev Vygotsky
- Eric Lenneberg
- Jerome Bruner
- Burrhus Frederic Skinner
- Jean Berko Gleason
- Jean Aitchison
- M.A.K. Halliday

Use the internet and books available to you to collect information on your linguist. Identify the area of language theory most commonly associated with them. Summarise your findings into a one- or two-page report for your class. All the reports can then be collated into a booklet.

## The functions of language

Another concept you will find useful when analysing child language data is function.

## Activity 20    What does language do?

Individual

Write down all of the spoken language encounters you have had since you woke up this morning.

Pair work

In pairs, share your findings and describe the purpose of each encounter. Summarise the different functions of your spoken language. Share your ideas about function with the class.

M.A.K. Halliday divided language use into seven functions:

1  Instrumental – satisfying material needs
2  Regulatory – controlling others' behaviour
3  Interactional – getting along with others

4 Personal – identifying and expressing the self
5 Heuristic – exploring the world
6 Imaginative – creating a world of one's own
7 Representational – communicating information.

## Activity 21 | Applying the terminology

Go back to your own list of language functions from Activity 20. Re-label them using Halliday's terms.

## Review

This brings us to the end of our exploration of spoken language development. In this section you have seen how different areas of language study – phonology, grammar, semantics and pragmatics – allow us to examine different aspects of speech as it is acquired by human beings. You have encountered new concepts to help you to think about child language data including stages of development and function. You have also been introduced to key theories of CLD that you can apply to data. You will not be asked to recount these theories in an exam.

You may be asked to analyse spoken CLD data at AS or A2. It is important to remember that this is data like any other and you should always take account of issues such as audience, purpose and specific context as well as concepts specific to language acquisition, particularly if you are tackling the topic at A2 as this will be part of your synoptic unit.

The most important thing you can do to consolidate your understanding of spoken language development is to expose yourself to as much child language as possible. If you don't have young cousins or siblings, you can find examples of children's speech on television, online, in language textbooks and out and about in the world.

# Literacy

As a starting-point, you are going to explore what you understand by the term 'literate'.

## Activity 22 | Surveying the word 'literate'?

**Class work**

Everyone in the class should write their own definition on a Post-it note and place it on the board. A student or the teacher should then read out the definitions and summarise the word as it is understood by the class. The whole class should then discuss the variations in definition.

## Activity 23 | Research

**Group work**

Using dictionaries and other resources available to you, find 'official' definitions of 'literate'. Are there varying opinions?

If you have access to the *OED online*, trace the origins of the word. How did Dr Johnson define it? How is it most often used today?

Have a look at the websites www.literacytrust.org.uk and www.ukla.org.uk. What are these organisations and why do they exist?

Read the following article from the *Guardian* (February 2007). Why is literacy a political issue?

# Poor maths and literacy skills cost £800m a year, survey finds

The *Guardian* has reported on research from Learndirect which has said that poor mathematics skills cost British adults more than £800m a year, according to a survey of 1000 adults. It also revealed that one in three workers – 14.6 million people – admit their inadequate numeracy and literacy skills have lost their company money. Half those questioned felt their basic maths and English skills let them down. Many said they did not know the difference between basic words or homophones such as 'there' and 'their'. Learndirect said £823m is lost each year due to inadequate basic skills – enough to pay the starting salaries of more than 40,000 new teachers.

The *Guardian* interviewed Judi James, a workplace expert, who said that around a third of people surveyed said they feel embarrassed, panicked or afraid when their basic skills let them down. Learndirect also estimated that 1.4 million workers in the UK believe they have missed out on a promotion, or even lost a job, due to a lack of basic maths or English skills.

Go to the website www.dfes.gov.uk and search for references to literacy. What is the government doing to improve national literacy levels?

In your groups present your findings to the class under the heading 'Why literacy is an important issue in the twenty-first century'.

For the purposes of your AS- and A-level studies, you need to understand how young children learn to read and write. As you have probably discovered, there is no simple answer to this question. However, there are various theoretical approaches you need to consider. The important difference between reading and writing and the acquisition of spoken language is that reading and writing need to be taught.

# Writing

## Learning to write

In pairs, take it in turns to read the paragraph above to each other. As one of you reads, the other should attempt to write down the passage using the hand that they would not normally write with.

When you have done this, discuss the challenges of learning to write. What do you remember about learning to write? What strategies did your teachers employ to help you? Did you enjoy writing at primary school? Do you enjoy writing now?

Share your observations with the rest of the class.

As with speech, research has shown that the ability to write happens in identifiable stages:

1 Drawing and sign writing
2 Letter-like forms

3 Copied letters
4 Child's name and strings of letters

5 Words

6 Sentences
7 Text.

## Research

As a class, collect as many examples of children's early writing as you can. These may be your own or the work of younger relatives or friends. If you know any primary school teachers, ask them if you could borrow examples of their pupils' work (you must get permission for this). If you have difficulty collecting data try the website www.ncaction.org.uk and search on English, Examples of Work. You will find lots of examples of children's work at various levels of ability.

In groups, share your data and identify what stage you think the young writers are at. Then consider the following questions.

- What do the children already know about writing?
- How is their writing functioning in terms of the language concepts (covered in more detail on pages 6–18 and 23–26)?
- What type of text is the child attempting to write?
- Are they aware of audience and purpose?

In your groups, create informative posters of your findings and present them to the class.

**Activity 26**  **Assessing writing**

This text was written by Anna in Year 1 at primary school. Imagine you are Anna's teacher. How would you assess this piece of writing? What comments would you make and how would you feed these back to Anna?

Discuss your ideas with the class. How would you, as teachers, ensure that Anna had a positive learning experience?

owns The Gods disied to get a anml For eth Yir so thy go twev anmuls and The Gods Put themin a ras ties whir the anmls The PiJ The ox The Reak and the dragn and a tigeu and a hrysaRam anda muky and a doG ana snak and hru. and The Rat wan Biks Thoe gat Tupt on The oxs bak and The ox sru he was winig but the Rat Jupt qof and The PiG was The 4 Loosur

## Spelling

As you will have noticed, mastering the English spelling system is challenging at all levels. Spelling is always interesting when you are analysing children's writing. As with speech, you must take care not to use a **deficit model** when discussing children's work – look for the logic behind what they have done. Researchers have identified four stages of development in spelling.

1 **Pre communicative**
   - The child knows that symbols can be used to say something.
   - The child uses a range of symbols – invented, numbers, upper and lower case.
   - The child does not make sound–symbol connections.

2 **Semi phonetic**
   - The child is beginning to make sound–symbol connections.
   - The child knows about word boundaries (spaces between words).
   - The child may shorten some words.

3 **Phonetic**
   - The child uses sound–symbol connections consistently (this of course gives rise to spelling mistakes owing to the irregular nature of English spelling).
   - The child uses known words.

4 **Transitional stage**
   - The child uses visual strategies.
   - The child uses mostly conventional spelling.
   - Place holding – the child will write letters in place of a word that is not known.

**Activity 27** | **Analysing spelling**

Using the data you collected for Activity 25 and the other texts in this section, write a report on patterns of spelling that you have observed.

## The writing context

**Activity 28** | **Discussing your own writing output**

Consider all the writing you have done in your lifetime. Who was the audience and what was the purpose? How much writing have you done in a 'real world' context rather than an educational context? Have you ever written a story for anyone other than a teacher?

**Narrative** is one of the first discourses we encounter. We are told stories from an early age, much of our speech involves recounting stories and events from our lives. Narrative is also an important part of our early writing experience. There are many models for **narrative structure**. Here is one (devised by linguist Michael Hoey) that you might find useful.

- **Situation** – What was the situation?
- **Problem** – What was the problem?
- **Solution** – What was the solution or response?
- **Evaluation** – How successful was the solution?

The following text was written by Lesley, aged 10, at school.

> **The Dead Pigeon**
> Today, at afternoon play, just when we were coming back into school, Mrs B. found a pigeon on the floor, next to the Haygreen Lane side. Some children had gone in but I was there when Gary Destains said,
>
> 'Hey up! There's a pigeon on floor.'
>
> We all rushed up but Mrs B. shouted,
>
> 'Stop. Come back and let me look what's happened to it, poor thing.' I just thought it was resting a bit but Dobbie said, 'It's dead'.
>
> It was. When Mrs B. picked it up, its neck just flopped over.
>
> 'Poor thing,' I said to Dobbie.
>
> She lifted it up with its wings, and they were like big, lovely grey fans. I didn't know wings were so lovely and big, with so many feathers especially.
>
> When we had gone in, we were just sitting in our class and telling Mrs Sanderson and the others about it, when Mrs B. came and held it up with its lovely grey wings. I was sorry for it, poor thing, and Mrs Sanderson was sad. And we all were.

## Activity 29   Analysing children's writing

Write an analysis of this text, focusing particularly on the structure of the narrative and any techniques the writer has used to enhance the narrative. You should also evaluate the writer's language in terms of grammar, lexis, semantics and pragmatics.

Here is another narrative, this time an imagined one by a ten-year-old boy. The contributions of the adult listening to the story are given in brackets.

> A donkey and a giraffe ... came out [uh-huh] And ... the ... giraffe said, 'Hi! Would you like to play with me?' And ... the donkey said, 'No! I'm mad' [uh-huh] And ... she said, 'What happened?' ... and ... the donkey said, 'Well, I made a box to keep my things in.' [uh-huh] 'And I found a penny. And I put it in the blo-box but now I can't find the penny' [uh-huh] ... and ... and ... the giraffe said, 'Well, maybe it's at school! Remember? You took it to school!' And the donkey said, 'How do you know? I think you're the one that took the penny.' [uh-huh] And the gi-giraffe said ... um ..., 'No I didn't.' And ... oh ... she said, 'How do you know?' He said, 'Well ... you know, I remember you took it' [uh-huh] And ... then she thought about it for a while and she s-said ..., 'Well, friends don't steal! I'm sorry I was mad at you! Now let's go play.'

## Activity 30   Telling stories

Track the different things the boy does with language as he tells the story. For example,

> 'A donkey and a giraffe' identifies the characters; giraffe initiates a conversation with a question/invitation to play; negative response plus personal remark, 'I'm mad'; question, followed by hesitations; note use of 'Well' to begin utterance. And so on.

What do you learn from this transcript about the ways young children tell stories?

## Activity 31  A ruined house – text for analysis

Here is a story written by a Year 2 child. It was based on a story about a house read to the class earlier. The child's story was written in exam conditions for the purposes of a SATs test.

Write an analysis of this piece of writing. Remember to explore different areas of language study as well as discussing the context of the writing. Remember also to avoid deficit model observations. What does this child understand about narrative structure?

A Ruined house

Once there was a street called Newstree
it was an old Street I fownd a Ruined
House. It has levs herlee evvy Whte it
cooks like a Rustey house It was bilt
in 1996 i thihc It was now a brosenhouse I
will go in side it but it mite have bug
inside it. lets opun the door rrvrrrr
when I went inside it mait a surt of a
krac husee I rownd a fire it was on I
was rely hot I am swating cobs and I
went to the ccubit and I saw ...
"a spidr"! a big one I did.

## Theory on the stages of writing development

One theoretical approach to the writing process that students find useful when analysing text is that put forward by B.M. Kroll (1981). Kroll identified four stages of development.

1  **The preparatory stage** – Children master the physical skills needed to write and the basic principles of the spelling system.

2 **The consolidation stage** – Children write as they speak. They tend to use short, declarative sentences, grammatically incomplete sentences or longer sentences linked by simple conjunctions such as 'and', 'so', 'then'.

3 **The differentiation stage** – An awareness of the differences between writing and speech. Increased confidence in using conventions and grammatical structures associated with writing. Sentences become more complex with more subordinate clauses and sophisticated connectives. Style becomes more suited to audience and purpose.

4 **The integration stage** – The writer develops a personal voice and adapts to the requirements of different situations. These skills continue to develop into adulthood.

| Activity 32 | ## Applying the theory |

Revisit the written texts you have studied on pages 252–256. Can you apply Kroll's stages of development to them? To what extent do you feel your own writing reflects the integration stage?

| Activity 33 | ## Further text for analysis |

The following text was written by a Year 2 pupil. It is about a book that he has read in class. Write a detailed analysis of the text. Remember to acknowledge context and the content of the piece.

The text says:
I don't like the writing because the writing you don't know which one to read first. I like the pictures.

# Reading

**Activity 34**

**Individual**

## Your own reading

Individually, write down a list of your current reading repertoire. Consider the types of reading material you don't read. Are there types of text that you have read in the past that you no longer choose to read? What has shaped your current reading choices?

**Group work**

Discuss your findings in small groups and then report back to the class.

**Activity 35**

**Pair work**

## Reading together

In pairs, take it in turns to read a children's fiction book to each other.

How did this feel? What happened to your voice whilst you were reading? Write down everything you can remember about learning to read at primary school. Discuss your observations with the class.

**For further discussion:** How did learning to read at primary school differ from your experience of reading at secondary school?

Reading is an essential activity for language development. It is one of the best ways of increasing your vocabulary and accessing ideas. Traditionally, at university, students 'read' subjects rather than 'studying' them.

Learning to read is therefore a crucially important stage of anyone's education. How we teach young people to read is a topic of much debate. Here are two articles concerning recent developments in the teaching of reading. Text A is from the *Times Educational Supplement* (2006); Text B is from the *Daily Mail* (2005).

**Text A**

# G-oo-d-b-ye 2-00-6

**Adi Bloom**

• • • • • • • • • • • • • • • • •

The debate over synthetic phonics dominated the headlines for primary teachers this year. If there is one lesson all primary teachers have learnt over the last year it is to recognise synthetic phonics. The reading method dominated the primary world in 2006.

In March, Jim Rose, former head of primary at Ofsted, published the results of his review into the teaching of reading. He recommended introducing synthetic phonics at the age of five and providing 20-minute phonics lessons every day. The Government accepted the report entirely.

**Text B**

# How Synthetic Phonics Works

Synthetic phonics has been described as a 'back to basics' way of teaching children to read and it will be the focus of the Government's literacy review. The system teaches pupils to recognise the sounds of individual letters, and then blends of letters such as 'sh', 'th' and 'ee'. Gradually pupils build up to 'decoding' whole words from their constituent parts, for example 's-t-r-e-e-t'. Those in favour of synthetic phonics say it teaches children very quickly how to read almost any word they encounter. But critics of the method have argued that while children can read individual words they often do not understand what the words mean. Synthetic phonics proved hugely successful in trials involving 300 schoolchildren in Clackmannanshire, Scotland, that were evaluated earlier this year. By the age of 11, those children taught using synthetic phonics were three years ahead of their peers in reading skills. Phonics was the dominant teaching system until the 1960s when new methods arrived, such as teaching children to learn whole words without mastering the alphabet 'by rote'. The Government's national literacy strategy involves a combination of phonics with other methods.

## Activity 36
**Group work**

### The reading debate

In small groups, discuss why the way we teach reading is contentious. Why do you think there is still debate in the twenty-first century about how to do it? Can you remember any reading experiences that were particularly successful when you were learning to read?

## Approaches to teaching reading

In 1998 Ann Browne identified these three basic approaches to the teaching of reading.

- **Bottom up model** – Text is decoded by matching letters to sounds and building up these sounds to form a word. Words are then put together to form sentences.
- **Top down model** – Readers predict the meaning of a text from what they already know about the structure and meaning of language. They use their knowledge of the world, stories and visual clues to get the meaning of a text. Then they progress to letter and word recognition.
- **Interactive model** – This puts the two approaches together. Readers assume a text is meaningful and predict meaning using contextual knowledge. They also apply their knowledge of sounds, letters and words to help them understand.

Within these basic models many specific approaches to the teaching of reading have been developed. We will look at a few here.

# Phonics

As you will have gathered from the articles you read earlier, the phonics method of teaching reading is widely used at the moment. Phonics is, very basically, to do with the matching of sounds to symbols in order to allow children to build up words: for example,

- 'c-a-t' spells 'cat'
- 'd-o-g' spells 'dog'
- 'm-a-n' spells 'man'.

In English, a high proportion of the commonest words pose problems, they cannot be sounded out. Here are twenty of the commonest words. Try sounding them out.

- the
- to
- that
- was
- with
- of
- in
- it
- on
- his
- and
- is
- he
- are
- they
- a
- you
- for
- as
- at

There is no simple one-to-one relationship between our phonemes and the 26 letters of the alphabet. Vowels pose problems. Try pronouncing these words:

- plag
- glame
- clure
- chench
- gatter
- mald.

The rime unit is a more reliable guide to pronunciation than individual letters: for example,

- look – cook
- please – pleasure
- would – should
- jumped – landed.
- to – who

Children need to learn many words as sight words. They must also use analogy and prediction. To be able to read you need motivation, background knowledge, rewards, interesting texts, social interaction, strategies, teacher input, collaboration, books, relevance.

**Activity 36**

**Group work**

## Research phonics

To find out more about the complexities of phonics, research the websites

- www.bbc.co.uk/schools/wordsandpictures/phonics
- www.literacytrust.org.uk/Database/Primary/phonics.html

# Reading schemes

Are you familiar with Letterland? Then you already know about reading schemes. Reading schemes are specially written to help children with their reading. They include deliberately chosen vocabulary, high frequency words, and graduated progression through a series of books or booklets. These are often colour coded to show progression.

There is much debate surrounding the use of reading schemes as opposed to 'real books'. To find out more visit www.literacytrust.org.uk/pubs/solity.html.

# Collaborative reading

Research has shown that children learn to read more effectively if they collaborate with others. Collaboration can include working with other pupils, teachers, parents or siblings. Recently it has been suggested that children learn most effectively when they read aloud, rather than being read to.

The following transcript is of an A-level English Language student (Rachel) helping a seven-year-old primary pupil with her reading. They are reading an excerpt from *The Jolly Pocket Postman*.

**Key**

R    Rachel
P    Pupil
(.)  Brief pause          |  Overlapping speech

---

P    once upon a summers (.) morning (.) the jolly postman walk up (.) yyyeard
R    shall we try that word again?
P    (.) postman
R    no this one
P    walk?
R    what do you do in the morning? (3 seconds) wwwoke
P    woke (3 seconds) jp (.) yawning
R    – yeah –
P    (.) cooked his breakfast (.) fed the dog (.) read [spoken as present tense] the (3 seconds) package (.) paper!
R    urn-hum
P    kissed the frog  | [laughter]
R                    | uurrgghh and then look that star means you go down to there and it says (.) only joking
P    [sing-song] only joking (.) so it means there's a flower there and you go from that one to go to there
R    yep
P    [sing-song] oflly joking [laughter] got-his-coat-and (2 seconds) grabbled
R    [inaudible]
P    huh?
R    what do you what am I doing?
P    (.) grabbed-his-hat (2 seconds) for his (.) phoned
R    very nearly
P    s-so does it have one of these on every one?
R    it has some letters (.) on each page (3 seconds) well on some pages (.) we'll | get to those I know (.) it's funny isn't it
P                                                                                  | haha
P    [high-pitched] I'm late
R    shall we carry on?
P    (3 seconds) got his coat and grabbed his hat (.) fbund (.) his (.) tray
R    nearly
P    (3 seconds) ttry
R    shall we split it up? (2 seconds) what's that part?
P    tyy-red
R    ty-uh
P    tyre (.) was (.) pain [throaty sound] (.) painted

R    what does that |

P                 | pain [inaudible] –ake

R    what's that?

P    pink (.) pinky (.) I can't read it!

R    I bet you can (.) how about if I put that (.) do you know what that word is?

P    (2 seconds) uunmimm

R    no?

P    pancake

R    that's it so you can

P    f-flat

R    urn hum

P    [inaudible mumbling followed by big breath] blowww me (.) down (.) uh (.) can you hold that up? (3 seconds) blow me up (3 seconds) went back for an-other cup

R    (.) cup of tea

P    yeah but it doesn't say another cup of tea on there

R    (3 seconds) no it doesn't [inaudible]

P    ri-ot (.) ribbuhl (.) robbed

R    (.) rubbed

P    rubbed-his-cane (.) chain

R    sound it out

P    ch(.)chin

R    yep

P    (.) scratched his had (.) head

R    uh huh

P    and walked to walk inside

R    let's go back to these two

P    to walk (.) inside

R    (.) in?

P    in (.) s-stead

R    walked to work instead (.) right shall I read this next page or do you want to have a go?

P    you read it

## Activity 38   Research phonics

**Pair work**

In pairs, take the role of pupil and student. Read the transcript aloud. What do you notice about the interaction between student and pupil?

**Individual**

Individually, write an analysis of the transcript, commenting on the ways in which the student attempts to encourage the pupil to read. How successful is she? In what ways is the pupil interacting with the activity? Remember to address ideas and concepts from language study wherever you can.

The transcript on page 262 is of a group of primary school children who have been asked to discuss the poem 'hist whist' by E.E. Cummings.

**hist whist**

hist    whist
little ghostthings
tip-toe
twinkle-toe

little twitchy
witches and tingling
goblins
hob-a-nob    hob-a-nob

little hoppy happy
toad in tweeds
tweeds
little itchy mousies

with scuttling
eyes    rustle and run    and
hidehidehide
whisk

whisk    look out for the old woman
with the wart on her nose
what she'll do to yer
nobody knows

for she knows the devil    ooch
the devil    ouch
the devil
ach    the great

green
dancing
devil
devil

devil
devil

        wheeEEE

## Activity 39    Collaborative reading

**Group work**

In small groups, read the poem and discuss it. What do you think it means?

Now read the transcript on pages 263–264. How did your discussion compare with the primary children's?

Make notes in response to the following questions.

- What strategies do the children use to makes sense of the poem?
- Which aspects of the poem appeal most to the children?
- How does the collaboration work? What roles do the children adopt?
- Are the children using a bottom up, top down or interactive approach to this text?

[Rustles, door creaks and closes. Whispers]

| | |
|---|---|
| Hazel | D'ya understand? |
| Matthew | Yes, I understand |
| Simon | Hm |
| Various | Sh…sh [inaudible whispers] All right … right |
| H | Right – it's about thisss – ghosts and it goes creak and he goes disappearing under the boat floorboards. |
| M | But what gets me is hist whist |
| Jenny | What does that mean? |
| M | The wind or something |
| J | Couldn't be the wind. The wind doesn't make two sounds like that |
| H | The pot – the cooking pot |
| S | Yes – sh – hish whish sh – sh – sh-er |
| H | It could be the wish in the book – it could be the wish it meant |
| S | It could be a wishing [inaudible] Hist whist [whispers] hist whist |
| M | Little ghostly things |
| S | What ghostly? |
| M | Snake |
| S | Yeah |
| H | Snakes in the pot! |
| M | Yeah snakes! |
| Various | In the pot … hist … whist |
| J | Whist! |
| M | Whist! |
| H | Ghosts! |
| Several | Ghosts [whispers] ss – ss-ss ss-ss-ss-ss-ss-ss-ss |
| J | Oh for she knows the devil oh the devil ouch |
| H | I saw the devil at the pictures |
| J | the devil oh the great green dancing devil, devil, devil wheese – what does that mean, then? |
| S | Dancing devil! |
| J | All put together? |
| H | Well I don't know |
| J | The dancing … the green devil dancing round her |
| S | Yeah |
| J | Dancing round the pot |
| S | Aah … yeah |
| H | and she makes it all her own and everything |
| S | for she knows the devil ouch, the devil – ouch |
| H | The snakes … how she knows so it could – be – that |
| J | It could be the woman with all the snakes on her head |
| S | I know that, I know that – something like somebody caught by the devil |
| H | Yeah |
| J | Or someone's got a mind they're going to do something what the devil wishes 'em to do |
| H | Yeah! |
| M | And the witch is like a devil is she … she spells |
| S | Well one … does the wi…does the witch |

| M | the devil's … she's a devil's witch |
|---|---|
| J | Like do de… the witch is devil's thing so wha… what's this story – the poem's trying to say – is that cos she's a witch, cos sh…er…the devil – cos she's the really – what the devil |
| H | She's the devil witch … the devil |
| J | … wanted her to do |
| S | [notices the Sleep switch on the tape recorder] Sleep, let's go to sleep!! [giggles] |
| H | Oh be quiet Matthew! [noise from Matthew presumably] |
| J | So that's what that story |

## Children's books and media texts

As we have seen, young children like to play with language. It is a common misconception amongst A-level students writing about children's books that they contain only 'simple' words and are 'straightforward'. Consider the words

- supercalafragelisticexpealidocious
- muchness
- diagon alley.

Why do these appeal to young readers?

| **Activity 40** | **Language in stories for children** |
|---|---|
| **Individual** | Research and collect a range of children's books. Analyse their use of language using all of the language concepts (covered in more detail on pages 6–18 and 23–26). What patterns of language use can you identify? What contextual factors influence the language use (consider gender, purpose of text, when the texts were written, etc.). |
| **Class work** | As a class, watch an episode of *Teletubbies* or read some of the children's stories and look at some of the language activities on www.bbc.co.uk/cbeebies or www.bbc.co.uk/schools. Make notes on the contexts and language features used in these stories. |
| **Individual** | From your research, write a guide to analysing the language of children's books for A-level English Language students. Make sure your audience know what sort of language features to look out for. |
| | How do the texts you have studied in this section on reading (pages 257–264) reflect what you already know about children's acquisition of language? |

## Computer literacy – a quick note

When did you first use a computer? In primary schools today ICT is an integral part of the teaching of Literacy. Keyboard skills and the manipulation of software are an essential part of early learning.

**Discussion:** For which written tasks do you use a pen and for which a keyboard? Do you think there should be more computers in schools? Is the pen, as writing technology, defunct? How has ICT changed the way we write?

In this section you have explored the topics of children's writing and children's reading. The level of expertise you need in this area will depend upon the specification you are following, but texts written for children can be set for analysis in various exam units not simply those dealing specifically with CLD.

You should now be aware of key issues surrounding the teaching of reading and writing. You should also have identified the way in which writing for children reflects their own language development. In an exam you might be asked to analyse transcripts of children reading, possibly with adults. It is important to consider the role of interaction and collaboration in these cases. You may have to analyse an example of children's writing. Again you will be expected to apply all your knowledge of texts, not simply issues specific to the topic. Always remember to unpack the context of a reading or writing text as you would any other, taking particular account of context, audience and purpose. You should always consider and apply the range of language concepts, as well as specific topic knowledge, particularly if you are tackling this topic in your synoptic unit.

Through the activities you have completed in this section you have been introduced to a range of sources of reading and writing data. You should continue to use these to further your expertise in this area.

# Model exam question and advice

Here is an exam question followed on pages 266–267 by a student's answer and examiner's comments.

### Exam question
The extract gives examples of typical utterances spoken by children aged two and children aged three. Discuss what this data illustrates about the language abilities of children of these ages and how their ability has developed between the ages of two and three.

| Age Two | Age Three |
|---|---|
| Teddy on floor. | You put that on there. |
| That stuck now. | Me got lots of cars like Jimmy. |
| Mummy gone out. | Mummy want me to go in the garden. |
| No daddy go. | Where you going with that red shovel? |
| Open it. | Daddy comed to see me in the garden. |
| Put in box. | I can see mummy and daddy in the mirror. |
| Look my dollie. | Mary went in the Wendy house with me and Paul. |
| What it doing? | Why you do that for? |
| Fall down car. | Can me put it in like that? |
| My mouse eating. | It doesn't go that way, it goes this way. |

## Student's response

At the age of two most children are at the stage known as the two word stage. Extract F illustrates the abilities of a two year old. This particular child[1] shows an example of negation[2] as he/she recognises[3] negatives: 'No daddy go'. The two year old child also shows examples of deixis because he/she uses pronouns to replace nouns: 'That stuck now'.[4]

The main sentence mood this child uses is declarative because he/she is observing things and making conversation: 'Teddy on floor'; 'That stuck now'. The child also uses a lot of imperatives[5] as he/she is instructing someone to do something: 'Open it'. One interrogative sentence is shown: 'What it doing?'[6]

The two year old child also knows how to use possessive adjectives: 'Look my dollie'; 'My mouse eating'.

The child knows how to say words in the present tense with an 'ing' ending: 'My mouse eating'. An irregular past tense is shown: 'Mummy gone out'.[7]

All of the sentences used by the two year old are simple sentences with the determiners missed out. The child of three shows the use of deixis: 'You put that on there'. This child is at the telegraphic stage. The main sentence moods used by the three year old are declarative sentences: 'Me got lots of cars like Jimmy'; 'Mummy want me to go in the garden'. The three year old also uses a lot of interrogative sentences: 'Where you going with that red shovel?'; 'Why you do that for?' The three year old gives commands shown by the use of imperative sentences: 'You put that on there'.[8]

Unlike the two year old, this child tends to use many pronouns: 'You put that on there'; 'Me got lots of cars like Jimmy'. Sometimes the child says 'me' instead of the first person pronoun 'I' because he/she does not completely understand how to use pronouns yet.[9]

The three year old child understands how to form a regular past tense with the 'ed' ending but tends to use this ending for irregular past tenses which is Gill[10] Berko-Gleason's theory known as analogy. The child over-generalises one rule: 'Daddy comed to see me in the garden.'

Compound sentences[11] are shown in the three year old's language: 'Mary went in the Wendy house with me and Paul'. The three year old does not miss out all of the determiners.

The use of adverbial phrases are shown in the three year old's vocabulary: 'Daddy come to see me in the garden'; 'Mary went in the Wendy house with me and Paul'.[12]

The child knows the rule of how to end a plural with the letter 's': 'I got enough of those apples now'. Also the child knows how to use abbreviations: 'It doesn't go that way, it goes this way'.[13]

As shown in extract F, a child's ability develops quite a lot between the ages of two and three. The child begins to use pronouns, understands how words are made into plurals, and understands how to form regular past tenses. At three years old the child has learnt how to use compound sentences with a continuer unlike the two year old child. The three year old child has learnt how to use abbreviations.

## Examiner's comments

1 Assumes that the utterances come from one child (which they do not). Shows the importance of reading the question carefully.
2 Does not build on 'two word stage' but moves onto another topic.
3 'Recognises' should be 'uses'. It is also more important to say how negatives are formed at each age.
4 This paragraph is very fragmented, as if the candidate has not planned the answer.

5 The data suggests nothing about the frequency of these utterances. Mistake arises from the assumption in 1.
6 There are several missed opportunities for explaining how the moods are constructed.
7 'Past tense' should be 'past participle'. Needs to connect with inflections in general.
8 Again the moods are correctly spotted but needs to put the two ages together and comment on typical development.
9 Connect this with typical development of pronoun usage over the two ages.
10 Jean.
11 Misunderstands that 'and' links 'me' and 'Paul', not two clauses and so the sentence isn't compound.
12 Adverbials are correctly identified but should be highlighted and connected with development of clause elements.
13 Implies that the child is deliberately abbreviating and misses changes in formation of negative.

### Overall comment

The candidate understands and accurately describes many of the features shown in the data, making clear use of quotations. The short paragraphs indicate weak organisation and underdeveloped points. The comments are not rooted firmly enough in knowledge of typical linguistic abilities at these ages although the candidate knows which features are important.

Grade: D/C

## Activity 41  Exam practice

Write a plan for the exam question and then write the essay, basing improvements on the examiner's comments.

# Sources for further research

**Really useful books**
- David Crystal (1987) *The Cambridge Encyclopedia of the English Language.* Cambridge: Cambridge University Press.
- Jean Sitwell Peccei (1994) *Child Language.* London: Routledge.
- Jean Aitchison (1987) *Words in the Mind.* Oxford: Blackwell.
- Steven Pinker (1999) *Words and Rules.* London: Weidenfeld & Nicholson.

**Really useful websites**
- www.bbc.co.uk – Check out Cbeebies and Learning English sections.
- www.universalteacher.org.uk – Lots of revision materials for every module in A-level English Language.
- www.ncaction.org.uk – the National Curriculum website. Click on the English menu to access examples of children's writing with commentaries. Great for revising Early Reading and Writing.

# Language change

You can be in no doubt that language changes. You have all studied Shakespeare and so are well aware that the language we use today has changed a lot since the seventeenth century. You will also be aware that you do not use the same words now that you did as a child. Can you remember the words you used to describe something as 'good' when you were ten?

Your study of language change involves the exploration of three main areas:

- How language changes – looking at the changes that take place across the range of language concepts (covered in more detail on pages 6–18 and 23–26)
- Why language changes – how change in society influences changes in the language
- Attitudes to language change – the different ways in which people respond to and debate changes in language use.

## How language changes

Read the following statement. Why do you think such a society exists?

> The Society aims to encourage high standards of written and spoken English, and in so doing defend … the language against debasement and changes.
>
> (The Queen's English Society, founded 1972)

Just in case you were in any doubt that English has changed, take a look at the following.

> Hwæt! We Gardena in geardagum,
> þeodcyninga, þrym gefrunon,
> hu ða æþelingas ellen fremedon.

This is the opening of *Beowulf,* an epic poem written in the eighth century, and one of the earliest examples of written English. Here is a word-for-word rendition in Modern English.

> Listen! We of the Spear-Danes
> in days of yore, of the kings of the people
> the glory have heard, how those princes deeds of valour performed.

---

**Activity 42** | ## Identifying change

What changes between Old English and Modern English can you identify here?

Why do you think the Modern English version has more words than the original? Are there features of the Old English that remind you of other European Languages? Is Old English in any way similar to Modern English?

What does the initial word 'Listen' suggest about context?

In November 2007, a film version of *Beowulf* was released. What social, cultural and technological changes can you think of that have made the transition from Old English text to action movie possible?

You can hear an audio reading of *Beowulf* in Old English at
www.bl.uk/learning/langlit/changlang/activities/lang/beowulf/beowulfpage1.html

But you don't have to look back to Anglo-Saxon times to see how English has changed. Changes occur over very much shorter periods of time. Texts A and B below are two advertisements for make-up which appeared in *Good Housekeeping* with only 60 years between them.

**Text A – 1996**

# Bare just became more beautiful.

## Estée Lauder invents
# Enlighten
## Skin-Enhancing Makeup

Discover a new kind of make-up.

So weightless and flexible it floats on the skin's surface – never drying or settling into pores or fine lines. So sheer it gives you the look of impeccable skin, invisibly.

Feels comfortable hour after hour. So innovative it compensates for oiliness or dryness. Enlighten is oil free, soothes even sensitive skin, protects with a non-chemical SPF 10.

**Text B – 1935**

## So unnecessary!

A shiny nose is so unnecessary! End that powder-puff habit once and for all with *Elizabeth Arden's No-Shine*. Just a touch of it on your nose in the morning, fluff on your powder and you're safe all day. And our fashion scout tells us that a bit on the forehead has helped more than one bright young girl to present a smooth unshining brow to the world beneath her new Autumn hat.

### Elizabeth Arden's
*No-Shine*
4/6, 10/6.

## *Face Powder must be used and not seen.*

*It must give a soft, lovely finish and not a coated look. It must blend imperceptibly with your skin. It must be pure and fine. In other words . . . it must be* **Elizabeth Arden's powder.** *One of the nicest things about Miss Arden's powder is that it comes in a big box . . . which lasts and lasts and lasts, because you need so little . . . and it stays on so long.*

*Flower Powder 6/6*
**Ardena.**

**Activity 43**  Comparing adverts

Read the advertisements on page 269 carefully, either on your own or in pairs, and write down any changes in the language that you notice. Then compare your notes with the ones below.

## Model notes on make-up advertisements

- These words and phrases from 1935 sound slightly dated: 'powder-puff', 'fashion scout', 'fluff on', 'bright young girl', 'Miss Arden's powder', 'one of the nicest things'.
- The technical-sounding lexis 'non-chemical SPF 10' was probably not used in 1935.
- Much is quite similar, many words and phrases haven't changed in meaning:

| 1935 | 1996 |
|------|------|
| smooth | sheer |
| pure and fine | impeccable |
| imperceptibly | invisibly |
| soft and lovely | soothes even sensitive skin |

- Name of product is more punning in 1996: 'Enlighten' versus 'No-Shine'.
- The 1996 text stresses newness: 'new kind', 'innovative'. The 1935 text stresses economy: 'it comes in a big box', 'need so little'.
- The 1996 text is sexier: 'Bare just became more beautiful' versus 'smooth unshining brow'.
- **Phonology:** More alliteration in 1996: 'Bare just became more beautiful', 'skin's surface', 'soothes even sensitive skin'. Repetition of name in 1935: 'Elizabeth Arden', 'Elizabeth Arden's No-Shine', 'Miss Arden's powder'.
- **Grammar:** Both use repeated structures: in 1935, 'It must …'; in 1996, 'So …'. The 1996 text uses more ellipses with subject of sentences frequently omitted: [It is] 'So weightless …'; [It] 'Feels …'.

The result is that the 1996 advertisement seems more casual than the 1935 one.

**Activity 44**  Investigating language change in advertising

Now investigate how language has changed in the three advertisements on pages 271–273. They are all adverts for Persil. Text A is from 1939, Text B is from 1954 and Text C is from 2005. This time there are no answer notes, though you might find it helpful to follow the structure used for the advertisements for make-up. Make sure that you consider the different social contexts in which the adverts were produced.

**Text A**

**Text B**

**Text C**

The **only** pre-treatment we recommend is **Life.**

Persil's new formula is so powerful in tackling tough stains like mud and grass, there's no need to pre-treat hundreds of stains. Just throw your clothes in and see them come out brilliantly clean and white. Result!

**new no need to pre-treat** on 100's of everyday stains.

**Persil**

www.dirtisgood.co.uk

273

## Activity 45 — Identifying change in magazines

**Group work**

This exercise will give you more practice in identifying language change. Texts A and B are pages from popular music magazines, one from the 1980s and one from 2007. For both magazine pages, you should identify

- *what* exactly the pages are – context
- *where* the language has changed
- *how* it has changed – refer to the appropriate language areas (lexical, semantic, grammatical, orthographic, etc.)
- *why* it has changed – you may need to make some educated guesses here!

**Text A**

In groups, read through the pages and write down your observations on a piece of paper. You have 5 minutes!

When your group has finished, the piece of paper should be passed on to another group for further observations to be recorded, until all groups have commented on the document. There is no need to duplicate observations. Only add new ones to the piece of paper! While the paper is circulating, groups should continue to analyse the texts. When the process has been completed, the class should discuss its findings.

**Text B**

# BITZ

This issue the *Bitz* Award For Best Song Title Of The Fortnight goes to Liverpool band **It's Immaterial** for their "A Gigantic Raft (In The Philippines)". The single features a Welsh choir, needless to say.

Watch out for a single called "High Rise" by **The Trainspotters**. Why? Well, it's actually a track Mike Read made in the late '70s, so, like we said, watch out.

**Kajagoogoo** have a new single out on February 20 called "Lion's Mouth".

**Simple Minds** are playing yet another night at London's *Hammersmith Odeon*. March 19 is the extra date and it'll be the final night of their tour.

Talking drums? "Din Daa Daa (Trommeltanz)" by **George Kranz** is a rather odd record that consists mainly of this German bloke going "din daa daa", "rat-atat-a-tat", "wallop" and "bash". There are also some keyboards added by a chap who rejoices in the name of Dismal Witting. Expect to hear it down your local disco soon.

"Moving" is the last album ever from **The Raincoats**. Why? Because they've split up.

# CAROL SINGING

Carol Kenyon: hawk of the town.

More solo singles. **Carol Kenyon** was the session singer who did the inspired wailing on **Heaven 17**'s "Temptation". Since then she's recorded her own solo single, "Warrior Woman" which has just been released.

**Dee C. Lee** used to be in **Wham!** until she left and got replaced by Pepsi. Then she sang with **The Style Council** and now, well next week actually, her first solo single is being released. It's called "Felina Wow Wow" and she wrote it herself.

# SACRE BLEU!

"Cafe Bleu" is the rather continental title of **The Style Council**'s first LP which Paul Weller, Merton Mick and their chums have just completed. There's no release date announced yet but on February 10 their new single, "My Ever Changing Moods", will be unveiled. Expect some live dates soon under the title, "Council Meetings".

**J.B.'s All-Stars,** the group formed by ex-Special **John Bradbury,** have just released their second single. It's called "Backfield In Motion" and is apparently a re-working of "the classic Mel And Tim number" (whoever *they* are).

It's nearly Valentine's Day and already *Bitz* has come over all soppy. "A Gift For Valentine's Day" is a special, limited edition, 4-track, romantically packaged, 12-inch record by **Billy Joel** and there are 20 of them simply yearning to find a place in your heart and on your turntable. *(Oh, shut up! — Ed.)* To win one, just write the name of Billy's girlfriend on a postcard and rush it to: **Smash Hits Billy Joel Competition,** 52-55 Carnaby Street, London W1V 1PF. Is Billy's girlfriend: Jerry Hall, Cyndi Lauper or Christie Brinkley? You've got 'till February 16 to tell us.

# TRADING PLACES

The Clash: (l-r) Paul Simenon, Pete Howard, Joe Strummer, Vince White, Nick Sheppard.

Ah, they come and they go. It's been a bit of a fortnight for it: groups splitting up and re-forming all over the shop. First off, **The Clash** (above). You may remember that last autumn Paul Simenon and Joe Strummer chucked guitarist Mick Jones out of the group. Well now, just in time for their tour, they've bounced back with not one, but two new guitarists: Vince White from London's Finsbury Park and Nick Sheppard from Bristol. Drummer Pete Howard, who played with them in the USA last year, has also joined the group. It's rumoured that former Clash drummer, Topper Headon — fined £3 the other week for being "staggering drunk while walking his mongrel dog' — is working on an LP with Mick Jones.

Meanwhile, the former members of **BowWowWow** — who haven't been up to much since they split with Annabella last summer — have just re-emerged under the rather wiggy name, **The Chiefs Of Relief.** No record yet, but lots of live shows.

Up in Scotland, there's all sorts of re-shuffling going on. **The Bluebells** have split up. So have **Altered Images.** Again. And this time it looks like it's for good. Johnny McElhone and Tony McDaid are to form another band, we hear, while Steve Lironi has nipped down to London for "talks with other musicians". Clare Grogan will be continuing as a solo artiste and concentrating on her film career. *Comfort And Joy*, the new Bill Forsyth film that she's in, will be shown at the Cannes film festival this summer and should be on general release here by the end of the year. She's also now signed to a theatrical agent.

**Orange Juice,** of course, split up yonks ago. But now they're back with a new single called "Bridge". The group is now just Edwyn Collins and Zeke Manyika, although they'll be adding to the line-up for some live dates in the spring. Former members David McClymont and Malcolm Ross are both now involved in the usual "solo projects".

Remember **Gene October**? You don't. Lead singer of early punk group **Chelsea**, he's now donned a shirt, tie and jacket and made a solo single with another ex-punk, **Glen Matlock** who was once a Sex Pistol. It's called "Don't Quit".

**Daryl Hall and John Oates** will be in Britain in March to play some concerts: Brighton *Centre* (March 6), Birmingham NEC (7) and Wembley Arena (9). Tickets are on sale now.

Since their last video caused such a fuss, the **Rolling Stones** have made their new one, "She Was Hot", in Mexico with the same director, Julien Temple.

# HAPPY BIRTHDAY

**Tony Butler** of **Big Country** (27) on February 3
**Alice Cooper** (36) on February 4
**Alan Lancaster** of **Status Quo** (35) on February 7
**Peter Gabriel** (34) on February 13
**Mark Fox** of **Haircut One Hundred** (27) on February 13

## Activity 46   Modernising nineteenth-century English

Here are two versions of the opening paragraph of Thomas Hardy's *The Mayor of Casterbridge*. The first is what Hardy wrote in 1886 whilst the second is an attempt at a modern 'translation' of the paragraph.

### Hardy's version

One evening of late summer, before the nineteenth century had reached one-third of its span, a young man and woman, the latter carrying a child, were approaching the large village of Weydon-Priors, in Upper Wessex, on foot. They were plainly but not ill clad, though the thick hoar of dust which had accumulated on their shoes and garments from an obviously long journey lent a disadvantageous shabbiness to their appearance just now.

### A modern 'translation'

One evening in late summer, about the year 1830, a young man and woman were approaching the large village of Weydon-Priors, in Upper Wessex, on foot. The woman was carrying a child. They were plainly but not badly dressed, although the thick coating of dust on their shoes and clothes from an obviously long journey made them look unfortunately shabby just now.

Make a list of the changes the 'translator' has made. You will notice a few, though not many changes of vocabulary and some changes of phrasing. The main effect of the changes is to make the passage 'lighter'. Look, for instance, at the effect of the change from 'lent a disadvantageous shabbiness to their appearance' to 'made them look unfortunately shabby'. What grammatical changes has the 'translator' made here?

This comparison is not intended to suggest that the modern version is better, but it does highlight the difference between the English Thomas Hardy used in novels in 1886 and that used today.

## Activity 46   Texts to modernise

Here are three short passages for you to 'translate'. The first is the opening of another well-known Hardy novel, *The Woodlanders* (1887), the second is from Samuel Pepys' diary (1666), the third is from Robert Greene's *Carde of Fancie* (1587). Your 'translations' should enable present-day readers to accept them as being contemporary texts. When you have completed your versions, comment on the changes you made and on any difficulties that you encountered.

### Text A

The rambler who, for old association's sake, should trace the forsaken coach-road running almost in a meridional line from Bristol to the south shore of England, would find himself during the latter part of his journey in the vicinity of some extensive woodlands, interspersed with apple-orchards. Here the trees, timber or fruit-bearing as the case may be, make the wayside hedges ragged by their drip and shade, their lower limbs stretching in level repose over the road, as though reclining on the insubstantial air.

**Text B**

So I down to the waterside and there got a boat and through bridge, and there saw a lamentable fire. Poor Michells house, as far as the Old Swan, already burned that way and the fire running further, that in a very little time it got as far as the Stillyard while I was there. Everybody endeavouring to remove their goods, and flinging them into the river or bringing them into lighters that lay off.

**Text C**

There dwelled in the Citie of Metelyne, a certain Duke called Clerophontes, who through his prowesse in all martiall exploites waxed so proude and tyrannous, using such mercilesse crueltie to his forraine enimies, and such modelesse rigour to his native citizens, that it was doubtfull whether he was more feared of his foes for his crueltie, or hated of his friends for his tyrannie.

Your work so far in this section will have shown you that the evidence for language change can be examined in a number of different ways. You can look for changes in

- vocabulary and meaning (lexis and semantics)
- spelling and punctuation (orthography)
- morphology and syntax (grammar)
- sounds and pronunciation (phonology).

If you want to learn more about the history of the English language and gain a chronological view of the changes that have occurred from the very earliest days to the present, then there are a number of very good and readable books that you could consult. The classic one of these is A. C. Baugh and T. Cable's *A History of the English Language* (Routledge), which contains lots of detailed examples, particularly of lexical developments, together with a section on American English. Two more-recent books you should consult are *The Stories of English* by David Crystal (Allen Lane) and *The Adventure of English* by Melvyn Bragg (Hodder & Stoughton). There are also numerous websites that you can access. The following are recommended:

- www.bbc.co.uk/routesofenglish
- www.bllearning.co.uk/live/text
- www.bbc.co.uk/voices.

**Activity 48**

**Group work**

## A language timeline

Research major chronological events in the development of the English language. Using the resources listed above and any others you have access to, work in groups to produce illustrated timelines of the history of the English language.

## Lexis and semantics

Lexical and semantic changes in English are perhaps the easiest to spot. New words come into use all the time and words that are no longer useful disappear. Words also frequently change their meanings. Read the following advertisement from the 1 January 1831 edition of the *Courier* and list all the words which are no longer in use or seem to have changed their meaning.

# FAMILY LINEN AND SHAWL ESTABLISHMENT
## 21, PICCADILLY, MANCHESTER

•

R. HOSKIN begs to apprise the Ladies of Manchester and Neighbourhood, that, according to his usual custom at this season of the year, he will submit to their inspection the whole of his Stock of FURS, consisting of Pelerines, Mantillas, Boas, and Muffs, of every description at Cost Price. R.H. has just received some very elegant designs in SHAWLS, a great variety of very choice colours, in Gros-de-Naples, Gauze Scarfs and Handkerchiefs, Tissues and Ærophanes. A choice assortment of FRENCH MERINOS and FLOWERS; several Bales of REAL WITNEY BLANKETS; a few boxes of very prime Irish Linens. Also, very Rich Black Veils, Thread and Gymp Laces, all of which R.H. flatters himself (from having selected them with the most scrupulous care) will give the most decided satisfaction to purchasers, and secure to him a continuance of that patronage he has so liberally experienced.

The English lexicon (or word-stock) has vastly expanded in the last 200 years and continues to do so. Recent influences have been the rise of feminism, the electronic revolution and the immigration into Britain of settlers whose first language is not English.

To understand why language changes look at the following list of words. They all entered the dictionary during the twentieth century. Classify them according to the social phenomena that brought them about. You should end up with a list of social contexts that influence language change. Use a good dictionary to find out what the words mean and when they were first used.

- Fingerprint
- Teddy bear
- Tarmac
- Suffragette
- Allergy
- Borstal
- Jazz
- Schizophrenia
- Vorticism
- Tank
- Fascism
- Robot
- Gigolo
- Surrealism
- Television
- Penicillin
- Neutron
- Nylon
- Tupperware
- Bikini
- Big Brother
- Discotheque
- Stoned
- Psychedelic
- Hovercraft
- Catch-22
- Miniskirt
- Workaholic
- Watergate
- Punk rock
- Blairite
- Aids
- Glasnost
- Ethnic cleansing
- Alcopop

You need a good understanding of historical periods in order to appreciate the context of an old text. For example, what do you know about the 1930s? This Craven A cigarette advertisement on page 279 appeared in the *Tatler* in 1933. What details of the text indicate that it is from this era?

The first Cork-Tipped Cigarette . . . again first with the patented wrapping of moisture-proof "CELLOPHANE" . . . and *now*, first with the exclusive "EASY-ACCESS" inner FOIL wrapping. This progress demonstrates once again Carreras' constant aim to do everything "a little better."

IN THE **NEW** 'EASY-ACCESS' FOIL PACKING

**CRAVEN "A"**

*made specially to prevent sore throats*

| Activity 49 | ## Researching historical context |
|---|---|
| Group work | It is a good idea to identify periods of history about which you know very little. As a class, divide the decades of the twentieth century between you and research social context and major historical events. Produce a fact sheet for your decade and create a class booklet of useful contextual information. You can then do the same for the sixteenth, seventeenth, eighteenth and nineteenth centuries. |

## How new words are formed

Here are some of the ways in which new words, neologisms, are formed in English.

- Compounding – Teapot, blackboard, laptop
- Eponym – Hoover, Dyson

**279**

- Affixation – Hoodie
- Conversion – We no longer 'send a text', we 'text'
- Acronym – ASBO, AIDS, EMO
- Blending – E-mail, brunch
- Clipping – Blog, bus, phone
- Back formation – 'Editor' produces 'to edit', 'burglar' produces 'burgle'
- Borrowing – Karaoke, déjà vu

For more on these processes, turn to pages 6–7 or consult the Glossary.

## Activity 50 — Applying the terminology

**Pair work**

In pairs, generate your own list of new words and identify the way that they have been formed. To get you started, think about new words to do with technology.

## Activity 51 — Analysing new words

The following words are new additions to the English language or have recently changed their meaning. What do you think they mean? What word-formation processes do they illustrate? How many of them do you think will stand the test of time?

- burn
- manga
- blamestorming
- wannabe
- gastropub
- WMDs
- blog
- iPod
- pimp

## Activity 52 — Semantic shift

This activity will provide you with a fascinating glimpse, decko, shufty or butcher's into the way meanings have changed over the years. Here are definitions of three words from three different dates: 1951, 1996 and 2015. The 2015 definitions were all invented by English teachers.

|  | Bell | Grief | Window |
|---|---|---|---|
| 1951 | n.  A metal device designed to give a ringing tone when struck. | n.  A feeling of woe and bereavement. | n.  A rectangular opening in a wall for admitting light and air. |
| 1996 | vb. To call someone by using a telephone. | n.  Excessive authoritarian aggravation as in 'You're giving me grief'. | n.  A space in one's programme, an opportunity. |
| 2015 | vb. To attach an electronic device to a convict licensed to be outside prison. | n.  An indoor sport based on fighting to the death with bare hands. | vb. To perceive hidden meaning or implications in an apparently innocuous statement. |

Research the words below and provide similarly accurate definitions of them for the three years 1951, 1996 and 2015. You will need a 1951 edition of a suitable dictionary, or a historical dictionary like the *OED online* (www.oed.com).

- bad
- bonk
- ace

- house
- gay
- grass

- wasted
- queen
- sky

- thatcher
- monkey
- awesome

## Review

In this section you have begun to explore the way that language changes and identified a range of reasons for this change. You should now be aware that an understanding of context, be it social, cultural or historical, is crucial to understanding the process of language change. You have specifically explored how words are formed. You will need to apply this new terminology in the exam. You have also encountered changes in meaning over time. If you meet a word in an old text that you think you understand, always be aware that it may have changed its meaning. As always, the context in which it appears will help you decide whether a 'semantic shift' has taken place.

You have also compared texts in this section. In the exam you may be asked to analyse a single text or to compare texts of similar genres. In both cases always explore the context first. What do you already know about the text type? Are you aware of a modern equivalent to the old text that is being presented?

## Why do words change?

You will have obviously noticed that words do change meaning over time. There are four main reasons for this.

- Words simply die or are abandoned, because they are no longer needed – 'stomacher', 'bassinet' and 'galantine' are examples of this.

- Words are replaced because of fashion or other cultural influences – 'teacher' may be in the process of being replaced by 'learning facilitator' or 'library' by 'learning resources centre'.

- Existing words alter their meaning to take account of changes in society. There are two important processes that can occur when words change their meaning over time. These processes work in opposite ways: sometimes the meaning of a word broadens and sometimes it narrows. An example of the former process is 'butcher', which meant originally only 'killer of goats', whilst 'doctor' is an example of the latter. 'Doctor' used to mean 'teacher' or 'learned man', not solely, as today, 'learned in medical matters'. There is a remnant of the original meaning in the university degree of Doctor of Philosophy (PhD).

This brief explanation should suggest to you the questions you need to ask of a document or passage when looking at lexical or semantic change.

- Are there any words or expressions no longer in use? What reasons can you suggest for their disappearance?

- Are there any words or expressions still in use today, but which clearly had a different meaning when the passage was written? What did they mean then? What reasons can you suggest for this change?

To give you an indication of how alert you have to be when looking at this aspect of language change, look at these annotated examples of Jane Austen's English, quoted in David Crystal's indispensable *Cambridge Encyclopedia of the English Language*.

> The supposed inmate of Mansfield Parsonage
> – 'inmate' had not yet developed its sense of someone occupying a prison.
>
> Her regard had all the warmth of first attachment
> – 'regard' had a much stronger sense of 'affection'.
>
> She was now in an irritation as violent from delight as …
> – 'irritation' could be caused by a pleasurable emotion.

A good etymological dictionary (such as *OED online*) will always show you how words have changed their meaning over time.

## Activity 53 — Language for the future

**Pair work**
**Group work**

The following text is the opening of *A Clockwork Orange* by Anthony Burgess. He wrote it in 1962. Here his character Alex is speaking Nadsat, an imagined 'youthspeak' of the future that Burgess has created.

Work in pairs or small groups. What do you think the new words and phrases mean? What methods has Burgess used to create his new language? What social changes might Burgess have imagined taking place to create the new language?

Now predict the future. What social, cultural and political changes might take place in the next 50 years. How will these affect the English language?

> What's it going to be then, eh?'
>
> There was me, that is Alex, and my three droogs. that is Pete, Georgie, and Dim. Dim being really dim, and we sat in the Korova Milkbar making up our rassoodocks what to do with the evening, a flip dark chill winter bastard though dry. The Korova Milkbar was a milk-plus mesto, and you may, O my brothers, have forgotten what these mestos were like, things changing so skorry these days and everybody very quick to forget, newspapers not being read much neither. Well, what they sold there was milk plus something else. They had no licence for selling liquor, but there was no law yet against prodding some of the new veshches which they used to put into the old moloko, so you could peet it with vellocet or synthemesc or drencrom or one or two other veshches which would give you a nice quiet horrorshow fifteen minutes admiring Bog And All His Holy Angels and Saints in your left shoe with lights bursting all over your mozg. Or you could peet milk with knives in it, as we used to say, and this would sharpen you up and make you ready for a bit of dirty twenty-to-one, and that was what we were peeting this evening I'm starting off the story with.
>
> Our pockets were full of deng, so there was no real need from the point of view of crasting any more pretty polly to tolchock some old veck in an alley and viddy him swim in his blood

while we counted the takings and divided by four, nor to do the ultra-violent on some shivering starry grey-haired ptitsa in a shop and go smecking off with the till's guts. But, as they say, money isn't everything.

The four of us were dressed in the height of fashion, which in those days was a pair of black very tight tights with the old jelly mould, as we called it, fitting on the crotch underneath the tights, this being to protect and also a sort of a design you could viddy clear enough in a certain light, so that I had one in the shape of a spider, Pete had a rooker (a hand, that is). Georgie had a very fancy one of a flower, and poor old Dim had a very hound-and-horny one of a clown's litso (face, that is), Dim not ever having much of an idea of things and being, beyond all shadow of a doubting thomas, the dimmest of we four. Then we wore waisty jackets without lapels but with these very big built-up shoulders ('pletchoes' we called them) which were a kind of a mockery of having real shoulders like that. Then, my brothers, we had these off-white cravats which looked like whipped-up kartoffel or spud with a sort of a design made on it with a fork. We wore our hair not too long and we had flip horrorshow boots for kicking.

'What's it going to be then, eh?'

There were three devotchkas sitting at the counter all together, but there were four of us malchicks and it was usually like one for all and all for one. These sharps were dressed in the height of fashion too, with purple and green and orange wigs on their gullivers, each one not costing less than three or four weeks of those sharps' wages, I should reckon, and make-up to match (rainbows round the glazzies, that is, and the rot painted very wide). Then they had long black very straight dresses, and on the groody part of them they had little badges of like silver with different malchicks' names on them – Joe and Mike and suchlike. These were supposed to be the names of the different maichicks they'd spatted with before they were fourteen. They kept looking our way and I nearly felt like saying the three of us (out of the corner of my rot, that is) should go off for a bit of p01 and leave poor old Dim behind, because it would be just a matter of kupetting Dim a demi-litre of white but this time with a dollop of synthemesc in it, but that wouldn't really have been playing like the game. Dim was very ery *ugly* and like his name, but he was a horrorshow filthy fighter and very handy with the boot.

'What's it going to be then, eh?'

## A word about dictionaries

As students of language change, the dictionary is your best friend. You should acquaint yourself with how dictionaries work. A good dictionary will give you information about a word across the range of language concepts. It will also tell you something about its etymology.

## Activity 54 | How do dictionaries change?

Pair work

The text on page 284 is taken from Dr Johnson's dictionary of 1755. Find the equivalent page in a modern dictionary. In pairs, note down all the changes that have taken place. Try to identify changes from all areas including graphology, phonology, grammar, semantics, pragmatics and discourse.

## OBD

**OA'RY.** *adj.* [from *oar*.] Having the form or use of oars.

His hair transforms to down, his fingers meet,
In skinny films, and shape his *oary* feet. *Addison.*

The swan with arched neck,
Between her white wings mantling, proudly rows
Her state with *oary* feet. *Milton.*

**OAST.** *n. s.* A kiln. Not in use.

Empty the binn into a hog-bag, and carry them immediately to the *oast* or kiln, to be dried. *Mortimer.*

**OATCA'KE.** *n. s.* [*oat* and *cake*.] Cake made of the meal of oats.

Take a blue stone they make haver or *oatcakes* upon, and lay it upon the cross bars of iron. *Peacham.*

**OA'TEN.** *adj.* [from *oat*.] Made of oats; bearing oats.

When shepherds pipe on *oaten* straws,
And merry larks are ploughmens clocks. *Shakesp.*

**OATH.** *n. s.* [*aith*, Gothick; áð, Saxon. The distance between the noun *oath*, and the verb *swear*, is very observable, as it may shew that our oldest dialect is formed from different languages.] An affirmation, negation, or promise, corroborated by the attestation of the Divine Being.

Read over Julia's heart, thy first best love,
For whose dear sake thou then did'st rend thy faith
Into a thousand *oaths*; and all those *oaths*
Descended into perjury to love me. *Shakespeare.*

He that strikes the first stroke, I'll run him up to the hilts as I am a soldier.
—An *oath* of mickle might; and fury shall abate. *Sha.*

We have consultations, which inventions shall be published, which not: and take an *oath* of secrecy for the concealing of those which we think fit to keep secret. *Bacon.*

Those called to any office of trust, are bound by an *oath* to the faithful discharge of it: but an *oath* is an appeal to God, and therefore can have no influence, except upon those who believe that he is. *Swift.*

**OA'THABLE.** *adj.* [from *oath*. A word not used.] Capable of having an oath administered.

You're not *oathable*,
Altho' I know you'll swear
Into strong shudders th' immortal gods. *Shakespeare.*

**OATHBREA'KING.** *n. s.* [*oath* and *break*.] Perjury; the violation of an oath.

His *oathbreaking* he mended thus,
By now forswearing that he is forsworn. *Shak. Hen.* IV.

**OA'TMALT.** *n. s.* [*oat* and *malt*.] Malt made of oats.

In Kent they brew with one half *oatmalt*, and the other half barleymalt. *Mortimer's Husb.*

**OA'TMEAL.** *n. s.* [*oat* and *meal*.] Flower made by grinding oats.

*Oatmeal* and butter, outwardly applied, dry the scab on the head. *Arbuthnot on Aliment.*

Our neighbours tell me oft, in joking talk,
Of ashes, leather, *oatmeal*, bran, and chalk. *Gay.*

**OA'TMEAL.** *n. s.* An herb. *Ainsworth.*

**OATS.** *n. s.* [aten, Saxon.] A grain, which in England is generally given to horses, but in Scotland supports the people.

It is of the grass leaved tribe; the flowers have no petals, and are disposed in a loose panicle: the grain is eatable. The meal makes tolerable good bread. *Miller.*

The *oats* have eaten the horses. *Shakespeare.*

It is bare mechanism, no otherwise produced than the turning of a wild *oatbeard*, by the insinuation of the particles of moisture. *Locke.*

For your lean cattle, fodder them with barley straw first, and the *oat* straw last. *Mortimer's Husbandry.*

His horse's allowance of *oats* and beans, was greater than the journey required. *Swift.*

**OA'TTHISTLE.** *n. s.* [*oat* and *thistle*.] An herb. *Ainsf.*

**OBAMBULA'TION.** *n. s.* [*obambulatio*, from *obambulo*, Latin.] The act of walking about. *Dict.*

**To OBDU'CE.** *v. a.* [*obduco*, Latin.] To draw over as a covering.

No animal exhibits its face in the native colour of its skin but man; all others are covered with feathers, hair, or a cortex that is *obduced* over the cutis. *Hale.*

**OBDUC'TION.** *n. s.* [from *obductio*, *obduco*, Latin.] The act of covering, or laying a cover.

## OBE

God should be so *obdurate* as yourselves,
How would it fare with your departed souls? *Shakesp.*

Women are soft, mild, pitiful, and flexible;
Thou stern, *obdurate*, flinty, rough, remorseless. *Shakesp.*

To convince the proud what signs avail,
Or wonders move th' *obdurate* to relent;
They harden'd more, by what might more reclaim. *Milt.*

*Obdurate* as you are, oh! hear at least
My dying prayers, and grant my last request. *Dryden.*

2. Hardned; firm; stubborn.

Sometimes the very custom of evil makes the heart *obdurate* against whatsoever instructions to the contrary. *Hooker.*

A pleasing sorcery could charm
Pain for a while, or anguish, and excite
Fallacious hope, or arm th' *obdurate* breast
With stubborn patience, as with triple steel. *Milton.*

No such thought ever strikes his marble, *obdurate* heart, but it presently flies off and rebounds from it. It is impossible for a man to be thorough-paced in ingratitude, till he has shook off all fetters of pity and compassion. *South.*

3. Harsh; rugged.

They joined the most *obdurate* consonants without one intervening vowel. *Swift.*

**OBDU'RATELY.** *adv.* [from *obdurate*.] Stubbornly; inflexibly; impenitently.

**OBDU'RATENESS.** *n. s.* [from *obdurate*.] Stubbornness; inflexibility; impenitence.

**OBDURA'TION.** *n. s.* [from *obdurate*.] Hardness of heart; stubbornness.

What occasion it had given them to think, to their greater *obduration* in evil, that through a froward and wanton desire of innovation, we did constrainedly those things, for which conscience was pretended? *Hooker, b.* iv.

**OBDU'RED.** *adj.* [*obduratus*, Latin.] Hardned; inflexible; impenitent.

This saw his hapless foes, but stood *obdur'd*,
And to rebellious fight rallied their pow'rs
Insensate. *Milton's Paradise Lost, b.* vi.

**OBE'DIENCE.** *n. s.* [*obedience*, Fr. *obedientia*, Latin.] Obsequiousness; submission to authority; compliance with command or prohibition.

If you violently proceed against him, it would shake in pieces the heart of his *obedience*. *Shakespeare's K. Lear.*

Thy husband
Craves no other tribute at thy hands,
But love, fair looks, and true *obedience*. *Shakesp.*

His servants ye are, to whom ye obey, whether of sin unto death, or of *obedience* unto righteousness. *Rom.* vi. 16.

It was both a strange commission, and a strange *obedience* to a commission, for men so furiously assailed, to hold their hands. *Bacon's War with Spain.*

Nor can this be,
But by fulfilling that which thou didst want,
*Obedience* to the law of God, impos'd
On penalty of death. *Milton's Paradise Lost, b.* xii.

**OBE'DIENT.** *adj.* [*obediens*, Latin.] Submissive to authority; compliant with command or prohibition; obsequious.

To this end did I write, that I might know the proof of you, whether ye be *obedient* in all things. *2 Cor.* ii. 9.

To this her mother's plot
She, seemingly *obedient*, likewise hath
Made promise. *Shakesp. M. W. of Wind.*

He humbled himself, and became *obedient* unto death. *Phil.* ii. 8.

Religion hath a good influence upon the people, to make them *obedient* to government, and peaceable one towards another. *Tillotson, Serm.* 3.

The chief his orders gives; th' *obedient* band,
With due observance, wait the chief's command. *Pope.*

**OBE'DIENTIAL.** *adj.* [*obedientiel*, Fr. from *obedient*.] According to the rule of obedience.

Faith is such as God will accept of, when it affords fiducial reliance on the promises, and *obediential* submission to the command. *Hammond.*

Faith is then perfect, when it produces in us a fiduciary assent to whatever the gospel has revealed, and an *obediential* submission to the commands. *Wake's Prep. for Death.*

The *Oxford English Dictionary* is available online. It is the most accessible and comprehensive record of the English language to date. Take the tour of the dictionary and learn how to use it. Extracts from this dictionary have already appeared on exam papers. The dictionary can be found at www.oed.com.

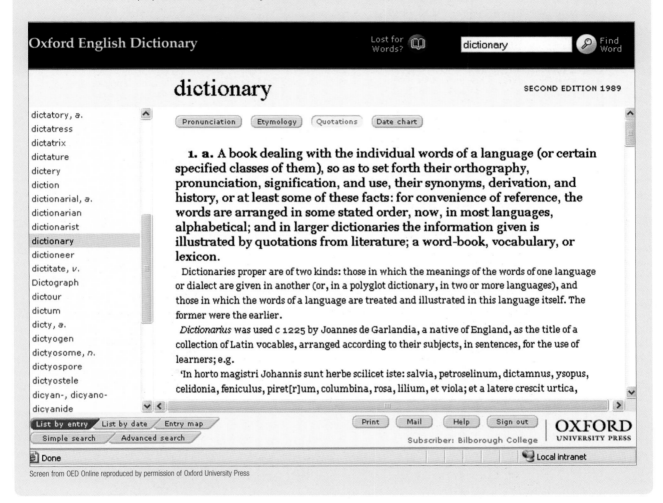

Screen from OED Online reproduced by permission of Oxford University Press

## Exam practice

The following activity will provide you with a good initial approach to tackling old texts in the exam.

## Activity 55 — Dr Hall's patient

The text on page 286 is an extract from the medical notes of John Hall, who was Shakespeare's son-in-law. He practised as a doctor in the early 1600s. First, unpack the context of these passages as fully as you can. Think about audience, purpose, time, genre and any modern equivalents you may be aware of. You should indicate the meanings of the words as used in the passage. Again, refer to a dictionary if you are unsure. Make notes on all the examples of language change that you can find.

158     *Select Observations*

jected, and procured three stools, which gave great ease. She often took the Gelly of Harts-horn in Broth, altered with Antiscorbutic Herbs. At the hour of sleep she took this : Rx *Aq. Cord. frig. Sax.* ʒi. *Syr. Sceletyrb. Forest. coch.* ii. The third day I thus purged her : Rx *Man.* ʒi. *Rhabarb* ʒi. *Crem. Tartar.* Əi. *Syr. Sceletyrb. Forest.* ʒi. *Aq. Cichor.* ʒiii. *Misc.* This gave four stools. For her thirst she used the Decoction of Harts-horn. And thus she was cured.

### Observ. LXVIII.

The Lady *Rainsford*, aged about 62, cruelly tormented with the Stone, Fever, Thirst, Pain of the Back, was cured as followeth: Rx *Pul. Holland.* ʒi. *Tereb. Cypr.* ʒii. *Misc. f. Pil.* Of which was given ʒi made in five Pills. Rx *Ol. Scorpion.* ʒi. *Amygd. dulc.* ʒii. With this her Back was anointed. Rx *Decoct. comm. pro Clyst.* ʒxii. *Elect. Lenit. & Diaphœnic.* à ʒi. *Syr. Ros. sol.* ʒiii. *Misc.* This gave two stools. Six hours after it came away, was given another prepared only of the said Decoction, red Sugar ʒiv. and Butter ʒiv. But note, every third hour she took the following : Rx *Spec. Liberant.* ʒi. *Syr. Papav. erratic.* ʒß. *Hypos. q. s.* She rested quietly this night. Rx *Rhab. pul.* ʒii. *Aq. Fumitor.* ʒviii. *bul. ad quartam Col. adde Tart. Cryst.* Əi. *Syr. Diaserios* ʒn. *f. Haust.* This gave five stools. The following day she had a Clyster framed only of Oil of Linseed. At bed time she took this : Rx

*upon English Bodies.*     159

Rx *Spec. Liberant.* Əii. *C. C. præp.* Əi. *Tinctur. Coral,* Əß. And so in the morning she was well.

### Observ. LXIX.

Doctor *Thornberry*, Bishop of *Worcester*, aged about 86, *Febr.* 1. 1663. was long tormented with a Scorbutic wandering Gout, falsly imagined by his Physician to be a true Gout, as appeared not only by the frequent Change of his Urine, both in colour and substance, but also livid spots in his Thighs. He had very unquiet Nights from salt and sharp humors, and Vapors ascending to his Head ; and if he did sleep, it was with terror, which happened from the sudden slaughter of one in his Family, which did much terrify and perplex his Spirits, and afflicted him grievously with Melancholy. His Pain lay sometimes in his Knee, otherwhiles in his Foot, without any tumor in the Foot, but about the Knee and Instep there was great swelling, and after in the Feet. I said he might be eased, but never perfectly cured, which I effected as follows. I omitted purging, he being very weak, and having been before purged. He had a Gelly framed of Harts-horn, with Knuckles of Veal, Partridg, Raisins, Dates, and Antiscorbutic Herbs. It being strained, there was added a little Tincture of Saffron and Alkermes, with Sugar-candy to sweeten it. He took the Juyce of Scurvy-grass prepared in Wine twice or thrice a day. For the Pain and Tumor

# Spelling

English spelling is relatively unchanging; by the eighteenth century, in fact, it had reached more or less the state in which we find it today and there have been only minor alterations since then. This has not stopped those in favour of spelling reform, though. There is a long history of attempts to 'reform' the spelling system of English and make it more 'logical', from John Hart in 1569 to the Simplified Spelling Society (www.spellingsociety.org.uk) of today. Sir Isaac Pitman in the late nineteenth century founded a journal devoted to spelling reform called the *Speler* which gave a religious dimension to the cause. It was

> 'Devoated tu the Wurship and Luv ov the Lord God and Saivier Jesus Christ … The Investigashon ov Spiritiual Tru'th; Speling Reform; Shorthand; Pees on Er'th'.

By the mid-twentieth century, many people had begun to make fun of the reformers, as you can see from this extract from Dolton Edwards' *Meihem in ce Klasrum* (1946).

In 1951 we would urg a greit step forward. Sins bai this taim it would have ben four years sins anywun had used the leter 'c', we would sugest that 'National Easy Languag Wek' for 1951 be devoted to substitution of 'c' for 'th'. To be sur it would be som taim befor peopl would bekom akustomd to reading ceir newspapers and buks wic sutsh sentenses in cem as 'Ceodor cought he had cre cousand cistles crust crough ce cik of his cumb.'

In ce saim maner, bai maiking eatsh leter hav its own sound and cat sound only, we kould shorten ce language still mor. In 1952 we would elimineit ce 'y'; cen in 1953 we kould us ce leter to indikeit ce 'sh' sound, cerbai klarifaiing words laik yugar and yur, as wel as redusing bai wun mor leter al words laik 'yut', 'yore', and so forc. Cink, cen, of al ce benefits to be geind bai ce distinktion whitsh wil cen be meid between words leik:

ocean now writen oyean
machine now writen mayin
racial now writen reiyial

Al sutsh divers weis of wraiting wun sound would no longer exist, and whenever wun kaim akros a 'y' sound he would know exaktli what to wrait.

Kontinuing cis proses, year after year, we would eventuali hav a reali sensibl writen langug. By 1975, wi ventyur to sei, cer wud bi no mor uv ces teribl trublsm difikultis, wic no tu leters usd to indikeit ce seim nois, and laikwais no tu noises riten wic ce seim leter. Even Mr. Yaw, wi beliv, wud be hapi in ce noleg his drims fainali keim tru.

The main variation in contemporary English spelling is between British English and American English and we can all recognise differences between the two varieties. Decide whether the words in the following list are spelt in the British way or spelt in the American way or spelt this way in both varieties.

- color
- torpor
- ax
- acknowledgment
- recognize
- honour
- honorary
- center
- diarrhoea
- appal
- encyclopedia
- civilise
- catalog
- monologue
- jewelry
- tyre
- ameba
- skilful
- massacre
- somber

If you are unsure, you may need to consult *Webster's Dictionary of American English* or change the spell check facility on a PC to US English.

It was the arrival of printing in England in the late fifteenth century that helped to establish the fixed patterns of English spelling which over the next 300 years or so became regularised into the system as we know it today. The consequence of this is that the conventions of English spelling reflect how the language was pronounced several centuries ago rather than how it is pronounced now.

The next activity shows you how to investigate spelling changes.

## Activity 56  Investigating spelling changes

In the extract on page 288 William Caxton (the man who brought printing to England from Europe) is writing in 1490 about a group of merchants who were trying to sail from the Thames ('tamyse') to Zealand in the Netherlands, but were becalmed and so went ashore to try to buy some eggs. They had considerable difficulty in making themselves understood, as the housewife thought they were speaking French, not merely a different dialect of English!

> It happened that certayn merchauntes were in a shippe in tamyse, for to have sayled over the see into zelande, and for lacke of wynde, thei taryed atte forlond, and went to lande for to refreshe them. And one of theym named Sheffelde, a mercer, cam in-to an hows and axed for mete; and specyally he axed after eggys. And the goode wyf answerde, that she coude speke no frenshe. And the marchaunt was angry, for he also coude speke no frenshe, but wolde have hadde egges, and she understode hym not. And thenne at laste a nother sayd that he wolde have eyren. Then the goode wyf sayd that she understode hym wel. Loo, what sholde a man in these dayes now wryte, egges or eyren?
>
> Note: forlond = headland    mercer = textile dealer    axed = asked

List the words that Caxton spells differently from Modern English. You should end up with about 45 words.

Can you identify any patterns in the spelling? Here are just two of the categories that you can use to sort out the patterns of late-fifteenth-century spelling:

- words that have an 'e' ending
- words that have a double consonant (shippe).

You should be able to find other categories as well.

Do the spellings tell us anything about the way some words might have been pronounced?

When words are used more than once, are they always spelt in the same way? Is there any consistency in the spelling? For instance, what class of words have 'e' at the end?

# Grammar

We are not going to look at the history of English grammar in this section; there are many books you can consult on this subject, as mentioned on page 267. Remember, though, that the most dramatic changes in English grammar occurred before the end of the Middle Ages. These two dates of particular interest.

- **1542:** Publication of *A Short Introduction of Grammar* by William Lily.

  'This remained the national grammar for several centuries and versions of it were used in English schools down to the nineteenth century. Although written in English, it was essentially a grammar of Latin, but it provided the basic introduction to grammar that … Shakespeare was brought up on.' (Dick Leith)

- **1762:** Publication *of A Short Introduction to English Grammar* by Robert Lowth. This book, which had an enormous influence on the teaching of grammar almost to the present day, stressed the notion that there was only one correct grammar for English. It was almost as if, for Bishop Lowth, grammar was next to godliness. Lowth laid down rules (such as never put a preposition at the end of a sentence) and illustrated them by examples.

You will know from your studies that it is impossible to 'fix' a language. It is constantly in a state of flux. You will also know that different dialects of English have different grammars, as do different national Englishes. For example, look at these differences in the grammar of American English and British Standard English.

| American | I've just gotten these new jeans. |
| British | I've just got these new jeans. |
| American | It's ten after six. |
| British | It's ten past six. |
| American | He dove into the sea. |
| British | He dived into the sea. |

## How to recognise grammatical change

One of the difficulties you might face when asked to identify changes in grammar in a passage or a document is to know exactly what you should be looking for. Here are some of the more important questions, together with some very brief examples, that you can use to examine any passages you may encounter. Ask yourself whether there are any differences between the passage you are analysing and Modern English in:

- verb inflections – pleaseth/pleases, gotten/got, think'st/thinks
- formation of the past tense – my life is run its course/my life has run its course, I am come/I came
- use of modal and auxiliary verbs – especially 'do'
- the personal-pronoun system – thou/thee/ye
- the relative-pronoun system – Our Father which art in heaven/Our Father who art in heaven
- formation of negatives – see not/I do not see, I cannot see no longer/I cannot see any longer
- formation of questions – seest thou?/do you see?
- noun and adjective endings or inflections – mankinde/mankind
- formation of plurals – shoon/shoes
- sentence structure – co-ordination or subordination
- the use of prepositions.

This is not, of course, an exhaustive list, but it does cover the main areas of grammatical change you are likely to encounter.

## Activity 57    Analysing grammatical change

The following short quotations and extracts illustrate grammatical forms and constructions that are no longer found in modern English. Turn them into acceptable contemporary English and comment on the grammatical changes that you have had to make to do this. The spelling has already been modernised for you.

### Seventeenth century
- Do thou meet me presently at the harbour. (presently = immediately)
- If thou be'st valiant.
- No, I hear not your honest friend.
- If she will return me the jewel, I will give over my suit. (suit = courtship)
- What are you here that cry so grievously?

(All from Shakespeare's *Othello*)

### Eighteenth century

- There lived a good substantial family in the town. (Daniel Defoe)
- Even the streets round the Pump room are pulling down for new Edifices. (Fanny Burney)
- A gentleman sat smoking a pipe at the door, of whom Adams inquired the road. (Fielding)
- The principal design of a Grammar of any Language is to teach us to express ourselves with propriety in that Language, and to be able to judge of every phrase and form of construction, whether it be right or not … . (Lowth)
- Would it not be hard that a man who hath no ancestors should therefore be rendered incapable of acquiring honour? (Fielding)

Finally, here is a longer extract from *The Arte of English Poesie*, by George Puttenham (1589). The extract has been left unaltered, so you may need to comment on changes in lexis and spelling as well as in grammar.

But after a speech is fully fashioned to the common vnderstanding, and accepted by consent of a whole countrey and natiõ, it is called a language, and receaueth none allowed alteration, but by extraordinary occasions by little and little, as it were insensibly bringing in of many corruptiõs that creepe along with the time; of all which matters, we haue more largely spoken in our bookes of the originals and pedigree of the English tong.

## Phonological change

The main change in the way that English was pronounced took place gradually in the fifteenth century and was known as the Great Vowel Shift. No one is quite sure why this shift took place, but the effects are fairly clear.

Here is an example of how a sentence was probably pronounced before this change took place.

And saw it is team noo to say hose narma is on the show and if the sarma fate can doe the daunce toneet that hath such farma aroond the toon.

Here's what it sounds like in modern English.

And so it is time now to see whose name is on the shoe and if the same feet can do the dance tonight that has such fame around the town.

Pronunciation change, however, has been a feature of English throughout its history. This is due, in part, to population shifts and migration, and it is still going on today. Research by Paul Kerswill and Ann Williams (2005) has shown that not only do children in the new town of Milton Keynes pronounce words differently from their parents, many of whom are not native to the town, but they also speak differently from the original inhabitants of this area of Buckinghamshire. Their speech more closely resembles that of children 50 miles away in London and of children throughout the south-east of England.

| Word | Buckinghamshire 1950 | Milton Keynes parents | Milton Keynes children |
|------|----------------------|------------------------|-------------------------|
| arm | arrm | arrm | ahm |
| fill | fill | fill | fiw |
| three | three | three | free |
| feather | feather | feather | fevver |
| night | noit | noit | naa-it |
| round | raind | raind | round |
| woman | umman | woman | woman |
| letter | le'er | le'er | le'er |

To read more about this research go to www.bbc.co.uk/threecounties/voices2005.

Migration of peoples can also account for the differences in the American and British pronunciations of English.

## Activity 58  American English

Try reading aloud the following passage. There are at least sixteen words in it that Americans pronounce differently from Standard English speakers. Do you know how Americans pronounce the words in italics?

> *Can't* you give me the *address* of the *leisure* centre in *Derby*? The hotel *clerk* couldn't answer my *inquiry* and I've got to get there by the fastest *route* if I'm to keep to *schedule* to see the *ballet* at *half* eight. And another thing! All I've had to eat today has been a *tomato* and *herb* omelette made with *margarine* not butter and a *banana* fritter with *yoghurt*.

## Activity 59  Variations in British English

Here are a number of words whose pronunciation in British English is still a matter of dispute. (*Dis*pute or dis*pute*?) Investigate the most common pronunciation in your area for each word. Does it vary according to the age, gender, ethnic origin or educational level of the speaker?

- economics
- controversy
- homosexual
- dilemma
- privacy

- status
- scone
- apparatus
- migraine
- ate

- often
- forehead
- archipelago
- schedule
- lieutenant

- evolution
- (n)either
- gooseberry
- wrath
- medicine

Can you think of any other words to add to this list?

This could form the basis of a language investigation.

Today we have much more understanding of how spoken language changes. Thanks to developments in sound recording we have substantial archives of spoken English from the last 100 years.

# Received Pronunciation and Estuary English

Received Pronunciation or RP is an accent associated with privilege. It is used by only about 3% of the population but was adopted by the BBC in the 1950s and is therefore often referred to as BBC English or sometimes the Queen's English. There is some recent evidence that even the Queen is modifying her accent, as the article on the facing page from the *Daily Telegraph* (2006) suggests.

Estuary English is a name given to the form(s) of English widely spoken in and around London and, more generally, in the south-east of England – along the River Thames and its estuary. Middle-class speakers wishing to avoid the connotations of RP and sound more 'down to earth' might adopt Estuary English instead. To find out more about the features and context of Estuary English go to http://www.phon.ucl.ac.uk/home/estuary/whatis.htm.

# Pragmatics

Social conventions and codes of behaviour have a great influence on the language. Can you think of any words that you could not have said in front of your teacher 50 years ago that you can now? What subjects can we talk about now that we couldn't have in the past? Of course, change isn't all one way. Think about political correctness. What are we not allowed to say today? What words are taboo? Do taboos change?

Here are two letters to the *Daily Express*, written in 1926.

### The Best English
The purest English is spoken in Inverness.

R. Hadden, Brixton SW9

### Our Aliens
If 'G.A.T.' is one of those who is obliged to work for a living, which I very much doubt, how would he like it if one of his 170 Russian refugee friends came along, undercut his wages and took his job from him to starve or go on the dole? I think he would change his views a bit then.

This is what is happening in thousands of cases. Let England deport all her aliens, and I venture to suggest there will be plenty of work for our unemployed and no shortage of houses for our own people to live in.

R.A.P.

Here is an advert from the *Lady's Realm* (1899).

# TOO STOUT
For years I was a very bad figure, with rolls of fat upon the stomach and hips, was short of breath, and a positive misery to myself. Almost by accident I became possessed of a remedy which has cured me, and will send particulars for stamped addressed envelope.

**Mrs Moore, 1 Borough Road, London S.E.**

# How Queen's English has grown more like ours

**By Neil Tweedie**

As the common tongue continues its inexorable slide towards a new dark age of glottal stops and 'innits', news comes that even the Queen is drifting slowly down river towards Estuary English.

A scientific study of Christmas broadcasts to the Commonwealth since

> The Queen in 1998 had become 'definitely less upper class'

1952 suggests the royal vowel sounds have undergone a subtle evolution since the days when coal was routinely delivered to Buckingham Palace *in sex*.

Her Majesty may not be quite ready to engage in fully-fledged Bermondsey banter with Jade Goody, but her speech has nevertheless followed the general trend from cut-glass URP (Upper Received Pronunciation) towards the more

democratic Standard Received Pronunciation and its close relative, Standard Southern British English.

The findings are contained in the *Journal of Phonetics*, which, in addition to the Queen, addresses such topics as, 'The temporal domains of accent in Finnish' and 'Perceptual correlates of Cantonese tones'.

Jonathan Harrington, Professor of Phonetics at the University of Munich, and author of the study on the Queen, said his team had conducted a thorough acoustic analysis of all the Christmas broadcasts during her reign.

'We chose the broadcasts because it is very rare indeed to find high-quality recordings of a person's voice stretching back over such a long period,' he said. 'The changes in the Queen's speech have been very, very slow, but they are there nevertheless.

'In 1952 she would have been heard referring to "thet men in the bleck het". Now it would be "that man in the black hat".

'Similarly, she would have spoken of the citay and dutay, rather than citee and dutee, and hame rather than home. In the 1950s she would have been lorst, but by the 1970s lost.'

And indeed, the

Queen's first Christmas broadcast was pure Dartington Crystal.

She began: 'As he [King George VI] used to do, I em speaking to you from my own hame, where I em spending Christmas with my femly.'

Prof Harrington said he did not believe the changes in the royal delivery were a conscious attempt to lower social barriers.

'Half a century ago the social classes were much more demarcated.

'That changed with the social revolution of the 1960s and 1970s and the much greater blurring of boundaries,' he said.

'I don't think the Queen changed consciously at all. What the study suggests is that we all participate in sound changes, whether we like it or not. The Queen has merely altered her way of speaking in line with her host community in south-east England.'

But did that mean that she would soon be mixing it with Jade darn the Dog n' Duck?

'She may be drifting slowly downstream towards Estuary, but she has a very, very long way to go before she gets anywhere near the open sea.'

The historian and royal biographer Kenneth Rose said the Queen's accent had undoubtedly changed during her reign.

'She has become definitely less upper class – dropping an octave and coming nearer to her own "Queen's English", by which I mean nearer to Standard English,' he said.

'There have always been variations in royal speech. The Queen Mother was the embodiment of the upper class lady in the first class compartment, while George V was more like a hoarse country gentleman.

'Edward VIII adopted a kind of upper class cockney, talking of "moi house", but after his marriage began to sound more American.

'About two or three years ago I was sitting next to the Queen at tea and she remarked that some of her grandchildren talked Estuary. I think she was talking about the Phillips children – but then Princess Anne always sounded a little suburban.

'And then there's Prince Edward, who sounds a bit Estuary – whereas the Dukes of Kent and Gloucester are proper country gents.'

And was Her Majesty happy about the Estuarisation of the Royal Family.

'She was absolutely neutral on the subject.'

Is one bovvered? Does one look bovvered? One thinks not. 'A merry Christmas and a happay New Yeah.'

## Activity 60 | Changing contexts

In pairs, identify specific features of language change illustrated by the texts on pages 292 and 293. How do these changes reflect changes in attitudes and values over the last century? To what extent has the discourse of each of these texts changed?

For each text, try to find modern examples of similar texts for comparison. Write an analysis comparing the modern examples to the ones above. What does such comparison tell us about the nature of language change over time?

## Activity 61 | Language in advertising

Write an analysis of this Kleinerts advertisement. Remember to start by unpacking the context and then identify how this influences the features of language change. The advert appeared in a woman's magazine in the late 1930s.

# Global English

More than 380 million people speak English as their first language. English today is probably the third largest language by number of native speakers, after Mandarin Chinese and Spanish. If you combine native and non-native speakers it is probably the most commonly spoken language in the world.

The countries with the highest populations of native English speakers are the United States (215 million), United Kingdom (58 million), Canada (17.7 million), Australia (15 million), Ireland (3.8 million), South Africa (3.7 million) and New Zealand (3.0–3.7 million). Countries such as Jamaica, Nigeria and Singapore also have millions of native speakers of dialect continuums ranging from English-based creoles to more standard versions of English. India has the highest population of speakers of English as a second language. David Crystal suggests that if we combine native and non-native speakers, India now has more people who speak or understand English than any other country in the world.

## Activity 62 — Researching global English

**Individual**

How did English get to be so widespread? Research this using reference books and the internet (start with www.bbc.co.uk/radio4/routesofenglish).

Collect data on different world Englishes. You can find radio stations from around the world online (try www.world.english.org), you may be able to access English-speaking television from around the world, you may have songs by English-speaking artists from around the world. Identify the types of English and some of their key features. Remember it is not just accent that will differ, but spelling, lexis, meaning and cultural reference.

**Class work**

As a class, pool your findings to make a map of English as it is used around the world.

Debate or discuss in class the question 'Is the global nature of English a good thing?' What are the cultural, political, economic, educational and social implications of the continuing dominance of English as a world language? Do you think English will continue to be such a powerful language?

**Individual**

Write a newspaper article arguing the case either for or against Global English.

## Review

In this section you have completed your exploration of the way that language changes across the range of language concepts. You have practised analysing texts and used a range of resources to support your study of this topic. You should also understand how important dictionaries are to the study of this topic.

The global nature of the English language is a very important topic and may be specifically mentioned in your exam specification.

# Language change debates

## Prescription and description

How do you respond to these examples of language use?

- 10 items or less.
- We have much to be thankful for.
- To boldly go where no man has gone before.
- Tomato's, potato's and carrot's.
- Keep apart two chevrons.
- With whom will you attend?

How do you respond if someone tries to 'correct' your English?

In terms of attitudes to language use and language change, opinions can be placed along a continuum from prescriptive to descriptive.

| Activity 63 | Entering the debate |
|---|---|

Read the following series of texts which presents a range of views on language use. Text A is from the *Guardian* (October 2003), Text B is from *Eats, Shoots and Leaves*, by Lynne Truss, Text C is David Crystal's response (posted on his blogspot) to criticism from John Humphrys.

How would you describe the opinions being expressed? Which, if any, do you agree with?

**Text A**

# Not I. It's me

**Texting, lazy jargon, management-speak: never has the English language been so abused. But a new book called *Between You And I* is pointing out the worst errors – and demanding higher standards. In his introduction John Humphrys explains why bad English makes him cross.**

The story is told in journalistic circles of a crowd of journalists gathered outside the house of a very important man, all of them waiting for a very important announcement. The great man's butler came to the door, drew breath and bellowed: 'Would the press go around to the tradesman's entrance and will the gentleman from the *Times* please come with me!'

Ah, those were the days: the days when the *Times* was not just a newspaper but an institution. Pompous, stuffy and old-fashioned it might have been, but it was respected throughout the world for its high standards. It was the newspaper of record. When the *Times* spoke, the world took note. It got things right.

So when, a few years ago, I was asked to write my first column for the *Times* I was flattered and agreed immediately. On the morning of publication I opened my copy. The headline above one of the stories on my page read: 'Work Comes Second For Tony And I'. In case you did not know, newspaper headlines are written not by the contributors but by sub-editors.

I was shocked. That a sub on the *Times* should commit such a howler was beyond belief. It was time, perhaps, to give up and accept that the battle for good English had been lost. It was all over. But then the letters began to arrive: a trickle that became a torrent. The readers were as shocked as I had been. And that reassured me. There are still many people out there who care enough for the English language to register their protest when they see it being desecrated. Many battles have been lost, but the war is not yet over.

Perhaps it should be. Perhaps those of us who recoil at the incorrect use of 'I' in a great newspaper are pedants. There is, after all, a danger that if we old fogies have our way the language will be treated as though it were a precious artefact in a museum. It will be guarded day and night, protected from potential vandals. No one must be allowed to touch.

Like any other organism, language changes. It lives in the real world and gets knocked about from time to time. It adapts in order to survive. Look up almost any word in the Oxford English Dictionary and you can follow the journey that it has taken over the centuries, changing its precise meaning as it twists and turns with the passing of time. Often its present meaning bears little relationship to its original one. It is silly to imagine that this evolution can be halted. It is even sillier to try.

But that is different from hoisting the white flag and surrendering to linguistic anarchy. A degree of discipline is not a constraint; it is a liberation. The more clearly we are able to express ourselves, the less room there is for ambiguity. The more elaborate and the more precise our vocabulary, the greater the scope for thought and expression. Language is about subtlety and nuance. It is powerful and it is potent. We can woo with words and we can wound. Despots fear the words of the articulate opponent. Successful revolutions are achieved with words as much as with weapons.

When words with distinct meanings become synonymous with each other – flaunt and flout, for instance – we begin to lose the capacity for discriminated expression. When we are cavalier about where we place the word 'only' in a sentence we risk destroying its meaning.

All this matters more in written than in spoken English. I have always felt it a little unfair for parliamentary sketch writers to mock John Prescott by reproducing his garbled sentences verbatim in print. It might be difficult to follow him on the page, but he is capable of making a powerful speech. His audiences may not follow every point in his argument, but they know exactly what he means. I once saw him sway an audience at a Labour party conference and win a crucially important vote that had been thought lost. He spoke from the heart and not the head and there is nothing wrong with that.

Flowery language from the pen of a poet is one thing; written English as a means of everyday communication is another. It

should be plain and simple and accurate. It should use no more words than are needed to do the job and they should be the right words. We all have our own pet hates. One of mine is the relatively recent and altogether hideous American import 'met up with'. I have offered a bottle of the best bubbly to anyone who can explain how that differs from 'met'. The bottle sits in my office to this day.

Then there is the tendency to use nouns as verbs. 'Impact' is a good (by which I mean bad) example. 'Fast track' was bad enough when it was overused as a noun. It is unspeakable as a verb.

This is all of a piece with our lazy acceptance of jargon, using words for merely instrumental purposes rather than for genuine expression. It is not new. Orwell made the point in his classic essay, Politics and the English Language. Political speeches, he said, 'consist less and less of words chosen for the sake of their meaning and more of phrases tacked together like the sections of a prefabricated hen-house.'

Politicians have a lot to answer for, but the real villains are business people. Management speak has been infiltrated into our lives, a loathsome serpent crawling into

our bed at night and choking the life out of our language. It is an outrage that the phrase 'human resources' was not strangled at birth. I hate it for its ugliness and its sloppiness. A moment's thought tells you that 'resources' are exploited, used up, squeezed for every last drop of value and then replaced. Are we really meant to regard human beings in that light? It seems we are.

Less offensive, but equally dreary, is all the mumbo-jumbo surrounding 'delivering objectives' by 'thinking outside the box' or 'stretching the envelope' by 'building on best practice'. What does it all mean? I doubt that anyone really knows, least of all the people who use it. They tend to be middle managers striving to impress their bosses or, possibly, each other. The people at the top, in my experience, tend to communicate clearly. Maybe that's why they made it to the top in the first place. Lazy use of language suggests lazy thinking.

This hen-house language might not matter if it were confined to the business world. But it has escaped, like some malign virus, and is infecting us all. I would love to claim that the BBC, with its proud history of championing good English, is fighting back. Sadly, it is not. We have been suborned. A colleague of mine interviewed a young man who was applying for a job in his department. He asked him what he had been doing since he left Cambridge. He was told: 'Proactively networking.'

He should have had him thrown out of the building on the spot or, better still, publicly executed, his body left to hang in the lobby of Television Centre as a warning to others. Instead he gave him the job. The young man is now, I have no doubt, a middle manager telling his colleagues how he can 'progress' his latest challenge – or some such rubbish.

There are so many threats to the survival of good, plain English that it is not easy to be optimistic. Email has a great deal to answer for. Punctuation is no longer required and verbs are abandoned with the speed of a striptease artiste late for her next performance. Text messaging is worse – much worse. Yet I have seen it suggested that students be allowed to use 'texting' abbreviations in examinations. Ultimately, no doubt, we shall communicate with a series of grunts – and the evolutionary wheel will have turned full circle.

**Text B**

Either this will ring bells for you, or it won't. A printed banner has appeared on the concourse of a petrol station near to where I live. 'Come inside,' it says, 'for CD's, Video's, DVD's and Book's.'

If this satanic sprinkling of redundant apostrophes causes no little gasp of horror or quickening of the pulse, you should probably put this book down at once.

**Text C**

Note my phrasing. You really are getting me wrong, you know, and your ascription of the various views to me in your Chapter 1 is so far from the truth that it is virtual linguistic character assassination! When *The Fight for English* came out, and an *Observer* journalist rang around for soundbites [the article appeared under the heading 'Language guru takes on queen of commas'], you are quoted as saying that I say 'rules don't matter that much'. I have never said that, ever. I don't know where you would have got that idea from. Of course rules are important. I say so myself in many places. I've written two grammars of English where the importance of rules is repeatedly stressed. I know exactly how many grammatical rules there are in English. I teach courses on grammar. To say to a linguist that he or she doesn't like rules is simply absurd.

What I'm against are *artificial* rules – rules which have no basis in reality, or only a limited basis, but which people hang on to like grim death despite the fact that the language has changed (which means the grammar has changed, which means that the rules have changed). All the ones you mention, such as the split infinitive, the end-placed preposition, the use of initial conjunctions, the dangling participle, the use of *only*, and so on, are like this. You acknowledge that some of these are silly, but you hang on to others. If, as you now say, 'context is everything' (p. 148), then – for example – you have to allow that some dangling participial constructions and some non-adjacent *only*-placements are perfectly OK, because the context makes it perfectly clear what is being said.

'Context is everything'. I say almost exactly that on p. 152 of *The Fight for English*, and in many of my other writings. And it is this, along with several other things you say in your new book, which leads me to believe that actually our two positions are not as far apart as you may think.

In her 1996 Reith Lectures, 'The Language Web', Jean Aitchison used three metaphors to describe the various attitudes expressed by those opposed to language change:

- **The crumbling castle** – Here English is regarded as a once great building that has been eroded by misuse and neglect. It implies a 'golden age' of English.

- **The damp spoon** – 'Incorrect' usage of English is offensive and impolite, like placing a damp spoon in the sugar. It is done but it is to be regretted. A decline in standards.

- **The infectious disease** – Misuse of English spreads like a disease until we are all infected. It needs a cure.

## Activity 64 Research and report

Research current attitudes to language usage. First, devise a questionnaire that you can use to interview family and friends about their language prejudices. Is there such a thing as 'Bad English'? What annoys them about the way people use language today? Do they think language is changing for the better or worse? Has their own language use ever been criticised? Is spoken language subject to different rules than written language? You might want to provide them with examples of non-standard language use to prompt their reactions.

Jean Aitchison called her 1991 book *Language Change: Progress or Decay?* Using your own primary research and other sources available to you, write a report or an essay using her title.

# Computer-mediated communication (CMC)

You already know a lot about the relationship between language and technology and how modern technology is affecting English. As frequent users of modern technology you have a lot of expertise in this area. Computer-mediated communication (CMC) has obviously had a huge effect on the English language. Texts, e-mails, MSN and so on have all had an impact on our changing language, what it looks like and how we use it. Thanks to modern technology language is perhaps changing faster than ever. However, it has been suggested that innovations such as text messaging do not so much affect the language itself as the way we use it. Do you agree?

## Activity 65 Language technology

Taking a historical perspective, think of all the technologies that have had an effect on language – the printing press, the pen, the telephone, the word processor, etc. Describe, in your own words, how each one you can think of has affected language use.

Research and collect a range of CMC data. This could be texts, MSN conversations, e-mails, blogs, podcasts or anything else you can find. Underline all the examples of changing language you can identify. Classify these language features using the language concepts. On which levels do most changes occur? Consider pragmatics. Are there certain language functions that you wouldn't conduct using texts or e-mail? How often are texts or e-mails misunderstood by the recipient? Why does this happen?

## Review

In this final section you have been introduced to some of the key debates surrounding language change and to some important personalities involved. Language debates happen all the time on personal, local, national and international levels. Look out for language issues being discussed on television, the radio, the internet and in local and national newspapers.

In an exam you may be asked to analyse texts that raise these issues or you might be asked to write an essay or article that engages with a particular language debate. In this section you have practised both of these approaches.

In most exam specifications language change appears as part of the synoptic unit. It is therefore important that you make a detailed consideration of context and apply the range of language concepts when you are asked to analyse a text. Always consider audience and purpose. You will encounter examples of both old and new texts in the exam. Your choice of what to analyse should be informed by your understanding of genre, not simply your preference for old or modern texts.

Language change is happening all around you. Keep your eyes and ears open during your course and keep a record of changes you observe. These can be used to support discursive essays or to provide evidence of your own research in an analysis.

# Model exam question and advice

The passage below was set for comment in an examination. Beneath it are suggestions for *some* of the points that you could make to impress the examiner. The text is an edited letter written by Queen Elizabeth I to her cousin, King James VI of Scotland, in 1587. Elizabeth is trying to justify her decision to have James's mother, Mary, Queen of Scots, executed. Perhaps because of the subject-matter of the letter, Elizabeth is writing in quite a tortuous style.

To my deare brother and cousin, the kinge of Skotz.

Be not caried away, my deare brother, with the lewd perswations of suche, as insteade of infowrming you of my to nideful and helples cause of defending the brethe that God hath given me, to be better spent than spilt by the bloudy invention of traitors handz, may perhaps make you belive, that ether the offense was not so great, or if that cannot serue them, for the over-manifest triall wiche in publik and by the greatest and most in this land hathe bine manifestly proved, yet the wyl make that her life may be saved and myne safe.

Your commissionars telz me, that I may trust her in the hande of some indifferent prince, and have all her cousins and allies promis she wil no more seake my ruine. Deare brother and cousin, way in true and equal balance wither the lak not muche good ground whan suche stuf serves for ther bilding. Suppose you I am so mad to truste my life in anothers hand and sent hit out of my owne?

Make account, I pray you, of my firme frindship loue and care, from wiche, my deare brother, let no sinistar whisperars, nor busy troblars of princis states, persuade to leave your surest, and stike to vnstable staies. And so, God hold you ever in his blessed kiping, and make you see your tru frinds. Excuse my not writing sonar, for paine in one of my yees was only the cause.

Your most assured lovinge sistar and cousin,

ELIZABETH R.

Spelling:

- patterns of words ending in 'e' – deare, suche, brethe
- the use of 'u' and 'v' as both vowel and consonant – serue/serves, loue, vnstable
- representation of vowels and dipthongs – bine/nideful, traitors/way, sinistar/whisperar
- individual variation within passage – perswations/persuade
- s/z variation – Skotz/handz/telz, perswations/commissionars.

**Lexical items:** Changes in usage and meaning of
- words – lewd, invention, staies
- idioms and phrases – better spent than spilt, make account, greatest and most, your most assured
- metaphors – good ground … for their bilding, stike to vnstable staies.

**Grammar:**
- word-order changes – wither the lak or not, pain in one of my yees was only the cause, suppose you
- use of prepositions – trust my life in anothers hand
- verb inflections – God hath given, your commissionars telz me
- formation of plurals – handz, troblars, yees.

## Activity 65 — A complete exam question to attempt

The following passage is from a book called *The History of Myddle* which chronicles the life of a small English town. The book was written over a period of years after 1700, but was not published until more than a century afterwards. The events described in this passage took place around 1701.

By referring in detail to the passage, describe and comment on some of the changes which have taken place in English spelling, vocabulary and grammar since it was written.

> One William Cleaton married a daughter of this Reynolds, and soe beecame tenant of this farme, and had a lease for the lives of himseife, his wife, and Francis, his eldest son. Her lived in good repute, and served severall offices in this parish. Hee had 4 sons. 1. Francis, who displeased his father in marrying with Margaret Vaughan, a Welsh woman. 2. Isaac who married a daughter of one White, of Meriton, and had a good portion with her. 3. Samuell, who married Susan, the daughter of Thomas Jukes, of Newton on the Hill. 4. Richard, an untowardly person. He married Annie, the daughter of William Tyller, a woman as infamous as himselfe. Richard Cleaton soone out run his wife, and left his wife bigge with child.
>
> Richard Cleaton went into the further part of this County; and below Bridgnorth hee gott another wife, and had severall children by her. At last, Anne Tyler, his first wife, caused him to bee apprehended, and indicted him att an Assizes at Bridgnorth upon the statute of Poligami. Shee proved that shee was married to him, but could not prove that hee was married to the other woman, but only that he lived with her, and had children by her. The other woman denied that shee was married to him; and thereupon the Judge sayd 'Then thou art a whore.' To which shee answered 'the worse luck mine my lord.' Cleaton was acquitted, and went out of the country with the other woman, and I never heard more of him.

## Further texts for analysis

The following texts are letters pages from popular music magazines. Text A is from *Smash Hits* (1983), Text B is from *Kerrang* (2007). By detailed reference to the texts and to relevant ideas from language study, write about how these texts show changes in language over time. You should take account of context in your answer.

Use the following approach to structure your written response:

1 What is the text? How has the role and function of these types of text changed over time? How would you describe the audience and purpose of each text – are they the same?

2 Unpack the context. The *Kerrang* text is from 2007, the *Smash Hits* text is from 1983. What are the social, political, technological differences between these two years?

3 Apply the full range of language concepts – group the changes you identify using as many of the concepts as you can. Always give examples of language features you identify.

4 Are the changes predictable, considering the context? Does anything surprise you?

5 What have you learnt about language change through exploring these texts. Do your findings tie in with research you have done previously? Do they raise any language issues?

**Text A**

Dear **Black Type,**

I would like to complain about the stupid names that people give themselves when they write to *Smash Hits*. So far we have seen letters from such THINGS as: Mona Lisa, Simon le Bon's Nose, A French Fry, The Panoramic Banana, The Green Chicken From The Raving Monster Loony Green Chicken Alliance, David's Striped Braces, Marc Almond's Eye-Liner, Andrew Ridgeley's Jeans, Oakey's Black Leather Trousers, The Anti-Headbanging Society, Flash And The Pan's Brown Shoe, Wham Bam I Am A Wham! Fan, John Taylor's Guitar, A Person Trying Desperately To Be A Seagull, Suggs' You-Know-What, A Smurf Lost In Buckinghamshire, Andy Pandy's Ex-Girlfriend, Paul Weller's Sense Of Humour, The Key To The Cage I'd Like To Lock Zoo In Every Thursday Night From 7.25 'Til 8 O'Clock, A Red Rhino and A Pink Hippopotamus, to name but a few! These stupid idiots probably spend all their free time trying to think up silly names for themselves. I think it is disgusting!
*A Paradisical Sock, Australia.*

**Disgusting, is it? Little do you realise, oh foolish piece of foreign footwear, that most of these persons just happen to be very close friends of the Black Type. Send me holiday postcards from places like Droitwich and Sidcup, that sort of thing. Particularly A Person Trying Desperately To Be A Seagull (little known fact: his real name's Darren so you can see why he's adopted this clever disguise). Anyway, push off.**

Why on Earth can't newspaper photographers leave Boy George alone? There have been numerous photos of "Boy George Without His Make-Up". Who cares? OK so these type of pictures may please some people but that proves how small-minded they are. What if Boy George decides not to wear make-up when he goes out? It's not exactly a big sensation so why can't they allow him some privacy? After all, it's the *personality* and not *looks* that count in the end, and Boy George has one of the greatest personalities ever.
*Carole, The Culture Fan, Thornton Heath.*

I feel I must be speaking for a lot of people when I say how sick I am about the continuous harassment of Boy George by the media, and in particular one newspaper.

It seems that this paper will stop at nothing to sprawl his name over its front page, reporting such important matters as "Boy George In Airport Row" and, more recently, Boy George hitting a photographer with an umbrella.

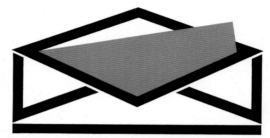

# LETTERS

Write to: Smash Hits Letters, 52-55 Carnaby Street, London W1V 1PF. The best letter gets a £10 Record Token.

Now I know a lot of people will say that George is a media personality and he's brought it on himself, but surely there are more interesting items to report. Give the lad some time to himself.
*Andy Smith, Larkhall.*

**Does seem a bit ridiculous. About the only story we haven't been served up is "My Life With Boy By Pop Chameleon's Friend's Brother's Windowcleaner's Auntie Who Lives In Mozambique". Can't be long though. I reckon his only real hope is to send R. H. Meredith's Grandad on ahead . . .**

This is a picture of my Grandad taken whilst listening to the *Top Forty Show* some weeks ago. Believe it or not he is unbelievably happy that Culture Club are Number One for the sixth week running. His name is George and he thinks Culture Club are smashing and is forever pinching my Soft Cell tapes. He even goes as far as to put *Top Of The Pops* on full blast each week so we are deafened by the sound of music. I'll have to sign off now as he has just stolen my "Seven And The Ragged Tiger" LP and I don't want it scratched.
Yours sufferingly,
*R. H. Meredith, Forestgate, London E7.*

**Brilliant! What a man! Does he actually go to Tesco's dressed like this? He *does*? Take this £10 Record Token immediately in case you never see your Duran LP again. We *must* have more of these! Any other photos of parents or grandparents being unbelievably trendy? Any Toyah lookalikes? Frankie Goes To Hollywood impersonators? This is what we want.**

I bet no-one has got a Gran like mine. My Gran's a Duran Duran fan, buys all their singles, albums and every magazine with them in. She watches every pop TV programme with them on it, and has been to four Duran Duran concerts. She has even covered the spare bedroom with pictures of them, and has T-shirts with them on. Her favourite is Simon le Bon and both her bed quilt and pillow case has a picture of Simon on it. She listens to their records nearly all day.

There is one problem, though. My Grandad can't stand Duran Duran, especially Simon and Andy.
*Limahl's Underpants, Dunfermline.*

OK People, you can safely say that the correspondence on who has the trendiest parents can stop now 'cause my Mum wins hands down. No she *doesn't* like Duran Duran, The Style Council or even Wham!. Oh no, *mes comarades*, all of those are far too untrendy for my Mum. She is the proud owner of "Kiss Me" by Tin Tin, "Send Me An Angel" by Real Life and "So Many Men So Little Time" by Miquel Brown (all 12" of course). She has been to no less than five pop concerts in the past 3 months and is an avid Japan fan. She came with me to see Aztec Camera's gig for the *Whistle Test* and met Roddy Frame and Campbell Owens after the show. And she goes to *Christopher's Nightclub* (plug plug) every week. Beat that!

*An Aztec Camera & Alarm Fan, Kingswinford.*
P.S Please send me a £10 record token as my mum is dying to get her hands on a copy of the new Cocteau Twins LP.

**Cocteau Twins. Get off. *Passé,* mate. Old news. We're looking for people with parents who are actually members of Einsturzende Neubaten or play the oxy-acetylene welder with The Legendary Luton Kippers.**

The recent banning of "Relax" by Frankie Goes To Hollywood by the BBC has brought up some interesting points.

Firstly the hypocrisy and double standards displayed by the BBC. During the last few months they have promoted at least two singles that deal exclusively and obviously with sexual activity. I refer to "Tonight I Celebrate My Love" and "Move Over Darling". "Relax" is far better to dance to and generally superior to the other two. Do the lyrics of a song have to resemble pages of a biology book to receive airplay?

Secondly, a record that reaches Number 1 in the charts should not be excluded from the national airwaves of a nationally-owned broadcasting company. Why should the majority be dictated to by the minority?

Third point. The vast majority of Radio 1 listeners are under 25. Why should we be dictated to by a small group of middle-aged businessmen?
*Tony Smith, Cheadle Hulme, Cheshire.*

I was furious to learn that DJ Mike Read has banned "Relax" by Frankie Goes To Hollywood on the grounds that "the music is great and they are an exciting and competent band but I find the lyrics overtly obscene". It's not enough that the prat is acting as a judge and jury by telling us what is obscene but, in the same breath, he also sees fit to inform us what is exciting and competent as though his opinion is *fact*. The man obviously thinks he is God.

What concerns me is that the BBC let him get away with it, proving that these DJs have a huge say in deciding which singles receive air-play. Remember this is the man who gave endless plugs to songs like "Happy Talk" and "Orville's Song" and was almost responsible for their becoming hits, at which point he would gleefully remind us: "I told you this would be a hit single, didn't I?"

I also read recently that Mike Read had a wheel clamp fixed on his sports car. It's a pity they didn't fix one on his mouth, but then I suppose they couldn't find one big enough.
*Derek, Bristol.*

42

## Text B

WRITE: FEEDBACK!, PO Box 2930, London, W1A 6DZ.
E-MAIL: kerrang@emap.com
TEXT: KFEEDBACK followed by your message and name to 63333 (charged at normal operator rates)
MESSAGE US: www.myspace.com/kerrangmagazine

# FEEDBACK

### ROCK FOR LIFE!

JOIN ANNETTE and Naomi in supporting the Kerrang! and Samaritans' 'Rock For Life' campaign by purchasing a Rock For Life dog tag! Available from the Samaritans website www. samaritans.org/kerrang or by calling 01227 811656, the tags cost £2 each plus P&P with no minimum order. Samaritans provide 24-hour confidential emotional support for people who are experiencing feelings of distress or despair. If you feel you need someone to talk to, email jo@samaritans.org or call 08457 90 90 90.

### PRETTY DECENT PROPOSAL

I'D JUST like to tell the world that last night I proposed to my gorgeous missus onstage at the Funeral For A Friend gig in Leeds. Thankfully, she said yes! Please print how downright fantastic the band and their tour manager are for letting me do it. Cheers!

**CHRIS, VIA MYSPACE.**

### HAPPY IS THE NEW BLACK

THIS ISN'T really a complaint, more of a suggestion, but could you PLEASE print more rock that's a little... happier? I mean it pisses me off that people associate rock music with darkness and evil so much, so couldn't you do more articles about bands like Bowling For Soup and All-American Rejects who make songs that are upbeat and cheery as well as kick ass rock?

This whole dark scene of rock is so overrated. Not only is the word 'black' overused way too much in rock, but there's so much rock nowadays that's all about self-harm, suicide, or death, so it wouldn't hurt to have a few cheery articles, would it? Thanks for the awesome Fall Out Boy and Blink 182 posters (K!1155), by the way.

**ELLIOTT, SURREY VIA EMAIL.**

### STOP CRYING YOUR HEARTS OUT

ONE MESSAGE to all My Chemical Romance fans... STOP IT AND GET SOME SLAYER! Laters, People.
**LITTLE HARRY HARDCORE, VIA MYSPACE.**

### NOT SUCH A SCARY MARY

THE PICTURES of Biffy Clyro in last week's issue (K! 1159) are absolutely gorgeous. Did it take long to wash all those inky equations off of Simon Neil's delicious body? I also noted that he has very attractive feet for a man. Not at all Hobbit like, and no obvious hair. Lovely.
**MILLIE, VIA EMAIL.**

### HYBRID WEE-WEE

I'M A huge Linkin Park fan. I was 11 when 'Hybrid Theory' came out and they've been in my top five ever since. Anyway, getting to the point is it just me or does the back cover of 'Minutes To Midnight' look like they're all going for a piss in the sea? And more disturbingly Phoenix is comparing sizes with Brad.

**JORDAN, VIA EMAIL.**

### ESCAPE ARTISTS NEVER SMELL

HEY THERE! This is my picture of me meeting Gareth from Funeral For A Friend at their first gig of the tour in Bristol. I look like I'm gonna kiss his neck and I was stroking his face, he was terrified! But my God did he smell good, nice shaving cream!
**CALLAM 'DOOGLE' LAWLESS.**

### WE ARE FAMILY

A FEW weeks ago I was in Oxford Street and I saw Ryan Ross from Panic! At The Disco with his little sister (Kate). They are both really nice and I got both their autographs and a hug.
**VIOLET, DUBLIN VIA TEXT.**

## RANT OF THE WEEK
## Planet Rock

IS IT just me that finds the whole 'Live Earth' concert thing a bit hypocritical? Do organisers and bands like Foo Fighters not realise that they are going to be playing their instruments, through amps (using electricity), and that all of the shows are going to be broadcast to millions by different TV companies etc, using yet more electricity?

Then there's flying the bands in their private jets to the different locations, then the car from the airport... using yet more fossil fuels. Then the transport of the fans, the printing of the tickets on paper... Oh deary me, Doesn't it kinda defeat the object of the 'save the world' shite?
**DANIELLE, VIA MYSPACE..**

(STIMULANTS)  THIS ISSUE WAS CREATED BY... COSMO'S HIGH FIVES, BANDITS KING KONG, THREE CHEERS FOR THE ROCK IN THE CHOPPY OCEAN, SOFTER THAN SOFT TOWELS, HANGING OUT WITH THOSE LOVELY BEARDED BLOKES THE MIRIMAR DISASTER, GOTH BLOW-UP DOLLS, HAIRY BUT WITHOUT THE HONEY PART, L WORD SEASON 4 - FRANKIE'S BACK!, LAUGHING AT MURDER MISTRY'S CRAP SLOGANS, MAKING GOTHS CRY, POISON 'BEAT ME UP' ARROW, SUNSHINE DAYS OFF, CHEAP FRUIT, FRUIT BOOTS, GOODBYE TO ICELAND TIL AUGUST, ALL WORK AND NO PLAY MAKES DAN A DULL BOY, ALL WORK AND NO PLAY MAKES DAN A DULL BOY...

| Activity 66 | # A final look at language change |
|---|---|

Here is an article that appeared in *Wife and Home* magazine in 1954.

Write a detailed analysis exploring what this text demonstrates about language change using the approach outlined above. For this text you should also consider what a modern equivalent would be like. You could even find one for comparison.

### Expecting Elizabeth

**DAPHNE HAYES continues her series and tells you about the early months of her pregnancy.**

Peter, my husband, was thrilled when he received my letter while he was abroad telling him about the baby – all the more so because it was obvious that I was very happy about it.

'Take care of yourself, darling,' he wrote, 'and don't do anything silly that might bring complications.'

I remembered our anxiety about Kainche, the Indian girl, who had been pregnant while accompanying us on an expedition in India during the first year of our marriage. She had led a very arduous life – and her baby had been born without any trouble.

'Surely it's not likely that I should face a miscarriage, Mrs. Oldroyd?' I asked my landlady. 'My husband is quite concerned.'

'Don't you worry your pretty head about such things, love,' she replied. 'I'll see you don't do any heavy lifting or anything that might harm that precious baby.'

I remembered that she had once told me she had a threatened miscarriage when she was expecting her first child, so I asked her what happened.

'It was at about the third month,' she told me. 'I had a sudden loss, like a period, and I knew that wasn't right, so I went straight to bed and got my neighbour to telephone for the doctor. When he came he said I'd done absolutely the right thing. He kept me in bed for a week and I didn't lose the baby. That was about the time I came across my first copy of WIFE and HOME and I've read it ever since.'

And that was how *I* came to read WIFE and HOME. Mrs. Oldroyd lent me the current issue, and I went straight to my newsagent and ordered it for myself. I devoured every word of the mothercraft pages, including the maternity series. How helpful and encouraging it was to read about another woman going through the same experiences. Little did I think then that I would one day be writing a series myself.

Obeying the doctor's orders, I made an appointment with the dentist. He found that several fillings were needed and one extraction.

'I am expecting a baby,' I told him. 'Is it safe to have a tooth out?'

'Much safer than keeping a decayed tooth in your mouth,' he replied. 'The poison from that tooth would get into your bloodstream and that would not be good for your baby.'

He explained to me while he worked on the first filling that the reason why the teeth often decay more quickly in pregnancy than at other times is that the baby takes a lot of calcium from his mother's body to build his own bones and teeth. One of the chief sources of calcium is milk and that is why every expectant mother is advised to drink at least one pint of milk a day.

I am not very fond of milk, but my good Mrs. Oldroyd was always bringing me up tempting little blancmanges and milk puddings, just to encourage me 'to do my duty by Elizabeth' as she put it.

My diet sheet told me that I must be sure to take the vitamin pills I obtained free from the welfare clinic. This, the dentist explained, would ensure that my bloodstream absorbed the much needed calcium. If I didn't do this, not only would my baby suffer, but I should probably find myself getting most unpleasant cramp.

Mrs. Oldroyd kept me up to scratch in following my diet. She used to provide me with my main meal in the middle of the day, the others I prepared myself with the aid of a gas ring. Fortunately, I like salads and I practically lived on them. During the winter when lettuces were scarce and dear, I used shredded raw cabbage or sprouts, watercress, raw celery, grated raw carrot and turnip, etc.

I didn't have to ask Mrs. Oldroyd not to put bicarbonate of soda in the water when she cooked greens for me. She had learned from WIFE and HOME years ago, she said, that this destroys the vitamins and that greens should be cooked as quickly as possible in the minimum of water to preserve the full food value.

I never had any cravings for highly seasoned foods like pickles, chutneys and sauces, as I believe some women do, although they are not good for the expectant mother. Nor had I been in the habit of having more than an occasional drink, so it was no hardship to cut out alcohol. In fact, I was lucky in that I naturally liked most of the things that were good for me, such as wholemeal bread, cheese and fresh fruit.

Meat was still rationed, so I could not eat more than was good for me, but I preferred a little of the best quality to large helpings of a cheaper cut. I am very fond of eggs, and I knew that these, with fish, offal and cheese, would supply the necessary protein when meat was off the menu.

EVERY DAY I took Mrs. Oldroyd's dog for a good brisk walk over the common. Having only my own two rooms to keep tidy, I didn't get much exercise through housework, so I knew that the walk was essential. I bought a good sensible pair of brogues and put away my high heeled shoes 'for the duration.'

I had sometimes noticed pregnant women tottering along on high-heeled sling back shoes and thought how foolish they looked. My doctor told me later that they are also dangerous because as the expectant mother gets bigger her balance is altered and there is risk of a fall if she wears unsuitable shoes, to say nothing of the backache they produce.

PRESENTED BY OUR MATERNITY DOCTOR

# Glossary

**Abstract language** language that conveys ideas, emotions or thoughts. It is usually applied to nouns or noun phrases that represent concepts, not concrete objects. A phrase like 'firm commitment' may sound very definite but it is an intention or an idea and so is abstract. *p 102*

**Accent** usually refers to characteristic features of regional pronunciation or social class. It also refers to deviations from Received Pronunciation in the speech of people whose first language is not English. The term can also be used to denote emphasis on a particular word or syllable. In written French, for example, it refers to signs added to individual letters to indicate their pronunciation. *pp 16, 51, 117, 174, 292*

**Accommodation (theory)** expresses the idea that, in general, people will adapt their language so that it is close to the way other people are using language. For example, if two people are talking and one participant's language would normally be more formal, they will adapt their language to a more informal style in order to make the other participant feel more comfortable. The term is connected with issues of politeness, convergence and social variation. *p 58*

**Acronym** refers to the use of the initial letters of a group of words or a phrase as shorthand for the words themselves. When said aloud an acronym makes a new word, e.g. Acquired Immune Deficiency Syndrome becomes AIDS, Anti Social Behaviour Order becomes ASBO. *pp 8, 280. See also Initialism.*

**Active voice** *p 15. See Voice.*

**Affect** emotional force of a word or words. *p 42*

**Affixation** addition of a prefix or suffix to a word or morpheme to make a new semantic or grammatical form (e.g. **re**turn, **in**formal, sing**ing**, walk**ed**). *pp 8, 280*

**Agreement** grammatical term that expresses the way in which verb forms change according to the tense and the person to which the verb refers: when it is the standard form it has 'agreement'. For example, in Standard English, 'he goes' shows agreement of verb and person whereas 'he go' does not. *p 77*

**Alliteration** repetition of the same initial sound within a group of words, e.g. **s**ing a **s**ong of **s**ixpence. *pp 18, 69, 193, 270*

**Allophone** one of two or more different pronunciations of the same **phoneme**. *p 16*

**Ameliorative change** change in meaning of a word from negative/unpleasant to positive/pleasant associations. *p 8*

**Analogy** as a general term means that there is a similarity between two objects or ideas. In linguistic terms it refers to one of the methods for creating new words by finding a similarity with an object or idea that already exists. For example, a crane (for building) is tall and thin like the bird. A computer window is like the window in a building – in shape and in function. As a process, analogy also works for other changes in language. For example, the plural of 'hippopotamus' is 'hippopotami' if it follows the Greek pattern of making plurals but by analogy with other English plural formations 'hippopotamuses' can also be used. *pp 34, 85, 259*

**Anaphoric reference** cohesive device by which a pronoun is substituted for and *refers back* to a previous noun or noun phrase to avoid clumsy repetition. *pp 40, 41, 114*

**Antithesis** rhetorical term referring to the use of contrasting ideas or words. *p 45*

**Antonym** word with opposite meaning to another word. *pp 8, 106*

**Aspect** verb form which conveys information about the duration of an action, and whether it was completed or continuous. *p 13*

**Assonance** repetition of the same vowel sound with different consonants, e.g. feel, heap, chief. *p 18*

**Asymmetry** as a general term is where two parts of an object that are expected to be the same are different from each other. In linguistic terms it applies to two specific features. The first is a lack of similarity in the status of two speakers – therefore their language use will be different. It is also used to apply to terms for men and women that were once, or are expected to be, equal but are not equal. For example, 'lord' has high status but 'lady' has a lower status linguistically. You might say 'cleaning lady' but you would never say 'cleaning lord'. *p 99*

**Audience** the specific category of reader or listener that a text is *intended* for. Audiences can be categorised in a number of different ways, e.g. by age, gender, specific interest group, level of expertise. *pp 2, 67, 148, 162, 236, 249*

**Authorial voice** implied author (rather than 'real' author) of fictional text who comments directly on character and action to the reader. *p 36*

**Babbling** refers to the stage in spoken language development where children practise forming the sounds of language. They produce strings of sounds that resemble spoken language but do not yet form words. *p 235*

**Back formation** process of forming a new word, usually a verb, from a noun that already exists. The noun will sound as if it ends in 'er', and this phoneme is removed to form the verb, e.g. 'burglar' becomes 'to burgle', 'editor' becomes 'to edit'. This type of word formation is relatively rare. *pp 9, 280*

**Back-channel behaviour** alternative (rather clumsy) term for response tokens. *pp 64, 131*

**Binary opposition** describes the way in which two terms are seen as paired opposites in order to make understanding the world simpler, e.g. male/female, black/white, old /young. A set phrase that states these binary opposites is called a **binomial expression**, e.g. life and limb, up and down. Sometimes these terms are a remnant of a phrase with both Germanic and French origins, e.g. the legal phrase 'without let or hindrance'. Binary opposition also has relevance to gender theories, e.g. it is considered 'natural' for the order to be male then female in binomial expressions such as man and wife, Mr and Mrs, lords and ladies. *p 56*

**Black English Vernacular (BEV)** describes a dialect that is influenced by Afro-Caribbean, Creole or patois languages. It is a social rather than a regional dialect as it is not specific to a particular regional area, but more likely to be found in urban communities. Related terms are African American English or Black American English, or Ebonics. *p 77*

**Blending** word formation process where two words are 'blended' or merged together to form a new word, e.g. blending 'breakfast' and 'lunch' produces 'brunch'. *pp 8, 280*

**Booster** has a similar meaning to intensifier, a word that strengthens other terms, e.g. really, hugely, massively. *p 63*

**Borrowing** describes the process where the English language appropriates a word from another language, usually because no English word exists to describe the concept, activity or thing to be described, e.g. déjà vu, karaoke, pizza, Schadenfreude. *pp 8, 280*

**Branching** a left-branching sentence opens with a number of subordinate clauses, and *ends* with a main clause; a right-branching sentence *opens* with a main clause, and ends with a number of subordinate clauses. *p 12*

**Cataphoric reference** cohesive device whereby a pronoun is used to substitute for and *refer forward* to a noun or noun phrase in the next clause or sentence. *pp 40, 41*

**Child directed speech (CDS)** describes the variety of language that adults use when talking to very young children. This is thought to be instinctive and also resembles the way we often talk to our pets. It has distinctive features such as rhetorical questions, diminutive endings, repetition, tag questions and exaggerated intonation. *p 236*

**Cliché** overused or stereotyped phrase. *p 10*

**Clipping** process of forming a new word by removing a morpheme from an existing word. The existing word is shortened or 'clipped', e.g. 'telephone' becomes 'phone', 'omnibus' becomes 'bus'. *pp 8, 280*

**Closed network** group of speakers that do not generally engage in speech with speakers of other dialects or accents. This means that other language forms will not influence their language. *p 134. See also Social network.*

**Closing** technical term for the phrases that are used to end a conversation. They are often formulaic and are related to politeness features. Several phrases may be exchanged before a closing is successful, e.g. 'thanks for calling', 'see you later', 'so that is sorted then' or 'speak to you again soon'. The person who initiates or succeeds in the closing is demonstrating that they have the power to decide when the conversation is over. *p 89*

**Co-constructed** term particularly associated with Jennifer Coates's research. She discovered that women will often finish each other's utterances or will divide a turn or utterance between several speakers, in contrast to the usual assumptions about conversation: that it is constructed through clear turn taking. *p 64*

**Code** describes the particular language features that are used in a specific social group or a specific context. As with Morse code or secret codes, it may be difficult for others to understand or it may just describe the typical features. *p 58. See also Elaborated code and Restricted code.*

**Code switch** describes how speakers can change between the languages of different language groups. Almost everyone can switch automatically, for example, when conversing with two speakers who might require different levels of formality or when changing accent or lexis according to the person you are talking to. *p 58*

**Coherence** refers to the overall sense and meaning of a text. *pp 8, 40*

**Cohesion** refers to the way a text fits together via grammar, syntax, lexis and sound patterning. Specific instances of cohesion are called **cohesive devices**. *pp 8, 40, 69, 157. See also Anaphoric reference and Cataphoric reference.*

**Collocation** phrase or group of words habitually used together. *p 10*

**Communicative competence** is similar to code switching. It describes how a speaker has command of a variety of communicative styles. It expresses the proficiency or competence with which a speaker communicates with other speakers. *p 58*

**Competition** describes the viewpoint that the male conversational style depends upon competing with other speakers to have control of the conversation. This theory sees male conversation as being a matter of competing for the 'floor' and maintaining their turn, until they have finished or are interrupted. This style is considered to be focused on relaying anecdotes or opinions. *p 64*

**Compounding** process of forming new words by adding two existing words together, e.g. black + board = blackboard. *pp 8, 85, 279*

**Computer-mediated communication (CMC)** refers to any form of written or spoken communication that takes place through the medium of computer-assisted technology. This includes e-mails, texts, telephone ordering services, online shopping, MSN. This variety of communication has some similarities to speech in that it is often quick, uses non-standard grammar and spelling and can appear temporary. It is very often written but can be manipulated in ways that traditional writing can't. It has changed the way we communicate more substantially than the actual language we use. *p 299*

**Conative function** refers to language which is focused on the addressee with the intention of exerting influence. *p 21. See also* **Persuasive function** *and* **Function of language**.

**Concept of correctness** refers to the way a piece of writing will be judged, which is closely connected to the discourse type and context. So, for example, writing published in a newspaper would need to conform to a different standard of spelling and grammar rules than a letter or a scribbled note. This is closely related to the audience expectations and the status of the discourse. High-status discourses would be expected to demonstrate high levels of correctness, whereas low-status or personal discourses would not necessarily demand the same level of correctness. *p 85*

**Connective** grammatical term used to describe words that link clauses. An alternative term is 'conjunction'. There are co-ordinating connectives that join two equal clauses, e.g. and, then, so, but, or, for. There are also subordinating connectives which are used with subordinate clauses, e.g. because, while, as, who, which, although, after. *pp 77, 256*

**Connoted meaning** associated meaning. *p 4*

**Consonance** repetition of final consonant or consonant group. *p 18*

**Content words** grammatical units (parts of speech) conveying semantic meaning, e.g. nouns, adjectives, verbs, adverbs. *p 9*

**Context** parts of a text preceding or following a particular passage; (more generally) a situation or event within its temporal, social, locational or cultural setting. *pp 2, 27, 52, 189, 242*

**Context bound** refers to terms that are used because they are expected in that context or words and phrases that make sense only in that context. *p 63*

**Contrasting pairs** refers to a dual or repeated pattern in language. This is done for linguistic effect and is a particular feature of skilful and persuasive spoken language, e.g. 'Some people believe football is a matter of life and death. I can assure you it is much, much more important than that', or 'It was the best of times, it was the worst of times'. *p 140*

**Convergence** refers to the tendency for speakers to move towards each other linguistically when talking together and might affect their dialect, register and accent. It's normally done unconsciously. *pp 58, 125.* Downward convergence refers to one speaker adjusting their language to the more non-standard forms of the other – adjusting it downwards. For example, a person living in London when phoning their

parents back home in Leeds might unconsciously adopt more of their parents' accent and dialect. *p 77*

**Conversational implicature** implicit rather than explicit meaning of an utterance, e.g. 'I'm cold' really meaning 'Shut the window'. *pp 24, 133*

**Conversational maxims** four 'rules' for successful conversation (maxims of quality, quantity, relevance and manner) as described by H.P. Grice (1975). *p 23*

**Conversational styles** are the different ways that people use conversation, the functions people expect from the conversation, the roles they take and the content they expect them to have. For example, Tannen found that men expect conversations to have transactional purposes, to convey information or show expertise, whereas women's conversational style centres around interpersonal functions of sharing feelings, supporting and being inclusive. *p 64*

**Co-operation** in conversation theory describes the way in which turn taking and conversational roles work. It includes features such as minimal response (e.g. mmm/yeah/ I know) to show listening and positive feedback or agreement. It may include simultaneous speech where two participants say the same thing together to show listening and support. *pp 64, 126. See also* **Conversational styles** *and* **Co-constructed**.

**Co-operative principle** part of Grice's theory of conversation. His intention was to describe and explain how conversations work, how different individual participants can work together to create a successful conversation. He devised four conversational maxims that describe how a coherent discourse between different contributors is created. He termed this coherence the 'co-operative principle', and identified the various factors that contribute to creating a complete discourse. *p 133*

**Copula deletion** describes a feature of some non-standard dialects. The copula is a verb that links the subject and the complement. The subject is the main person or thing that the sentence is about. The complement is a term that describes the subject. The verb/copula links the two. So, in 'you are lovely', for example, 'you' is the subject, 'are' is the copula, 'lovely' is the complement. Some dialects delete this copula and say 'you lovely', or say 'you my girl' where Standard English would say 'you are my girl'. *p 82*

**Corpora** is the plural form of 'corpus' and refers to computer-based 'banks' of twentieth- and twenty-first-century spoken and written language held at various universities, where researchers and publishers often share resources and expertise. *p 9*

**Covert prestige** describes the attitudes of a group that consider a non-standard dialect to have more prestige than the standard dialect. So, for example, in particular social groups, the more a person uses slang terms, the more he or she is held in high esteem by other members of the group. *p 77*

**Creative function** is associated with productivity in language and has links with the imaginative function of children's language. *p 21. See also* **Function of language**.

**Creole** describes a variety of language that has formed from the contact of European languages with another, especially African, language. *pp 78, 295*

**Critical Period Hypothesis** theory, put forward initially by Lenneberg, that there is a time limit on acquiring a first language. Children who do not acquire the rudiments of language, especially grammar, by a certain age will never be able to do so. There is some debate over when this critical period might be: some suggest adolescence, others suggest it may be as young as four. *p 236*

**CVCV** refers to a cluster of sounds that children find easier to pronounce than other combinations. It stands for 'Consonant, Vowel, Consonant, Vowel' as in the utterance 'Mama' or 'Dada'. Children will often alter the pronunciation of words to form this pattern. *p 239*

**Declarative** describes a sentence that makes a statement, e.g. 'The dog is sitting on the chair.' *pp 53, 256*

**Deficit model/Deficit prescriptive evaluation** describes the way in which adults often look at the negative aspects of children's language before acknowledging what they have achieved. This is the process of identifying what someone can't do, before identifying what they can do, e.g. if your teacher only picked out the spelling mistakes in an essay you had written and did not comment on the content. This term is also used in gender theory of language to describe the view that women's spoken language is deficient, and that to be taken seriously women must learn to speak like men. *pp 63, 240, 253*

**Deletion** describes the way that young children remove more challenging sounds from words to make them easier to pronounce. These might include final consonants, unstressed syllables or consonant clusters. *p 239*

**Denoted meaning** 'dictionary' definition giving precise meaning. *p 4*

**Dense social network** *p 58. See* **Social network**.

**Descriptive** describes an open attitude to language use. A descriptive approach suggests that language use is not wrong or incorrect but appropriate to context, e.g. 'We was sitting' as a spoken utterance is not incorrect but a frequent feature of informal spoken English. *p 296*

**Descriptive function** can either be a factual and informative account or be associated with the representational function of language whereby the writer or speaker re-creates and constructs an imagined version of the real world. *p 21. See also* **Function of language**.

**Diachronic change** change over time; historical change. *p 1*

**Dialect** describes the particular words, phrases or grammatical structures associated with a particular region or group. These will be consistent enough to form a distinctive variation in the common language. Regional dialects are the most familiar but there are also social, cultural and occupational dialects. *pp 16, 51, 117, 288*

**Dialogic** adjective from 'dialogue'. In relation to Bakhtin, it refers to the interactive nature of all language, whether spoken or written. *p 34*

**Difference model** is used in gender theory of language. It describes the view that male and female language use is simply about difference in language choices. It was developed in contrast to the deficit model: the view that women's language is deficient in some way. A third model is the dominance model: the theory that difference in language use between genders is more to do with power relations because in society the male dominates the female. *p 63*

**Dimeter** verse line of four syllables, of which two are stressed. *p 20*

**Directive** in a linguistic context refers to a given order, like a command. *pp 63, 124*

**Discourse** is used to describe text types. It refers to the structure of the text and the conventions or typical features. It is therefore used to classify specific types of text. So speech discourse is a type of text that has a specific structure and particular features. In written texts narrative will have a particular discourse, because it might have typical lexis, grammar, structure, etc. *pp 6, 54, 225, 239*

**Discourse community** group of people using the same sorts of discourse, e.g. lawyers who are proficient in legal discourse. It is similar to a speech community but discourse could include written as well as spoken discourse. *p 7*

**Discourse marker** lexical item that is specific to a particular discourse type. It is often used to describe terms that signpost the text, create cohesion and help the audience to follow the way the text works. For example 'well', 'so', 'as I said' are all discourse markers of speech that can signal a change of topic. *pp 10, p 99, 131*

**Discourse structure** describes the way in which a particular type of text is structured. For example, a narrative will often have a chronological structure. An argumentative essay will start with an introduction, present one view, then the opposite view and end with a synthesis of the various viewpoints. A conversation will be structured by the participants and will shift from topic to topic according to the contributions. It may have side-sequences, where a new, related topic is introduced before returning to the main topic. *p 53*

**Dissonance** clashing consonant sounds. *p 18*

**Divergence** is the opposite of convergence and refers to the tendency for speakers to move away from each other linguistically when talking together. It might affect their dialect, register and accent. Unlike convergence, it's normally done consciously. *pp 58, 125*

**Dominance model** is a term in gender theory which links the differences in male and female language to the dominant roles males often have in society. It holds links between research into gender and power. It sees women's language use as created by asymmetric exchanges, finding that there is a similarity between women's language use and that of the less powerful participants. *p 63. See also Difference model.*

**Dominant discourses** describes the debates, thoughts or priorities of a society and the language it uses to describe them. For example, the dominant discourses of a society may be in terms of duty or it may view things in terms of individual freedoms and personal happiness. 'Dominant discourses' describes how powerful groups, whether their power is instrumental or influential, use language to influence the way ideas are discussed and perceived. Another example is how education or the health service is described in business terms. In this dominant discourse, a college might offer an 'educational product', not 'courses', and education would be described as an 'industry'. The use of these terms will influence the values and goals of those who work within it or judge it. *p 57. See also Discourse.*

**Double negative** sentence that uses two negative constructions, e.g. 'Don't never do that' or 'I don't know no one'. Some accounts of grammar disapprove of this use: it is described as illogical as two negatives produce a positive statement. Other views on language use see this as a way of accentuating the negative statement. In some dialects a double negative would be considered as standard use. *p 77*

**Dynamic verbs** describe action, e.g. running, singing, playing, lying. *p 13. See also Stative verbs.*

**Elaborated code** term formulated by Basil Bernstein and used in sociolinguistics to describe a style of language use associated with formal situations and characterised by explicitness, lack of dependence on the external context, syntactic complexity, and individuality of expression. An elaborated code is normally more comprehensible to an outsider than a restricted code. *p 134*

**Elicitation** asks for a response from the listener or reader. It means 'bring out' or 'draw out'. It is therefore a key part of educational talk, where teachers draw out an answer or response from the students. It could also be used in other contexts. *p 88*

**Elision** speech feature where the speaker misses out sounds in a word, e.g. a final sound ('doin' instead of 'doing'), an initial sound (''appen' instead of 'happen'), or a sound in the middle of a word ('don't' instead of 'do not'). *p 53*

**Ellipsis** omission of whole words from an utterance or sentence because they are grammatically implied. For example, it is sufficient to reply 'Yes I can' to the question 'Can you cook?' The word 'cook' is redundant because it is implied. This is a normal feature of spoken English. *pp 40, 53, 270*

**Eponym** word that has been formed using the name of a person or company that invented or popularised something, e.g. Hoover, Biro, Sandwich. *p 279*

**Estuary English** variety of English spoken in the South of England. It is a mixture of London and Standard English. It is often regarded as having replaced Received Pronunciation as the variety of English used by people in various positions of power, including the media. *p 292*

**Etymology** study of the origins of words: how words are formed and how they acquire meaning. A good dictionary will give you the etymology of a word as well as its current meaning. *pp 5, 283*

**Euphemism** word or words which soften or even hide meanings, e.g. 'passed away' instead of 'died', 'killed by friendly fire' instead of 'killed by troops on the same side'. Euphemisms are also often used to avoid direct and explicit language referring to sex or sexual parts of the body. *pp 56, 118*

**Evaluative function** is associated with the expressive function in that it involves judgement and the communication of subjective attitude and opinion. *p 22. See also Function of language.*

**Evaluative lexis** way of expressing an opinion about the object or concept being discussed. Adjectives are often evaluative lexis, e.g. lovely, great, super. *p 64*

**Exclamative** describes a sentence or utterance that conveys an emotion such as surprise or warning. In written texts exclamatives are marked with exclamation marks; in speech they are marked by intonation. They may not always be marked in transcripts. In terms of sentence structure they could be questions, statements or imperatives. *p 53*

**Exclusion** omission of a word, especially a grammatical unit, that does not affect the meaning of an utterance. Children do this during the telegraphic stage of their language development. For example, 'We go shops tomorrow' omits the auxiliary verb, preposition and article but the meaning is clear. *p 243*

**Expletive** swear word or exclamation in the form of an oath or vulgar word. *p 64*

**Expository function** function associated with argument and the communication of attitude and opinion. *p 21. See also Function of language.*

**Expressive language** language which conveys emotion, attitude or opinion; creative language. *p 1*

**Face** in linguistic terms relates to politeness theory and most people's desire to be approved of by others. This is comparable to its use in the idiom 'lose face', meaning to be made to feel foolish in front of others. *p 14*

**Face needs** describes the need that most people have to feel they have a positive status in the company of others. *p 64*

**Face-threaten** describes the way in which some language use threatens the need to be seen positively by others and therefore threatens the sense of self-esteem. Face-threatening acts are actions or speech that impose on other people. *p 65*

**Facework** effort made so that others feel comfortable and maintain their positive face or self-esteem. *p 64*

**False start** refers to a non-fluency feature found in spontaneous conversation when someone starts to say something, stops and then starts again. It is not stammering and can be quite natural when someone is thinking what to say as they are speaking. *pp 54, 131*

**Feedback** is how a participant in a conversation shows that they are listening and agree with the other contributions to the conversation. It might be a word or sound or repeating terms. *p 53*

**Filler** refers to a sound or word that while it does not necessarily add to the conversation, maintains the speaker's turn, while they decide what to say next. A filler might be a word like 'so' or a sound like 'um' or 'er'. Pauses in conversation are referred to as silent/unfilled or voiced/filled. *pp 53, 131*

**Focalisation** describes the way in which a writer uses different strategies to focus and communicate point of view, usually in prose fiction. *p 36*

**Fourteener** verse line of fourteen syllables, of which seven are stressed. *p 20*

**Frame** set of contextualisation clues enabling a speaker to recognise a situation. Frame and schema theory refers to a more advanced stage of recognition when the speaker already possesses a mental model (schema) of a situation. *p 24*

**Framing** term for the way in which a concept or phenomenon will be described. For example, you might frame a debate about immigration in terms of economic benefit or conversely in terms of invasion. Framing is linked to dominant discourses in the way it restricts and defines the language available to discuss an idea or presupposes the attitudes of the audience. *p 99*

**Fronting** inverting normal word order for purposes of emphasis. *p 12*

**Function of language** The overall function of language is to communicate meaning through its systems and structures. Many distinguished linguists have listed and described the range of language functions, yet their accounts overlap at times. This entry lists 21 language functions and each has its own separate entry in the glossary. You are advised to look up each term as and when you need to, rather than trying to absorb and memorise them all at once. Be ready for some overlap in these functions. Commonly encountered descriptions of language function include the following: referential; descriptive; conative; expressive; phatic; metalingual; poetic; instrumental; informative; regulative; interactional; personal; heuristic; representational; pragmatic; creative; expository; persuasive; transactional; social; evaluative. *pp 21, 22, 248, 249*

**Function words** grammatical units or 'parts of speech' (e.g. pronouns, conjunctions, prepositions and determiners) which connect content words and create coherent meaning. *p 9*

**Functional language** language which communicates information and gets things done. *p 1*

**Genderlect** term used to describe the way in which genders speak, but more specifically how women speak. It is a way of viewing women's language choices as equivalent to a dialect or a sociolect. *pp 6, 51*

**Genre** way of classifying or describing texts that share content, function or form, e.g. diaries, letters, novels. Genres can be divided into sub-genres. For example, the genre of novels includes the sub-genres of adventure novels, mystery stories, romantic novels. *pp 13, 69, 164, 281*

**Glottal stop** sound used to replace a 't' in some accents. Whereas a 't' is made with the tongue behind the teeth, a glottal stop is made by the back of the tongue on the roof of the mouth, as in words like 'bottle'. In the International Phonetic Alphabet (IPA) a glottal stop is sometimes represented by a shape like an upside-down question mark or by an apostrophe. *p 76*

**Grammar** component or system of language which relates to form and structure, rather than to meaning and sound. *pp 1, 2, 51, 225, 235*

**Grapheme** smallest unit in the writing system of a language; letter or symbol which can be a visual representation of sound. In English there is no one-to-one relationship between grapheme and phoneme. *p 2*

**Graphology** refers to language as a semiotic system, creating meaning through textual design, signs and images. Or more simply, it refers to any aspect of the form and/or appearance of a text that modifies meaning in any way. *pp 69, 225*

**Great Vowel Shift** name given to a major change in the pronunciation of the English language that took place in the fifteenth century. *p 290*

**Hedge** refers to a feature found in spontaneous conversation when a speaker wants to soften what they are saying, e.g. 'I think', 'I guess', 'sort of'. Hedges can also function to get support from the listener, e.g. 'if you see what I mean'. *pp 61, 131*

**Heteroglossia** Greek word literally meaning 'different tongue'; term used by the Russian linguist Michael Bakhtin to describe the multivoiced nature of spoken and written language. *p 34*

**Heuristic function** language function identified by Halliday in young children's speech, e.g. 'Tell me why'. *pp 21, 249. See also Function of language.*

**Hexameter** verse line of twelve syllables, six of which are stressed. *p 20*

**Hinglish** variation of English which may have similar features to a pidgin, as it is a mixture of languages such as Hindi or Urdu and English. *p 77*

**Holophrastic stage** name given to the stage in a child's language development when they are able to use individual words. They cannot yet form sentences so they manipulate individual words, or holophrases, for a wide variety of functions. *pp 235, 242*

**Hypercorrection** describes the way a person might use a very correct form of language, possibly unnecessarily correct or overcorrect. *p 74*

**Hyponym** Lexical meaning can be understood as a system of categories. The most generalised meaning is the hyponym (e.g plant), the next level of semantic refinement (e.g. flower) is the superordinate category and the most specific level of meaning (e.g. rose) is the subordinate category. *p 8*

**Iambic pentameter** verse line of ten syllables, five of which are stressed. Also referred to as 'blank verse'. *p 19*

**Ideology** set of ideas held by a group, usually a system of ideas, or the study of these ideas. *p 102*

**Idiolect** refers to the fact that each individual has a specific way of using language. Everyone has their own idiosyncratic way of speaking (idiolect) which is the sum of all the influences on their language. *pp 6, 51, 133*

**Idiom** phrase in a language that does not have a literal meaning (e.g. 'raining cats and dogs') or phrase that is used in a set way (e.g. 'tall, dark and handsome', where the language users would understand the meaning of the words as a set phrase). 'Idiom' is linked with the term 'idiomatic' as being particular to an individual situation. *pp 56, 301*

**Imaginative function** language function identified by Halliday in young children's speech, e.g. 'Let's pretend...'; later associated with the creative or productive function of language. *pp 21, 249. See also Function of language.*

**Imperative** describes sentences that are commands. It is a grammatical term so it refers to the structure as well as the function. Imperatives have a specific form: the person addressed is the subject of the verb, but is missed out or 'understood'. Therefore these sentences start with the verb. 'Shut the door', 'Be quiet now', 'Pass me that book' are all imperatives.

Bald imperatives often sound rude. Directives and commands relate to the same function, but use other sentence forms and may be mitigated. For example, 'Could you shut the door?' has the same function as 'Shut the door' but is mitigated by using the interrogative form and so is a directive, not strictly an imperative. *p 53*

**Imperative mood** verb form which expresses a command or instruction. *p 14. See also Mood.*

**Indicative mood** verb form which conveys factual information. *p 14. See also Mood.*

**Influential power** type of power that seeks to influence the audience, e.g. advertising or the media. *p 99*

**Informative** describes a text with the primary purpose of conveying information. Other purposes might be persuasive, entertaining, instructive. *pp 88, 201*

**Informative function** language function identified by Halliday in young children's speech, e.g. 'I've got something to tell you'; later associated with the referential function of language and the ideational metafunction. *p 21. See also Function of language.*

**Initialism** describes a phrase or term made up of initials, e.g. CD, FAQ, tb (meaning 'text back'). It is common in computer-mediated texts for ease of communication and to refer to computer-related terms, e.g. SMS. *p 85*

**Instrumental function** language function identified by Halliday in young children's speech, e.g. 'I want...'. *pp 21, 248. See also Function of language.*

**Instrumental power** power that is somehow institutionalised, e.g. owing to the hierarchy in a workplace or undertaking teacher/student, doctor/patient, policeman/suspect roles. *p 91*

**Intensifier** word that strengthens the expression of another word, e.g. very, really, so. *p 63*

**Interactional function** language function identified by Halliday in young children's speech, e.g. 'Me and you'; later associated with the interpersonal metafunction. *pp 21, 248. See also Function of language.*

**Interactivity** term used to describe discourses that allow exchange between the participants or allow the reader to manipulate the text. So text-messaging is interactive because there is an exchange between the two participants. Web pages may be interactive if they allow the reader to navigate around the site. *p 83*

**Interior monologue** literary representation of the feelings and thought processes of a character. *p 36*

**International Phonetic Alphabet** *See IPA.*

**Interpersonal** usually contrasts with 'transactional'. It describes the type of communication that is largely focused on social functions, e.g. exchanging views, feelings, phatic conversation. *pp 21, 53*

**Interrogative mood** verb form which asks a question. *pp 14, 53. See also Mood.*

**Interruption** refers to a non-fluency feature found in spontaneous conversation and is simply when someone wants to butt into the conversation. *pp 53, 124*

**Intertextuality** describes the fact that all texts are 'in dialogue' with other texts via echoes, allusions, references or rewriting. *p 34*

**Intonation** describes the varying patterns of tone and pitch in spoken English. The way we 'intonate' an utterance can change its meaning. So 'You have done your homework' can have a variety of meanings depending on how we pronounce it and stress different words or syllables. *pp 61, 226, 235*

**Intransitive verbs** *p 15. See Transitive verbs.*

**IPA (International Phonetic Alphabet)** was first developed in the late nineteenth century by the International Phonetic Association, the most recent revision being in 2005. It uses symbols (based on the Roman alphabet) to represent the sounds of any language in the world. Names are given to vowels, consonants and diphthongs according to where they are produced in the mouth. Other markers (diacritics) can be used to indicate sound variants. The most common vowel sound, as in pic**tu**re, **u**nhappy, terr**or**, has its own name (schwa) and is represented by an upside-down 'e' – ə. *pp 17, 76*

**IRF structure** describes the three-part exchange between two groups that is common in a teaching discourse but might also appear in child directed speech. The three parts are initiation, response, feedback. The dominant participant initiates exchange (e.g. by asking a question), gets a response from the other participant and gives feedback on how acceptable the response is. This is an asymmetric exchange where the dominant participant controls the discourse and the other participant's response. *p 89. See also Response mechanism.*

**Irony** rhetorical figure of speech or trope in which a speaker or writer uses words which seem to contradict the actual context (i.e. saying the opposite of what is really meant), usually for comic or satiric or sarcastic purposes. *p 44*

**Jargon** pejorative or negative term used to describe specialist language. It implies language use that is unnecessarily complicated and aims to exclude those who are not part of the group who understand the lexical terms. *p 88*

**Language variation** general term used to describe how language might have different features, owing to a range of factors. It assumes the same basic language but includes some differences, particularly in lexis, phonology and grammar. *p 49*

**Latent vocabularies** *p 240. See Vocabulary.*

**Left-branching sentence** *p 12. See Branching.*

**Lexis** (origin: the Greek for 'word') refers to the vocabulary or word-stock of a language. *pp 1, 2 ,50, 133, 222, 225*. **Lexicon** has a similar meaning, but can also refer to a dictionary. *pp 8, 278*. **Lexeme** and **lexical item** are interchangeable terms meaning 'word'. *pp 2, 10*. **Lexical semantics** means the study of the meaning of words. *p 4*

**Linguistic concepts** all the terms and ideas related to the study of language. *p 54*

**Linguistic determinism** is a theoretical viewpoint. It states that language dictates or determines the way that we perceive the world, i.e. the words we use to describe the world can influence our perception of it. *p 55*

**Linguistic variables** items of language that might vary, e.g. accent, past-tense formation, lexical items. *p 58*

**Loan word** word borrowed from another language which becomes part of the new language, e.g. pizza (from Italian). *p 8*

**Loose social network** *p 58. See Social network.*

**Maxim** *See Conversational maxims.*

**Melodramatic** describes a text that is sensational in content and contains stereotypical characters and actions (both good and evil). *p 181*

**Metafunction** term used by the linguist Michael Halliday to describe the three key overarching functions of language. The ideational metafunction conveys information about everything that's happening in the world; the interpersonal metafunction represents the relationship between the addresser and the addressee; the textual metafunction refers to whatever spoken or written mode is used to enable communication to take place. *p 21. See also Function of language.*

**Metalingual function** function that focuses on the language itself. *p 21. See also Function of language.*

**Metaphor** figure of speech which is an implicit comparison based on certain shared attributes, e.g. 'He's a real wet blanket'. *pp 4, 45, 118, 140, 247* **Conceptual metaphor** is applied by cognitive linguists to what they regard as basic 'life' metaphors which seem to be built into the human imagination, e.g. death is sleep, sport is war. *p 45*

**Metonymy** figure of speech or trope in which a single term stands for everything associated with it, e.g. 'the press' includes all newspapers. *p 44*

**Metre** regular patterning of stressed and unstressed syllables in verse. *p 19*

**Metrical patterns** variants or deviations from regular patterning in verse to create a particular effect. *p 19*

**Minimal response** feature of speech and turn taking where responses are very short. Responses may be words or noises like 'mmm' and are usually considered to show active listening, although some minimal response or delayed response can indicate the opposite. *p 65. See also Response token.*

**MLU** stands for 'mean length of utterance'. In spoken language, counting someone's total number of words said and then dividing by their actual number of utterances gives a mean or average length for each utterance. The mlu is useful in providing statistical evidence when assessing how much or how little someone speaks. It is often used when assessing power or control in conversation or when analysing children's language. *p 135*

**Modality** describes state or mood and, in linguistics, is used to define **modals** which express the mood of a verb. These **modal verbs** are any of the group of English auxiliary verbs (can, could, may, might, shall, should, will, would, must) that are used with the base form of another verb to express distinctions of mood, e.g. 'Can I leave now?' compared with 'May I leave now?'. **Modal auxiliaries** can also function in politeness strategies to soften directives or express requests in a more formal register, e.g. 'Would you help?' *pp 13, 63, 124, 246*

**Mode** channel of communication within a text, e.g. spoken or written. *pp 21, 51, 160*

**Modifier** word which alters or changes the meaning of another word it is linked with. A modifier is often an adjective used with a noun, but not always. It can go in front of the other word or after it. The terms 'pre-modifier' and 'post-modifier' describe the positioning, e.g. in 'good girl', 'good' is a pre-modifier. *p 90*

**Mood** range of verb forms conveying information (indicative), giving commands (imperative) or asking questions (interrogative). *p 13*

**Morpheme** smallest grammatical unit in a language. A **free morpheme** is one that makes sense on its own; it is a word, e.g. 'hand'. A free morpheme cannot be broken down any further. A **bound morpheme** is one that needs to be 'bound' or attached to another to form a word, e.g. 'y', as in handy (= hand + y). Morphemes are used to change the grammatical functions of words, e.g. the morpheme 's' makes nouns plural, the morpheme 'ed' puts verbs into the past tense. *p 10*

**Morphology** study of the structure of words and their roots, stems and affixes (or morphemes). Morphology is an integral part of grammar. *pp 10, 82, 277*

**Multiplex network** *pp 58, 129. See Social network.*

---

**Narrative** story or storytelling. *pp 10, 35, 167, 253*

**Narrative perspective/voice** both refer to the angle or point of view from which a story is told. This may be autobiographical (first-person narrative voice) or told by an **omniscient narrator** or by a participating observer (third-person narrative voice). *pp 30, 36*

**Narrative structure** the way in which a narrative is organised with relation to events, participants, time frame and voice. William Labov's narrative structure theory provides a useful methodology. *pp 37, 253*

**Negative face** is used in politeness theory to describe the way in which speakers aim not to impose on others. It is 'negative' in contrast to 'positive politeness', which describes compliments or other ways of actively raising another person's esteem in the group. *p 64. See also Face.*

**Neologism** word new to a language. New words are formed all the time in English in a variety of ways, including compounding, clipping, blending, back formation, affixation and acronyms. *pp 8, 85, 279*

**Non-fluency features** features of speech where the utterances or exchanges temporarily lose fluency, e.g. pauses, repairs, interruptions or repetition. They are common because speakers are thinking as they speak and so sometimes rephrase their comment as they are producing it. *p 53*

**Non-standard dialect** any dialect which differs from Standard English. Standard English is the accepted 'correct' English which is used when writing textbooks, newspapers, etc. It is the English used as the norm in teaching in English-speaking institutions and it is the English used to teach non-native English speakers. In fact, many native speakers use some forms of non-standard dialect in their daily lives, particularly in spoken language. Most common are the double negative, e.g. 'I didn't know nobody' (standard: 'I didn't know anybody' or 'I knew nobody'), and the non-standard past continuous tense, e.g. 'I was sat' (standard: 'I was sitting'). *p 133*

**Norm** in linguistics describes the accepted or expected way in which something would be said or written. *pp 36, 58, 133, 235*

**Noun phrase** phrase such as 'the blue lagoon'or 'pride and prejudice' which contains one or more key words that are nouns but may also include the definite article (the), indefinite article (a), adjectives or connectives. Titles of books, plays and films are often noun phrases. *p 85*

---

**Observer's paradox** refers to the unnatural effect on speakers when being observed or recorded. The very act of observation produces the opposite effect of what is desired: natural speech/interaction. *pp 59, 119*

**Onomatopoeia** phonological feature that mimics the sound it describes, e.g. 'bang' or 'buzz'. *pp 17, 69*

**Orthography** refers to the study of spelling and the writing system of a particular language. *pp 76, 277*

**Overextension** describes the way that young children often use a word to refer to something beyond the scope of the word's specific meaning. There will usually be a logical semantic connection between the child's use of the word and its accepted meaning, e.g. a child may use 'apple' to refer to any type of fruit. *p 241*

**Overgeneralisation** occurs where a child grammatically overextends a feature of language. For example, a child may learn the grammatical pattern 'ed' for the formation of the regular past tense and apply it to all verbs, as in 'we wented'. *p 242*

**Overlap** refers to a non-fluency feature found in spontaneous conversation. It is like an interruption but intended to support the speaker rather than butt into the conversation. *pp 54, 131*

---

**Paradigmatic and syntagmatic axes** represent (in diagrammatic form) the fact that all language users work within two frameworks – the words available for choice (paradigmatic axis) and the structure or form of the language into which these choices fit (syntagmatic axis). *p 2*

**Passive voice** *pp 15, 245. See Voice.*

**Patois** describes a language form based on a mixture between a dominant language and a minority language. It is often a language that is primarily colloquial; it may or may not have a formal grammar or other features of standardisation. *p 79*

**Pejorative change** change in meaning of a word from positive/pleasant to negative/unpleasant associations. *p 7*

**Perlocutionary acts** situations where language has a concrete effect. An example would be any speech that has a legal consequence, such as 'I now pronounce you husband and wife', where the words create part of the contract, although the couple also sign a written contract. Similarly, when a judge says 'I sentence you to three years in prison', the sentence is enforced in other ways but the words function as an action and have some standing of their own. *p 91. See also Speech act theory.*

**Personal function** language function identified by Halliday in young children's speech, e.g. 'Here I come'. *pp 21, 249. See also Function of language.*

**Persuasive function** All language is persuasive to a greater or lesser degree, depending on the audience, purpose and context, ranging on a continuum or cline from a dictionary definition to posters on a shop front declaring 'Fire-damaged goods!! SALE!!!! EVERYTHING MUST GO!!!' *p 25. See also Function of language.*

**Phatic function** function that establishes social contact and maintains communication in any given interaction. Phatic tokens like 'Hi' and 'See you' are part of everyday speech. The term 'phatic communion' was coined by an anthropologist to describe this kind of social behaviour. *pp 21, 53. See also Function of language.*

**Phonaesthesia** the expressive element in sound patterning. *p 17*

**Phoneme** smallest individual unit of sound in a language. There are 44 phonemes, or sounds, in English. They can be transcribed using the phonetic alphabet. *pp 2, 259. See also IPA.*

**Phonetics** recognised way of classifying the vocal sounds in a language. Writing something phonetically means using the alphabet and other symbols to indicate how a word was pronounced, e.g. 'gonna', 'cuz'. *pp 17, 225. See also IPA.*

**Phonics** describes the use of the sound system of English to teach children to read. Children are encouraged to 'sound words out', e.g. C – A – T. There has been much debate in recent years about how effective this is as a method of teaching. In schools it is often used in combination with other methods of teaching. *p 259*

**Phonology** study of the sounds in language. As well as pronunciation, it includes the way sound patterning is used in written and spoken English. *pp 2, 76, 225, 277.* **Phonological features** may include alliteration, repetition, rhyme. *pp 1, 69*

**Pidgin** language that is a mixture of a dominant language and a minority language, and is used by speakers who do not share a common language. It generally has a limited lexis and grammar. It may primarily be spoken rather than written. When a pidgin develops grammatical forms and standardisation it is called a creole. *p 78*

**Pivot grammar/marker** refers to words that are characteristic of children's two-word utterances. These are words that tend to be used in fixed positions and are not replicated in adult grammar, e.g. 'all-gone' biccy, 'more' biccy. *p 243*

**Poetic function** function that incorporates the aesthetic, productive and creative functions of language, and is ultimately a development of the imaginative function Halliday identified in young children's speech. *p 21. See also Function of language.*

**Politeness**, in linguistics, is used to describe certain language forms and behaviours. **Politeness forms** soften requests and show respect for others. *pp 93,*

124. Robin Lakoff formulated this into her politeness principle, which suggests three 'rules' we follow in order to smooth interaction: don't impose, give options, make your receiver feel good. p 133. These principles form part of the politeness strategies, which also can involve adjusting your language to reduce the linguistic distance between yourself and another. p 58. Common politeness markers are 'please', 'thank you', 'I'm sorry to bother you but...', 'I'm afraid (you've got that wrong/you owe me some money, etc.)'. p 63

Political correctness describes a variety of language use that is deliberately constructed to avoid giving offence to particular persons or social groups. It was popularised in the USA and has been attacked for being overly sensitive and politically divisive. (Consider the banning of 'Baa Baa Black Sheep' in schools.) It is an important concept as it highlights the power of language to exclude. It was also responsible for raising societal awareness about language use. pp 55, 292

Positive face desire to be seen in a positive light by other people. It is part of politeness theory and may include compliments, thanks or other language features that make others feel valued. It contrasts with 'negative' politeness, which attempts to reduce the way the person is imposing on others. p 64. See also Face.

Pragmatic function general description of language used to achieve specific practical purposes, and associated with the transactional function. Much everyday communication is pragmatic in function and purpose. p 21. See also Function of language.

Pragmatics study of implied meaning and how social context affects the meaning of language. It has been defined as 'not what is said but what is understood'. This area of language study also includes assumed knowledge, politeness, taboo and 'reading between the lines'. When a teacher says 'You're late!' what do they really mean? pp 23, 65, 123, 225, 245

Preposition term which conveys a sense of the position of two objects, e.g. like, by, with, from, to. pp 53, 288

Prescriptive describes an attitude to language use that embraces ideas of 'correctness' and 'right usage' in language. A prescriptivist might criticise the use of slang or split infinitives, or may accuse informal language use of being 'lazy', 'sloppy' or just 'bad English'. The prescriptive attitude is at the opposite end of the continuum to the descriptive attitude. p 296

Prestige general term that means something has high status. In language terms, some dialects (e.g. Standard English) have more prestige than others. pp 58, 124. See also Covert prestige.

Presupposition specific type of pragmatic meaning where a statement may convey an assumption that is not directly stated. For example, 'When did you last beat your wife?' presupposes that you have a wife and have beaten her. 'Would you let your wife and servants read it?' presupposes you are male and you have a wife and servants. p 99

Productive role term for the role played in a language exchange by the participant who has the main function, i.e. produces the main language contributions. p 94. See also Receptive role.

Prolect term used to describe occupational language. p 51. See also Dialect, Idiolect, Sociolect.

Prosody describes the phonology or sounds of speech, including the rhythm and intonation. p 83

Pull-quote technique adopted by magazine subeditors in which a short interesting or thought-provoking snippet from an article is extracted and highlighted in an eye-catching way with the intention of enticing the readers to read the whole article to discover its significance. p 207

Purpose In terms of writing for A-level English Language, purpose within texts can be divided into the following broad categories: writing to entertain, writing to persuade, writing to inform and writing to advise/instruct. It should be noted, however, that texts rarely, if ever, have a single purpose, e.g. persuasion texts often contain elements of information and/or entertainment. It is often more helpful to regard texts in terms of their primary (most significant) purpose and their secondary (or less significant) purpose(s). pp 2, 53, 162, 249

Rank order is associated with Halliday's systemic grammar. The idea of a rank scale or order relates to larger units and smaller units in discourse, ranging from sentence, clause, phrase, to word and morpheme. p 11

Reader-response theory useful theory which explores the relationship between author, text and reader. The basic premise is that reading a text is a dynamic and complex experience in which the reader is active rather than passive, in a variety of ways. p 37

Reading position/readerly text, writing position/ writerly text The differences here are between texts where the reader's expectations are matched and texts where the writer's desire to innovate leads to the reader's expectations of a text being (excitingly, one hopes) disrupted. p 27

Received Pronunciation (RP) describes an accent used by less than 3% of English speakers. It has traditionally been the accent of royalty and 'BBC' English, i.e. the accent of Prince Charles or the actors in the film Brief Encounter. pp 58, 133, 292

Receptive role term for the role played in a language exchange by the participant who primarily listens or receives the language contribution of the other participant. p 94. See also Productive role.

Referential function p 21. See Function of language.

Register describes variations in language according to the 'user' (defined by variables such as social background, geography, gender and age), and variations according to 'use' (in the sense that each speaker has a range of varieties and chooses between them at different times and in different contexts). pp 8, 145, 167

Regulative function language function identified by Halliday in young children's speech, e.g. 'Do as I tell you'. pp 21, 248. See also Function of language.

Repairs non-fluency feature of speech when speakers correct themselves in their utterance. p 53

Repetition non-fluency feature of speech when speakers repeat a word or phrase. p 53

Representational function function associated with the creative and productive functions of language, and in particular with the representation of speech and thought. p 249. See also Function of language.

Response mechanism is used to describe any response in a conversation. p 135. It can be forceful, as in an interruption, but in linguistics more often refers to a response token used by participants to encourage other speakers. This can be a simple response such as 'yes', 'mm', 'OK', supportive laughter, or a positive response such as 'great', 'brilliant', 'cool'. p 131

Restricted code sociolinguistics term, formulated by Basil Bernstein, for a style of language use associated with informal situations, characterised by linguistic predictability and by its dependence on context and on the shared knowledge and experience of the participants for conveying meaning. p 134. See also Elaborated code.

Rhetoric comes from the Greek techne rhetorike, meaning the art of speech. It acquired a more specialised meaning associated with persuasion and was later used in written as well as spoken language. pp 17, 42

Rhyme literally, a 'phonetic echo in verse'; regular repetition of selected sounds in verse. End rhyme is full rhyme at the end of a line. Half-rhyme is echoing of final consonants with different vowels. Internal rhyme is full rhyme within a line, rather than at the end. Eye rhyme is visual, not phonetic repetition, e.g. slough/ rough. Feminine rhyme refers to repetition of unstressed final syllables. Masculine rhyme refers to repetition of stressed final syllables. pp 18, 19, 69

Rhythm patterning of stressed and unstressed syllables, usually in poetry but sometimes in prose. p 18

Right-branching sentence p 12. See Branching.

Rime unit refers to the sound–spelling correspondence in words that is important for children when they are learning to read. In contrast to phonics, rime units take spelling into account. For example, sounding out will not provide the pronunciation of 'fleet' and 'meet' but children can spot the spelling pattern that produces a specific sound. p 259

Schema p 24. See Frame.

Scheme name for a rhetorical device such as antithesis. p 45

Schwa the sound like the vowel sound in 'the' in IPA. It is represented by an upside-down 'e' – ə. p 76. See also IPA.

Script is borrowed from the term for a play script and describes any repeated speech forms. Scripts are particularly common in occupational contexts. They may be written down and read as, with a play script, and be dictated by the company. Or it may be that in an occupational context the person in the occupational role will repeat their contribution in more or less the same form each time. For example, in a shop or restaurant the same form of words might be used with each customer. pp 89, 138

Semantic change describes the process words undergo when they change their meaning over time. For example, the word 'wicked' has changed its meaning and is now often used to mean 'great' or 'good'. pp 7, 145, 277

Semantic field group of words or terms related to the same area of meaning. The word 'net' belongs to the semantic fields of computers, but also to the semantic fields of fishing and hair. If we can identify the context of a word we can pin down the 'field' to which it belongs. pp 6, 57

Semantic grammar is used when analysing the two-word utterances of children. Where the grammatical connection between the two words is unclear we can look at the meaning connection between them in order to understand the utterance. p 243

Semantics study of meaning connections between words. It may also include the study of meaning devices such as metaphor, allusion, connotation and juxtaposition. For example, the meaning of the word 'dress' changes as soon as we connect it with other words such as 'party' or 'wound' or 'down'. The meanings of words are not fixed but can change according to context. pp 4, 45, 241

Semiotics study of the cultural signs and symbols used in text. It can refer to language use as well as the use of images. This is important to the way we 'read' text. We are influenced not only by what is written but by the images and symbols that accompany it. p 4

Service encounter technical term for any occupational exchange that involves the role of service such as in shops or restaurants. Such exchanges generally have the same structure, e.g. a greeting, a question so that the customer can ask for what they want, then a closing. pp 21, 89

Sight words words that young children need to learn by recognising them 'on sight' as they cannot be learnt using phonics. These are words where there is no correspondence between spelling and pronunciation, e.g. through, because. p 259

**Simile** extended metaphor in which the comparison between entities is explicit, e.g. 'The old man walks like a snail'. *p 45*

**Social context** general term that describes any social situation that might influence language use. *pp 5, 49, 57, 245*

**Social function** function associated with the interactional and phatic functions of language, and also part of the interpersonal metafunction. *p 22. See also Function of language.*

**Social network** general term that describes the connections between the members of a social group. A dense social network describes people who maintain contacts with the same narrow group of people, while a loose social network is the opposite where there is more mixing between social groups. A multiplex network describes a network whose members interact with each other in more than one context, e.g. work and sporting activity. *p 58.*

**Social variety** language variety created by social differences, rather than geographical differences, e.g. upper-class language. Speakers have little conscious degree of control over these background features of their language. *p 50. See also Stylistic variety.*

**Sociolect** language variety linked to any sort of social group, e.g. the language of local football supporters, friendship groups or work-based associations. *pp 6, 51*

**Sociolinguistics** term for the study of language variation as a result of social context. It also covers all the technical terms and concepts related to it. *p 49*

**Speech act theory** derives from the work of philosophers Austin and Searle (1962, 1969). Speech acts perform at three levels: the words themselves are a locutionary act; whatever the words are doing has illocutionary force; and the result of the speech act on the addressee is the perlocutionary effect. To perform successful speech acts a speaker must have authority to speak, must be able to speak appropriately and must be sincere, thus achieving felicity conditions. *p 91. See also Perlocutionary acts.*

**Speech community** group of people who use the same variation of language. *p 57*

**Standard English (SE)** variety of English recognised as the norm for spoken and written English. It is the predominant variety of English used in education. It grew out of the need for countrywide and later worldwide communication in English. *pp 51, 133, 288*

**Standard form** form recognised and understood throughout the English-speaking world. It is important to remember that Standard English can be spoken in any accent. *pp 71, 119*

**Standard Scottish (SSE) and Northern Irish (NIE)** refer to the standard varieties of English used in Scotland and Northern Ireland. These varieties contain lexical and grammatical features that make them distinctive. *p 71*

**Stative verbs** describe states of existence, of being, seeming or becoming. *p 13. See also Dynamic verbs.*

**Stream of consciousness** primarily a literary technique; can also be described as an interior monologue. *p 36*

**Stylistic variety** language variety linked to an individual's personal preferences (e.g. poetic, humorous) or to narrow social groups (e.g. the language of local football supporters, friendship groups or work-based associations). Speakers have a conscious degree of control over these styles. *p 50. See also Social variety.*

**Subordinate category** *p 8. See Hyponym.*

**Superordinate category** *p 8. See Hyponym.*

**Syllabic verse** verse form where the metrical patterning depends on the number of syllables per line of verse, not on the balance and number of stressed and unstressed syllable. *p 20*

**Synecdoche** trope where a part stands for a whole, e.g. 'All hands on deck!' *p 44*

**Synonym** word with the same or similar meaning as another word. *p 8*

**Syntactic parallelism** pattern in language closely allied to contrasting pairs. Essentially it is when the order of words (syntax) is repeated close by. This is done for linguistic effect and can be a feature of good or persuasive writing. Often it is a feature of skilful and persuasive spoken language. For example, 'I came, I saw, I conquered' and 'This was not a terrorist attack against the mighty and the powerful. It was not aimed at Presidents or Prime Ministers. It was aimed at ordinary, working-class Londoners, black and white, Muslim and Christian, Hindu and Jew, young and old.' *pp 12, 140*

**Syntagmatic axis** *p 2. See Paradigmatic and syntagmatic axes.*

**Syntax** structure of the sentence, including word order and grammatical relationships. *pp 1, 2, 71, 145, 242*

**Synthetic personalisation** is used to describe the way some public texts manufacture a relationship with the audience. It can be created by the use of personal pronouns (particularly I/you/we), personal details, mitigation, and typical features of speech. *pp 36, 99*

---

**Taboo** describes any subject that a cultural or social group may consider beyond the realms of discussion. It is also used to refer to topics that people find it difficult to talk about. For this reason we develop ways of indirectly referring to taboo topics, e.g. euphemism. Taboo topics may include sex, money, death, disease. *pp 56, 292*

**Telegraphic** describes the stage of child language development when a child's utterances resemble a telegram, i.e. lexical items that have purely grammatical functions may be omitted. (This is sometimes called the 'telegrammatic' stage.) The meaning of the utterance is clear but the syntax is incomplete in comparison to adult norms, e.g. 'me go bed now'. *pp 235, 243*

**Tense** means of expressing time relations in the verb form. *p 13*

**Tetrameter** verse line of eight syllables, four of which are stressed; also called octosyllabic verse. *p 20*

**Text** passage of written or spoken language. This term can also refer to multi-modal extracts. *p 31*

**Text type** refers to the genre of the text in question. *pp 22, 162, 281*

**Tone** term describing the way in which a writer's language choices are tailored to the requirements of genre, purpose, audience and situation. *p 193*

**Topic setting** relates to speech. It simply describes the way in which the subject of the conversation is established: what it is and who introduces it. *p 52*

**Transactional function** language function associated with practical matters, getting things done, e.g. visiting the bank, shopping, going to the doctor. It is linked with pragmatic function of language. *p 21. See also Function of language.*

**Transactional language** aims to convey information, to get something done. It contrasts with interpersonal language, whose aim is developing relationships. *p 54*

**Transcript** specific way in which speech is recorded in writing so that it can be studied. It has its own layout and notation. It is set out in a similar way to a play script with the speaker in the left margin. Everything that is spoken is written, including false starts, repairs, fillers, pauses, interruptions and simultaneous speech. A vertical line is used to show simultaneous speech or interruptions. Pauses are marked with brackets () with the time in seconds between them if appropriate, e.g. (1). *pp 22, 51, 125, 232*

**Transitive verbs** have a grammatical subject and an object. Intransitive verbs have only a grammatical

subject. According to Michael Halliday, transitivity is an important part of the ideational metafunction of language because it links people, actions and situations. *p 15*

**Trimeter** verse line of six syllables, three of which are stressed. *p 20*

**Trinomial** is used to describe a set phrase of three terms, e.g. tall, dark and handsome. *p 56*

**Trope** figure of speech in rhetoric. *p 43*

**Turn taking** feature of conversation. In a co-operative conversation the participants take turns to contribute an utterance. *pp 53, 237*

**Two-word stage** stage in a child's language development where they can put two words together to create meaning. As soon as two words are placed together in an utterance both a grammatical and a semantic connection is formed. This is a powerful stage for children as they can create a wide variety of meanings using just two words. *p 235*

---

**Underextension** is the opposite of overextension. It describes what a child is doing with language when they apply a word to something more specific than its normal meaning. For example a child may use the word 'banana' only to refer to an actual banana and not to a picture of one. *p 241*

**Unities** three requirements of conventional (classical) storytelling concerning place, time and action. Scenes should be in a set place, all the events should take place within a stipulated time and there should be nothing in the plot that is irrelevant to its development. *p 182*

**Utterance** stretch of spoken language, brief or extended. *pp 2, 112, 131, 225, 235*

---

**Vague language** term used to describe words such as 'like', 'kind of', 'whatever'. *p 131. See also Hedge.*

**Variety** refers in linguistic terms to a type of written or spoken language use. There are endless varieties of language use. A variety is often associated with a particular context, e.g. formal language, slang, medical language, creole. *pp 6, 49, 239*

**Vernacular** refers to plain, everyday, ordinary language, also to the standard native language of a country or locality, as opposed to learned or literary language. It is sometimes used to describe a variety of everyday language specific to a social group or region, e.g. the vernaculars of London. *pp 74, 134*

**Virtuous errors** features of children's language use that may appear to be 'mistakes' in comparison to the adult norm but are logical and appropriate to the child's stage of development, e.g. 'the bird flied'. 'Virtuous error' is a useful phrase for writing about children's language as it avoids suggesting that the child is doing something 'wrong'. *p 242*

**Vocabulary** words a speaker of a language has at their disposal. We all have vocabularies that we use frequently. These are our active vocabularies. However we also know a lot of words that we do not use often, words that we understand but do not necessarily use. These are called latent or passive vocabularies. *pp 2, 56, 118, 215, 235, 240*

**Voice** verb form which reveals whether or not the grammatical subject took action (active voice) or received/felt the action (passive voice). *pp, 13, 15, 245*

---

**Writerly position** *p 27. See Reading position/ readerly text, writing position/writerly text.*

**Writerly text** *p 27. See Reading position/ readerly text, writing position/writerly text.*

# Acknowledgements

The publishers would like to thank the following for their kind permission to reproduce copyright material:

*Monty Python* Pet shop sketch © Python (Monty) Pictures Ltd; *The BFG* by Roald Dahl, Jonathan Cape Ltd & Penguin Books Ltd; 'Musée des Beaux Arts' from *Collected Poems of W.H. Auden*, Faber and Faber Ltd, © The Estate of W.H. Auden; 'Mrs Midas' from *The World's Wife* by Carol Ann Duffy, Pan Macmillan, London, © Carol Ann Duffy, 1999; 'I have a dream' from *The Penguin Book of Historic Speeches*, ed. Brian MacArthur, by permission of the Estate of Martin Luther King, Jr, Inc.; *The Cat That Could Open the Fridge* by Simon Hoggart, 2004, Atlantic Books; 'New York to Detroit' from *The Collected Dorothy Parker*, by permission of Gerald Duckworth & Co Ltd; 'Mind your language, critics warn BBC' by Anushka Asthana and Vanessa Thorpe, in the *Observer*, © Guardian News & Media Ltd 2007; *The Waste Land* by T.S. Eliot, Faber and Faber Ltd, © The Estate of T.S. Eliot; *White Teeth* by Zadie Smith, Hamish Hamilton, 2000, © Zadie Smith, 2000, reproduced by permission of Penguin Books Ltd; *Persuading People: An Introduction to Rhetoric*, 2nd ed. 2005, by Robert and Sue Cockcroft, Palgrave Macmillan; Conversation transcript by Emily Taylor; *Politics and the English Language* by George Orwell (Copyright © George Orwell, 1946) by permission of Bill Hamilton as the Literary Executor of the Estate of the late Sonia Brownell Orwell and Secker & Warburg Ltd; *Sociolinguistics: An Introduction to Language and Society* by Peter Trudgill, Penguin Books, 1974, rev. ed. 1983, © Peter Trudgill, 1974, 1983, reproduced by permission of Penguin Books Ltd; *You Just Don't Understand* by Deborah Tannen, Little, Brown Book Group; *Women in their Speech Communities* by Jennifer Coates and Deborah Cameron, Pearson Education; *The Lost Prince* by Cindy Dees, cover art used by arrangement with Harlequin Enterprises Ltd. All rights reserved. ® and ™ are trademarks of Harlequin Enterprises Ltd and/or its affiliated companies, used under license. Trademarks marked with a ® are registered in the United States Patent and Trademark Office, the Canadian Intellectual Property Office and/or other countries; New South Wales' Policy relating to gender-neutral expression, by permission of New South Wales Parliamentary Counsel's Office; 'What would Beth Ditto do?' reproduced in facsimile from *G2* supplement, © Guardian News & Media Ltd 2007; *Lady Chatterley's Lover* by D.H. Lawrence, Penguin Books, reproduced by permission of Pollinger Ltd and the Estate of Frieda Lawrence Ravagli; *The Killing Jar* by Nicola Monaghan, published by Chatto & Windus, reprinted by permission of The Random House Group Ltd; 'Schoolchildren now speak the Queen's Hinglish', *Daily Mail*, 1 December 2006, © Associated Newspapers; Black and white talk by permission of Georgia Copeland; 'Words of a Jamaican Laas Moment Them' from *Hot Earth, Cold Earth* by James Berry, Bloodaxe Books, 1995; *The Lonely Londoners* by Samuel Selvon, reproduced by permission of Althea Selvon; BookCrossing homepage with permission; *Talking from 9 to 5* by Deborah Tannen, Little, Brown Book Group; Classroom language investigation by permission of Ben Shaw; 'The Form and Function of Threats in Court' by Sandra Harris, published in *Language and Communication* 4 (4), 1984, © Elsevier; 'Fight to Save the Queen's English', *Sunday Express*, 24 September 1995, Northern & Shell Media Publications; Tony Blair's resignation speech, transcript © Guardian News & Media Ltd, 2007; Christian Aid advertisement reproduced by permission of Christian Aid and Shop agency, image © Panos Pictures; Staff and students at Bilborough College; 'Imagine', words and music by John Lennon, © 1971 Lenono Music. Used by permission of Music Sales Ltd. All Rights Reserved. International Copyright Secured; 'Reeling Fulham in Dogfight', AFP, 11 April 2007; 'Northerners have the last laff' by Ben Fenton, *Daily Telegraph*, 28 March 2007, Telegraph Media Group Ltd; 'Are Women Really More Talkative Than Men?' from Mehl et al., *Science* 317:82 (2007). Reprinted with permission from AAAS; 'Female chatterbox?' by Mark Henderson and Richard Mabey, in *The Times*, 6 July 2007, © NI Syndication, London; 'Physician Self-disclosure in Primary Care Visits',

*Archives of Internal Medicine,* vol. 167 no. 12, 2007, AMA; 'Yackety Yak' by Trisha Torrey on blog trishatorrey.com; *Notes from a Small Island* by Bill Bryson, Black Swan, reprinted by permission of The Random House Group Ltd; Facsimile pages from *Crap Towns* by David Finch, Pan Macmillan, London, © David Finch, 2003; *Cider with Rosie* by Laurie Lee, Hogarth Press, reprinted by permission of The Random House Group Ltd; 'Her Big Chance' from *Talking Heads* by Alan Bennett, BBC Books, reprinted by permission of The Random House Group Ltd; 'Just another conquest' by permission of Thomas Cummings; 'A Life in the Day' – Frank Lampard, in *The Sunday Times*, London © NI Syndication, London (16 October 2005); 'Drip, drip, drip…' by Jeremy Clarkson, in *The Times*, London, © NI Syndication, London (25 February 2007); Eulogy to Diana, Princess of Wales, reproduced by permission of Earl Spencer; 'Liverpool', in *Hotline*, January–March 2007, reprinted by permission of Tony Naylor, use of page facsimile by permission of River Publishing Ltd; 'The Pirate Queen's Retreat' by Catherine Mack, in *The Observer*, 8 April 2007, © Guardian News & Media Ltd 2007; Feature on Russell Brand, in *Hotline,* January–March 2007, reprinted by permission of Dominic Midgely; 'Text like a teenager' by permission of Beth Barrett; 'Let your fingers do the talking' by Tim Dowling, in *The Guardian,* 20 March 2007, © Guardian News & Media Ltd 2007; 'Strategies for Communicating' by Eve Clark, in *Child Development*, 49, 4 (December 1978), Bailey-Blackwell; 'The Truth about Lying' from *Quirkology* by Richard Wiseman, Pan Macmillan, London, © Richard Wiseman, 2007; 'Poor Maths and Literacy Skills' by Rebecca Smithers, in *Guardian Unlimited*, 21 February 2007, © Guardian News & Media Ltd 2007; Child's writing on page 252 by Anna Michel; 'How Synthetic Phonics Works', *Daily Mail*, 3 June 2005, © Associated Newspapers; 'Goodbye 2006' by Adi Bloom, in *TES*, 22 December 2006; 'Jolly Pocket Postman' transcript by permission of Rachel Doherty; 'hist whist' is reprinted from *Complete Poems 1904–1962* by E.E. Cummings, edited by George J. Firmage, by permission of W.W. Norton & Co. © 1991 by the Trustees for the E.E. Cummings Trust and George James Firmage; Craven A cigarette advertisement reproduced by permission of British American Tobacco; *A Clockwork Orange* by Anthony Burgess, Jonathan Cape, reprinted by permission of The Random House Group Ltd; OED online, © Oxford University Press; Dr John Hall's Select Observations, by permission of Shakespeare Birthplace Trust; 'Meihem in ce Klasrum' by Dolton Edwards, © 1946 by Dolton Edwards. This story originally appeared in *Astounding Science Fiction Magazine*; 'How the Queen's English has grown more like ours' by Neil Tweedie, *Daily Telegraph*, 4 December 2006, © Telegraph Media Group Ltd; Kleinert's advertisement reproduced by permission; 'Not I. It's Me.' by John Humphrys, from the introduction to *Between You and I: A Little Book of Bad English* by James Cochrane, Icon Books Ltd; Extract from David Crystal's blog reproduced by permission of the author; *Eats, Shoots and Leaves* by Lynne Truss, Profile Books Ltd, 2003; Facsimile pages from *Kerrang!* and *Smash Hits* reproduced by permission of Emap Performance; Persil advertisements from 1939, 1954 and 2005 reproduced by permission of Unilever PLC.

Images are reproduced by permission of the following:
Beth Ditto: Sarah Lee, copyright Guardian News & Media Ltd 2007; Cathy Mack: copyright Guardian News & Media Ltd 2007; Clare Island: image by © Ladislav Janicek/zefs/Corbis; Russell Brand: image by © Rune Hellestad/Corbis; The Queen: image by © UPPA Luke Macgregor/dpa/Corbis; Dictionary extract: from 'School Days' Collection © Getty Images.

Every effort has been made to trace copyright holders of material reproduced in this book. Any omissions will be rectified in subsequent printings if notice is given to the publisher.